C000318463

# Tolley's Corporate M
# Homicide: A guide to compliance

# Tolley's Corporate Manslaughter and Homicide: A guide to compliance

by

Andrea Oates, BSc
Freelance health and safety writer and former researcher at the Labour
Research Department (LRD).

LexisNexis®
Tolley

## Members of the LexisNexis Group worldwide

| | |
|---|---|
| United Kingdom | LexisNexis Butterworths, a Division of Reed Elsevier (UK) Ltd, Halsbury House, 35 Chancery Lane, London, WC2A 1EL, and London House, 20–22 East London Street, Edinburgh EH7 4BQ |
| Argentina | LexisNexis Argentina, Buenos Aires |
| Australia | LexisNexis Butterworths, Chatswood, New South Wales |
| Austria | LexisNexis Verlag ARD Orac GmbH & Co KG, Vienna |
| Benelux | LexisNexis Benelux, Amsterdam |
| Canada | LexisNexis Canada, Markham, Ontario |
| Chile | LexisNexis Chile Ltda, Santiago |
| China | LexisNexis China, Beijing and Shanghai |
| France | LexisNexis SA, Paris |
| Germany | LexisNexis Deutschland GmbH, Munster |
| Hong Kong | LexisNexis Hong Kong, Hong Kong |
| India | LexisNexis India, New Delhi |
| Italy | Giuffrè Editore, Milan |
| Japan | LexisNexis Japan, Tokyo |
| Malaysia | Malayan Law Journal Sdn Bhd, Kuala Lumpur |
| Mexico | LexisNexis Mexico, Mexico |
| New Zealand | LexisNexis NZ Ltd, Wellington |
| Poland | Wydawnictwo Prawnicze LexisNexis Sp, Warsaw |
| Singapore | LexisNexis Singapore, Singapore |
| South Africa | LexisNexis Butterworths, Durban |
| USA | LexisNexis, Dayton, Ohio |

© Reed Elsevier (UK) Ltd 2008

Published by LexisNexis Butterworths

A CIP Catalogue record for this book is available from the British Library.

ISBN 9780754530664

Typeset by Letterpart Ltd, Reigate, Surrey

Printed and bound by William Clowes Limited, Beccles, Suffolk

Visit LexisNexis Butterworths at www.lexisnexis.co.uk

# Preface

This book aims to guide employers through the provisions of the Corporate Manslaughter and Corporate Homicide Act 2007 (CMCHA 2007), which will come into force on 6 April 2008 and which has been described as probably the most significant piece of health and safety legislation since the Heath and Safety at Work etc. Act 1974.

CMCHA 2007 will be enacted in response to the situation where thousands of people have lost their lives in workplaces, as a result of work-related activities and in public disasters, but only a handful of small companies and sole traders have ever been convicted of corporate manslaughter following a work-related death.

CMCHA 2007 aims to ensure that companies (and other organisations) are held to account when a death at work has been caused as a result of gross failings by their senior management. Although it is aimed at the worse cases of corporate failure, and the Home Office has estimated that around 10 to 13 additional prosecutions may result from the change in the law, many commentators believe that there will be a larger number of cases.

Barrister Gerard Ford specialises in manslaughter and is widely seen as a leading expert in the field of regulatory crime. He believes that CMCHA 2007 will make it much easier to successfully prosecute medium and large companies, as well as public sector organisations, for corporate manslaughter because 'it removes the need to pierce the corporate veil and find a directing mind'. Although there are a number of areas that will no doubt be tested in appeal cases in due course he says that: 'The runway to a conviction will be much easier for the prosecution to find in the future once the Act comes into force'.

CMCHA 2007 will remove what has proved to be a major stumbling block in corporate manslaughter prosecutions – the need to identify a 'directing mind' or someone at the very top of the company who can be said to embody the company in his or her actions – which has become known as the 'identification principle'. In order to secure a corporate manslaughter conviction, it has been necessary to show that a single individual at the top of the company is personally guilty of manslaughter before the company can be convicted, and if this cannot be shown, the company escapes liability.

According to the Ministry of Justice (MoJ), CMCHA 2007:

- will make it easier to prosecute companies and other large companies when gross failures in the management of health and safety lead to a death, by delivering a new, more effective basis for corporate liability;

- reforms the law so that a key obstacle to successful prosecutions (that is the identification principle) has now been removed. It means that both small and large companies can be held liable for manslaughter where gross failures in the management of health and safety cause death, not just health and safety breaches;

- complements current law under which individuals can be prosecuted for gross negligence manslaughter and health and safety offences, where there is direct evidence of their culpability; and

- lifts Crown immunity to prosecution.

Each year, more than 200 people are killed at work. According to the latest Health and Safety Executive (HSE) statistics, in 2006/07 alone, 241 workers lost their lives, and 90 members of the public were killed. On top of these figures are railways-related deaths involving members of the public, and deaths on the road, in the air and at sea. For example, the HSE estimates that there are more than 20 deaths every week which are caused by road traffic accidents involving someone at work.

While most work-related deaths occur in 'hazardous' industries such as sea fishing, construction, manufacturing, agriculture and areas such as waste management and quarrying, employers outside these high-risk sectors need to be aware of CMCHA 2007, and their responsibilities under existing health and safety legislation. Work-related deaths unfortunately occur throughout the economy, with work activities resulting in the deaths of members of the public as well as employees. For example:

- Ken Farr was killed in 2002 when he was out shopping with his family, including his three-year-old daughter. A horizontal swing barrier hit his car and smashed through the windscreen as he was driving into an Asda supermarket car park.

- Six-year-old Samuel Adams was killed at the newly opened Trafford Centre in Manchester in October 1998 while on a family day out. A heavy balustrade in the arena area of the Centre fell on him. The managing company had opened the centre without carrying out appropriate risk assessments to ensure the safe removal and replacement of the railings around a stage area.

- Fifteen-year-old William Kadama and 14-year-old Gameli Akuklu were just two of several children and adults to have drowned in a swimming pool where there were not enough lifeguards on duty. The two boys died while taking part in a summer play scheme at the Metropolitan Police Training College at Hendon in 2002.

The book:

- looks at calls for, and the history of, reform of the law of corporate manslaughter, setting out details of failed prosecutions in a number of public disasters and accidents with loss of life involving large organisations; as well as cases involving manslaughter convictions of small companies and sole traders (**Chapter 1**);

- provides an overview of statutory health and safety legislation (**Chapter 2**). CMCHA 2007 sets out a range of factors for juries to consider when assessing an organisation's culpability, and this includes a failure to comply with health and safety legislation;

- provides a summary of the law of negligence and the common law duty of care, looking particularly at employers' and occupiers' duties (**Chapter 3**). CMCHA 2007 sets out the offence of corporate manslaughter (corporate homicide in Scotland) with reference to negligence and common law duties of care;

- sets out the law on individual liability for gross negligence manslaughter and culpable homicide (which applies in Scotland) (**Chapter 4**). Although CMCHA 2007 does not include secondary liability for the offence of corporate manslaughter (or homicide), individuals can still be directly liable for the offence of gross negligence manslaughter (or culpable homicide);

- explains how CMCHA 2007 changes the existing law on corporate manslaughter, sets out the views of employers' organisations, trades unions and safety campaigners; summarises the main requirements of CMCHA 2007 and examines the Act in detail, with reference to the MoJ guidance on the Act, and provides advice and commentary from legal experts (**Chapter 5**);

- describes how health and safety legislation is, and CMCHA 2007 will be, enforced and what penalties can be imposed. It looks particularly at how work-related deaths are investigated and prosecuted, and outlines the role of the various enforcement agencies and prosecuting authorities (**Chapter 6**);

- outlines when and how coroners inquests and public inquiries take place (**Chapter 7**); and

- looks at the wider corporate accountability of directors and senior managers, including an examination of the HSE and Institute of Directors (IoD) guidance on directors' duties (**Chapter 8**).

The final chapters of the book, **Chapters 9–14** look at particular sectors of the economy: construction, transport, agriculture, energy and utility supply, manufacturing, and public services.

These chapters:

- set out the views expressed by employers' organisations, trades unions and legal experts on how CMCHA 2007 is likely to impact on these sectors, together with advice for employers on what they can do to protect themselves from a manslaughter conviction;

- provide examples of cases involving manslaughter convictions of either companies or individuals in that sector, where these have occurred;

- refer to sector specific legislation that applies, although generally this is not examined in detail. The exception to this is in construction, both because of the high rate of fatalities in the industry, and because the legislation sets out duties in relation to clients as well as contractors; and

- provide examples of cases of work-related deaths and health and safety prosecutions highlighted by the HSE in these sectors.

## Acknowledgements

Many people and organisations have helped by providing invaluable information and advice for this book and they are acknowledged throughout it. In particular, I would like to thank David Bergman, Director at the Centre for Corporate Accountability (CCA) (www.corporateaccountability.org) for his help, advice and for giving permission to use information from the CCA's comprehensive database of work-related deaths and prosecutions, and briefings on the law of manslaughter and culpable homicide (in Scotland) and on directors' duties.

Also, many thanks to Lawrence Bamber, Consultant Editor of *Tolley's Health and Safety at Work*, and to Professor Frank Wright, Professor of Law at Warwick Law School, University of Warwick, for taking the time and trouble to read through and comment on a draft of the book. Finally, I would like to thank Rebecca Casey and Alan Blanchard at LexisNexis Butterworths for their help and support during the writing and editing of the book.

**Andrea Oates**
December 2007

# Contents

# Table of Statutes

# Table of Statutory Instruments

# Table of Cases

## A

## B

## C

## D

## E

## F

## G

# W

# Chapter 1

# Background

## Overview

### 1.1

This chapter looks at the need for reform of the law on corporate manslaughter. It:

- contains the most recent Health and Safety Executive statistics on deaths at work;

- compares the number of work-related deaths in recent years with the number of successful prosecutions;

- Provides details of the few cases of work-related deaths involving corporate manslaughter convictions (all against small companies);

- Examines the failure of, or lack of, corporate manslaughter prosecutions in a number of public disasters and accidents with loss of life involving large organisations which led to calls for reform:

  o the sinking of the P&O Ferry, the Herald of Free Enterprise;

  o the fire at Kings Cross Underground Station run by London Underground Ltd (LUL);

  o the explosion at the Piper Alpha Platform owned by Occidental Petroleum;

  o the Clapham train crash which occurred under British Rail;

  o the sinking of the Marchioness pleasure boat after it was hit by the Bowbelle dredger owned by South Coast Shipping Ltd;

  o the Southall Rail train crash involving Great Western Trains; ➡

○   the Ladbroke Grove train crash involving Thames Trains and Network Rail (formerly Railtrack plc);

○   The Hatfield Rail train crash involving Network Rail (formerly Railtrack plc) and Balfour Beatty; and

○   The Potters Bar derailment involving Network Rail (formerly Railtrack plc) and Jarvis.

It also outlines the history of reform leading to the Corporate Manslaughter and Corporate Homicide Act 2007 (CMCHA 2007), which will come into effect on 6 April 2008, examining:

- the 1996 Law Commission proposals: *Legislating the Criminal Code: Involuntary Manslaughter*;

- the government's 2000 consultation paper: *Reforming the Law on Involuntary Manslaughter: The Government's Proposals*;

- the 2005 draft Corporate Manslaughter Bill, published in March 2005;

- the Home Affairs and Work and Pensions Committees' scrutiny of the draft Bill, which began in October 2005;

- the government's response to the Committees' report;

- The Scottish Executive Expert Group review of culpable homicide, which was established in April 2005 and reported in November 2005;

- the Corporate Manslaughter and Homicide Bill, published in July 2006; and

- the Bill's passage through Parliament to gain Royal Assent on 26 July 2007.

Finally, it summarises the provisions of CMCHA 2007, which are examined in more detail in CHAPTER 5.

## Calls for Reform

**1.2**    CMCHA 2007 will become law on 6 April 2008, and it will have been enacted in response to a situation where thousands of people have lost their lives in UK workplaces, and in public disasters, yet only a handful of small companies, and not a single large company, have ever been successfully prosecuted for corporate manslaughter.

### A Comparison of the Number of Work-related Deaths and the Number of Successful Prosecutions

**1.3**    Every year more than 200 people are killed at work, and many more in work-related incidents. According to the main organisation responsible for enforcing health and safety laws, the Health and Safety Executive (HSE), the majority of these are preventable.

The latest statistics published by the HSE in July 2007, which are based on provisional figures, show that between April 2006 and March 2007, 241 workers were killed, and a further 90 members of the public were killed by work-related activities (excluding railways-related deaths involving members of the public).

A sectoral breakdown of the number of deaths of employees and self-employed workers in the year from April 2006 to March 2007 is provided in table 1 (below):

| Table 1: Sectoral breakdown of work-related deaths | | |
|---|---|---|
| Industry/service sector | Standard industrial classification (SIC) | Number of deaths of workers 2006/7 (provisional figures) |
| Agriculture, forestry and fishing | A, B | 34 |
| Extractive and utility supply industries | C, E | 10 |
| Manufacturing industries | D | 35 |
| Construction | F | 77 |
| Service industries | G–Q | 85 |
| Total for all sectors | | 241 |

*Source:* Health and Safety Commission (HSC) and National Statistics, *Statistics of Fatal Injuries 2006/07.*

In addition, the HSE estimates that up to a third of all road traffic accidents involve somebody who is at work at the time, which may account for over 20 fatalities and 250 serious injuries every week (see chapter 10).

And the HSE statistics do not include work-related deaths at sea and on inland waterways, nor those which occur in the air. These are recorded separately by the Marine Accident Investigation Branch (MAIB) and Civil Aviation Authority (CAA) (see chapter 10). Fifty-six deaths occurred on UK vessels in 2006, and there were 14 fatalities as a result of helicopter, microlight, gyroplane and gliding accidents (although not all these fatalities were work-related).

Between 1992 and 2005, 3,425 workers were killed, yet over the same period only 34 work-related manslaughter prosecutions were brought against companies, and only six succeeded – all against small companies or sole traders (see 1.33 and 1.34). (A manslaughter conviction against a seventh company was later overturned on appeal). (There have also been prosecutions taken against individual directors, officers and workers involved in work-related deaths – see CHAPTER 4).

### Concern about the Level of Fines and how Seriously Health and Safety Breaches are Viewed

**1.4**      Instead, where prosecutions have been taken against companies, they have tended to be been taken under health and safety legislation. The HSE's most recent report on offences and penalties, *Health and Safety Offences and Penalties Report 2004/2005,* shows that the average penalty imposed by the courts following a work-related death was £42,795[1] and in many cases fines have been far lower.

In September 2006, the Amicus section of the general UNITE union highlighted what it called the 'scandal' of a £200 fine which following the death of Dean Thomas, who was crushed to death in a paper mill in 2003 after an untrained assistant pressed the wrong button. The company, JR Crompton Ltd, had gone into administration and the judge in the case said that the fine would have been £250,000 had the company still been operating[2].

Many feel that health and safety fines, particularly where someone has been killed, are generally far too low, and comparisons have been made between sentencing and penalties for work-related deaths, and those for other corporate misdemeanours.

For example, the Communication Workers Union (CWU) included in its evidence to the October 2005 Home Affairs and Work and Pensions Committee (HAWPC), which scrutinised the Government's draft Corporate Manslaughter Bill[3], the following:

> 'When Royal Mail was convicted in 2003 for three health and safety offences following the death of a member of the public in a horrific accident at the Bridgend Delivery Office the Court imposed fines of £200,000 and this compares poorly with the power of the Postal Regulator who may impose massive fines. After missing its 2004 targets, Royal Mail paid out £50 million in compensation fines for failing to meet quality of service targets which never hurt anyone'.

In addition, some feel that breaching health and safety law is not seen as a serious criminal offence. The Law Society of Scotland (the Society) pointed out in its submission to the Scottish Executive Expert Group review of the law on corporate liability for culpable homicide:

> 'Whilst conviction for an offence under health and safety legislation may ensure that a company receives a substantial penalty, does it

attach the social stigma which some argue is appropriate for offences of this nature? Some may perceive a conviction under health and safety legislation as a lesser breach of the criminal law or almost quasi-criminal in nature. It may not attract the same stigma as a conviction for culpable homicide whether at common law or under statute.'

So there have been calls, particularly from organisations including trades unions, civil liberties groups, and those representing bereaved families, that when a company's gross management failing causes death it should be liable for a more serious offence than that available under health and safety legislation, and it should be possible to successfully prosecute companies for corporate manslaughter.

[1] This figure excludes certain industries: chemicals, mining, offshore work and railways.
[2] Amicus press release 14/9/03.
[3] House of Commons Home Affairs and Work and Pensions Committees, *Draft Corporate Manslaughter Bill Written Evidence*, October 2005 (Ev 194).

## Employers' Views

**1.5**    Employers' organisations have also recognised that the law as it stood was not satisfactory. For example, the Engineering Construction Industry Association (ECIA), which represents contractors building large and complex process plants, such as oil refineries and chemical plants, told the HAWPC: 'ECIA recognises the existing law's shortcomings in being able to bring serious organisational failings to account and the need to resolve them through new law'.[1]

In its response to the Home Office Consultation Document: *Corporate Manslaughter, the Government's Draft Bill for Reform*, June 2005, the Confederation of British Industry (CBI) commented:

'We understand the perceived need to introduce an effective legal sanction to deal with serious management failings that lead to fatalities overcoming the 'Identification' principle [see below]. Clearly it cannot be right that corporate liability can only apply if all elements of the offence can be proved against one member of the directing mind of the company.'

And the Institute of Directors (IoD) acknowledged that 'the current state of the law on involuntary manslaughter is unsatisfactory. Public confidence in parts of the business community has been damaged as a result of some tragic and heavily publicised accidents'.[2]

[1] House of Commons Home Affairs and Work and Pensions Committees, *Draft Corporate Manslaughter Bill Written Evidence*, October 2005 (Ev 3).
[2] House of Commons Home Affairs and Work and Pensions Committees, *Draft Corporate Manslaughter Bill Written Evidence* October 2005 (Ev 44).

## The Government View

**1.6**    The government summarised the need for reform in its introduction to the draft Corporate Manslaughter Bill, which was published in

March 2005, admitting that there was 'public concern that the law is not delivering justice, a feeling that has been underlined by the lack of success of corporate manslaughter prosecutions following a number of public disasters'.

The public perception that justice is not being done, and that the law dealing with corporate manslaughter is inadequate, has been heightened because a number of disasters which did not result in a corporate manslaughter prosecution were followed by inquiries which severely criticised the organisations involved and found them seriously at fault; and because there were subsequent successful prosecutions under the Health and Safety at Work etc Act 1974 (HSWA 1974) and other health and safety legislation.

Announcing the Bill, the then Home Secretary Charles Clarke said:

'This Government is committed to delivering a criminal justice system that commands the confidence of the public. A fundamental part of this is providing offences that are clear and effective. The current laws on corporate manslaughter are neither, as a number of unsuccessful prosecutions over the years stand testament.The Government is committed to reforming this area of the law and today's draft Bill marks an important step in delivering that commitment.'

In addition to ensuring that companies are properly held to account when a death at work has been caused as a result of gross failings by their senior management, the intention is that the new law will also act as a deterrent against failing to meet health and safety standards, and provide a driver for ensuring safe working practices – thereby reducing the incidence of work-related death and injury.

## The 'Identification Principle'

**1.7**    The key problem with the law in existence before CMCHA 2007 (coming into force on 6 April 2008) is the need to show that a single individual at the top of a company is personally guilty of manslaughter before the company can be prosecuted. This has become known as the 'identification principle'. It requires that a 'directing mind' – that is someone at the very top of a company who can be said to embody the company in his or her actions and decisions – has to be identified, and shown to be guilty of manslaughter. If this cannot be shown, the company escapes liability.

In the May 2000 Consultation Document, *Reforming the law on involuntary manslaughter: The government's proposals* (see 1.11), the government set out the problem with the law in this area:

'The governing principle in English law on the criminal liability of companies is that those who control or manage the affairs of the company are regarded as embodying the company itself. Before a company can be convicted of manslaughter, an individual who can be "identified as the embodiment of the company itself" must first be shown himself to have been guilty of manslaughter. Only if the individual who is the embodiment of the company is found guilty can the company be convicted. Where there is insufficient evidence to convict the individual, any prosecution of the company must fail. This principle is often referred to as the "identification" doctrine.

'There can often be great difficulty in identifying an individual who is the embodiment of the company *and who is culpable*. The problem becomes greater with larger companies which may have a more diffuse structure, where overall responsibilities for safety matters in a company can be unclear and no one individual may have that responsibility. In such circumstances it may be impossible to identify specific individuals who may be properly regarded as representing the directing mind of the company and who also possess the requisite *mens rea* (mental state) to be guilty of manslaughter: in such circumstances, no criminal liability can be attributed to the company itself.'

The situation is different from health and safety offences, where there is no requirement for *mens rea*. Organisations are considered to be vicariously liable for actions by their employees that give rise to a breach of health and safety law (see CHAPTER 2).

The Law Commission's Consultation Paper No 135 on involuntary manslaughter (see 1.9) explains that in the leading House of Lords case on the nature of the identification principle, *Tesco Supermarkets Ltd v Nattrass*[1], Lord Reid describes the distinction between it and vicarious liability:

'[A corporation] must act through living persons, though not always one or the same person. Then the person who acts is not speaking or acting for the company. He is acting as the company and his mind which directs his acts is the mind of the company. There is no question of the company being vicariously liable ... He is an embodiment of the company ... and his mind is the mind of the company. If it is a guilty mind then that guilt is the guilt of the company.'

What the identification principle has meant in practice is that only a very small number of small companies and sole traders have been convicted of the offence of corporate manslaughter, while a number of high profile cases against large companies have all failed. It became increasingly clear with these cases that the law was failing to operate flexibly in a way that recognised the reality of decision making in large organisations, with complex management structures and lines of control, and was not providing proper accountability or justice for victims.

According to the HSE, responding to the Law Commission's Consultation Paper No 135 on involuntary manslaughter, death or personal injury resulting from a major disaster is rarely due to the negligence of a single individual. In the majority of cases the disaster is caused as a result of the failure of systems controlling the risk, with the carelessness of individuals being a contributing factor.

## The History of Reform

**1.8**    CMCHA 2007 has been awaited a very long time. It was back in 1994 that the Law Commission, the independent body set up by Parliament to review and recommend reform of the law in England and Wales, published a consultation paper, *Criminal law: Involuntary manslaughter,* setting out provisional proposals for reforming the law on involuntary manslaughter. In light of the responses to its consultation, it then published its 1996 report, *Legislating the Criminal Code: Involuntary manslaughter*, which is examined below.

### The Law Commission *Legislating the Criminal Code: Involuntary Manslaughter*

**1.9**    The report looked at the criminal liability of those who kill when they do not intend to cause death or serious injury and considered what 'frame of mind or will' ought to be required if criminal liability is to be imposed for unintentional killing.

It set out that there are only two general homicide offences under the current law:

- murder – which requires proof of intention to kill or cause serious injury; and

- manslaughter – which includes all other forms of unlawful killing and is therefore extremely broad, too broad in the view of the Law Commission.

The report set out that:

> 'Although it is a single offence, manslaughter is commonly divided by lawyers into two separate categories, "voluntary" and "involuntary" manslaughter. The first of these describes cases where the accused intended to cause death or serious injury, but is excused liability for murder because some mitigating factor may be present. In the present project we are concerned only with the second type, "involuntary" manslaughter. This expression covers cases where there was no intention to kill or to cause serious injury, but where the law considers that the person who caused death was blameworthy in some other way'.

There are two cases where a person who causes a death unintentionally is sufficiently blameworthy to attract serious criminal sanctions:

- 'unlawful act manslaughter', arises where the person who causes death was engaged in a criminal act which carried with it a risk of causing some, perhaps slight, injury to another person;

- 'gross negligence manslaughter' is committed where a death is caused through extreme carelessness.

## Main recommendations

**1.10**    The report's main recommendations were to abolish the offence of involuntary manslaughter, and to replace this with two new offences:

- 'reckless killing' which would carry a maximum penalty of life imprisonment and would require a person to unreasonably and consciously decide to run a risk of causing death or serious injury; and

- 'killing by gross carelessness', which would require proof of three matters:

    (i)   there must be an obvious risk of causing death or serious injury, of which the accused need not actually have been aware, as long as he was capable of appreciating it;

    (ii)  his conduct must have fallen far below what could reasonably be expected in the circumstances, intended to cause some unlawful injury to another person or was reckless; and

    (iii) that a death was caused.

The recommendations proposed four degrees of general criminal homicide: murder, voluntary manslaughter, reckless killing and killing by gross negligence, in addition to offences aimed at specific situations, such as causing death by dangerous driving.

With regard to corporate manslaughter, it recommended a new offence of corporate killing, broadly corresponding to the individual offence of killing by gross carelessness.

The offence would be committed when the organisation's conduct in causing the death fell far below what could reasonably be expected of the organisation. Unlike the individual offence, the corporate offence should not require that the risk be obvious, or that the defendant be capable of appreciating the risk.

The Law Commission's recommendations included the following:

- a company would be guilty of corporate killing if a death was caused 'by a failure in a way in which the corporation's activities are managed or organised to ensure the health and safety of persons employed in or affected by those activities';

- it should be possible for a management failure on the part of a corporation to be a cause of the person's death even if the immediate cause is the act or omission of an individual;

- the offence should apply to any corporation, but not a corporation sole[1], nor to an unincorporated body, or an individual, even as a secondary party. However, individuals within a company could still be liable for the offences of reckless killing and killing by gross carelessness, as well as the company being liable for the offence of corporate killing; and

● it should apply where the English courts have jurisdiction and there should be no requirement of consent to bring a private prosecution.

The Law Commission's website is at www.lawcom.gov.uk.

[1]   According to *Reforming the law on involuntary manslaughter: The government's proposals*, a corporation sole is 'a corporation constituted in a single person in right of some office or function, which grants that person a special legal capacity to act in certain ways. Examples include many Ministers of the Crown and government officers, for example the Secretary of State for Defence and the Public Trustee and a bishop (but not a Roman Catholic bishop), a vicar, archdeacon, and canon.'

## Home Office: Reforming the Law on Involuntary Manslaughter: The Government's Proposals

**1.11**   It was not until May 2000, following the judgement in *R v Great Western Trains*[1] (see 1.34), which followed the 1997 Southall train crash and an unsuccessful attempt by Andrew Dinsmore MP in April 2000 to create a new criminal offence of corporate killing for companies and company officers using the Ten Minute Rule Bill[2], that the government published its own consultation document – *Reforming the law on involuntary manslaughter: The government's proposals*. This was based on, but went further than, the Law Commission recommendations.

The consultation document acknowledged that the present law in the area of 'involuntary manslaughter' – which the then Home Secretary Jack Straw described as being 'where an individual kills as a result of some blameworthy act on their part but without actually intending to cause death or serious injury' – was unclear, and where corporations were concerned, ineffective.

The government accepted the vast majority of the Law Commission's proposals, outlined in *Legislating the Criminal Code: Involuntary manslaughter*. The consultation document therefore concentrated on areas where the government came to a different conclusion to the Law Commission, or considered that a further explanation of the proposals was necessary, and it invited comment on the proposals.

It considered reform of the criminal law in England and Wales 'used to prosecute those who kill when they do not intend to cause death or serious injury, but have:

(i)   committed a crime which was only intended to result in some minor injury, but which, unforeseeably, led to death; or

(ii)   been extremely careless or negligent; or

(iii)   reckless as to whether death or serious injury occurred.

With regard to corporate liability, the government accepted the Law Commission's proposal for a new offence of corporate killing, subject to the following:

It consulted on whether the offence should apply to 'undertakings' rather than solely to corporations. An 'undertaking' is used in HSWA 1974, and has been taken to mean 'any trade or business or other activity providing employment'. This would widen the remit of the offence to cover schools, hospital trusts, partnerships and unincorporated charities, in effect, applying the offence of corporate killing to all employing organisations.

It also consulted on whether there should be application of Crown immunity[3] to the offence of corporate killing. It proposed that the same standards would be applied to Crown bodies, with access to enforcing authorities permitted; but rather than applying criminal liability, the courts would be allowed to make a declaration of non-compliance with statutory requirements, requiring immediate action to rectify the shortcoming identified.

It proposed that the new offence would be investigated and prosecuted by the health and safety enforcing authorities, possibly other enforcing authorities as appropriate – such as those dealing with particular forms of transport – as well as the police and the Crown Prosecution Service (CPS).

The government also proposed that action should be capable of being taken against a parent or other group companies where it could be shown that their own management failures were a cause of the death concerned. And it asked for comments on:

● the proposal that 'any individual who could be shown to have had some influence on, or responsibility for, the circumstances in which a management failure falling far below what could reasonably be expected was a cause of a person's death, should be subject to disqualification from acting in a management role in any undertaking carrying on a business or activity in Great Britain'; and

● whether it is right in principle that officers of undertakings, if they contribute to the management failure resulting in death, should be liable to a penalty of imprisonment in separate criminal proceedings.

The consultation period closed in September 2000, but it was not until 2005 that the government published a draft Corporate Manslaughter Bill.

In the intervening period, the then Director for Public Prosecutions (DPP) David Calvert-Smith, QC, repeated his call for a change in the law in November 2001. He demanded reform 'to make it easier for the criminal courts to bear down on negligent treatment of employees in the workforce' after Euromin and its general manager, Richard Martell, were acquitted of gross negligence manslaughter following the death of Simon Jones[4].

Simon was killed on his first day at work unloading cargo in a ship at Shoreham Docks, after being sent there by Brighton-based employment agency Personnel Selection.

The prosecution was taken after a ruling in March 2000 by the Divisional Court[5] that the CPS should reconsider its earlier decision not to prosecute. It was the first successful judicial review[6] of a decision not to prosecute for manslaughter over a workplace death.

However, the company and its general manager were acquitted of manslaughter and Euromin was instead found guilty of two offences under HSWA 1974 and fined £50,000 plus £20,000 costs (see CHAPTER 4 for full details of this case).

Attempts were made to introduce an offence of corporate manslaughter by amending the Criminal Justice Bill in 2002/2003, but although the then Home Secretary David Blunkett repeated the government's intention to bring forward a Bill at this time, no timescale was set out.

In January 2005, there was another unsuccessful attempt at legislation when a Private Members Bill on the issue of directors' duties was brought by Stephen Hepburn MP (see CHAPTER 8).

[1]   (1999) (unreported).
[2]   The UK Parliament website at www.parliament.gov.uk explains that in the House of Commons, Bills introduced under the ten-minute rule in the House of Commons are a way in which backbench MPs can introduce legislation. However, as there is little parliamentary time available, they mainly provide the opportunity for MPs to test Parliament's opinion on a particular subject. The rule allows a brief introductory speech of no more than ten minutes and one of the same length opposing the motion.
[3]   There are a number of government bodies and quasi-government bodies which have been able to claim immunity from prosecution because they are said to be acting as a servant or agent of the Crown.
[4]   *R v Martell & Euromin Ltd* (2001) (unreported).
[5]   *R v Director of Public Prosecutions, ex parte Jones* [2000] IRLR 373.
[6]   Judicial review is explained on the Judiciary of England and Wales website – of judges, magistrates and tribunal members in England and Wales – which can be found at www.judiciary.gov.uk:
      "Judicial review is a type of court proceeding in which a judge reviews the lawfulness of a decision or action made by a public body. In other words, judicial reviews are a challenge to the way in which a decision has been made, rather than the rights and wrongs of the conclusion reached."
      It explains that a public body may be able to make the same decision again, as long as this is done lawfully. In the case of a work-related death, the family of the person killed can apply for a judicial review if a decision has been taken not to prosecute. Guidance on this procedure is available on Her Majesty's Courts Service website at www.hrcourts-service.gov.uk.

## Corporate Manslaughter: The Government's Draft Bill for Reform

**1.12**    So, despite strong support for reform of the law, it was not until March 2005 that the government at last published its draft Corporate Manslaughter Bill. It also provided an overview of the responses received during its 2000 consultation exercise, which showed that there was support for:

- reform of the law;

- a wide application of the offence to cover all undertakings, rather than applying solely to corporations as originally proposed by the Law Commission; and

- the removal of Crown immunity.

With regard to the issue of individual liability, it reported that on the one hand, many respondents considered that disqualification and imprisonment were 'draconian measures which would lead to scape-goating, a culture of blame, and a risk-averse environment'. But on the other, many victims' support groups, trades unions and individuals argued that without any individual liability, the corporate offence would lack sufficient deterrent force:

> 'Many of these argued that without individual penalties, officers within large companies would not be sufficiently concerned by the prospect of a large corporate fine to take greater personal responsibility for health and safety. These arguments were frequently related to the need to introduce a statutory requirement for companies to have nominated health and safety directors'.

There was some support for a specialist unit to investigate all work-related deaths, and agreement that whichever agency was responsible for investigating and prosecuting the new offence, detailed working protocols would be necessary to ensure effective joint working.

In setting out the government's draft Bill, the then Home Secretary Charles Clarke said that:

> ' ... the proposals need to strike a careful balance. Companies and other organisations must be held properly to account for gross failings by their senior management which have fatal consequences. On the other hand, as an offence of homicide, corporate manslaughter charges must be reserved for the very worst cases of management failure.'

*Key proposals contained in the draft Bill*

**1.13**    The main proposals in the draft Bill are set out below:

13

THE OFFENCE

*Scope of the offence: duty of care*

**1.14**    The offence would apply where a duty of care is owed at common law (in the context of the law of negligence (see CHAPTER 3)).

This duty of care is owed by, for example:

• employers to employees;

• transport companies to passengers; and

• manufacturers to the users of products.

The offence proposed would apply where an organisation owes a duty of care:

• as an employer or occupier of land; and

• when supplying goods or services or when engaged in other commercial activities (for example, in mining or fishing).

*Management failure by senior managers – a new test*

**1.15**    A new test to replace the need to find a 'directing mind' of a company personally guilty of gross negligence would look more widely at failings within the senior management of an organisation.

An organisation would be guilty of the new offence if 'a gross failing by its senior managers to take reasonable care for the safety of their workers or members of the public caused a person's death'.

The requirement in the new offence for a management failure on the part of its senior managers was intended to replace the identification principle 'with a basis for corporate liability that better reflects the complexities of decision taking and management within modern large organisations, but which is also relevant for smaller bodies'.

It focuses on the arrangements and practices for carrying out the organisation's work rather than any immediate negligent act by an employee, and applies to management failings by an organisation's senior managers, either individually or collectively. But organisations would not be liable on the basis of any immediate, operational negligence causing death, or the 'unpredictable, maverick acts of its employees'.

The government said that it had not replaced the requirement to identify a single, directing mind with the need to identify several, but provided a different basis of liability that focuses on the way the activities of an organisation were in practice organised or managed. The new offence would be targeted at strategic management, not failings at a relatively junior level.

The definition of a senior manager includes those who play a role in making management decisions about, or actually managing, the activities of the organisation as a whole or a 'substantial part' of it. The person must also play a 'significant role'.

*Gross breach of the duty to take reasonable care*

**1.16**    The organisation would need to have owed a duty of care to the victim (see 1.14); and the management failure would have to amount to a gross breach of the duty to take reasonable care. The offence requires the same high threshold that the law of gross negligence manslaughter requires: a gross failure that causes death, involving conduct that falls far below what can reasonably be expected in the circumstances.

The draft Bill provided a framework for assessing an organisation's conduct, including a clear link with standards imposed by health and safety legislation, and guidance on how these should be discharged.

APPLICATION

*To corporations*

**1.17**    The new offence would apply to all companies incorporated under company law and other types of incorporated body. Parent companies, as well as subsidiaries, would be liable to prosecution where a duty of care is owed to the victim in respect of one of the activities covered by the offence, and a gross management failure by its senior managers caused a death.

*To the Crown and other government bodies*

**1.18**    The offence would apply to bodies incorporated under statute or Royal Charter, such as local authorities, NHS trusts, and many non-departmental public bodies. Government bodies and other Crown bodies would also be liable to prosecution. The draft Bill included a schedule of a list of particular Crown bodies to which the offence applies.

However, the offence would not hold the government or public bodies to account for matters of public policy or uniquely public functions, such as the custody of prisoners. Decisions involving matters of public policy would be outside the scope of the offence, and deaths relating to public policy decisions which have been taken after weighing up financial, social or political considerations would not be subject to the new offence.

The government explained that 'the offence does not apply to activities that the private sector either does not do, or cannot do without particular lawful authority, which are areas more appropriately subject to other lines of accountability ... Government departments and other public authorities are subject to a range of accountability mechanisms including through Ministers in Parliament, the Human Rights Act [1988], public inquiries and other independent investigations, judicial review and Ombudsmen.'

## To unincorporated bodies

**1.19**   The draft Bill did not apply the offence to unincorporated bodies such as some types of partnership, trades unions, and some registered friendly societies, which do not have a distinct legal personality. However, it kept this position under review.

And while police authorities are incorporated bodies and would be covered by the new offence, police forces are not incorporated and would not be covered by the new offence. The government said that it did not intend in principle for police forces to be outside the scope of the offence, and that the legislation should in due course extend to them.

## To individuals

**1.20**   The offence would not apply to individual directors or others. The government argued that proceedings for manslaughter, or under health and safety law, would continue to be possible against individuals where their conduct makes them liable under other, existing legislation (see chapter 4).

## Sanctions

**1.21**   Organisations found guilty of corporate manslaughter would face an unlimited fine, and the courts would be able to impose remedial orders, allowing the court to specify remedial action to be taken to address the failures that led to a death within a specified time.

## Extent

**1.22**   The new offence would apply to England and Wales. The Bill did not cover Scotland and Northern Ireland at that time. The explanatory notes to the Bill said:

'Criminal law in Northern Ireland is the responsibility of the Secretary of State for Northern Ireland and is a devolved matter in Scotland. The Secretary of State intends to consult Northern Ireland on the proposal that the Bill's provisions should also extend to that juris-diction. Scottish Ministers will be consulting separately on proposals for reforming Scottish law'.

## House of Commons Home Affairs and Work and Pensions Committee Report

**1.23**   The draft Corporate Manslaughter Bill was then subject to pre-legislative scrutiny[1] by a sub-committee of the House of Commons Home Affairs and Work and Pensions Committees, which started taking evidence in October 2005.

The committee was supportive of the reform of the law on corporate manslaughter, and although it urged the government to introduce an actual Bill by the end of the 2005/06 Parliamentary session, it outlined a number of concerns regarding the draft Bill, saying:

'We are concerned that the current drafting of the Bill may not satisfy those who have previously felt so let down by the law'.

The committee made a total of 57 recommendations. Its key concerns were that:

- although the removal of Crown immunity was welcomed, some of the exemptions were too broad, particularly the proposed exemption for deaths in police custody and prisons;

- there should be provision to prosecute an individual for contributing to the offence of corporate manslaughter;

- a wider package of corporate sanctions should have been considered;

- there should not be a requirement to obtain the consent of the DPP before a private prosecution can be brought;

- the offence should have a wider territorial application;

- the proposed basis for liability is overly complicated and the civil law concept of a duty of care in negligence should be removed from the Bill, since it is inappropriate to adopt a civil law concept as the basis for a criminal offence;

- the restriction of management failure to that by senior managers has reintroduced some of the problems of the 'identification principle' and that 'management failure' should be used as a basis for liability; and

- juries should be assisted by being required to consider whether there has been a serious breach of health and safety legislation and related guidance, or other relevant legislation, which would allow them to assess whether a corporate culture that encouraged, tolerated or led to that management failure existed.

The report also warned that the draft Bill could create incentives to treat health and safety less seriously, by allowing senior directors to delegate decisions on health and safety to more junior staff in order to avoid the risk of prosecution.

The committee also looked at whether the offence would cover fatal damage to health, which resulted from sustained exposure to hazardous substances, or as a result of contracting a disease with a long latency, in addition to deaths resulting from immediate injury. It concluded that it was satisfied that the Bill would apply in these circumstances, but urged the government to ensure that sufficient resources and appropriate procedures would be in place so that prosecutions could be brought for deaths related to occupational health causes.

The government replied to the committee in March 2006 saying that the government had taken on board the recommendation to introduce a simpler test to define corporate culpability, based on the concept of 'management failure' and would look at reframing the test.

Although the government said that it would not create a secondary offence for individual directors or managers complicit in corporate manslaughter; it said that directors whose companies were found guilty of corporate manslaughter could be barred from their posts in future, and it agreed to look at further legislation on the disqualification of directors.

It also said that the legislation would not be extended to cover prisons, the armed forces or senior civil servants. On exemptions in the Bill, the government said it would look again at 'where the line should be drawn between those public functions whose management should be subject to scrutiny in the criminal justice system and those where strategic accountability lies properly through other means'.

---

[1]   Pre-legislative scrutiny allows Parliament to examine and make recommendations about legislative proposals before a Bill is introduced to Parliament.

## Scottish Executive Review of Scots law

**1.24**    At the same time as developments were taking place in Westminster, the Scottish Executive was also examining the operation of the law in Scotland. Although criminal law on culpable homicide differs from the law of manslaughter elsewhere in the UK, the same issues of identifying a directing mind had arisen in Scotland.

In April 2005, the Scottish Executive established an Expert Group, consisting of representatives from business and trades unions, academia, the public sector and the legal profession, to review Scots law on corporate liability for culpable homicide. This took into account the proposals set out in the government's draft Corporate Manslaughter Bill. The Group reported on 17 November 2005.

### Background to the review

**1.25**    The report sets out that an average of almost 40 workers and members of the public are killed through work each year in Scotland, and many more if deaths on the railway, and those resulting from past exposure to asbestos, fires in workplaces, food poisoning as a result of 'commercial sources' of food, the sea fishing industry and road deaths while people are at work are included.

In Scotland an organisation can be convicted of a common law crime, and may be prosecuted on a charge of culpable homicide, which applies where there was not intention to kill, but behaviour was so reckless with complete disregard or indifference to potential dangers and possible consequences, that the law considers there is responsibility for the death.

Only one prosecution of a company for the crime of culpable homicide has taken place in Scotland[1].

The gas supply company Transco was charged with the homicide of Andrew and Janette Findlay and their children 13-year old Stacey and 11-year old Daryl who died on 22 December 1999 when a massive explosion destroyed a family house in Larkhall, Lanarkshire[1].

An investigation by the HSE had found that the iron mains pipe running through the front garden of the house had ruptured, and gas leaking from the main had found its way into the under-floor void and subsequently the kitchen, where it ignited. The blast also caused extensive damage to neighbouring properties.

The company challenged the competency, relevancy and specification of the charges, and claimed that if the prosecution proceeded to trial, the Lord Advocate would be acting incompatibly with the appellant's rights under certain articles of the European Convention on Human Rights and Fundamental Freedoms.

At the first hearing the complaints of lack of specification were not insisted on and the challenges in respect of competency and relevancy were confined to culpable homicide – Lord Carloway ruled against the company, stating:

'It may well be that in England there is a need to identify a particular person who could, if charged, also have been guilty of manslaughter, before a company can be found to have committed that crime. It is not a requirement under the Scots law of culpable homicide'

However, the company then appealed to the Criminal Court of Appeal and the charge was subsequently dismissed, although Transco was later successfully prosecuted under HSWA 1974 ss 3 and 33 and was fined £15 million.

Until the Appeal Court judgement[2], the Scottish Executive and Crown Office had believed that this area of the law was adequately covered by the Scottish common law offence of culpable homicide.

Again the 'identification principle' proved to be a barrier to a successful prosecution. The Expert Group report sets out why the court dismissed the charge:

'There are a number of problems associated with this identification principle. For example, the attribution of liability is associated with the conduct and states of mind of individuals. In organisations with complex, dynamic and diffuse organisational structures, it may be difficult to identify individuals at a senior level who are sufficiently directly involved to enable their state of mind to constitute the *mens rea* of the organisation. This makes it difficult when prosecuting an offence at common law to pinpoint the controlling mind in any but the simplest type of organisation. It is further complicated by the fact that corporate structures, the make-up of groups and the positions held by individuals, inevitably change over time. The Court considered that the relevant individuals must be the same throughout the commission of the offence.

In addition, in considering the allegations which the prosecution had identified as demonstrating Transco's guilt, the Court expressly stated that the law in Scotland does not recognise the principle of "aggregation", whereby conduct and states of mind of a number of people over a period of time, none of whom individually could be said to have possessed the necessary *mens rea,* might nevertheless be accumulated so that they collectively could provide the necessary *mens rea* which is then attributed to the body'.

The key problem in the *Transco* case was that the criminal actions or inactions of those in positions of sufficient authority could not be identified in a way that could trigger corporate liability. It was not possible to aggregate offences over a long period of time, over which responsibilities for health and safety had changed between different people.

The Expert Group report said that the implication of the judgment is that complex organisations cannot in practice be prosecuted for culpable homicide. It said that this was a gap in criminal law that needed to be addressed by amending the law so that such organisations could be prosecuted for culpable deaths arising from their activities.

[1]  *Transco plc v HM Advocate* 2004 SLT 995, 2004 SCCR 1. See Centre for Corporate Accountability (CCA) website at www.corporateaccountability.org/manslaughter/scotland/main.htm#Transco.
[2]  [2005] HCJAC 1, 2005 SLT 211, 2005 SCCR 117.

*Expert Group Comments on the draft Bill for England and Wales*

**1.26**     In looking at how the law should be reformed, the Group looked at the draft Corporate Manslaughter Bill for England and Wales, but felt strongly that it was not an appropriate model for Scotland for the following reasons:

• the proposed Home Office offence is based on the English offence of manslaughter by gross negligence which applies where a duty of care is owed at common law, which is 'materially' different from the common law of corporate homicide in Scotland. It would be difficult to import the concept of 'duty of care' into Scots criminal law;

• the senior management test could perpetuate problems with the identification principle by still requiring identification of an individual or individuals who were the 'controlling mind'. It could also encourage organisations to transfer management decisions lower down the management chain to avoid those falling within the definition of senior management;

- whether senior managers sought to cause the organisation to profit from the failure should not be relevant to whether an offence had been committed, although it could be taken into consideration when sentencing;

- a secondary offence covering individual directors or managers should be included;

- any offence should apply equally to public and private sector bodies; and there should be more extensive removal of Crown immunity; and

- a range of penalties other than fines and remedial orders should be available.

*Expert report conclusions*

**1.27**  The Expert Group concluded and recommended the following:

- there should be a new statutory offence of corporate killing for organisations guilty of recklessness which results in the death of employees or members of the public;

- an offence should make organisations responsible for actions or omissions by their agents which result in death. An organisation should be liable where it fails to put in place policies, practices and systems to ensure the health and safety of its employees and those affected by its activities – this could include allowing or failing to prevent a corporate culture to exist which encourages, tolerates or leads to an offence taking place;

- there would be a due diligence defence where an organisation could show that policies and procedures which should have prevented an incident taking place were in place, and there was a corporate culture in place, reinforcing the policies and procedures;

- a secondary offence for individual directors or senior managers whose actions or omissions significantly contributed to death (this was recommended by a majority of the group);

- the offence should cover incorporated bodies and should extend, as far as practically possible, to all Crown bodies;

- the legislation should apply equally to deaths in Scotland caused by organisations based outside Scotland, and vice versa (again a majority recommendation);

- further consideration should be given as to whether the scope of the offence should be limited to death or extended to cover serious injury and occupational illness;

- a wide range of penalties should be available to courts when sentencing organisations, including corporate probation, equity fines and community orders; as well as penalties for individuals including disqualification and imprisonment;

- adequate resources need to be made available to ensure full investigation and enforcement of any new legislation which is not to the detriment of existing HSE, police and local authority resources for preventative work; and

- government monitoring of the practical impact of any legislative changes to ensure that they have had the intended result.

The Scottish Executive considered measures to make corporate homicide an offence, but then announced that since the Westminster Bill covered reserved matters of health and safety, it would apply to Scotland. Causing some surprise when it was published – as it had been widely assumed since reform of the law was first discussed by the Law Commission that there would be separate legislation for Scotland – the government's Corporate Manslaughter and Corporate Homicide Bill extended to the whole of the UK, including Scotland, as well as Northern Ireland.

## Culpable Homicide (Scotland) Bill

**1.28**    This development was criticised by organisations including the Scottish TUC (STUC). It supported a Private Member's Bill put forward by Karen Gillon, Labour MSP for Clydesdale, in the Scottish Parliament which would have introduced separate legislation for Scotland. Despite cross-party support, the *Culpable Homicide (Scotland) Bill* ran out of time. Ian Tasker, Assistant Secretary (Health and Safety) at the STUC, said that discussions concerning the reintroduction of the Bill were continuing, and the STUC hoped that there would be the same level of cross-party support, particularly in the light of the Stockline case (see CHAPTER 12), despite the change of administration. The main difference between it and CMCHA 2007 is that it would apply to individuals as well as organisations, and liability could be attributed to an organisation on the basis of any manager. In addition, the Bill sets out a maximum penalty of life imprisonment for a person found guilty of culpable homicide.

However, in response to a question in the Scottish Parliament from Karen Gillon about how the Scottish Executive believes that Scotland's law on culpable homicide can be developed, Mr Kenny MacAskill, the Cabinet Secretary for Justice said on 22 November 2007:

'We have no plans to change the common law on culpable homicide. We consider that the Corporate Manslaughter and Corporate Homicide Act 2007 addresses the problem identified by the *Transco* case. The Act sends a robust message to organisations that failures to meet their duty of care to employees and the public will not be tolerated. That Act comes into force in April, and our priority is to ensure its successful implementation.'

## The Corporate Manslaughter and Corporate Homicide Bill

**1.29**   In July 2006, the government introduced its final Bill, the Corporate Manslaughter and Corporate Homicide Bill, which made provision for a new offence of corporate manslaughter, called corporate homicide in Scotland. This would apply to companies and other incorporated bodies, government departments and similar bodies and police forces.

Introducing the Bill, the then Home Office Minister Gerry Sutcliffe said that the government would look be looking to refine the definition of the new offence of corporate manslaughter to ensure that it focused on the overall picture of how an organisation's activities were managed by its senior managers, rather than focusing on the actions of one individual, or failings at junior level.

An organisation would be guilty of the new offence if someone were to be killed as a result of the gross failure of an organisation's senior managers to, for example:

- ensure safe working practices for their employees (eg that staff are properly trained and equipment is in a safe condition); and

- maintain the safety of their premises (eg ensuring that lifts are properly maintained and fire precautions taken).

It would also cover organisations providing goods and services to members of the public, the construction, use or maintenance of infrastructure or vehicles, or when operating commercially.

The Bill lifted Crown immunity so that Crown bodies – such as government departments – as well as other public sector organisations, including police forces, would be on an equal footing with the private sector when carrying out similar activities.

The new offence would be clearly linked to the standards required under existing health and safety laws. It would not apply to circumstances where an organisation does not owe a duty of care or to certain public and government functions whose management involve wider questions of public policy and are already subject to other forms of accountability.

For example, it would not apply to strategic decisions about the spending of public money or activities like statutory inspection, holding prisoners in detention, the response of the emergency services, policing or child protection.

Again, the Minister indicated that there would be some further refining of the areas that the new offence would not cover during the Bill's passage through Parliament.

He confirmed that the penalty would be an unlimited fine, although the Bill would also give the courts power to impose a remedial order, which can already be imposed for health and safety offences, and would require the company to address the cause of the fatality.

Individual offences for 'aiding, abetting, counselling or procuring' and private prosecutions would be prohibited.

The offence would not apply to deaths occurring outside Britain, even if the management failure took place in Britain, or the death was the result of the conduct of a British company.

The final Bill was not hugely different to the draft Bill, although some changes were made in response to the House of Commons select committee report. The major change was, as outlined above, it was extended to cover Scotland (and Northern Ireland) as well as England and Wales.

In addition, the proposed offence would now apply to police forces in relation to their employees and other people working for, or performing services for, the organisation; and as an occupier of premises. Outside of this, operations, activities and training for dealing with terrorism, civil unrest and serious public disorder and other policing or law enforcement activities are exempt from the legislation.

And although the Home Office said that it would draw up a new 'senior manager' test, this was not included in the final Bill, and was still being looked at as the Bill progressed through Parliament.

## *The Bill's passage through Parliament*

**1.30**    As the Bill progressed through Parliament, a number of other changes were made:

- the 'senior manager' test was modified to a 'senior management' test;

- the new offence was extended beyond corporate bodies to unincorporated partnerships, trade unions and employer associations;

- a new form of sanction – publicity orders – were included; and

- deaths in custody and detention were included – this was to prove the most controversial part of the Bill, and a key demand of the House of Lords. After the Bill had gone through all its stages in the House of Commons and the House of Lords, it was passed between the two Houses a number of times until agreement could be reached on this issue. The government eventually tabled an amendment meaning that on the face of the Bill, the new offence would apply to deaths in custody. However, before this part of CMCHA 2007 comes into force, a further resolution must be agreed by both Houses of Parliament (known as the affirmative resolution procedure). The government is committed to passing the resolution, although the timetable for this has been set out as being between three and five years (see CHAPTER 5).

## The Corporate Manslaughter and Corporate Homicide Act 2007

**1.31** The Bill received Royal Assent on 26 July 2007 and almost all the provisions of CMCHA 2007 will become law on 6 April 2008 (apart from those relating to deaths in custody and detention (see 1.30) and publicity orders, which will come into effect once guidelines on their application have been drawn up. The Sentencing Advisory Panel published a consultation paper in November 2007 with proposals for sentencing for corporate manslaughter. In addition to guidance on fines, the paper also contained guidance on publicity orders. The final guidelines for judges, which will be produced by the Sentencing Guidelines Council, are expected to be ready by autumn 2008 (see CHAPTER 6).

According to the Ministry of Justice, CMCHA 2007:

- will make it easier to prosecute companies and other large organisations when gross failures in the management of health and safety led to a death, by delivering a new, more effective basis for corporate liability;

- reforms the law so that a key obstacle to successful prosecutions (that is the identification principle) has now been removed. It means that both small and large companies can be held liable for manslaughter where gross failures in the management of health and safety cause death, not just health and safety breaches;

- complements the current law under which individuals can be prosecuted for gross negligence manslaughter and health and safety offences, where there is direct evidence of their culpability; and

- lifts Crown immunity to prosecution. Crown bodies, such as government departments, will be liable for the first time. The Act will apply to companies and other corporate bodies, in the public and private sector, government departments, police forces and certain unincorporated bodies, such as partnerships, where these are employers.

A summary of CMCHA 2007 is provided below and CHAPTER 5 outlines the new Act in detail.

---

- The offence is called corporate manslaughter in England, Wales and Northern Ireland, and corporate homicide in Scotland.

- An organisation is guilty of the offence if the way in which it organises or manages its activities causes a death, and this amounts to a gross breach of a relevant duty of care it owed to the victim. ➡

---

- An organisation will only be guilty of the offence if the way in which its activities are managed or organised by its senior management is a substantial element of the breach – the senior management test.

- The offence applies where the organisation owed a duty of care to the victim under the law of negligence.

- It will apply to deaths in detention and custody, but this part of CMCHA 2007 will not be enacted on 6 April 2008, but in some three to five years time.

- The offence applies to corporations, government departments (and other bodies listed in a Schedule to CMCHA 2007), police forces, partnerships, trade unions and employer associations (where these are employers); but does not apply to corporations sole.

- Crown bodies are not immune from prosecution under CMCHA 2007.

- Public policy decisions, exclusively public functions and statutory inspections are excluded from the scope of the offence.

- The Act includes a number of exemptions: for certain military activities and for police and other law enforcement bodies in particular situations (including terrorism and civil unrest); in relation to responding to emergencies; and for statutory functions relating to child protection and probation functions.

- The Act sets out factors for the jury to consider when deciding if there has been a gross breach of a relevant duty of care. It must consider whether health and safety legislation was complied with; and it may consider whether the culture of the organisation tolerated breaches, and any relevant health and safety guidance.

- Consent of the DPP is needed for proceedings for the offence to be instituted.

- There is no secondary liability for the offence – so individuals will not be liable for aiding, abetting, counselling or procuring the commission of, or in Scotland, being art and part of, the offence.

- The Act abolishes the common law offence of gross negligence manslaughter in relation to corporations.

- An organisation found guilty of corporate manslaughter (or corporate homicide) faces an unlimited fine, and the courts will have the power to make remedial orders and publicity orders (the latter are expected to come into force in autumn 2008).

## Reaction to CMCHA 2007

**1.32**    Employers' organisations have generally welcomed CMCHA 2007. For example, the Construction Confederation said:

'We welcome the Corporate Manslaughter Act as a useful addition to existing provision and a proportionate response which rightly focuses on joint responsibility rather than targeting individuals. System failure is often at fault for accidents and this legislation recognises that, resisting the temptation to target individual directors. Moves to hold individual directors accountable would only have cut across the collective responsibility for the management of health and safety that should exist in organisations.

'It should be clear that this is not an escape clause for individual malpractice. Under the existing law, courts can already impose unlimited fines on companies and individuals where management failures cause death or serious injury under the Health and Safety at Work Act. The problem is they rarely do.'

But many trades unions and safety campaigners have either given a qualified welcome to the legislation, or have expressed disappointment, particularly with regard to the lack of individual liability.

The Trades Union Congress (TUC) says that despite the lack of individual liability for individual directors, it hopes CMCHA 2007 will mean the start of a change in safety culture at the top of organisations.

But construction union UCATT, along with some safety campaign groups, has called CMCHA 2007 a 'hollow victory':

'The Bill was a severe disappointment for UCATT as it failed to include clauses which would have allowed the imprisonment of company directors, if their negligence had led to the death of a worker. Without such clauses in the Bill, UCATT have argued there will not be a step change in safety in the construction industry, the most dangerous industrial sector in Britain. Both the Labour Party and the TUC have policy supporting the imprisonment of negligent directors (directors duties).'

Alan Ritchie, General Secretary of UCATT, added:

'Ultimately any legislation involving corporate manslaughter is to be welcomed. However this is a hollow victory. The legislation falls far short of Labour Party policy, passed following UCATT's motion at conference in 2006 which committed the party to campaign for director's duties and the possibility of imprisonment for negligent directors.'

And he said:

'The issue of director's duties will not go away because without them the construction industry will not become an appreciably safer industry. UCATT will continue to campaign for their introduction. It is the single most important piece of legislation to stop our members being killed at work'.

The charity and campaign group the Centre for Corporate Accountability (CCA) also sees CMCHA 2007 as a lost opportunity to some extent, but is more positive about its impact. According to the September 2007 issue of *Health and Safety at Work* magazine, its director, David Bergman said: 'We do think it will increase the chances of greater justice and accountability for work-related deaths' and the CCA hopes it will bring 'an end to the immunity that large and medium-sized companies have had over the years'.

And the public safety campaign group Disaster Action, which has campaigned for a change to the law for 16 years, said that the government's 2000 commitment to legislation that would 'provide for safer travel on the railways, in the air, at sea and on the roads, and will take forward proposals for revitalising health and safety at work' has now been honoured. It reacted to the new law saying:

'Parliament has taken a significant step towards ensuring that the safety of people is at the core of every corporation's culture. The central purpose of this law is to ensure that other companies should not replicate the sloppy corporate behaviour that led to the 'unlawful killing' of so many people on the Herald of Free Enterprise. This is not about scapegoating, nor retribution, but about what is just. The law will act as an important deterrent, offering the protection denied to those killed on the Herald and in numerous disasters that have followed'.

Executive Director, Pamela Dix added: 'The Act is a memorial to the hundreds of victims of unsafe corporate practices whom we represent. It will go some way to show that such dangerous practices are no longer to be tolerated.'

## Examples of Cases involving Corporate Manslaughter Convictions[1]

**1.33**

*OLL Ltd[2]*

In a December 1994 judgment, a company specialising in multi-activity holidays, OLL Ltd, and its managing director, Peter Kite, were convicted of gross negligence manslaughter. The managing director was sentenced to a term of three years' imprisonment (which was later reduced to two) and the company fined £60,000 after four students (aged between 16 and 17) were drowned on a canoeing trip in Lyme Bay. Kite was convicted on the principle of identification. This was the first successful prosecution of a company for gross negligence manslaughter, and the first time a director had received a prison sentence in relation to a work-related death. The management structure was simple and made the establishment of liability straightforward as Kite was the only managing director and he could be identified as the 'directing mind' with personal knowledge of the inadequate safety systems and the consequent risks.

## *Jackson Transport (Ossett) Ltd*[3]

In September 1996, the company and its managing (and sole) director, Alan Jackson, were convicted for the manslaughter of James Hodgson. James died in May 1994 after being splashed with highly toxic chemicals. He had been using steam pressure to clean a valve in a tanker blocked with the chemicals. The company had not provided personal protective clothing – James was wearing only a pair of overalls and a baseball cap. Special suits for protection were provided to tanker drivers, but they were in poor condition and there were no hats, visors or goggles available. Supervision and training were also lacking, there were no first aiders and no first aid equipment, and there were no procedures to ensure safe entry to the tank or rescue equipment for use in an emergency.

The company had drawn up a manual which detailed safe methods of cleaning out tankers, but this had been produced six years before James's death and had been forgotten.

Jackson was sentenced to 12 months' imprisonment and the company was fined £15,000 in respect of the manslaughter charge.

## *English Brothers Ltd*[4]

In August 2001, construction company English Brothers Ltd pleaded guilty to the manslaughter of Bill Larkman, a gang foreman, who died in June 1999 when he fell more than eight metres through a fragile roof to his death. Melvyn Hubbard, a director of the company, had pleaded not guilty, which was accepted by the prosecution. HSE inspectors had seen Larkman working at another English Brothers site without using the correct safety equipment, and had spoken to the company about its safety failings, but nothing was done to remedy the situation. The company was fined £25,000.

## *Teglgaard Hardwood (UK) Ltd*[5]

In February 2003, the company and one of its directors, John Horner, pleaded guilty at Hull Crown Court to the manslaughter of labourer Christopher Longrigg, who died in April 2000 when a stack of timber fell on him. The timber had been incorrectly stacked and had broken away from its ties.

The company was fined £25,000 and Horner was also given a 15-month prison sentence, suspended for two years. A charge of manslaughter was laid against John Horner's son, John, who was also a company director. However, criminal charges were not continued against him as the Crown believed this was inappropriate. It regarded his father to be the main source of company actions.

## *Nationwide Heating Services Ltd*[6]

Apprentice Benjamin Pinkham died in February 2003, five days after suffering 90 per cent burns when the storage tank he was cleaning at Princess Yachts International in Plymouth exploded.

In July 2004 Alan Mark, managing director of Plymouth-based Nationwide Heating Systems Ltd, was convicted of Ben's manslaughter and jailed for 12 months at Exeter Crown Court. Nationwide Heating Systems Ltd was also found guilty of manslaughter. Both Mark and the company had pleaded guilty to three health and safety offences: failing to make a suitable assessment of risks to the company's employees; failure to ensure the health and safety of Mr Pinkham and another apprentice, Jonathan Jarvis, inside the tank; and failure to provide a system of work in a confined space which was safe and without risk to health.

Princess Yachts pleaded guilty at an earlier hearing to two health and safety offences and was fined £90,000 with £10,000 prosecution costs.

## Keymark Services[7]

In December 2004, director Melvyn Spree and his company, Keymark Services, admitted the manslaughter and unlawful killing of Neil Owen and Benjamin Kwapong. The two men were killed in a crash on the M1 in Northamptonshire in February 2002 when lorry driver Stephen Law, who worked for the company and who was also killed, fell asleep at the wheel and crashed into seven vehicles.

Spree was jailed for seven years . Another director, Lorraine March received a 16-month prison sentence for conspiracy to falsify driving records, and the two directors were banned for life from holding such positions.

Company secretary Clare Miller was given 160 hours' community service, for the same charge. In addition, all of the company's 10 full-time drivers were prosecuted for a total of 400 different offences of breaching driving regulations and falsifying vehicle records. Three part-time drivers also received official cautions.

The company was fined £50,000 after pleading guilty to a corporate manslaughter offence. It also had its license to operate withdrawn by the Vehicle Inspectorate.

[1]   See Centre for Corporate Accountability (www.corporateaccountability.org) and Michael G Welham, *Corporate killing – A managers' guide to legal compliance* (Tolley, 2002); news.bbc.co.uk/1/hi/england/2809395.stm; news.bbc.co.uk/1/hi/england/2795789.stm; news.bbc.co.uk/1/hi/england/4066331.stm; House of Commons Library Research Paper 05/18 1 March 2005 Health and Safety (Directors' Duties) Bill, Edward Beale, Brenda Brevitt, Sally Broadbridge, Louise Butcher and Timothy Edwards; Statement issued by Northamptonshire Police on Operation Nuthatch (www.northants.police.uk).
[2]   *R v Kite and OLL Ltd* (1994) (unreported).
[3]   *R v Jackson Transport (OSIT) Ltd* (unreported).
[4]   *R v English Brothers* (unreported).
[5]   *R v Horner* (unreported).
[6]   *R v Mark* (unreported).
[7]   *R v Spree* (unreported).

# Failed and Non-prosecutions against Companies involved in Public Disasters

1.34

## The sinking of the Herald of Free Enterprise 1987

On 6 March 1987, the roll-on roll-off P&O European ferry the Herald of Free Enterprise, sank off the coast of Zeebrugge, Belgium, after setting sail with its bow doors open. As a result, 150 passengers and 38 crew were killed.

The immediate cause of the capsize was that the assistant bosun, who had responsibility for shutting the doors had fallen asleep, and the Chief Officer, who was responsible for ensuring the doors were shut, had failed to do this.

The campaign group Disaster Action[1] highlighted the following parts of the report of the public inquiry (known as the Sheen Report and officially entitled *MV Herald of Free Enterprise Report of Court No 8074*, Department of Transport) criticising P&O European Ferries management:

> 'By the autumn of 1986, the shore staff of the company were well aware of the possibility that one of their ships would sail with her stern or bow doors open. They were also aware of a very sensible and simple device in the form of indicator lights which had been suggested by responsible Masters ... The directors did not have any proper comprehension of what their duties were ... From top to bottom the body corporate was infected with the disease of sloppiness'.

The Sheen report was published in July 1987, but it was not until after an inquest jury returned verdicts of unlawful killing in 187 cases in November 1987 that the DPP ordered a police investigation.

In the prosecution case that followed against seven individuals and the company, *R v P&O European Ferries (Dover) Ltd*[2] the court found that there was insufficient evidence to convict any of the seven personal defendants with manslaughter, and the case against the company therefore also failed. The company was automatically acquitted at the same time as the directors. According to David Bergman, Director of the Centre for Corporate Accountability (CCA)[3], this 'highlighted a serious defect in the legal principle of corporate liability'.

The judge ruled that there was insufficient evidence to show that the risk of the ferry leaving port with its bow doors open was 'obvious and serious' (although the law on manslaughter has since changed – see CHAPTER 4). The judge also ruled that there was insufficient evidence of wrongdoing by a director or senior manager. The case failed because the various acts of negligence could not be aggregated and attributed to any individual who was a directing mind of the company. Disaster Action said that it believed that the failure by the police to undertake immediate inquiries was likely to have affected the quality of evidence brought before the court.

The *P&O* case was, however, a landmark decision in that it acknowledged that a company could properly be charged with manslaughter. The collapse of the case also first triggered demands for a reform of the law in this area, and was in part responsible for the 1996 Law Commission report (see above).

No other criminal prosecution was taken. At the time of Zeebrugge, HSWA 1974 did not apply to deaths at sea, and no appropriate charges under merchant shipping legislation were available. A new offence was created in the Merchant Shipping Act 1988 – the current legislation is the Merchant Shipping Act 1995 – in response to this situation (see CHAPTER 10).

### Fire at Kings Cross Underground Station 1987

A fire at King's Cross Underground Station on 18 November 1987 resulted in the deaths of 31 people and injured many more. The immediate cause of the fire was a lighted match which fell through the wooden treads of an escalator and set fire to what was described in the report of the Public Inquiry into the fire, chaired by Sir Desmond Fennell and known as the Fennell Report[4], as 'an accumulation of grease and detritus (dust, fibre and debris) on the tracks which constituted a seed bed for a fire'.

Although the police launched a criminal investigation, this concentrated on whether a member of the public had committed arson, rather than looking at whether London Underground Ltd (LUL), and/or its directors has committed an offence[5].

An inquest into the deaths was held a month before publication of the report of the inquiry in November 1988.

The report catalogued serious lapses on the part of the most senior company officers of LUL. The Director General of the Royal Society for the Prevention of Accidents (RoSPA) gave evidence to the Inquiry that: 'There had been a collective failure from the most senior management level downwards over many years to minimise the outbreak of fire and, more importantly, to foresee and plan for an uncontrolled outbreak of fire at an underground station with a real potential for large scale loss of life'.

The report said that management's approach to passenger safety was reactive rather than proactive, and that many of the shortcomings which led to the disaster had been identified in earlier investigations and in reports by the fire brigade, the police and the Railway Fire Prevention and Fire Standards Committee. Yet many recommendations had not been adequately considered by senior managers and there was no way to ensure that they were circulated, considered and acted upon. The report highlighted the belief that failure to carry through proposals resulting from earlier fines had contributed to the disaster.

However, the DPP ruled against manslaughter proceedings in May 1989, and following this, the Chief Inspector of Railways informed the King's Cross Family Action Group that there would be no prosecution under health and safety legislation.

## Piper Alpha Platform fire and explosion 1988

In July 1988, 167 workers were killed in a fire and explosion on the Piper Alpha oil and gas platform sited off the Scottish coast in the North Sea, operated by Occidental Petroleum.

The Cullen report[6] was published in November 1990 and concluded that the explosion was most probably caused by the ignition of flammable gas which had built up as a result of a leak from an injection pump. Night staff had tried to restart a gas pump without realising that a safety pressure relief valve had been removed for overhaul. The report found that this was because of weaknesses in Occidental's design and operation of the 'permit to work' system, including lack of training and written procedures. The system was 'habitually or frequently' not followed.

According to Disaster Action, Occidental had been made aware of the defects in its procedures after the death of a rigger in 1987[1]. The Cullen report was also critical of the company's lack of emergency procedures, and inadequate safety training.

Despite the findings of the public inquiry into the explosion, no criminal investigation into the conduct of Occidental Petroleum was considered. The campaign group set up by families of the men who died, The Piper Alpha Family Action Group, wanted to present their case to a Fatal Accident Inquiry, the Scottish equivalent of an inquest. However, Scottish law prohibited holding a Fatal Accident Inquiry and public inquiry into the same incident without an order by the Law Advocate, and no such order was made (see CHAPTER 7).

The Lord Advocate announced in 1991 that there would be no prosecution of Occidental Petroleum or any of its senior officers for manslaughter or health and safety offences.

## Railway crash at Clapham Junction railway station 1988

On 12 December 1988, a commuter train ploughed into a stationary train in a cutting near Clapham Junction railway station, killing 35 people and injuring nearly 500 more.

The immediate cause of the disaster was a loose wire in a signal which allowed the display of a green light instead of a red one, but the report of the public inquiry into the crash[7] by Sir Anthony Hidden was highly critical of senior management at British Rail for allowing 'positively dangerous' working practices.

Errors in the organisation were reported to go much wider and higher in the organisation than merely to be the responsibility of those who were working that day.

But in May 1990, the DPP announced that there would be no manslaughter prosecution against British Rail or any of its senior company officers.

British Rail was instead prosecuted for health and safety offences and fined £250,000. Commenting on the level of the fine, the judge said 'A swingeing fine could only be met by British Rail by either increasing the burden on fare-paying passengers or by reducing the finance available for improvements to the railway system'[1].

## The sinking of the Marchioness Pleasure Boat 1989

In August 1989, the *Bowbelle* dredger hit the *Marchioness* pleasure boat on the River Thames in London. Fifty-one people attending a party on the boat were killed.

A police investigation was carried out, although according to Disaster Action[8], this concentrated on whether the Captain of the *Bowbelle* was culpable, rather than investigating the conduct of the owners of the dredger, South Coast Shipping Ltd.

An investigation into the disaster was carried out by the Marine Accident Investigation Branch of the Department of Transport, and in April 1990, the DPP announced that the Captain of the *Bowbelle* would be prosecuted under the Merchant Shipping Act 1988 s 32, but two juries were subsequently unable to reach a unanimous verdict.

In July 1992, the owners of the *Bowbelle*, South Coast Shipping Ltd, and four of its directors, were acquitted of manslaughter. A magistrate ruled in the case, brought as a result of a private prosecution by the widower of a woman killed in the disaster, that the case could not go before the Crown Court because the evidence suggested that the collision was probably caused by the *Marchioness* changing course at the last minute rather than any alleged safety failures on the part of the defendants.

In April 1995, six years after the event, an inquest jury returned a verdict of unlawful killing, but the DPP announced that no new prosecution would take place, due to inadequate evidence.

## The Southall rail crash 1997

On 19 September 1997, a high speed train travelling from Swansea to London went through a red signal and collided with an empty freight train at Southall, killing seven people and injuring 151. The Automatic Warning System that would normally have alerted the driver if he passed a signal at danger was malfunctioning in one of the train's two power units.

According to a November 2006 report by Thompsons solicitors, *Corporate Manslaughter and Corporate Homicide Bill: Impact on major rail disaster cases*, which was published by the rail union, RMT, 'The underlying causes of the accident were the failure of Great Western Trains' maintenance systems to identify and repair an automatic warning system fault on the high speed train, the failure of Railtrack to put in place rules to prevent normal running of a train with the automatic warning system isolated and the failure of Great Western Trains to manage the automatic train protection pilot scheme.' A manslaughter prosecution was subsequently taken by the CPS against Great Western Trains, the passenger train operator[9].

The judge in the case, heard in the Central Criminal Court, ruled in a pre-trail hearing that a company could not be prosecuted for manslaughter by gross negligence unless a named person deemed to be a 'controlling mind' of the company was prosecuted, and no such person had been charged.

But he also said that even having a named director would have made no difference in this case, because no director was personally responsible for ordering the running of the train that crashed.

This case was also significant as the Attorney-General referred the legal issues to the Court of Appeal – the first time that an appeal court had considered the law relating to corporate manslaughter.

In July 1999, Great Western Trains (GWT) pleaded guilty to breaches of HSWA 1974 s 3(1), for failing to ensure that members of the public were not exposed to risks to their health and safety. A record fine of £1.5 million was imposed for 'a serious fault of senior management', but relatives of those killed called this 'derisory' in view of the company's £300 million turnover. The CPS dropped manslaughter charges against the driver of the train.

## Ladbroke Grove train crash 1999

On 5 October 1999, a Thames Trains train from Paddington passed a red signal at Ladbroke Grove and continued for some 700 metres into the path of a high speed train travelling from Cheltenham to Paddington. Thirty-one people were killed and another 139 were injured.

According to the Thompsons report, in this case, 'The underlying causes of the accident were deficiencies in the route training of the driver, poor sighting of a signal and a failure by Railtrack to respond to numerous previous SPAD's (signals passed at danger).' Lord Cullen was appointed to chair a Public Inquiry, which was held in two parts and looked at:

- issues relating to the crash;

- wider issues of safety management and the regulatory regime.

The inquiry took place in 2000 and reports were published in 2001 and included 163 recommendations.

A further Joint Inquiry into Train Protection Systems was related to the Southall and Ladbroke Grove crashes, and looked at train protection, warning systems and measures to prevent signals being passed at danger. This report was published in 2000, with 39 recommendations.

In October 2003, the HSE announced that it intended prosecuting Thames Trains for breaches of HSWA 1974 ss 2 and 3, relating to driver training. In December 2003, the company pleaded guilty and were fined £2 million plus costs in the Old Bailey in April 2004[10].

In December 2005, the CPS announced that there was insufficient evidence to prosecute any individual in relation to the crash, but that it intended to prosecute Network Rail Infrastructure Ltd (formerly Railtrack plc) under HSWA 1974 s 3.

On 31 October 2006, Network Rail pleaded guilty to charges under HSWA 1974. Breaches cited in the indictment against Network Rail included the visibility of signals, with part of a signal being obscured to drivers.

In March 2007, Network Rail was fined £4 million for breaches of health and safety law that led to the crash, and ordered to pay £225,000 in costs.

## The Hatfield Disaster 2000

On 17 October 2000, a London to Leeds train travelling at 115 mph went over a defective rail near Hatfield, shattering it and derailing the train. The rail had been identified as suffering from a form of metal fatigue, commonly found where track curves, 21 months earlier. The derailment led to the loss of four lives, and 70 people were injured.

While the immediate cause of the derailment was the fracture and then fragmentation of the rail, the HSE investigation found that the underlying causes were that Balfour Beatty Rail Maintenance Ltd (BBRML) failed to effectively manage the inspection and maintenance of the rail; and that Railtrack plc had failed to effectively manage the work of BBRML.

Manslaughter charges were then brought against both Network Rail (formerly Railtrack plc) and Balfour Beatty, together with executives from both companies[11].

Two executives from Balfour Beatty were charged with manslaughter and health and safety charges: Regional director until 11 August 2000 Anthony Walker and Civil Engineer Nicholas Jefferies, and three executives from Railtrack also faced manslaughter and health and charges: Alastair Cook, Infrastructure Contracts Manager of the London North East Zone, Sean Fugill, Area Asset Manager of the London North East Zone (South) and Keith Lea, acting track engineer of the London north east zone. Railtrack owned the East Coast Mainline at the time of the derailment. However, manslaughter charges against Network Rail were dropped in September 2004, and in July 2005 the judge in the case against Balfour Beatty and five rail executives dismissed manslaughter charges, five months into the trial.

Mr Justice Mackay, the trial judge commented 'This case continues to underline a long and pressing need for the long-delayed reform of the law in this area of unlawful killing'.

According to the DPP: 'The ruling turned on the level of negligence that the jury was being invited to consider, and the judge took the view that it was not sufficient to invite the jury properly to conclude that it was grossly negligent. He therefore directed the jury to find the defendants not guilty.'

Network Rail and Balfour Beatty were found guilty of breaching health and safety law. Network Rail was fined £3.5 million, a record for a rail firm on health and safety grounds, and Balfour Beatty was fined £10 million (although this was reduced on appeal to £7.5 million. They were also ordered to each pay £300,000 in costs. The individuals facing health and safety charges were found not guilty.

## The Potters Bar derailment 2002

The train derailment at Potters' Bar on 10 May 2002 led to the loss of seven lives and 76 people were injured as the rear coach of a passenger train from Kings Cross derailed after passing a faulty set of points just outside the station.

The investigation into the derailment began in July 2002 and was led by the British Transport Police (BTP) under the Work-Related Deaths Protocol, on the basis that a serious criminal offence could have caused the accident (see chapter 6). In March 2004, the HSE investigators took over the lead, since the emphasis of the investigation had turned to systems and procedures.

The immediate cause of the derailment was the failure of the points, which moved as the train passed over them, but an underlying cause was that they had been poorly maintained and were out of adjustment.

The CPS announced in October 2005 that after consideration of the evidence, it had advised BTP that there was no realistic prospect of conviction for an offence of gross negligence manslaughter against any individual or corporation following the Potters Bar train derailment.

Giving reasons for this decision, the Principal Legal Advisor of the CPS said:

> 'To bring a prosecution for gross negligence manslaughter, the CPS needed to have identified a specific individual as committing a breach of duty of care, which was so serious or gross as to be criminal to the level of manslaughter, as well as being a substantial cause of the deaths of the deceased. No individual was identified as having committed that breach of care, in the first instance because it was impossible to pinpoint when the faults occurred which caused the points failure. Without an individual being identified, no prosecution could proceed against a corporation'.

The case was then referred to the HSE, and in April 2006 responsibility for regulation of health and safety on the railway transferred to the Office for Rail Regulation (ORR).

The investigation into the derailment remains open until the Coroner's inquest is concluded, after which the ORR will consider whether there will be proceedings for breaches of HSWA 1974. The points were operated by Railtrack, now Network Rail, and maintained by the engineering company Jarvis.

On 23 February 2007, a high speed Virgin passenger train bound for Glasgow derailed at Grayrigg, Cumbria, killing one person, Margaret Masson, and injuring another 22. The cause of the crash was identified by the Rail Accident Investigation Branch (RAIB) as a faulty set of points. The deputy Coroner in the Potters Bar inquest postponed the inquest, linking it to the Grayrigg derailment, and also wrote to the Secretary of State for Transport, suggesting that a public inquiry should be held.

A report published by Network Rail in September 2007 confirmed that there had been failures in its track inspection procedures. An inspector had cut short a check of the track just before the broken set of points which later caused the crash and this had not been picked up by his supervisor.

There have been repeated calls for a joint public inquiry into the incidents at Grayrigg and Potters Bar following publication of the Network Rail report.

[1]   David Bergman, *The case for corporate responsibility – Corporate violence and the criminal justice system* (Disaster Action, 2000).
[2]   (1990) 93 Cr App R 72.
[3]   David Bergman, as above.
[4]   Investigation into the King's Cross Underground Fire, November 1988.
[5]   David Bergman, as above.
[6]   J Cullen, *The Public Enquiry into the Piper Alpha Disaster* (1990).
[7]   Department of Transport, *Investigation into the Clapham Junction Railway Accident* (1989).
[8]   David Bergman, as above.
[9]   *R v Great Western Trains Ltd* (1999) (unreported).
[10]  *Thames Trains Ltd v Health and Safety Executive* [2003] EWCA Civ 720; [2003] All ER (D) 310 (May).
[11]  *Network Rail and Balfour Beatty* (2005) (unreported).

# Chapter 2

# An Overview of Statutory Health and Safety Legislation

## Overview

### 2.1

> The Corporate Manslaughter and Corporate Homicide Act 2007 (CMCHA 2007) provides a range of factors for juries to consider when assessing an organisation's culpability, and this includes failure to comply with health and safety legislation:
>
> > 'The jury must consider whether the evidence shows that the organisation failed to comply with any health and safety legislation that relates to the alleged breach, and if so—
>
> (a)   how serious that failure was;
>
> (b)   how much of a risk of death it posed.'
>
> (CMCHA 2007 s 8(2)).
>
> The jury may also have regard to any health and safety guidance that relates to the alleged breach (CMCHA 2007 s 8(3)).
>
> This chapter therefore provides an overview of statutory health and safety legislation, which consists largely (but not exclusively) of the Health and Safety at Work etc Act 1974 (HSWA 1974) and regulations made under that Act, including the Management of Health and Safety at Work Regulations 1999, SI 1999/3242, which are important as they make explicit what employers must do to comply with their general duties.
>
> The chapter also covers health and safety legislation not made under HSWA 1974, such as that concerning fire safety, which was made under a Regulatory Reform Order, the Regulatory Reform (Fire Safety) Order 2005, SI 2005/1541.
>
> This section summarises regulations applying to the majority of workplaces which could be relevant when considering a corporate ➡

manslaughter conviction, together with legislation applying to a narrower range of workplaces, but dealing with particularly hazardous work, such as work in confined spaces.

It also includes a summary of the legislation covering the reporting of accidents and incidents at work; but it does not cover legislation, such as that dealing with display screen equipment, noise and vibration, which are unlikely to be of relevance in relation to workplace deaths, and therefore a conviction of corporate manslaughter or corporate homicide.

The House of Commons Home Affairs and Work and Pensions Committees which scrutinised the government's Draft Corporate Manslaughter Bill (see CHAPTER 1) looked at whether the offence would cover fatal damage to health resulting from sustained exposure to hazardous substances, or as a result of contracting a disease with a long latency, in addition to deaths resulting from immediate injury. It concluded that it was satisfied that the Bill would apply in these circumstances, but urged the government to ensure that sufficient resources and appropriate procedures would be in place so that prosecutions could be brought for deaths related to occupational health causes.

However, experts such as Professor Frank Wright, Professor of Law at Warwick Law School, believe that in reality, it would be very difficult to secure a corporate manslaughter conviction in the case of a death caused by long-term exposure to hazardous substances, such as asbestos for example, and in any case, since the legislation is not retrospective, it would be some years before a case testing this aspect of the law is likely to be brought.

This chapter therefore refers to legislation aimed at preventing deaths as a result of long-term fatal damage to health, such as the Control of Asbestos Regulations 2005, but does not examine it in detail.

Legislation dealing with particular industries, such as the railways, air, sea and road safety, the construction industry, mines, quarries and offshore legislation is referred to in the chapters dealing with particular sectors (see CHAPTERS 9–14), but is not examined in detail. However, the Construction (Design and Management) Regulations 2007 are set out in detail in the chapter looking at the construction industry, both because of the high fatality rate in the industry, and because the Regulations contain duties for clients as well as contractors (see CHAPTER 9).

## Health and Safety at Work etc Act 1974

**2.2** The main piece of health and safety law in the UK is the Health and Safety at Work etc Act 1974 (HSWA 1974), which applies to virtually all types of workplace and workers, although it does not apply to domestic servants.

It imposes duties on employers, the self-employed and employees; outlines the role of the Health and Safety Commission (HSC) and the Commission's enforcement arm, the Health and Safety Executive (HSE); sets out enforcement provisions (including powers to issue improvement and prohibition notices) and details the penalties for non-compliance. The enforcement of health and safety legislation is dealt with in more detail in CHAPTER 6.

HSWA 1974 lays down the general principles for the health and safety of employees and others affected by work activity and contains broad general duties. It acts as a framework, with more detailed regulations setting out requirements with regard to particular areas of health and safety – such as hazardous substances, workplace premises, work equipment, working time and personal protective equipment – being made under the 1974 Act.

Regulations are often published with an associated Approved Code of Practice (ACoP) providing practical guidance; or with Guidance on compliance with the regulations prepared by the HSE.

Codes of Practice do not have the same legal force as the regulations themselves, but they are considered 'admissible evidence' in criminal proceedings for contravention of a provision for which an associated Code of Practice is in force. They often set out the requirements in more detail than the regulations themselves. Failing to follow a code is not an offence in itself, but an employer must demonstrate that equally effective methods have been adopted to signal compliance with the law.

The HSC and the Institute of Directors (IoD)'s recently published guidance *Leading health and safety at work – leadership actions for directors and board members* (INDG 417) which clearly sets out its legal status:

'Although reference is made to existing legal obligations, following the guidance is not in itself obligatory. However, if you do follow it you will normally be doing enough to help your organisation meet its legal obligations. In considering liability under the Corporate Manslaughter and Corporate Homicide Act 2007, a jury must consider any breaches of health and safety legislation and may have regard to any health and safety guidance. In addition to other health and safety guidance, this guidance could be a relevant consideration for a jury depending on the circumstances of the particular case.'

This guidance is examined in more detail in CHAPTER 8.

**Summary of the Main Requirements contained in HSWA 1974**

**2.3**

---

- employers are required to ensure the health, safety and welfare of their employees (HSWA 1974 s 2);

- every employer with five or more employees must prepare a written health and safety policy (s 2);

- recognised trade unions have the right to appoint safety representatives, which the employer must consult on a range of health and safety issues (s 2);

- employers must ensure that work activities do not expose people other than employees (for example members of the public and employees employed by others) to health and safety risks (s 3);

- owners, occupiers and others who have control of premises must ensure that the premises and plant and machinery under their control may be used without risks to health and safety (s 4);

- designers, importers, suppliers and manufacturers have a duty to ensure that articles and substances used at work are safe and without risks to health (s 6);

- employees must take reasonable care for the health and safety of themselves and others at work (s 7);

- anything provided in the interests of health and safety must not be interfered with by anyone (s 8); and

- employers must not charge employees for any item of safety equipment or protective clothing required by law (s 9).

---

**Employers' Duties**

**2.4**    Under HSWA 1974 s 2, every employer must ensure the health, safety and welfare of all employees.

In particular, employers must:

- provide and maintain plant and systems of work so that they are, so far as is reasonably practicable, safe and without risks to health;

- make arrangements for ensuring, so far as is reasonably practicable, that articles and substances are used, handled, stored and transported safely and without risks to health;

- provide the necessary information, instruction, training and supervision to ensure, so far as is reasonably practicable, the health and safety at work of employees;

- maintain any place of work under the employer's control, so far as is reasonably practicable, in a safe condition and without risks to health, including safe access and egress; and

- provide and maintain a working environment which is, so far as is reasonably practicable, safe and without risks to health and provided with adequate facilities and welfare arrangements.

There have been a number of cases which have provided interpretation on how these duties should be applied. For example:

In the case of *Bolton Metropolitan Borough Council v Malrod Insulations Ltd*[1], which involved asbestos removal contractors, the High Court held that the duty to provide plant which is safe arises as soon as the plant is provided. The duty applies not only to employees who are 'at work', but also extends to employees who will be at work. In this case the contractors had unsuccessfully argued that they were not in breach of HSWA 1974 s 2 in providing unsafe plant for work involving the removal of asbestos because, at the time of the alleged offence, the work had not yet begun.

In *R v Gateway Foodmarkets Ltd*[2], the Court of Appeal ruled that a company is liable for a breach of HSWA 1974 s 2(1) even though at senior management or head office level, it had taken all reasonable precautions to avoid the risk of injury to an employee.

In this case, a store manager was attempting to free a lift which had jammed as a result of an electrical fault when he fell through a trap door into the lift shaft and was killed. The accident occurred as a result of a system of work adopted at one of its stores by the store's management without the knowledge of senior company personnel. The Crown Court had ruled that HSWA 1974 s 2(1) imposes strict liability, subject to 'reasonable practicability', and that the company was liable if its employee had caused a breach of the duty.

The company appealed, arguing that it was not liable under HSWA 1974 s 2(1) for the acts or omissions of an employee (in this case the store manager) who could not be regarded as the 'embodiment' of the company. It argued that embodiment was limited to the 'directing mind' of the company – a small number of senior head office personnel.

Rejecting the appeal, the Court of Appeal said that the breach of duty and liability under the section do not depend upon any failure by the company itself, i e those who embody the company, to take all reasonable precautions. Rather, the company is liable if there is a failure to ensure an employee's health and safety, unless all reasonable precautions have been taken – by the company or on its behalf.

[1]   [1993] IRLR 274.
[2]   [1997] IRLR 189.

## What is Reasonably Practicable?

**2.5**   The phrase 'so far as is reasonably practicable' has been interpreted in the courts as meaning that the costs of carrying out the health and safety measures must not be grossly disproportionate to the benefits to be obtained from doing it. Technical means and financial considerations can be taken into account.

In *R v Nelson Group Services (Maintenance) Ltd*[1], the Court of Appeal held that the fact that an employee carrying out work had done the work carelessly, or failed to take a precaution that should have been taken, does not of itself preclude the employer from establishing a reasonably practicable defence. This is a question of fact depending on the circumstances of each case. The employer must show that everything reasonably practicable has been done to ensure that a person doing the work has the necessary skill and instruction, safe systems of work have been laid down, there is adequate supervision and safe plant and equipment has been provided.

In *Davies v Health and Safety Executive*[2], an employer was prosecuted and fined after an employee reversed a JCB into a sub-contractor and killed him. The employer appealed against his conviction, arguing that HSWA 1974 s 40, was not compatible in this case with the presumption of innocence in Article 6(2) of the European Convention on Human Rights, which states that 'Everyone charged with a criminal offence shall be presumed innocent until proved guilty according to the law'.

The judge in the county court directed the jury that there was a legal burden on the employer to prove that, on the balance of probabilities, it was not reasonably practicable for him to do more than he had done to prevent the death of the sub-contractor.

The Court of Appeal held that this legal burden on the employer under section 40 to prove that it was not reasonably practicable to do more than had been done to satisfy the duty under section 3(1) was compatible with the presumption of innocence in Article 6(2). The court found that the imposition of a reverse legal burden of proof in section 40 is justified, necessary and proportionate.

[1]   [1999] IRLR 646.
[2]   [2003] IRLR 170.

## Health and Safety Policies

**2.6**    Section 2 of HSWA 1974 also requires every employer with five or more employees to prepare a written health and safety policy. This should detail the hazards present at the workplace, and the organisation and arrangements in force for carrying out the policy. It must be revised 'as often as appropriate' and brought to the notice of employees (HSWA 1974 s 2(3)).

The health and safety policy should set out the employer's aims and objectives for improving health and safety and how these will be met, and it should state the arrangements for monitoring the effectiveness of the policy. It should also set out all those persons in the organisation with health and safety responsibilities.

The HSE guidance document, *An introduction to health and safety* (INDG259) contains a model policy statement.

## Duties to Non-employees

**2.7**    Section 3 of HSWA 1974 obliges employers and the self-employed to conduct undertakings to ensure that people other than the employees (members of the public and persons employed by others, for example) are not exposed to risks to their health or safety. Again, a number of cases have established how these duties should apply. For example:

*R v Swan Hunter Shipbuilders Ltd*[1] established that the duty extends to the provision of information, instruction and training to persons who are not employees or in a contractual relationship with the employer.

In *R v Rhône Poulenc Rover Ltd*[2], it was held that the level of this duty will vary, from doing little more than warning the contractor of potential dangers and co-ordinating operations – where an employer subcontracts part of its undertaking to a contractor operating a comprehensive system of supervision and instruction – to taking the same precautions for the contractors' workers as for its own employees where the contractor is providing workers totally under the employer's instruction and control.

*RMC Roadstone Products Ltd v Jester*[3] showed that in order to establish a *prima facie* liability under HSWA 1974 s 3, the following three elements must be proved:

• that the defendant was an employer within the meaning of the 1974 Act;

• that the activity or state of affairs which gave rise to the complaint fell within the ambit of the defendant's conduct of the undertaking; and

• that there was a risk to the health and safety of persons, other than employees, who were affected by the conduct of that aspect of the undertaking.

If these three elements are proved, conviction will follow unless the defendant can satisfy the court that it did all that was reasonably practicable to comply with the duty imposed.

It is a question of fact in each case whether an activity, which causes a risk to the health and safety of people not in his employment, amounts to part of the employer's conduct of undertaking within the meaning of HSWA 1974. Anything which constitutes the running of a plant is part of the employer's undertaking, and this may, but will not always, include ancillary activities carried out by independent contractors.

The location where the activity takes place will normally be very important, possibly decisive. Therefore activities carried on by another person entirely separate from those of the employer (ie on separate premises) probably would not form part of the conduct of the employer's undertaking.

If an independent contractor is engaged to do work which does form part of the conduct of the employer's undertaking, the employers must stipulate whatever conditions are needed to avoid risks to health and safety and are reasonably practicable. If he omits to do so, he cannot say that he was not in a position to exercise control.

In *R v British Steel plc*[4], the Court of Appeal held that a corporate employer cannot avoid liability for an offence under HSWA 1974, s 3(1) on the basis that the company at the 'directing mind' or senior management level was not involved, having taken all reasonable care to delegate supervision.

British Steel had subcontracted two workers on a labour-only basis, with the company providing equipment and supervision, to reposition a section of steel platform. The two men had cut the platform free of nearly all its supports and it collapsed, killing one of them working underneath.

British Steel argued unsuccessfully that at directing mind/senior management level it had taken all reasonable care to delegate supervision of the operation to a section engineer in its employment. A company is liable under HSWA 1974 s 3(1) regardless of whether employees who commit acts or omissions are part of senior management.

In *Viasystems (Tyneside) Ltd v Thermal Transfer (Northern) Ltd*[5], which involved damage caused to a factory by a workman who was employed through a series of subcontracts to fit air conditioning, the Court of Appeal considered whether there could be dual vicarious liability, and decided that this was legally permissible.

It found that the second and third defendants were both vicariously liable for the negligence of the workman. The worker in question was employed by the third defendants, who had contracted to supply his labour to the second defendants for the purposes of carrying out work at the premises.

The court said that the long-standing assumption that liability must rest on one employer or the other made little sense in a modern context.

¹   [1981] IRLR 403 (CA).
²   10 November 1995 (CA) (unreported).
³   [1994] IRLR 330.
⁴   [1995] ICR 586.
⁵   [2005] IRLR 983.

## Consultation with Safety Representatives

**2.8**    Section 2(4) of HSWA 1974 made provision for regulations giving recognised trade unions the right to appoint safety representatives to be introduced. A trade union is recognised for the purposes of such regulations where the employer recognises the union for any collective bargaining purposes.

Section 2(6) of HSWA 1974 states that every employer must consult trade union appointed safety representatives 'with a view to making and maintenance of arrangements which enable him and his employees to co-operate effectively in promoting and developing measures to ensure the health and safety of their employees, and in checking the effectiveness of such measures'. Where requested by two or more safety representatives, the employer must set up a safety committee.

The Safety Representatives and Safety Committees Regulations 1977, SI 1977/500, set out in detail the functions of safety representatives and safety committees and employers' duties to consult with safety representatives.

The legal rights of safety representatives can be found in the 'Brown Book', which contains the regulations, code of practice and guidance on safety representatives and safety committees. The TUC has produced a version of this for training purposes which can be downloaded from its website at www.tuc.org.uk/extras/brownbook.pdf. Single hard copies of the Brown Book, officially entitled 'Safety Representatives and Safety Committees' (L87) can be purchased from HSE Books.

## Consultation with Employees

**2.9**    The Health and Safety (Consultation with Employees) Regulations 1996, SI 1996/1513, give non-union employees the same rights to consultation that union safety representatives have, but are more limited in other aspects. For example, there is no right to carry out inspections of the workplace. These Regulations apply either where there is no trade union organisation in the workplace, the union is not recognised in a workplace, or there is no recognition for a particular group of workers. The Regulations can be found online at www.opsi.gov.uk.

### Duties of Owners and Occupiers

**2.10**   Section 4 of HSWA 1974 states the general duties of owners, occupiers and others who have control of premises and sets out requirements concerning places of work. Such persons must ensure that premises and plant and machinery under their control may be used without risks to health and safety.

Section 5 of HSWA 1974 obliges persons in control of certain premises to prevent the emission of noxious or offensive fumes. This section applies to scheduled processes and specified noxious substances ranging from petrochemical works to smelting.

### Designers and Manufacturers

**2.11**   Section 6 of HSWA 1974 requires designers, manufacturers, importers and suppliers to ensure that the design and construction of articles and substances are, as far as is reasonably practicable, safe and without risk to health when properly used at work. There is also a duty to ensure that adequate information is available about the hazards of any article or substance, and the precautions required to control those hazards. This section was extended by section 36 of and Schedule 3 to the Consumer Protection Act 1987. 'Use' for articles now includes design, installation, commissioning, use, maintenance and dismantling. For 'substances' it includes storage, transport, use and disposal.

### Employees' Duties

**2.12**   Section 7 of HSWA 1974 sets out that every employee must take reasonable care for the health and safety of himself and other people at work. If there is a legal requirement on an employer to do certain things for reasons of health and safety, then the employee must co-operate with the employer to enable the employer to fulfil his legal duty.

Section 8 of HSWA 1974 prohibits interference by anyone with anything provided in the interests of health and safety at work.

### Duty not to Charge

**2.13**   Under HSWA 1974 s 9 the employer must not charge the employee for any item of equipment or protective clothing that is required by law.

## Management of Health and Safety at Work Regulations 1999

**2.14**   The Management of Health and Safety at Work Regulations 1999, SI 1999/3242, first came into effect in 1992 as part of the 'six pack' of regulations introduced as a result of the European Framework and Daughter Directives. They are important because they clarify what employers must do to comply with their duties under HSWA 1974.

Under SI 1999/3242:

- employers must carry out 'suitable and sufficient' risk assessments, which must be recorded where there are five or more people employed;

- there must be adequate arrangements for the effective planning, organisation, control and monitoring of health and safety measures;

- health surveillance is required where an identifiable and detectable condition related to the work is likely to occur, and surveillance is likely to increase the protection of employees;

- competent staff must be appointed to assist with health and safety;

- procedures for serious and imminent risk, specifying under what circumstances employees can stop work, must be established;

- employees must be provided with comprehensive and relevant health and safety information;

- employers in shared workplaces must co-operate and co-ordinate health and safety measures;

- temporary workers must be provided with information on the necessary skills needed to carry out work safely; and

- employers must assess the risks to the health and safety of new and expectant mothers and if there is a significant risk to health and safety after preventive measures have been taken, the employer must temporarily adjust the woman's hours or conditions, offer her alternative work, or give her paid leave from work.

## Risk Assessments

**2.15**     A central requirement of SI 1999/3242 is the carrying out of a 'suitable and sufficient' risk assessment (reg 3), in order to decide what health and safety measures are needed.

This should 'involve management, whether or not advisers or consultants assist', although specialist advice may be necessary, according to the ACoP.

The definition of 'suitable and sufficient' is further explained in the ACoP, which gives guidance on compliance with the Regulations. This indicates that the level of detail in the risk assessment should be determined by the risks and that there is no need to evaluate trivial risks.

A suitable and sufficient risk assessment should:

- correctly and accurately identify hazards;

- determine the likelihood and severity of injury or harm arising;

- identify any specific legal duty relating to the hazards;

- remain valid for a period of time; and

- enable decisions to be made about appropriate control measures.

The risk assessment must be recorded where there are five or more people employed. The ACoP states that, where appropriate, the document 'should be linked to other health and safety records or documents, such as the record of health and safety arrangements required by SI 1999/3242 reg 4 and the written health and safety policy statement required by HSWA 1974 s 2(3).

Recent guidelines issued by the HSE carry the key message that employers must spend less time 'dotting 'i's' and crossing 't's' and more time putting practical actions into effect. The guide spells out what is, and what is not expected, and provides advice and tips on five key elements to an effective risk assessment:

- identifying the hazards;

- deciding who might be harmed and how;

- evaluating the risks and deciding on precautions;

- recording findings and implementing them; and finally

- ensuring they are reviewed at regular intervals.

This is supported by four examples of what a risk assessment might look like. The examples help emphasise that risk assessment need not be difficult and the paperwork need not be long and complicated. For most, bullet points work very well.

Copies of *Five steps to risk assessment* (INDG163 (rev2)), are available from HSE Books. Alternatively the leaflet can be downloaded free from the HSE website at: www.hse.gov.uk/risk.

Examples are also available on the HSE website at www.hse.gov.uk/risk/examples.htm

A number of prosecutions taken by the HSE against companies involving work-related deaths have highlighted a lack of a suitable and sufficient risk assessment in place when the deaths occurred, and some have involved a prosecution under SI 1999/3242 reg 3, for example:

Prysmian Systems and Cables Ltd was prosecuted under HSWA 1974 s 3 and SI 1999/3242 reg 3 for failing to make a suitable and sufficient risk assessment of vehicle activities in the area where a fatal accident occurred in March 2001[1]. A contractor was killed while working on the site as a haulage/shunter driver. He was struck by a reversing fork-lift truck and crushed between it and the side of the HGV he was preparing to drive away in. The company was fined £20,000.

¹   See HSE Prosecutions Database at www.hse.gov.uk/prosecutions.

## Principles of Protection to be Applied

**2.16**   Employers must implement any preventive and protective measures on the basis of the following principles (SI 1999/3242 reg 4):

- avoiding risks;

- evaluating risks that cannot be avoided;

- combating risks at source;

- adapting the work to the individual, particularly with regard to workplace design, the choice of work equipment and working and production methods, with a view to alleviating monotonous work and work at a predetermined work-rate;

- adapting to technical progress;

- replacing the dangerous with safe or safer alternatives;

- developing a coherent overall prevention policy covering technology, work organisation, working conditions, social relationships, and the working environment;

- giving priority to collective over individual protective measures; and

- giving appropriate instructions to employees.

## Health and Safety Arrangements

**2.17**   SI 1999/3242 reg 5 requires employers to ensure that adequate arrangements are in place regarding 'effective planning, organisation, control, monitoring and review of protective and preventive measures'.

The HSE advises that an effective management structure into which health and safety needs are fully integrated must be a central part of the arrangements and that health and safety responsibilities must be understood and acted on at all levels.

These arrangements, as in the case of the risk assessment, must be in writing where there are five or more employees. Employers have to produce a written safety policy under HSWA 1974 s 2(3). The HSE says that 'good written safety policy statements should demonstrate that appropriate measures have been determined and applied'.

## Health Surveillance

**2.18**    SI 1999/3242 reg 6 requires employers to carry out health surveillance 'as is appropriate having regard to' the risks to the health and safety of employees as revealed by the risk assessment.

## Competent Staff

**2.19**    Under SI 1999/3242 reg 7 employers are required to appoint competent staff to assist in ensuring that the protective and preventive measures identified as necessary by the risk assessment are established. Competent employees should be appointed in preference to external sources for health and safety advice and assistance.

The Approved Code of Practice to SI 1999/3242 (see 2.26) gives further guidance on how to determine competence and says that this depends on the person having an understanding of best practice, an awareness of his own limitations, and a willingness and ability to supplement existing experience and knowledge.

Regulation 7 also requires that employers designate workers to implement fire-fighting procedures.

The HSE has published a leaflet for employers on when and how to get help on health and safety issues. *Need help on health and safety?* (INDG322) is a simple guide to assist employers identify health and safety problems in the workplace, and get the right help at the right time so they comply with their legal duties under health and safety law. The free leaflet is available from HSE Books or can be downloaded at www.hse.gov.uk/pubns/indg322.pdf.

## Serious and Imminent Danger

**2.20**    Procedures for serious and imminent risk, including specifying the circumstances in which employees can stop work or take other remedial action, must be established (SI 1999/3242 reg 8).

Also, a sufficient number of competent personnel, who have sufficient training and experience, must be nominated to implement the procedures. Again, these procedures must normally be written down.

Employers must arrange any necessary contacts with external services, particularly with regard to first-aid, emergency medical care and rescue work (SI 1999/3242 reg 9).

### Training and Information

**2.21**    Regulation 10 of SI 1999/3242 states that employees must be provided with specific 'comprehensive and relevant' information. Guidance to the Regulations states that employers may have to make special arrangements for employees with little understanding of English, or who cannot read English.

The HSE provides a telephone interpreting service and publishes a range of health and safety information in 30 other languages. There is an 'other languages' link on the front page of its website at www.hse.gov.uk

In the case of *Tasci v Pekalp of London Ltd*[1], the Court of Appeal held that the duty of an employer to train an employee not only involved giving a comprehensive explanation in ordinary language of the dangers involved but also involved some appraisal as to whether the employee understood the instructions and the dangers of the machine. (This case involved the use of woodworking machinery.)

[1]   (2001) Times, 17 January.

### Co-operation and Co-ordination

**2.22**    Employers and the self-employed sharing the same workplace must co-operate and co-ordinate safety measures (SI 1999/3242 reg 11) in order to ensure that health and safety legislation is complied with, and that all employees on the site are informed of the risks to health and safety from all the work activities taking place.

In addition, SI 1999/3242 reg 12 requires employers to ensure that any contract workers are provided with information about the risks and the health and safety measures taken.

### Temporary Workers

**2.23**    SI 1999/3242 implemented the requirements of a European Directive covering temporary workers and require employers to provide information on the necessary occupational qualifications or skills needed to carry out the work safely (and carry out any necessary health surveillance) to workers on fixed-term contracts (SI 1999/3242 reg 15).

### New and Expectant Mothers

**2.24**    Where there are women of child-bearing age in the workforce, any risk assessment must take account of how hazards may particularly affect the health and safety of new or expectant mothers (SI 1999/3242 reg 16). If there is a significant risk to health and safety after preventive measures have been taken, the employer must temporarily adjust the woman's hours or conditions, offer her alternative work, or give her paid leave from work.

## Young Workers

**2.25**   Young workers are particularly vulnerable at work and workplace fatalities in the 16 to 24 age range occur at a rate of more than one a month, according to a report in *Hazards* magazine[1]. A number of cases where manslaughter charges have been considered have involved the deaths of young people under 18, including Daniel Dennis.

> In December 2006, the High Court ordered the Crown Prosecution Service (CPS) to review its decision not to bring manslaughter charges against the employer of Daniel Dennis, who was killed in 2003 in his first week at work, aged only 17. An inquest into Daniel's death ruled that he was unlawfully killed when he fell through a skylight on the roof of a Matalan store while working for North-Eastern Roofing.
>
> In October 2007, Gwent CPS announced that it would prosecute Roy Clarke, the owner of North Eastern Roofing. The case is a landmark ruling as it is only the second case in which the courts have ordered the CPS to review a decision not to prosecute in the case of a workplace death. Daniel's family's efforts to have the case reviewed were supported by the general GMB union to which Daniel's father Peter belongs.

Employers have to protect young workers (defined as anyone under 18 years of age) from risks to their health and safety arising from lack of experience or maturity (SI 1999/3242 reg 19) and must not employ a young person for work:

- which is beyond their physical or psychological capacity;

- involves harmful exposure to radiation or toxins or carcinogens which chronically affect human health; or

- involves the risk of accidents which may not be recognised or avoided by young people by virtue of their inexperience; or

- where there is a risk to health from extreme cold or heat, noise or vibration.

In addition, the Working Time Regulations 1988, SI 1988/1833, control the working hours of young workers (see 2.57).

There is also legislation applying to employing children – the Children (Protection at Work) Regulations 1998[3] control the working time of children aged 14 and 15. The minimum age from which children are allowed to work is 14, although 13-year-olds may be allowed to do some light work which can be specified in local by-laws. Local bye-laws can impose further rules on occupations, hours, rest breaks and holiday times; but cannot override those specified in the Regulations. Model bye-laws issued by the Department of Health list the types of jobs from which children should be excluded, including delivering milk, collecting refuse, collecting money or canvassing from door to door and telephone sales. They also contain the type of permitted work for 13-year-olds. These include working in hairdressing salons, office work, working in cafes and restaurants and newspaper delivery.

¹   *Too young to die*, Hazards Magazine number 95, July/September 2006 www.hazards.org/
2young2die.

### Approved Code of Practice

**2.26**   The HSC ACoP to SI 1999/3242 is available from HSE Books.
The Regulations can be downloaded at www.opsi.gov.uk.

## Workplace (Health, Safety and Welfare) Regulations 1992

**2.27**   The Workplace (Health, Safety and Welfare) Regulations 1992,
SI 1992/3004, apply to virtually all fixed workplaces and lay down a wide
range of requirements relating to the structure and organisation of the
workplace, repair, maintenance, housekeeping, and facilities for staff.

The Regulations define a 'workplace' as any non-domestic premises
available to any person as a place of work, including: canteens, toilets,
parts of a workroom or workplace including a corridor or staircase or
other means of access or egress other than a public road, and a completed
modification, extension, or conversion of an original workplace. But
boats, ships, hovercraft, trains and road vehicles are excluded – although
the requirements in reg 13, which deal with falls and falling objects, apply
when aircraft, trains and road vehicles are stationary inside a workplace).
Building operations and engineering construction works and mining
activities are also excluded, with other legislation applying to these
(regs 2, 3 and 4).

They require employers to ensure that workplaces comply with the
following requirements:

- workplaces must be provided with sufficient ventilation, a reasonable temperature, and suitable and sufficient lighting;

- workrooms must be kept clean and meet minimum space standards;

- suitable workstations and seating should be provided;

- work equipment and systems should be maintained and kept in safe
working order;

- floors and traffic routes should be suitably constructed and kept free
from slip and trip hazards, and vehicles and pedestrians should be
kept separate;

- there should be protection against the risk of falls and falling
objects;

- windows should be made of safety materials and be capable of
being opened and cleaned safely;

- doors, gates, escalators and moving walkways should function
safely;

- workplaces must be provided with adequate toilets, washing facilities, drinking water, clothing accommodation and changing facilities where necessary, and rest and eating facilities; and

- non-smokers using rest facilities must be protected from discomfort from tobacco smoke.

Legislation banning smoking in enclosed workplaces and public places in England came into effect on 1 July 2007, following bans in Scotland, introduced in March 2006, Northern Ireland in April 2006 and Wales in April 2007. The legislation introducing smoke-free workplaces is set out in the Health Act 2006 Part 1 (ss 1–13) which contains broad provisions for smoke-free legislation, and provides legal powers to enable the more detailed aspects of smoke-free legislation to be dealt with by regulations.

Five sets of smoke-free regulations set out the detail of the smoke-free legislation:

- Smoke-free (Premises and Enforcement) Regulations 2006, SI 2006/3368;

- Smoke-free (Signs) Regulations 2007, SI 2007/923;

- Smoke-free (Exemptions and Vehicles) Regulations 2007, SI 2007/765;

- Smoke-free (Penalties and Discounted Amounts) Regulations 2007, SI 2007/764; and

- Smoke-free (Vehicle Operators and Penalty Notices) Regulations 2007, SI 2007/760.

Of particular importance with regard to preventing deaths at work are the provisions discussed below.

## Falls and falling objects

SI 1992/3004 reg 13 deals with falls or falling objects and requires that steps are taken to prevent, as far as is reasonably practicable, by means other than providing personal protective equipment, any person falling a distance likely to cause personal injury or being struck by a falling object likely to cause injury. Tanks or pits should also be, so far as is reasonably practicable, securely covered or fenced where there is a risk of a person falling in.

The ACoP to SI 1992/3004 outlines requirements relating to fencing or covers, ladders, roof work, falls into dangerous substances, changing of level, stacking and racking, loading and unloading, scaffolding and other measures. The Work at Height Regulations 2005, SI 2005/735, and the Construction (Design and Management) Regulations 2007, SI 2007/320, (see CHAPTER 9) also contain requirements to prevent falls.

A Purley company, RTAL Ltd, was fined £25,000 with £5,000 costs, and its managing director Terry Green was also fined £2,500 and ordered to pay costs of £500 in October 2007 after it admitted health and safety offences following the death of Andrew Taylor, who was killed by an 8 m fall from the RTAL factory premises in Tilbury[1]. He was working installing a kiln and fell from the edge of a fixed platform where a protective guardrail had been temporarily removed.

In this case, the company was charged under HSWA 1974 s 3(1) while Green was charged under s 37. Due to his neglect as director, the company had failed to take suitable and sufficient measures to prevent people falling, as required by the Construction (Health, Safety and Welfare) Regulations 1996, SI 1996/1592, (now superseded by the CDM Regulations 2007 (see CHAPTER 9).

## Windows and skylights

Windows and skylights should be designed and constructed to allow them to be cleaned safely (SI 1992/3004 reg 16). On average, two window cleaners are killed every year falling from ladders, according to the HSE.

## Workplace Transport

The Regulations require that workplaces should be organised so that pedestrians and vehicles can circulate in a safe manner – workplace transport is the second biggest cause of accidents in the workplace, accounting for about 70 fatalities each year.

The ACoP outlines requirements for the separation of people and vehicles, crossings, loading bays and signs (SI 1992/3004 reg 17). In essence, this brings the Highway Code into the workplace.

[1]   See HSE (Yorkshire and Humber) Press Release 8/10/07.

**2.28**   Workplace transport means any vehicle that is used in a work setting. It specifically excludes transport on the public highway; air, rail or water transport, and specialised transport used in underground mining.

The four main types of workplace transport accidents which employers and the self-employed need to prevent are:

● moving vehicles hitting or running over people;

● people falling off vehicles;

● vehicles overturning; and

● objects falling off vehicles.

The free booklet *Workplace transport: An overview* provides employers with a brief summary of the main issues that should be considered when planning workplace transport operations and can be downloaded from the HSE website at www.hse.gov.uk/pubns/tranindx.htm.

And HSE guidance on the safe operation of vehicles in the workplace, *Workplace transport safety: An employers' guide* (HSG136) provides advice on all aspects of workplace transport operations.

The guidance looks at general workplace transport safety issues and provides an introduction to workplace transport risk management. In particular, it offers information on assessing transport risks relating to site safety, vehicles themselves, and the people working with and around them and implementing a safe system of work. It also offers specific guidance on typical workplace transport operations and common risks. Throughout, the book provides practical examples of risk control.

Although primarily aimed at managers and supervisors, it is equally useful for safety and other union representatives, contractors, the self-employed and employees.

The HSE has proposed a new route map – an online tool – aimed at helping employers and workers manage workplace transport risk by providing a framework of current law with links to existing guidance, whilst filling any gaps with new guidance.

Several sets of regulations govern workplace transport and there are many guidance documents, some generic, others for specific industry sectors. The route map will aim to provide a clear path for all employers to follow best practice and meet their legal responsibilities, including setting out alternative ways to comply where these exist. It will focus specifically on site layout and design, vehicle selection and maintenance, personnel matters and management responsibilities.

The route map can be viewed at www.hse.gov.uk/consult/condocs/routemap.htm.

Glebe Mines Ltd was prosecuted and fined £25,000 after an employee of another company was killed after becoming trapped between a forklift truck and a mechanical loading shovel in March 2003[1]. Adequate systems for the control of visiting drivers were not in place, and the company had failed to conduct a suitable and sufficient assessment of the risks to employees and other persons from workplace transport.

## Doors and gates

Safety features should be incorporated for particular types of doors and gates (SI 1992/3004 reg 18).

Bruntwood Estates was prosecuted and fined £50,000 for breaches of HSWA 1974 and SI 1999/3242 after an 11-year-old child died after becoming trapped in the roll-up mechanism of an automated roller shutter door at a multi-storey car park owned and managed by Bruntwood in October 2000[2]. The health and safety risk assessment of the roller shutter door that had been carried out was not suitable and sufficient.

**Escalators and moving walkways**

Escalators and moving walkways should function safely, be equipped with any necessary safety devices, and be fitted with one or more emergency stop control which is easily identifiable and readily accessible (SI 1992/3004 reg 19).

**ACOP and guidance**

The HSE produces a free leaflet entitled *Workplace health, safety and welfare – A short guide for managers* (INDG244) summarising the legal requirements and providing practical advice on general workplace health and safety. This is available from HSE Books and can be downloaded at www.hse.gov.uk/pubns/whswindx.htm.

SI 1992/3004 (unamended) can be downloaded at www.opsi.gov.uk and is published, together with the ACoP, in *Workplace health, safety and welfare: Workplace (Health, Safety and Welfare) Regulations 1992 Approved Code of Practice* (L24) which is available from HSE Books.

¹   See HSE Prosecutions Database www.hse.gov.uk/prosecutions.
²   See HSE Prosecutions Database www.hse.gov.uk/prosecutions.

# Fire Safety Legislation – Regulatory Reform (Fire Safety) Order 2005

**2.29**    The majority of deaths in fires in the UK occur in dwellings, but according to the most recent *Fire Statistics Bulletin* (2005), twenty people died in fires in workplaces in 2005. According to these statistics, which can be found on the Department for Communities and Local Government website at www.communities.gov.uk, two people died in agricultural buildings, one in industrial premises, seven in trade, hotels, catering and repairs, and ten in other services, which includes public administration, hospitals, children's homes and homes for the elderly.

Fire safety legislation has been simplified, rationalised and consolidated, using a regulatory reform order, into one simple risk-based fire regime, applying to all buildings which the public might use (except for private dwellings): the Regulatory Reform (Fire Safety) Order 2005, SI 2005/1541, came into effect on 1 October 2006.

Responsibility for complying with SI 2005/1541 rests with the 'responsible person'. In a workplace, this is the employer and any other person who may have control of any part of the premises, e g the occupier or owner. In all other premises the person or people in control of the premises will be responsible. If there is more than one responsible person in any type of premises, all must take all reasonable steps to work with each other.

## Risk Assessments

**2.30**     The responsible person must carry out a fire risk assessment focusing on the safety in case of fire of all 'relevant persons'. It should pay particular attention to those at special risk, such as the disabled and those with special needs, and must include consideration of any dangerous substance likely to be on the premises.

The fire risk assessment will help to identify risks that can be removed or reduced, and to decide the nature and extent of the general fire precautions needed to protect people against the fire risks that remain. If five or more people are employed, the significant findings of the assessment must be recorded. The rules are enforced by the local fire and rescue authority which carries out regular inspections, with top priority going to those premises presenting most risk to the community.

## The Responsible Person

**2.31**     The 'responsible person', in relation to a workplace, is the employer, if the workplace is to any extent under his control. Where this is not the case, it is the person who has control of the premises (as occupier or otherwise) in connection with the carrying on of a trade, business or other undertaking (for profit or not); or the owner, where the person in control of the premises controls the carrying on by that person of a trade, business or other undertaking (SI 2005/1541 art 3). The responsible person must ensure that the duties in the Order are complied with in a workplace (art 5).

## General Fire Precautions

**2.32**     General fire precautions mean:

- measures to reduce the risk of and spread of fire;

- means of escape;

- measures for securing that, at all material times, the means of escape can be safely and effectively used;

- means for fighting fires;

- measures for detecting fire and giving warning in case of fire; and

- measures in relation to the arrangements for action to be taken in the event of fire on the premises, including instruction and training of employees and measures to mitigate the effects of the fire (SI 2005/1541 art 4).

## Exemptions

**2.33**     The Fire Safety Order 2005 does not apply in domestic premises, offshore installations, ships, fields, woods and other land forming part of an agricultural or forestry undertaking, aircraft, trains, vehicles, mines and borehole sites, some provisions do not apply to occasional or short-term work, and there are exemptions relating to means of transport (SI 2005/1541 arts 6, 7).

## Duties under the Order

**2.34**   The responsible person must take general fire precautions to ensure, so far as is reasonably practicable, the safety of employees, as well as non-employees, to ensure that the premises are safe (SI 2005/1541 art 8).

They must make a suitable and sufficient risk assessment in order to identify the general fire precautions needed to comply with the requirements and prohibitions set out in the order (art 9).

There are specific requirements relating to where dangerous substances are present, which are outlined in Schedule 1, and if young people are employed (Sch 2).

Assessments must be reviewed, kept up to date, and recorded where there are five or more employees, in licensed premises, and where there is an alterations notice requiring this (see art 29).

Preventive and protective measures must be implemented in accordance with the principles set out in Part 3 of Schedule 1:

- avoiding risks;

- evaluating the risks which cannot be avoided;

- combating risks at source;

- adapting to technical progress;

- replacing the dangerous by the non-dangerous or less dangerous;

- developing a coherent overall prevention policy covering technology, organisation of work and the influence of factors relating to the working environment;

- giving collective protective measures priority over individual protective measures; and

- giving appropriate instructions to employees (art 10).

The size of the undertaking and the nature of its activities must be taken into consideration when putting into effect appropriate arrangements for the effective planning, organisation, control, monitoring and review of the preventive and protective measures. Again these arrangements must be recorded as for the risk assessment (art 11).

The risk from dangerous substances must be eliminated or reduced (art 12).

Where necessary, due to the features of the premises, the activity carried on there or any hazard present, the premises must be equipped with appropriate fire-fighting equipment and fire detectors and alarms, and any non-automatic fire-fighting equipment must be easily accessible, simple to use and indicated by signs.

The responsible person, where necessary, must take measures for fire-fighting, and must nominate competent people to implement the measures, ensure that there are a sufficient number of such persons, and that their training and the equipment available to them are adequate. Any necessary contacts with external emergency services must be arranged (art 13).

Where necessary, there must be clear emergency exits and exit routes leading directly to a place of safety, ensuring that people can evacuate the building as quickly and safely as possible (art 14).

In the event of serious and imminent danger, where necessary there must be procedures, including fire drills, to be followed and competent people must be nominated to implement the procedures (art 15).

Where people are exposed to serious and imminent danger, they must be informed of the nature of the hazard and the steps to be taken to protect them from it. People must be able to stop work and immediately proceed to a place of safety in the event of their being exposed to serious, imminent and unavoidable danger, and they must be prevented from returning to a situation where serious and imminent danger remains (except in exceptional cases, which must be specified in procedures).

Additional emergency measures must be taken in respect of dangerous substances (art 16).

The premises, facilities, equipment and devices provided under SI 2005/1541 must be maintained so that they are in an efficient state, efficient working order and in good repair (art 17).

One or more competent people must be appointed to assist with the preventive and protective measures (art 18).

Information about the risks identified by the risk assessment, the preventive and protective measures, procedures and nominated people must be given to employees (art 19). Employers and the self-employed from outside undertakings must also be provided with information. Employees must be provided with training when they are first employed, and if they are exposed to new or increased risks (art 21)

Where there are two or more responsible persons, they must cooperate and coordinate with regard to complying with SI 2005/1541 (art 22).

Employees must take reasonable care of their own and others safety, cooperate with their employer and inform their employer or any other employee with specific responsibility for safety of any work situation they consider is a serious and immediate danger to safety, or of any shortcomings in the employer's protection arrangements for safety (art 23).

SI 2005/1541 is generally enforced by the local fire and rescue authority, although the HSE is the enforcement authority for nuclear installations, Crown premises, construction sites and ships, and the local authority enforces fire safety in sports grounds and stands (see CHAPTER 6).

Detailed guidance on SI 2005/1541 is available from the Department for Communities and Local Government (DCLG). This is targeted at specific areas of business including:

- offices and shops;
- premises providing sleeping accommodation;
- residential care;
- small and medium places of assembly;
- large places of assembly;
- factories and warehouses;
- theatres and cinemas;
- educational premises;
- healthcare premises;
- transport premises and facilities;
- open-air events.

These can be downloaded free of charge at www.communities.gov.uk/index.asp?id=1162101.

*Regulatory Reform (Fire Safety) Order 2005 – A Short Guide to Making your Premises Safe from Fire* is also available from the DCLG website at www.communities.gov.uk.

## Electricity at Work Regulations 1989

**2.35**    According to the HSE, around 1,000 accidents at work involving electric shock and burn injuries are reported annually and around 25 prove to be fatal. The three main hazards concerning electricity are:

- contact with live parts;
- fire; and

- explosion.

The HSE says that deaths and injuries arise from:

- the use of poorly maintained electrical equipment;

- work near overhead power lines;

- contact with underground power cables during excavation work;

- mains electricity supplies (230 volt);

- the use of unsuitable electrical equipment in explosive areas such as car paint spraying booths; and

- fires started by poor electrical installations and faulty electrical appliances.

Explosions can be also be caused by electrical apparatus or static electricity igniting flammable vapours or dusts.

The Electricity at Work Regulations 1989, SI 1989/635, are concerned with the prevention of danger from electric shock and burn, electrical explosion or arcing, or from fire or explosion.

The regulations require that:

- the strength and capability of electrical equipment is not exceeded;

- electrical equipment is protected where it could be exposed to:

  o mechanical damage;

  o the effects of the weather;

  o the effects of hot and cold temperatures;

  o wet, dusty or corrosive conditions; or

  o flammable or explosive substances;

- electrical equipment is properly insulated or suitably placed to prevent shocks and burns.

There are also requirements relating to earthing, the integrity of conductors, connections and joints, protection from excess current, means for cutting off the supply and for isolation, and requirements where electrical work is being carried out (including the competency of people carrying out the electrical work).

In practical terms, the HSE advises that some form of checking electrical equipment by a competent person must be arranged by the employer, although nothing is laid down in law as to how often equipment should be checked.

It also advises: 'The level of technical competence required will range from visual inspection of a cord grip on a plug (for which you could quickly train an employee) to the detailed testing of a major electrical installation for which you may need to engage a specialist'.

The National Inspection Council for Electrical Installations Contracting (NICEIC) enrols electrical contractors whose work is of an approved standard and surveys work to ensure it complies with the Institute of Electrical Engineers (IEE) Regulations, which do not have statutory force but indicate good practice.

## Portable Electrical Equipment

**2.36**    The HSE guide *Maintaining portable and transportable electrical equipment*, is aimed at employers, employees and the self-employed who use, or have control over, portable or transportable electrical equipment.

The guidance gives practical advice on how to maintain equipment in a safe condition and prevent accidents. It covers equipment that may be connected to either fixed mains or a locally generated supply, and that could result in an electric shock, burn or fire due to damage, wear or misuse.

The guidance applies to a wide variety of equipment, used in all environments, from electric drills and extension leads, to floor cleaners, pressure water cleaners and electric kettles. It includes advice on what the legal requirements for maintenance of electrical equipment can mean in practice and guidance on how to carry out a risk assessment in this area.

The maintenance strategy recommended by the guide is based on a straightforward, inexpensive system of visual inspections that can be undertaken by an appointed employee. In addition, a person with appropriate skill and technical knowledge should test equipment periodically.

Two free guidance leaflets are also available: *Maintaining portable electrical equipment in offices and other low risk environments* (INDG 236); and *Maintaining portable electrical equipment in hotels and tourist accommodation* (INDG 237).

## Electric Shock Risks

**2.37**    Provision should be made for dealing with electric shocks and is an element of first-aid training. Consideration should be given as to whether the display of an 'electric shock placard' is appropriate (this shows employees what to do in the event of an electric shock).

The HSE poster on emergency resuscitation in cases of electric shock takes account of the latest advice from the European Resuscitation Council. *Electric shock: First aid procedures*, provides basic advice on how to break the contact between an electrical source and a casualty and how to resuscitate someone who has received an electric shock.

The Memorandum of Guidance on the Electricity at Work Regulations 1989 (HSR 25) recommends that a poster containing emergency resuscitation procedures is placed at locations where there is a higher than average risk of electric shock, such as workplaces in electricity supply, generation, transmission and utilisation and companies carrying out electrical testing.

HSE publications on electrical safety can be downloaded at www.hse.gov.uk/pubns/elecindx.htm, and its electrical safety microsite is at www.hse.gov.uk/electricity/index.htm.

Nestlé UK Ltd was fined £220,000 in May 2003 and ordered to pay £30,000 in costs following the electrocution of a contractor's employee undertaking work at one of its factories in 1999. The contractor Monotronic Ltd, was also fined £25,000[1].

The HSE prosecuted both companies after the accident in which Anthony Allen, an electrician for Monotronic Ltd was electrocuted while pulling out redundant cables from trunking in the coffee plant in the factory.

Monotronic Ltd was charged with breaching HSWA 1974 s 2(1), for failing to ensure the safety of its employee.

Nestlé UK Ltd was charged with breaching HSWA 1974 s 3(1), for failing to ensure the safety of people not employed by them but affected by its work.

The HSE principal inspector Samantha Peace, commented on the case saying: 'Every company, however large or small, must ensure that contractors have safe systems of work and follow them. This is particularly important for electrical work.'

[1]  See HSE Press Release 3 June 2003.

## Gas Safety (Installation and Use) Regulations 1998

**2.38**    Every year about 30 people die from carbon monoxide (CO) poisoning caused by gas appliances and flues which have not been properly installed or maintained and a number of landlords and gas fitters have faced manslaughter charges following the deaths of tenants and other occupiers.

The Gas Safety (Installation and Use) Regulations 1998, SI 1998/2451, prohibit the installation of instantaneous water heaters, which have been the cause of a number of fatalities, unless they are room-sealed or fitted with a device to shut down the appliance before a dangerous quantity of combustion products, such as carbon monoxide can build up. They deal with the safe installation, maintenance and use of gas systems, including gas fittings, appliances and flues in domestic and commercial premises.

An ACoP, *Safety in the installation and use of gas systems and appliances* (L56) (1988 – reprinted in 2007 with references to new and updated legislation and new guidance), contains detailed guidance on the duties placed on those installing, servicing, maintaining or repairing gas appliances and other gas fittings, and apply to suppliers and users of gas, including some landlords.

The regulations contain requirements relating to:

- gas fittings – including the qualifications and supervision of operatives working on and installing gas fittings, a duty on employers and others to ensure that operatives are competent and a requirement that organisations employing gas fitters are registered under the Council for Registered Gas Installers (CORGI). There are also provisions concerning materials and workmanship, general safety precautions, protection against damage, existing gas fittings, emergency controls and maintaining electrical continuity;

- meters and regulators – including general provisions, meter housings, regulators, emergency notices and primary and secondary meters;

- installation pipework – safe use of pipes, enclosed pipes, protection of buildings, clogging precautions, testing and purging of pipes, marking of pipes, and large consumers;

- gas appliances – safety precautions, flues, access, manufacturer's instructions, room-sealed appliances, suspended appliances, flue dampners, testing of appliances and use of appliances;

- maintenance – duties of employers and self-employed persons; duties of landlords; and

- miscellaneous provisions – escape of gas, use of antifluctuators and valves, exception as to liability and exemption certificates.

There is an assessment regime for gas operatives undertaking commercial or industrial work. The national accredited certification scheme is administered by CORGI. A new gas installer registration scheme for domestic gas safety will come into effect by the end of July 2008 and this will include a strict framework, setting out performance and requirement criteria, to allow strong oversight of the new scheme by the HSE.

A number of gas fitters and landlords have been prosecuted after people have died of carbon monoxide poisoning as a result of faulty gas appliances.

Paul Clark, a landlord from Southsea in Portsmouth, was prosecuted and fined a total of £42,000, with additional prosecution costs of £18,000 at Winchester Crown Court for breaches of gas safety legislation which led to the fatal carbon monoxide (CO) poisoning of eleven-year-old Katie Overton in 2003[1].

The HSE reminded landlords of rented properties that gas appliances are subject to annual safety checks, and must also be maintained in a safe condition. This means gas boilers being serviced annually in accordance with manufacturers' instructions by a CORGI registered installer as well having annual gas safety checks carried out on them.

CHAPTER 13 sets out the legislation applying to the gas supply industry.

[1]   See HSE Press Release HSE/GNN/05/03 8 May 06.

## Provision and Use of Work Equipment Regulations 1998

**2.39**    The Provision and Use of Work Equipment Regulations 1998, SI 1998/2306, govern the selection and operation of machinery, tools and equipment and apply to work equipment used in all industry and service sectors. The Regulations first came into force in 1992 as part of the 'six pack' of regulations introduced to implement the European Framework and Daughter Directives.

The duties outlined in SI 1998/2306 reflect the way work equipment is used in industry, where there is not necessarily a direct employment relationship between users and the people who control its use, or where people control equipment but not its use.

The definition of 'work equipment' covers machinery, appliances, apparatus, tools and any assembly of components which function as a whole. The only exceptions are livestock, substances and private cars.

Although the case of *Knowles v Liverpool City Council*[1] did not concern SI 1998/2306, it was held that a flagstone used for repairing a pavement was 'equipment'.

The definition of 'use' covers starting, stopping, modifying, programming, setting, transporting, maintaining, servicing and cleaning.

The Regulations deal with risks from mobile work equipment, which includes fork-lift trucks, dumpers and tractors. These include: minimising risks from roll-over; preventing start up by unauthorised persons; providing a device for braking and stopping; and providing adequate devices to improve a driver's field of vision where necessary for safety. They also deal with power presses and woodworking machinery.

SI 1998/2306 is supported by an ACoP (L22) and there are additional ACoPs dealing specifically with power presses (L112) and woodworking machines (L114).

In summary, SI 1998/2306 requires that:

● work equipment must be inspected after installation and before being put into service for the first time;

● it must be suitable for the task for which it will be used, and maintained in good repair and proper working order; and

● those carrying out repairs, maintenance and servicing of work equipment must be properly trained.

SI 1998/2306 sets out a number of general requirements and employers must:

- ensure that work equipment is constructed or adapted so as to be suitable for the task for which it will be used (reg 4);

- take into account the working conditions and hazards when selecting equipment (reg 4);

- ensure that work equipment is maintained in an efficient state, in efficient working order and in good repair, and keep any maintenance logs on machinery up to date (reg 5);

- where the safety of work equipment depends on the installation conditions, ensure that it is inspected after installation and before being put into service for the first time; or after assembly at a new site or in a new location. Where work equipment is exposed to conditions causing deterioration which is liable to result in dangerous situations, ensure that it is inspected at regular intervals and each time that exceptional circumstances which are liable to jeopardise the safety of the equipment have occurred, so that health and safety conditions are maintained and that any deterioration can be detected and remedied in good time (reg 6).

- ensure that where there are specific risks involved, that use is restricted to those given the task of using it. Repair, modification, servicing and maintenance work must be carried out by those designated to perform such work and who have received adequate training (reg 7);

- ensure that appropriate information, instruction and training is given to employees and any supervisors or managers who are responsible for work equipment used at work (regs 8, 9); and

- ensure that work equipment complies with any relevant EU Directives (reg 10).

In addition, employers must ensure that the work equipment complies with more specific requirements outlined in SI 1998/2306 regs 11–24, which concern:

- dangerous parts of machinery (reg 11);

- protection against specified hazards (reg 12);

- high or very low temperatures (reg 13);

- control systems and devices (regs 14–18);

- isolation from sources of energy (reg 19);

- stability (reg 20);

- lighting (reg 21);

- maintenance operations (reg 22);

- markings (reg 23); and

- warnings (reg 24).

Part III of SI 1998/2306 requires employers and other duty holders to ensure that equipment is safe to use by preventing or controlling risks. This could involve, for example, the retro-fitting of roll-over protective structures (ROPS), falling object protective structures (FOPS), seat restraints (seat belts, lap belts, etc) and driver visibility aids such as mirrors.

A site foreman, building company director and the company itself all received fines for health and safety offences following the death of labourer Alex Hayden[2].

Alex died in August 2005 after the dumper truck he was driving fell down an embankment and toppled over. He had jumped from the truck after he lost control, but was crushed on landing. Staffordshire Police, who investigated the accident with the HSE said that he was not qualified to drive the truck and crucial safety measures had been flouted at the site on the City Park Trading Estate, Fenton.

Foreman Paul Nolan, who was responsible for health and safety at the location, was acquitted of manslaughter after a 13-day trial at Stafford Crown Court. He was convicted of failing to discharge a duty contrary to HSWA 1974 and fined £5,000 plus £1,000 costs. He had denied the charges.

Nolan was working for Denton building firm A & A Building Services who were carrying out demolition work, refurbishment of units and creating hard standings at the site. A & A Building Services director Darren Atkins, Nolan's manager, also denied contravening HSWA 1974 but was convicted and fined £15,000 plus £7,700 costs.

At a previous hearing, A & A Building Services admitted contravening HSWA 1974 and were fined £55,000 plus £6,000 costs.

[1] [1993] IRLR 588.
[2] See Staffordshire Police Press Release, 21 September 2007 and HSE Press Release 21 September 07.

# Lifting Operations and Lifting Equipment Regulation 1998

**2.40**    In addition to SI 1998/2306, the Lifting Operations and Lifting Equipment Regulations 1998, SI 1998/2307, contain specific requirements on equipment strength and stability; positioning and installation; marking; thorough examination and inspection and record keeping.

Duty holders must either have lifting equipment thoroughly examined by a competent person at intervals set out in the regulations – six months for equipment for lifting people and accessories (e g hooks and eyebolts) and 12 months for other lifting equipment. Alternatively, an examination scheme can be drawn up and intervals set for thorough examination based on a risk assessment.

Deco Marble and Granite Ltd of Park Royal, London was fined £3,000 at Southwark Crown Court in April 2005 following a prosecution brought by the HSE, after an investigation into an incident where a worker was killed on 26 September 2003[2]. The judge said the fine would have been potentially £80,000 if the company had not gone into liquidation.

Martin Dunleavy was crushed by several stone slabs from a bundle weighing approximately six tonnes. The slabs were being unloaded from a delivery lorry by crane when the chains used to lift the load became trapped. It was whilst Mr Dunleavy was trying to free the chains that the slabs tipped forward onto him.

Deco Marble pleaded guilty to breaching SI 1998/2306 reg 8(1), as well as HSWA 1974 s 2(1) and SI 1999/3242 reg 3(1).

The HSE principal inspector Mike Gibb, commenting on the case, said that the incident demonstrated the inherent dangers involved in moving and storing large heavy loads such as slabs of stone, and advised that:

> 'Firms receiving deliveries should consider the use of contract lifts where a crane hire firm can plan and coordinate all aspects of the lifting operations.
>
> All firms using and storing stone slabs should assess the risks from their current storage and handling arrangements. Toast-rack style storage is preferred to prevent toppling of slabs. Inclined A-frames can also be used provided the slabs are secure.'

[1]   See HSE Press Release 18 April 2005.

# Supply of Machinery

**2.41**   The Supply of Machinery (Safety) Regulations 1992, SI 1992/3073, provide common rules for machinery not covered by other regulations. The main responsibilities fall on the manufacturers and suppliers, and so are not covered in detail here. The regulations can be downloaded from the Office of Public Sector Information website at www.opsi.gov.uk.

*Junttan Oy v Bristol Magistrates Court*[1] involved the supply of a rig involved in the death of a sewage worker. The rig manufacturing company which supplied it argued that the magistrates' court had no jurisdiction to hear the case. It said the HSE had breached a European Machinery Directive by instigating proceedings under HSWA 1974 – where the maximum penalty for a breach was a fine of up to £20,000 – rather than SI 1992/3073, which implemented the Directive – where the maximum penalty for a breach was £5,000.

Although the HSE admitted that it had failed to follow the procedure under Article 7 of the Machinery Directive for withdrawing dangerous machinery from the market and reporting it to the European Commission, the High Court said that this was not a bar on prosecution. Article 7 requires member states to take steps if it considers that machinery is unsafe. In this case the machinery had been modified before the prosecution began, as a result of an HSE prohibition notice being served, so action under the article would have been meaningless.

The judge said that it could not have been intended that Article 7 should prevent a prosecution where a manufacturer of machinery may have committed a criminal offence, and he ruled that it had no relevance to enforcement action involving criminal proceedings.

However, he said that the HSE should have prosecuted under the Regulations, which provided for a specific statutory offence, rather than using HSWA 1974 s 6, even though the penalties were lower, remarking that these should probably be reviewed. He said that the conclusions reached would not necessarily apply if the offence had been one of manslaughter, nor did they affect a prosecution under HSWA 1974 s 3, which the HSE had also taken.

¹   [2002] EWHC (Admin) 566, [2002] 2 CMLF 37.

## Personal Protective Equipment at Work Regulations 1992

**2.42**   The Personal Protective Equipment at Work Regulations 1992, SI 1992/2966, lay down the type and standard of personal protective equipment (PPE) to be used when risks cannot be otherwise avoided and apply to all industries and services (apart from seagoing ships).

The regulations define PPE as 'all equipment (including clothing affording protection against the weather) which is intended to be worn or held by a person at work which protects them against one or more risks to health and safety, and any addition or accessory designed to meet that objective'.

In summary, the regulations require that employers:

- ensure that suitable PPE is provided to employees where risks to health and safety have not been adequately controlled by other means (the guidance makes it clear that PPE is a 'last resort'). Suitable PPE must be appropriate for the risks involved and conditions of work, take account of ergonomic requirements and the state of health of employees wearing it, fit properly, effectively prevent or adequately control risks and not increase the overall risk, and comply with other legislation (eg product safety legislation) (reg 4);

- ensure that where more than one type of PPE is necessary, the equipment is compatible (reg 5);

- carry out an assessment before choosing PPE to ensure it is suitable. This should include an assessment of risks not avoided by other means and of the necessary characteristics of the PPE, taking into account any risks created by the PPE itself. The assessment must be reviewed if there is reason to suspect it is no longer valid or there have been significant changes (regs 6, 7);

- ensure that any PPE provided to his employees is maintained (including being replaced or cleaned as appropriate) in an efficient state, in efficient working order and in good repair (reg 7);

- provide safe storage facilities for PPE (reg 8);

- provide information, instruction and training about the risks the PPE will avoid or limit, how the PPE should be used, and any action the employee must take to ensure that it remains in good repair and efficient working order. (Managers and supervisors must also be made aware of why PPE is being used and how it is to be used properly.) This includes practical demonstrations (reg 9); and

- ensure that PPE is being used properly by employees (reg 10).

Regulation 10 says that employees must use the PPE as trained to do so, and must report any loss or defect (reg 11). By virtue of section 9 of the HSWA 1974, no charge can be made to the worker for the provision of PPE which is only to be used at work.

*Fytche v Wincanton Logistics plc*[1] held that the regulations only require the employer to maintain or repair PPE so as to guard against the risk for which it was supplied, and not to any other risks which might arise. One of the judges said that the implications of a decision which went the other way would have meant that employers could be held liable for risks that could not reasonably have been foreseen. In this case, a tanker driver had been issued with safety boots with steel toecaps to protect his feet from heavy objects falling on them. His tanker became stuck in snow, and as he dug it free, one boot leaked through a tiny hole. He suffered frostbite and part of his toe had to be amputated as a result.

The PPE Regulations (as amended) concern the safety of PPE being put on to the market.

HSE guidance for employers who supply and use PPE at work is available in *Personal Protective Equipment (PPE) at Work Regulations 1992* (L25) and *A short guide to the Personal Protective Equipment at Work Regulations which* can be downloaded from the HSE website at www.hse.gov.uk/pubns/indg174.pdf.

In addition to the PPE Regulations, there is also law governing the use of respiratory protective equipment (RPE) which is contained in separate pieces of regulations, including the Control of Substances Hazardous to Health Regulations 2002, SI 2002/2677.

The regulations make specific requirements for the correct use of RPE at work. It must:

- be adequate and provide the wearer with effective protection;
- be suitable for the intended use;
- be 'CE'-marked;
- be selected, used and maintained by properly trained people;
- be correctly maintained, examined and tested; and
- be correctly stored.

Copies of *Respiratory protective equipment at work: A practical guide* (HSG53 2004) are available from HSE Books.

---

[1]   [2004] IRLR 817.

# Work at Height Regulations 2005

**2.43**   The latest HSE figures show that 45 people died as a result of a fall from height in the workplace in the year to March 2007.

The Work at Height Regulations 2005, SI 2005/735, apply to all work at height where there is a risk of a fall liable to cause personal injury and came into force in April 2005. The Regulations removed the old division between low and high falls, abolishing the 'two-metre rule'. Falls from any height must be prevented.

Under the regulations, duty holders must:

• follow the risk assessments carried out for work at height activities to make sure all work at height is planned, organised and carried out by competent people (regs 4, 5);

• follow the hierarchy for managing risks from work at height – take steps to avoid, prevent or reduce risks (reg 6);

• choose the right work equipment and select collective measures to prevent falls (such as guardrails) before other measures which may only mitigate the distance and consequences of a fall (such as nets or airbags) or which may only provide personal protection from a fall (reg 7); and

• ensure that guard rails, toe-boards, barriers or similar collective means of protection; working platforms; scaffolding; nets, airbags or other collective safeguards for arresting falls; personal fall protection systems; and ladders comply with requirements set out in the Schedules to the regulations (reg 8).

There are also specific requirements regarding work on or near fragile surfaces, falling objects, danger areas, and the inspection of work equipment and places of work at height (regs 9–13).

The HSE advises that:

'When a job requires work at height there needs to be a plan to work in a safe way. Simple precautions can prevent anyone working on or adjacent to fragile materials, such as roof lights or asbestos sheets. Precautions include:

• place platforms over fragile materials to work over them. Platforms must be at least 600 mm wide and supported by solid materials;

• either cover with a material capable of supporting weight or provide edge protection (ie hand rail, mid-rail and toe board) if working near fragile materials;

• where a roof will be removed the above precautions must be used and in addition it is possible to provide safety netting beneath the roof service to provide collective fall protection;

- when putting these precautions in place, or for jobs of short duration, harnesses may be an appropriate solution – but care must be taken to find a suitable fixing point;

- training courses are available for roofers that include basic health and safety; and

- a supervisor should be in charge of the work to ensure that safe systems of work are being followed.'

The *Work at Height Regulations 2005 – a brief guide* (INDG 401) has been published by the HSE to give a short introduction to the Regulations and how to work at height safely. It is aimed principally at small businesses and those not familiar with SI 2005/735. This is available on the HSE website at www.hse.gov.uk/pubns/indg401.pdf. It is also available free from HSE Books.

To assist the construction industry the HSE has also published *Question and answer brief for the construction industry on the Work at Height Regulations 2005* to explain what the Regulations mean in practice and the standards the HSE expects the industry to meet. It is available free on the HSE website at www.hse.gov.uk/construction/pdf/fallsqa.pdf.

SI 2005/735 is accessible via the HMSO website at www.legislation.hmso.gov.uk/si/si2005/20050735.htm. Printed copies are published by The Stationery Office Ltd (TSO) (tel: 0870 6005522; fax: 0870 600 5533; email customer.services@tso.co.uk).

The Electrical Contractors' Association (ECA) has also produced guidance on eliminating or reducing the risk of falls from stepladders to electricians and other engineering contractors.

*Practical alternatives to using stepladders* provides information on planning, risk assessment, competency, training and choosing temporary access equipment, and gives advice on the safe use of stepladders, if they are the chosen means of access.

The guidance is available to download free from the ECA website at www.eca.co.uk/files/hs/ECA_Practical Alternatives To Using Step Ladders.pdf.

The regulations do not ban ladders, as has been rumoured in some industries, but they do require that they are only used when all other safer alternatives for work at height have been ruled out, and they must be used sensibly. A risk assessment must show that the task is low risk and of short duration, or that there are site features that mean other equipment is not appropriate. If so, then ladders can be used.

The Work at Height (Amendment) Regulations 2007, SI 2007/114, came into effect on 6 April 2007 to bring workers paid to lead or train others in climbing and caving activities in the adventure activity centre within the scope of SI 2005/735.

¹  See HSE Press Release 14 March 2006.

# Radiation

**2.44**    The Ionising Radiations Regulations 1999, SI 1999/3232, set a limit on the dose of radiation to the whole body (effective dose) to which workers can be exposed in a calendar year.

The limit on the dose of radiation to the whole body (effective dose) to which workers aged 18 and over can be exposed is 20 millisieverts (mSv) in a calendar year. However, in special cases, a dose limit of 100mSv in five years may apply, with no more than 50mSv in a single year, subject to strict conditions.

For trainees the limit is 6mSv in a calendar year, and for any other person, including members of the public, the limit is 1mSv a year. The limit for the skin applies to doses averaged over an area not exceeding 1cm².

An Approved Code of Practice (ACoP) and HSE guidance on work with ionising radiation provides practical help for employers who need to comply with the *Ionising Radiations Regulations 1999 (IRR99): Work with ionising radiation* (L121). This sets out that the primary duties under IRR'99 are to:

*   undertake a suitable and sufficient risk assessment before starting any new type of work with ionising radiation;

*   restrict exposure to ionising radiations: firstly, through engineered means such as the use of adequate shielding, safety devices, containment and ventilation where these are reasonably practicable; also by the provision of systems of work and personal protective equipment as far as reasonably practicable;

*   maintain and examine engineering controls and personal protective equipment;

*   consider the risks to pregnant and breast-feeding employees and alter working conditions where appropriate;

*   consult (and appoint) one or more suitable radiation protection advisers as necessary;

*   designate controlled and supervised areas where necessary;

*   implement new dose limits; and

*   make arrangements for designating certain employees as classified persons, arranging for the assessment and recording of doses they receive and medical surveillance.

*Work with ionising radiations: Approved Code of Practice and Guidance* (L121) is available from HSE Books.

HSE guidance on planning for emergencies involving radiation releases with the potential to affect the public and the provision of information to the relevant public supports the Radiation (Emergency Preparedness and Public Information) Regulations 2001, SI 2001/2975.

(See also CHAPTER 13 which looks at legislation applying to the nuclear industry.)

## Diving at Work Regulations 1997

**2.45**   The Diving at Work Regulations 1997, SI 1997/2776, cover the whole diving industry, including groups of workers previously excluded from legislation such as journalists, scientists, archaeologists and recreational instructors. The means by which the industry must meet the standards set out in the regulations is set out in five ACoPs covering: commercial diving projects offshore; commercial diving projects inland/onshore; recreational diving projects; media diving projects, and scientific and archaeological diving projects. All working divers must have a qualification approved by the HSE.

Stoney Cove Marine Trials Ltd of Leicester was fined £7,500 and ordered to pay £40,000 costs at Warwick Crown Court on 23 December 2003 after pleading guilty to failing to ensure that divers on a recreational diving course were not exposed to risks to their health and safety, in breach of section 3(1) of HSWA 1974[1].

The prosecution followed an HSE investigation into the death of trainee diver Paul Gallacher who died in October 2000 while undertaking a Normoxic Trimix dive as part of a course being conducted by Stoney Cove Marine Trials, at Wastwater, Cumbria. The Normoxic Trimix diving course is governed by the International Association of Nitrox and Technical Divers (IANTD).

The company did not check Mr Gallacher's written diving records, in accordance with the IANTD Standards and Procedures to assess that he satisfied the prerequisites for attending the course. The site-specific risk assessment was not sufficient in that a number of items were not adequately recorded.

Commenting on the case, HSE principal inspector Mike Welham said that the company had failed to manage the diving operation where people were being taught technical diving in a remote location.

More information on diving is available on the HSE website at http://www.hse.gov.uk/diving/osd/acop.htm.

[1]   See HSE Press Release 23 December 2003.

## Work-related Violence

**2.46**   There were four work-related deaths as a result of acts of violence in 2006/07 according to the latest HSE fatal injury statistics.

The HSE defines work-related violence as including: 'Any incident in which an employee is abused, threatened or assaulted by a member of the public in circumstances arising from his or her employment'.

There is no general specific legislation on preventing violence at work, but the legal position is relatively clear. In addition to their common law duty of care, the HSE advises employers that if there is a significant risk of violence at work, the risk assessment which employers are required to carry out under SI 1999/3242 should include the risk of violence.

In addition, the Reporting of Injuries, Diseases and Dangerous Occurrences Regulations 1995, SI 1995/3163, (see 2.61) require employers to report physical injuries due to assault arising from, or in connection with, work to the HSE.

Also, as a result of campaigning by the fire brigades' union, FBU, in response to violence against its members, legislation protecting emergency workers was enacted – the Emergency Workers (Obstruction) Act 2006, which followed similar legislation introduced in Scotland in 2005. The 2006 Act covers England, Wales and Northern Ireland and makes it an offence to obstruct or hinder people providing emergency services, and although it does not specifically include "assault", as the Scottish legislation does, the union believes that the 2006 Act includes both physical and verbal abuse.

In its leaflet *Violence to staff* (IND(G)69L), the HSE sets out the following action plan for employers and employees to tackle violence:

**Step 1: Find out if there is a problem**

Ask staff whether they ever feel threatened or under great stress, either informally or through a short questionnaire. Staff should be told the results of the survey.

**Step 2: Record all the incidents**

By keeping a detailed record of all incidents, build up a picture of the problem. A simple report form can be used to record what happened, where, when, who was involved and any possible causes. Employees should be encouraged to report all incidents.

**Step 3: Classify all incidents**

Use headings – such as place, time, type of incident – to see who was involved and the possible causes. This should be checked for patterns.

**Step 4: Search for preventive measures**

The way jobs are designed can reduce the risk of violence; but find measures that are right for your workplace.

## Step 5: Decide what to do

Employees are likely to be committed to the measures if they help to design them and put them into practice. Try to balance the risks to employees against any possible side effects to the public. An atmosphere that suggests employees are worried about violence can sometimes increase its likelihood.

## Step 6: Put the measures into practice

Whatever measures are decided upon should be included in the safety policy statement so that staff are aware of it.

## Step 7: Check that the measures work

Once steps to reduce violence have been taken, check how well they are working. If violence is still a problem, go back through steps 2 and 3 and try to identify other preventive measures that could work.

*Work-related violence: managing the risk in smaller businesses* (HSG 229) offers examples of how some businesses have reduced the risk of violence to staff in retail, health and welfare, security and enforcement, and leisure/service providers and is available from HSE Books.

*Violence at work, a guide for employers* (INDG69 (rev)) is also available.

South West London Primary and St Georges Mental Health NHS Trust was fined £28,000 with £14,000 costs in May 2005 following an HSE prosecution brought against it after a junior member of staff working alone was killed by a psychiatric patient in June 2003[1]. The HSE said there were no clear procedures and inadequate measures in place to check on his safety, amounting to a significant management failure. It also said that the prosecution should send a strong message to other hospital trusts and organisations which have to manage potential violence at work that they must identify and manage the risks. (For further details of the case see CHAPTER 14).

The HSE violence microsite is at: www.hse.gov.uk/violence/index.htm and free leaflets can be downloaded at: www.hse.gov.uk/pubns/violindx.htm.

[1]   See HSE Press Release 5 May 2005.

## Work in Compressed Air Regulations 1996

**2.47**   The Work in Compressed Air Regulations 1996, SI 1996/1656, cover work such as tunnelling and civil engineering where there is danger of inundation or collapse and apply to construction work, but not to diving operations, which are subject to other legislation (see 2.45).

The health problems which can be caused by working in compressed air include decompression sickness (also known as 'the bends') and the more serious and potentially life-threatening Type 2 decompression sickness which affects the central nervous system; barotrauma, which can damage the ears and sinuses; and dysbaric osteonecrosis, a long-term, chronic condition damaging the hip or shoulder joints.

The Regulations provide a framework for the management of health and safety risks and set out requirements regarding:

• notification of the work to HSE;

• safe systems of work;

• competent persons undertaking various defined roles;

• provision of plant and equipment;

• health surveillance;

• compression and decompression procedures (including HSE approval of procedures);

• medical treatment;

• emergency procedures;

• fire precautions;

• provision of information, instruction and training; and

• maintenance of health and exposure records.

## Confined Spaces Regulations 1997

**2.48**    Under the Confined Spaces Regulations 1997, SI 1997/1713, employers must first try to avoid entry to confined spaces. Where this is not possible, they must:

• carry out an assessment of the risks associated with entering a confined space and draw up a safe system of work;

• limit entry to the confined space to employees who are competent for confined space work and who have received suitable training;

• verify, prior to entry, that the atmosphere in the confined space is safe to breathe;

• provide any necessary ventilation; and

• make sure suitable rescue arrangements are in place before anyone goes in to the confined space. These rescue arrangements should not involve risks to the safety of the people intended to carry out the rescue.

In addition to oxygen deficient atmospheres, employers must also consider all the other hazards associated with confined spaces, including:

• flammable substances and oxygen enrichment;

• toxic gases, fumes or vapour;

77

- the danger that people could be harmed by liquids getting into the space; and

- the flow of solid materials such as grain.

HSE guidance includes *Safe work in confined spaces* (INDG258) and *Confined Spaces Regulations 1997* (L101).

Carl Pointon, director of a meat rendering company, John Pointon and Sons, and the company recently escaped a manslaughter conviction, following the death of employee Glyn Thompson, who died after being overcome by fumes in a slurry pit.

The company was fined a total of £620,000 for breaches of the Confined Spaces Regulations 1997, SI 1997/1713, (as well as HSWA 1974 and SI 1999/3242). The company admitted not having a risk assessment.

Glyn died trying to rescue a colleague, Ivan Torr, who had slipped and fallen into a machine used for rendering animal carcasses.

## Pressure Systems

**2.49**   The Pressure Systems Safety Regulations 2000, SI 2000/128, deal with the prevention of serious injury from stored energy hazards associated with the containment of fluids under pressure, in pressure equipment and systems such as boilers, used in the workplace.

SI 2000/128 aims to prevent serious injury from the hazard of stored energy as a result of the failure of a pressure system or one of its components. The Regulations are concerned with steam and gases which are contained under pressure in excess of 0.5 bar above atmospheric pressure. They also cover fluids, which may be mixtures of liquids, gases and vapours, where the gas or vapour phase may exert a pressure in excess of 0.5 bar above atmospheric pressure.

Copies of *Safety of pressure systems: Approved Code of Practice* (L122) can be ordered online at: www.hsebooks.co.uk, or are available from HSE Books.

## Control of Substances Hazardous to Health Regulations 2002

**2.50**   The Control of Substances Hazardous to Health Regulations 2002, SI 2002/2677, apply to a substance (including a preparation):

(a)   which is listed in Part I of the approved supply list as dangerous for supply within the meaning of the Chemicals (Hazardous Information for Packaging and Supply) Regulations 2002, SI 2002/1689, and for which an indication of danger specified for the substance is very toxic, toxic, harmful, corrosive or irritant;

(b)   for which the HSC has approved a maximum exposure limit or an occupational exposure standard (note that these have now been replaced with workplace exposure levels (WELs);

(c)  which is a biological agent;

(d)  which is dust of any kind (except that which is a substance within head (a) or (b) above) when present in certain concentrations;

(e)  which, not being a substance falling within heads (a)–(d) above, creates a risk to health due to its chemical or toxicological properties and the way it is used or arises in the workplace.

SI 2002/2677 prohibits the use of a number of very dangerous substances for certain purposes. These are listed in Schedule 2. They do not apply to asbestos or lead, nor to ionising radiation since there are separate regulations which deal with these hazards (see 2.44).

The main requirements of the regulations are summarised below:

•  employers must carry out an assessment of the risks to health from exposure to any hazardous substance in the workplace. The assessment should cover storage, transport, use and disposal. An employer shall not carry on any work which is liable to expose employees or other persons on the premises to any substance hazardous to health unless an assessment of the risks to health and the steps which need to be taken to prevent or control those risks have been carried out;

•  hazardous substances should be eliminated from the workplace if reasonably practicable, or safer substitutes used;

•  if hazardous substances are used, or arise, and cannot be eliminated or substituted, control measures should be used to prevent or control the risk;

•  personal protective clothing or equipment should only be used as a last resort, if no other method of control is appropriate;

•  adequate control relies on compliance with WELs;

•  monitoring of exposure must be carried out where necessary to ensure the maintenance of adequate control of exposure, or to protect the health of employees;

•  health surveillance must be carried out where there is significant exposure to particularly hazardous substances and processes;

•  employees exposed to substances hazardous to health must be provided with information, instruction and training about the risks to health and safety, and the precautions which must be taken. This should include the results of monitoring and health surveillance where this has been carried out;

•  the Regulations apply to both chemical and biological agents, whether or not exposure to such biological agents is deliberate, such as for laboratory workers, or incidental, for sewage workers, cleaners and farmers;

- where containers and pipes used for hazardous substances are not marked under any relevant legislation, the employer must ensure that the contents, the nature of the contents and any hazards are clearly identifiable;

- in certain circumstances, employers must draw up detailed procedures for dealing with accidents, incidents, and emergencies that involve hazardous substances. This does not apply where the results of the risk assessment show that the quantities of hazardous substances (as long as they are not carcinogens) are such that there is only a slight risk to the health of employees, and the measures taken to control the risks are adequate; and

- employees must make full and proper use of any control measures or PPE provided.

*Dugmore v Swansea NHS Trust and Morriston NHS Trust*[1] showed that employers have an absolute duty to adequately control exposure to substances hazardous health, where this cannot be prevented. The qualification of reasonable practicability applies only to prevention, and not to the secondary duty of control.

*Control of Substances Hazardous to Health Regulations 2002: Approved Code of Practice and Guidance* (L5) (fifth edition, 2005) is available from HSE Books.

[1]  [2003] IRLR 164.

### Legionnaires' Disease

**2.51**   Legionnaires' disease is a type of pneumonia, named after a 1976 outbreak of severe pneumonia which affected a meeting of the American Legion. It is caught by inhaling small droplets of water suspended in the air containing the legionella bacterium, although most people exposed do not become ill and the disease does not spread from person to person.

It is uncommon but serious – infection with legionella bacteria can be fatal in approximately 12% of reported cases. This rate can be higher in a more susceptible population; for example, immuno-suppressed patients or those with other underlying disease. Certain groups of people are known to be at higher risk of contracting Legionnaires' disease, with the disease occuring more frequently in men than women; and in middle-aged or elderly people – it is uncommon in younger people and very uncommon in people under 20; and more commonly affects smokers and people with other chest problems.

About half the annually reported cases of Legionnaires' disease result from infections acquired in the UK. Although legionella is naturally widespread in water, for example ponds, it does not usually cause problems. Outbreaks from purpose-built water systems happen when temperatures are warm enough to encourage the growth of the bacteria, in cooling towers, evaporative condensers and whirlpool spas and from water used for domestic purposes in buildings such as hotels.

Most community outbreaks in the UK have been linked to cooling towers or evaporative condensers, part of air-conditioning and industrial cooling systems, which can spread droplets of water over a wide area.

In August 2002, seven people died and a further 180 people became ill as a result of an outbreak of legionella, the source of which was traced to the air conditioning unit at a council-owned arts and leisure centre, Forum 28, in Barrow-in-Furness, Cumbria.

Manslaughter prosecutions were then taken against Barrow Borough Council and their Design Services Manager. Although these were not successful, it was the first time that a manslaughter prosecution was undertaken against a corporation that was not a limited company. Both were also charged with offences under HSWA 1974 and were fined £125,000 and £15,000 respectively.

(See CHAPTER 14 for full details of the case.)

In order to prevent the occurrence of Legionnaires' disease, companies which operate these systems must comply with regulations requiring them to manage, maintain and treat them properly. Water must be treated and the system cleaned regularly.

An ACoP on the control of legionella bacteria in water systems gives advice on the requirements of HSWA 1974, SI 2002/2677 and relevant parts of SI 1999/3242. The Code includes:

- guidance on the requirement for getting competent advice;

- guidance on the duties upon suppliers of goods and services;

- references to a voluntary Code of Conduct for the water treatment industry; and

- a recommendation that routine sampling of cooling towers for legionella is carried out on a quarterly basis, together with guidance on action to be taken when legionella is detected in such systems. (Routine sampling of hot and cold water systems for legionella is not recommended.)

Copies of *The control of legionella bacteria in water systems: Approved Code of Practice and Guidance* (L8), and a free leaflet, *Legionnella's disease: A guide for employers* (IAC 27), are available from HSE Books.

The Notification of Cooling Towers and Evaporative Condensers Regulations 1992, SI 1992/2225, require that occupiers notify the local authority of 'notifiable devices' in writing.

These are cooling towers and evaporative condensers, except where they contain no water exposed to air and/or their water or electricity supply is not connected. The main purpose of such requirements is to assist in investigating outbreaks. There is no obligation for local authorities to maintain a register, although in many cases they will do so and it is expected that, whatever the form in which the information is collated, it will be made readily available.

## Chemicals (Hazard Information and Packaging for Supply) Regulations 2002

**2.52**   The regulations require that all chemical substances and preparations (ie mixtures of substances) used at work be classified according to their principal hazards. If substances fall into the danger categories set out in the Regulations, they must be safely packaged and supplied with information about the hazards, including environmental hazards. Information and any relevant precautions have to be shown on the label, and in more detail on safety data sheets. The ACoP is entitled *The compilation of safety data sheets* (L130). There are also Regulations applying to manufacturers and importers, concerning notification procedures for substances they intend to place on the market, the Notification of New Substances Regulations 1993, SI 1993/3050.

## Pesticides and Biocides

**2.53**   The use, supply, storage and advertisement of pesticides is regulated by a number of different regulations including the Control of Pesticides Regulations 1986, SI 1986/1510, and the Plant Protection Products Regulations 1995, SI 1995/887. The Pesticides Safety Directorate (PSD) (www.pesticides.gov.uk) is responsible for agricultural pesticides, while most non-agricultural pesticides are the responsibility of HSE. PPPR implements a European Directive on the regulation of products including agricultural pesticides and growth regulators. The use of pesticides is also regulated by COSHH (the Control of Substances Hazardous to Health). The Biocidal Products Regulations 2001, SI 2001/3050, control biocides, which are used to control, for example, cockroaches and rats, as well as wood rot. Examples include disinfectants, preservatives, pest control and antifouling products. *A guide to the Biocidal Products Regulations for users of biocidal products* (HSG215) is aimed at those who use biocidal products at work or home. This explains what biocidal products are, the authorisation process required before they can be sold for use in the workplace or the home, how to use them safely, what to do about any adverse reactions, and who is responsible for enforcing the Regulations. Sources of further information are also provided.

## Dangerous Substances and Explosive Atmospheres Regulations 2002

**2.54**   The Dangerous Substances and Explosive Atmospheres Regulations 2002, SI 2002/2776, control fire and explosion risks.

The main requirements are that employers and the self-employed must:

- carry out a risk assessment of any work activities involving dangerous substances;

- provide measures to eliminate, or reduce as far as is reasonably practicable, the identified risks;

- where it is not reasonably practicable to eliminate risks, apply measures, so far as is reasonably practicable, to control risks and to mitigate the detrimental effects of a fire or explosion or other harmful physical effects from dangerous substances;

- provide equipment and procedures to deal with accidents and emergencies; and

- provide employees with information and precautionary training in relation to dangerous substances.

Where explosive atmospheres may occur in a new workplace:

- the workplaces should be classified into hazardous zones and where necessary marked with a sign;

- equipment in classified zones should be safe and satisfy the requirements of the Equipment and Protective Systems Intended for Use in Potentially Explosive Atmospheres Regulations 1996, SI 1996/192; and

- the workplaces should be verified as meeting the requirements of SI 2002/2776, by a competent person, before coming into operation for the first time.

Six ACoPs to support the regulations cover:

- unloading petrol from road tankers (L133);

- design of plant, equipment and workplaces (L134);

- storage of dangerous substances (L135);

- control and mitigation measures (L136);

- safe maintenance, repair and cleaning procedures (L137); and

- dangerous substances and explosive atmospheres (L138).

A free leaflet, *Fire and explosion – How safe is your workplace: A short guide to the Dangerous Substances and Explosive Atmospheres Regulations* (INDG 370), is also available from HSE Books.

Howard Hawkins, the owner of a motor repair garage was found guilty of breaching section 2(1) of HSWA 1974. He was sentenced at Lewes Crown Court receiving a fine of £10,000 with costs of £15,000[1].

The prosecution followed the death of an apprentice mechanic, 18 year old Lewis Murphy, who died four days after becoming engulfed in flames in an explosion at the Anchor garage in Peacehaven, Sussex in February 2004.

The garage manager, Glen Hawkins, was acquitted of manslaughter after the Court of Appeal ruled in June 2005 that a statement which had formed the core of the prosecution's case should not have been admitted as evidence in the trial that had resulted in his conviction four months earlier.

The HSE inspector in the case commented that:

'In this case the garage employer apparently had little understanding of how highly flammable petrol is. Minimal attempts had been made to overcome the hazards associated with its handling. The joint investigation with Sussex Police found that no formal procedures were in place for transferring and storing highly flammable liquids or draining fuel from cars. Howard Hawkins had also failed to register his garage with HSE.

HSE issues simple guidance for petrol handling and storage in garages and we are always happy to advise on these matters. Most of the hazards of fuel removal can be mitigated by the use of a proprietary fuel retriever; providing a suitable container; eliminating static electricity; and capturing any petrol vapour displaced.'

*Health and safety in motor vehicle repair* (HSG67) provides practical advice on how to organise health and safety in garages and explains which laws apply to motor vehicle repair and how to comply with them. The HSE free leaflet/poster *Safe Use of Petrol in Garages* (INDG331) represents best practice and gives general guidance on petrol and fuel retrieval. Both are available from HSE books and the free leaflet can be downloaded from the HSE website.

¹   See HSE Press Release 11 March 2005 (updated 8 November 2005) and CCA database: www.corporateaccountability.org.

# Manufacture and Storage of Explosives Regulations 2005

**2.55**   The Manufacture and Storage of Explosives Regulations 2005, SI 2005/1082, require that:

- anyone manufacturing or storing explosives must take appropriate measures to prevent fire or explosion, to limit the extent of any fire or explosion, and protect persons, should one occur;

- in most cases a separation distance must be maintained between the explosives building and neighbouring inhabited buildings;

- with certain exceptions a licence is required for the manufacture or storage of explosives;

- licensing authorities have the power to refuse, revoke or modify licences in certain circumstances; and

- the supply of fireworks to anyone unable to prove they have a licensed or registered store available is prohibited. The amount of fireworks that can be kept without a licence or registration is limited.

# Control of Major Accident Hazard Regulations 1999

**2.56**   As a result of accidents like those below, a European Directive known as the Seveso Directive was adopted which resulted in UK regulations to control major accident hazards – the Control of Industrial Major Hazards Regulations 1984, SI 1984/1902. The current regulations, the Control of Major Accident Hazards Regulations 1999, SI 1999/743, implemented a European Directive known as Seveso II.

In June 1974, the Nypro (UK) site at Flixborough was severely damaged by a large explosion. Twenty-eight workers were killed and a further 36 suffered injuries. Prior to the explosion, it had been discovered that a crack in a reactor was leaking cyclohexane. The plant was subsequently shut down for an investigation which identified a serious problem with the reactor. Reactor No 5 was removed and a bypass assembly to connect reactors No 4 and No 6 was installed so that the plant could continue production.

On 1 June 1974, the bypass system ruptured, which may have been caused by a fire on a nearby pipe. This resulted in the escape of a large quantity of cyclohexane. The cyclohexane formed a flammable mixture and subsequently found a source of ignition. There was a massive vapour cloud explosion which caused extensive damage and started numerous fires on the site. Eighteen people died in the control room as a result of the windows shattering and the collapse of the roof.

In July 1976, at the Icmesa chemical company, Seveso, Italy, a bursting disc on a chemical reactor ruptured. A dense white cloud, of considerable altitude drifted offsite which included a small deposit of TCCD, a highly toxic material. The nearby town of Seveso, located 15 miles from Milan, had some 17,000 inhabitants. No human deaths were attributed to TCCD but many individuals fell ill, a number of pregnant women who had been exposed to the release had miscarriages, and many animals in the contaminated area died.

Under SI 1999/743, employers must take all measures necessary to prevent a major accident and limit their consequences to people and the environment and notify the competent authority of basic details about their activities.

SI 1999/743 is enforced jointly by a competent authority comprising the HSE, the Environment Agency and the Scottish Environment Protection Agency (SEPA).

SI 1999/743 apply where an establishment has a certain quantity of any substance specified in Schedule 1 or where the quantity could result from the loss of control of an industrial chemical process. There are two thresholds, known as lower-tier and top-tier, and the regulations operate at two levels depending on the quantities of dangerous substances at an establishment. They apply to enterprises rather than individual installations.

If the lower-tier threshold is exceeded, operators must notify the competent authority, take all necessary measures to prevent major accidents and report any that do occur and prepare a major accident prevention policy (MAPP). This should include the company policy on major accidents and detail the organisational structure, responsibilities and procedures for its implementation.

If any top-tier threshold is exceeded, there are additional duties. Operators must submit a written safety report to the competent authority.

Where operators are planning to build new top-tier establishments, information must be submitted to the competent authority before construction starts and they must wait for a response before building safety critical parts of the establishment. On-site and off-site emergency plans must be prepared and tested and safety reports and other information must be provided to the public.

The Regulations specifically require operators to consult their employees or safety representatives about the preparation of the on-site emergency plan.

Top-tier sites must also prepare a safety report showing that a MAPP has been put into effect; that major accident hazards have been identified; that the design, operation, construction and maintenance of the establishment have adequate safety and reliability to prevent or limit the consequences of major accidents; preparation and testing of on-site emergency plans and provision of certain information to the public.

A number of guidance publications on SI 1999/743 are available from HSE Books:

- *A guide to the Control of Major Accident Hazards Regulations 1999* (L111);

- *Major accident prevention policies for lower-tier COMAH establishments* (free information sheet); *Major hazard sites and safety reports* (C300); and *Major accident prevention policies* (Chemical sheet no 3);

- *Preparing safety reports* (HSG 190) and *Emergency planning for major accidents* (HSG 191) explains in detail how to draw up safety reports and how to prepare and implement emergency plans;

- *Leadership for the major hazard industries* (INDG277) is available free from HSE Books or can be downloaded from: www.hse.gov.uk/pubns/indg277.pdf.

Regulations on the Transport of dangerous goods are outlined in CHAPTER 10.

## Working Time Regulations 1998

**2.57**   The majority of workers are legally entitled to a maximum working week, paid holidays, and to breaks and rest periods, as a result of the Working Time Regulations 1998, SI 1998/1833. The regulations implemented the European Working Time Directive (and a European directive on young workers).

Most UK employees now have the right to:

- a maximum working week of not more than 48 hours, including overtime – the maximum working week (averaged over a 17-week period) is 48 hours, including overtime, unless a worker has voluntarily 'opted out' and agreed in writing to work more than this;

- a maximum of eight hours' night work – the maximum a night worker can work is eight hours' night work, averaged over a 17-week period, and this is an absolute limit where the work is particularly hazardous. Night workers are entitled to a free health assessment before carrying out night work, and at regular intervals thereafter;

- a daily rest period of 11 hours – workers are entitled to a daily rest period of 11 hours; a day off each week; and a rest break of at least 20 minutes if working more than six hours;

- a day off per week;

- a rest break if working more than six hours; and

- paid annual leave of 4.8 weeks (increasing to 5.6 weeks from 1 April 2009). The minimum amount was recently increased from 4 weeks to make paid time off for bank holidays additional to the existing four-week holiday entitlement.

### Excluded sectors and workers

**2.58**    The original regulations did not apply to workers in a number of excluded sectors: including air, rail, road, sea, inland waterway and lake transport, sea fishing, as well as the activities of doctors in training. The Working Time (Amendment) Regulations 2003, SI 2003/1684, implemented the European Horizontal Amending Directive and cover:

- non-mobile workers in the road, rail, air and sea transport sectors;

- mobile workers in the rail and non-HGV road transport sectors;

- offshore oil and gas workers; and

- doctors in training.

The amending regulations extended the Working Time Regulations 1998 to non-mobile workers in most of the previously excluded sectors. But the situation for mobile workers is more complicated, and there are specific regulations for some groups of workers. A mobile worker is defined as 'Any worker employed as a member of travelling or flying personnel by an undertaking which operates transport services for passengers by goods or road or air'.

Mobile workers involved in the road transport sector (if they are not covered by other working time directives – see below) are entitled to an average 48-hour working week, paid annual holiday, health assessments for night workers and provision for adequate rest.

If they are covered by other directives, they are entitled to health assessments (if a night worker) and paid annual leave.

The 2002 Road Transport Directive (RTD) makes provision in respect of breaks, rest periods and working time for those subject to 'the European drivers' hours regulations'. The RTD was implemented in April 2005 by the Road Transport (Working Time) Regulations 2005, SI 2005/639.

The Regulations introduced limits on weekly working time (excluding breaks and periods and availability) and a limit on the amount of night work. They also specify how much continuous work can be done before a break is taken, and introduce daily and weekly rest limits for the crew and travelling staff.

Working time for mobile staff must not exceed:

- an average 48-hour week (normally calculated over a four-month reference period although it can be extended to six months);

- 60 hours in a single week; or

- 10 hours in any 24-hour period if working at night (although this can be exceeded if in a collective or workforce agreement).

There is no opt-out of the maximum working week for mobile workers.

The Aviation Directive resulted in the Civil Aviation (Working Time) Regulations 2004, SI 2004/756, which limit the annual working time of mobile workers to 2,000 hours and restrict flying time to 900 hours. They provide for seven rest days per month, 96 rest days per year, paid leave and 'adequate' rest breaks. 'Appropriate' health and safety protection for all mobile personnel is also required.

The Seafarers' Directive provided for a maximum working week of 72 hours and 14 hours' rest in any 24 hours, or a minimum weekly rest requirement of 77 hours and 10 hours in any 24-hour period. It also provides for paid annual leave and health assessments. The Directive was implemented through the Merchant Shipping (Hours of Work) Regulations 2002, SI 2002/2125, which set out these provisions.

Doctors in training gained rights from 1 August 2004 (though the 48-hour week was to be phased in over five years).

There are still some groups of workers who are completely excluded from the Working Time Regulations – the armed forces for example.

And there are also "special case" exclusions which mean that some workers, including railway guards and platform staff are entitled to the 48-hour average working week, paid leave and night worker health assessments, but are excluded from limits on the amount they can work at night, rest breaks and rest periods.

The government's website www.direct.gov.uk has more detailed guidance on the Working Time Regulations, together with links to information on particular sectors and groups of workers.

## Manual Handling Operations Regulations 1992

**2.59** The Manual Handling Operations Regulations 1992, SI 1992/2793, apply to all workplaces (with the exception of seagoing ships). Manual handling operations are defined in these Regulations as 'any transporting or supporting of a load (including lifting, putting down, pushing, pulling, carrying or moving thereof) by hand or by bodily force'.

A load is defined in the guidance as a discrete moveable object, and includes people and animals.

The Regulations put the emphasis on the need for employers to assess the risk of injury from the manual handling of loads and establish a clear hierarchy of prevention and control measures.

Regulation 4 requires employers to, so far as is reasonably practicable, avoid the need for manual handling operations which involve the risk of injury to employees. The guidance outlines how manual handling operations can be eliminated by redesigning the task to avoid moving the load or by automating or mechanising the process.

Where it is not reasonably practicable to avoid the need for manual handling, a suitable and sufficient assessment of manual handling operations must be carried out.

Copies of *Manual handling: Manual Handling Operations Regulations 1992 (as amended) – Guidance on Regulations* (L23), are available from HSE Books, as is the free publication *Getting to grips with manual handling: A short guide* (INDG 143).

## Public Interest Disclosure Act 1998

**2.60** The Public Interest Disclosure Act 1998, which amends the Employment Rights Act 1996 and came into effect on 2 July 1999, gives workers legal protection if they raise issues of serious concern about their workplace, including safety concerns, with their employer. Workers have protection against victimisation or dismissal if they 'blow the whistle' and can take their case to an employment tribunal.

A dismissal of any worker making a protected disclosure is automatically unfair, regardless of the length of service.

A former train driver and safety representative, Laurie Holden, was awarded compensation of £55,000, including a payment for aggravated damages and injury to feelings, after he won an unfair dismissal case against train company Connex. He had resigned from Connex after suffering stress and complained that he was victimised for blowing the whistle about signals passed at danger (SPADs) and other safety issues.

## Reporting work-related deaths

**2.61**   The Reporting of Injuries, Diseases and Dangerous Occurrences Regulations 1995, SI 1995/3163, require that deaths at work must be recorded, notified and reported by a 'responsible person' to the enforcing authority, which may be the HSE or the local authority environmental health department.

There is a facility to report all cases to a single point, the Incident Contact Centre (ICC), so employers do not need to be concerned about which office and which enforcing authority should be reported to.

Postal reports should be sent to: Incident Contact Centre, Caerphilly Business Park, Caerphilly, CF83 3GG.

Internet reports can be made at: www.riddor.gov.uk or www.hse.gov.uk

Telephone reports can be made to 0845 300 9923, faxed reports to 0845 300 9924 and emailed reported to riddor@natbrit.com. (Railway incident-reports should be made to 0207 282 3910.)

SI 1995/3163 requires that 'responsible persons' (normally employers) must notify enforcing authorities by the quickest means possible (normally the telephone) of the following the death of a person as a result of an accident arising out of or in connection with work.

The written report (or report by telephone if approved by the HSE) must be submitted within 10 days to the enforcing authority, in addition to the notification. Gas incidents must be reported within 14 days. There is a prescribed form (Form 2508) for making reports.

Accidents include non-consensual physical acts of violence done to a person at work, and suicides on, or in the course of the operation of a railway, tramway, vehicle system or guided transport system. Deaths arising from gas incidents must be notified, as must deaths where a vehicle was involved.

The employer must report the death of an employee if it occurs within a year of the person suffering a reportable injury.

Records of deaths must be kept for three years, and employers are required to keep records in an accident book.

The HSE has issued an updated leaflet giving employers advice on how to report health and safety incidents and how to use the HSE's incident contact centre. Copies of *RIDDOR reporting: what the incident contact centre can do for you* (MISC310 (rev1)) are available from local HSE offices, local authority offices or HSE Books.

## First aid

**2.62**  The Health and Safety (First-Aid) Regulations 1981, SI 1981/917, provide that employers are under a general duty to make adequate and appropriate first-aid provision for employees if they are injured or become ill at work (reg 3). This includes providing first-aid equipment and arranging for first-aiders or an appointed person to administer first aid.

# Chapter 3

# The Law of Negligence and the Common Law Duty of Care

## Overview

3.1

---

The Corporate Manslaughter and Corporate Homicide Act 2007 (and the Ministry of Justice guidance on the Act, *A guide to the Corporate Manslaughter and Corporate Homicide Act 2007*) sets out the offence of corporate manslaughter (corporate homicide in Scotland) with reference to negligence and common law duties of care (see 3.2).

Although it outside the scope of this book to provide a detailed description of the law in this area, a brief summary of the law of negligence and the common law duty of care is provided in this chapter, particularly with regard to an employer's common law duty of care to their employees, together with examples of judgments.

The chapter also briefly looks at the duties of occupiers of premises, as set out in the Occupiers' Liability Acts of 1957 and 1984, and at the requirement for employers to take out employers' liability insurance under the Employers' Liability (Compulsory Insurance) Act 1969 and the Employers' Liability (Compulsory Insurance) Regulations 1998.

---

## The Corporate Manslaughter and Corporate Homicide Act 2007

### The Offence of Corporate Manslaughter (Corporate Homicide)

**3.2** The Corporate Manslaughter and Corporate Homicide Act 2007 (CMCHA 2007), which comes into force on 6 April 2008, sets out that an organisation is guilty of the offence of corporate manslaughter (or corporate homicide) if the way in which it manages or organises its activities causes a death and this amounts to a gross breach of a relevant duty of care it owed to the victim (CMCHA 2007 s 1(1)).

The Ministry of Justice (MoJ) guidance explains that:

'The offence is concerned with the way in which an organisation's activities were managed or organised. Under this test, courts will look at management systems and practices across the organisation, and whether an adequate standard of care was applied to the fatal activity.'

### Causation

**3.3**    The way in which the organisation's activities were managed or organised must have caused the death. The usual principles of causation in criminal law apply – the management failure need not have been the sole cause of death; it need only be a cause. However, it must have made more than a minimal contribution to the death and an intervening act must not have broken the chain of events linking the management failure to the death. An intervening act will only break the chain of causation if it is extraordinary.

The MoJ guidance provides further guidance on causation. It advises that although it will not be necessary for the management failure to have been the sole cause of death ' "but for" the management failure (including the substantial element attributable to senior management), the death would not have occurred'.

It also sets out that the law does not recognise very remote causes, and in some circumstances, an intervening act may mean that the management failure is not considered to have caused the death (see CHAPTER 4 which sets out case law developments with regard to causation in manslaughter cases with reference to a briefing produced by the Centre for Corporate Accountability (CCA)).

### 'Gross Breach' – Falling Far Below what can Reasonably be Expected

**3.4**    In order to amount to a 'gross' breach of duty of care, the conduct of the organisation must have fallen far below what can be reasonably expected in the circumstances (CMCHA 2007 s 1(4)).

### Relevant Duty of Care

**3.5**    The offence only applies where an organisation owed a duty of care, under the law of negligence, to the person who died, reflecting the common law offence of gross negligence manslaughter. The Act lists the following as a 'relevant duty of care':

- a duty owed to its employees or to other persons working for the organisation or performing services for it;

- a duty owed as occupier of premises;
- a duty owed in connection with:
  - ○ the supply by the organisation of goods or services (whether for payment or not);
  - ○ the carrying out by the organisation of any construction or maintenance operations;
  - ○ the carrying out by the organisation of any other activity on a commercial basis; or
  - ○ the use or keeping by the organisation of any plant, vehicle or other thing.

In addition, a relevant duty of care arises where the organisation is responsible for the safety of person in custody or detention (CMCHA 2007 s 2(1), (2)). However, extension of the offence to deaths in custody will not come into effect on 6 April 2008, but within three to five years of the other provisions coming into effect.

More guidance is available in the explanatory notes to the Act. The following are 'relevant' duties under CMCHA 2007:

- the duty to provide a safe system of work for employees; the breach of a duty owed to other people whose work the organisation controls or directs, but who are not formally employed, such as contractors, volunteers and secondees can also trigger the offence;
- duties to ensure that buildings the organisation occupies are kept in a safe condition;
- duties owed by organisations to their customers, such as those owed by transport providers to their passengers and by retailers for the safety of their products; it also covers the supply of services by the public sector, such as NHS bodies providing medical treatment;
- the duty of care owed by public sector bodies to ensure that adequate safety precautions are taken, when repairing a road for example, even where duties do not arise because they are not supplying a service or operating commercially; and
- the duty of care owed by organisations, such as farming and mining companies, for example, which are carrying out activities on a commercial basis, though not supplying goods and services.

The MoJ guidance explains that statutory duties owed under health and safety law are not 'relevant' duties for the new offence – only a duty of care owed in the law of negligence. It goes on to explain:

> 'In practice, there is a significant overlap between these types of duty. For example, employers have a responsibility for the safety of their employees under the law of negligence and under health and safety law (see for example section 2 of the Health and Safety at Work etc

Act 1974 and article 4 of the Health and Safety at Work (Northern Ireland) Order 1978). Similarly, both statutory duties and common law duties will be owed to members of the public affected by the conduct of an organisation's activities.

The common law offence of gross negligence manslaughter in England and Wales and Northern Ireland is based on the duty of care in the law of negligence, and this has been carried forward to the new offence. In Scotland, the concepts of negligence and duty of care are familiar from the civil law.'

The offence applies where the duty of care owed under the common law of negligence has been superseded by statutory provision (including where this imposes strict liability). For example, the duty of care owed by an occupier, which is now owed under the Occupiers' Liability Acts 1957 and 1984 and the Defective Premises Act 1972 (CMCHA 2007 s 2(4)) is included. (The Defective Premises Act places a duty on landlords to take reasonable care to ensure that tenants and others are safe from personal injury or disease caused by a defect in the state of the premises. The Act is not examined in detail in this publication).

The MoJ guidance sets out that in some cases where a person cannot be sued under the civil law of negligence, the new offence may still apply. For example, this would be the case where a 'no fault' scheme for damages has been introduced.

And the offence is not affected by common law rules precluding liability in the law of negligence where people are jointly engaged in a criminal enterprise ('ex turpi causa non oritur actio') – for example where there is illegal employment – or because a person has accepted a risk of harm ('volenti non fit injuria') (CMCHA 2007 s 2(6)).

## A Brief Summary of the Law of Negligence and the Common Law Duty of Care

**3.6**    Common law is based on, and develops as a result of, decisions or judgments made in the courts, which establish 'precedents'. In the system of legal precedent, lower courts are bound by the decisions of higher courts. These decisions or judgements are recorded in *Law Reports.*

The House of Commons Home Affairs and Work and Pensions Committees report on the Draft Corporate Manslaughter Bill, *First Joint Report of Session 2005–06 Volume 1: Report* set out that the concept of a 'duty of care' has been developed by the civil courts through judgments made in relation to the law of negligence.

### The Tort of Negligence

**3.7**    Negligence is one of three principle torts or 'civil wrongs' (the others being trespass and nuisance) and has been defined as careless conduct injuring another. It arises where the following elements are present:

- there is a duty of care owed by the defendant to the plaintiff;

- there is a breach of that duty;

- damage, loss or injury has resulted from or been caused by that breach.

## Duty of Care

**3.8**    Under common law, the circumstances where a duty of care is considered to exist are not fixed; although the courts have set down types of relationships where a duty of care is clearly owed. These are:

- by an employer to his employees to take reasonable care for their health and safety. Employers must take reasonable care to protect their employees from the risk of foreseeable injury, disease or death at work. If an employer knows of, or ought to have known in the light of current knowledge, a health and safety risk, they will be liable if an employee is injured, killed or made ill as a result of that risk, and they had failed to take reasonable care;

- by an occupier of buildings and land to people in or on, or potentially affected by the property;

- by transport companies to their passengers;

- by public bodies to members to the public – particularly where a service is being provided to the public – in certain circumstances.

In the famous case, *Donoghue v Stevenson*[1], it was held that a manufacturer could owe a duty of care to a consumer. (This case involved a decomposing snail in a bottle of ginger beer.)

The House of Commons Committee which examined the government's draft Bill (see CHAPTER 1) set out that the question of whether a 'duty of care' does exist as generally determined by reference to three broad criteria:

- Is the damage foreseeable?

- Is the relationship between the defendant and victim sufficiently proximate; and

- Is it fair, just and reasonable to impose such a duty.

[1]   [1932] AC 562.

## Employer's Common Law Duty of Care

**3.9**    An employer owes a duty of care to take reasonable care of their employees' health and safety. In addition, a duty of care is often found to exist to people who are not employees. And where employees are working at another place of work, whether the employer is liable will depend on whether they have any control over the premises. Barrister Cressida

Murphy, writing in *Tolley's Employment Law* points out that '... if an employee is injured whilst lent to another, temporary, employer, the employee can still maintain an action against his permanent employer, even though he may also have a right of action against the temporary employer'.

In the case of *Wilsons & Clyde Coal Co Ltd v English*[1], the House of Lords identified an employer's duties under common law as being three-fold: providing competent staff, adequate material and a proper system and effective supervision, although according to Professor Richard A. Buckley in *Buckley: The Law of Negligence*, more recently: 'the tendency has been to adopt a unified approach'.

The standard of care, and therefore negligent conduct, depends on the conduct of a hypothetical 'reasonable man'. What is reasonable depends on what a person ought to know, and based on that knowledge, what actions are reasonable.

This involves looking at, on the one hand, the likelihood of harm being caused, and the seriousness of the harm should it occur; and weighing this up with, on the other hand, the difficulty and expense, and other disadvantages of taking precautions. It can be summarised as:

- foreseeing the existence of a risk;

- assessing the magnitude of the risk; and

- taking reasonable precautions.

As Murphy sets out, in *Thompson v Smiths Ship Repairers (North Shields) Ltd*[2] it was held that 'the correct test to apply was what would have been done by a reasonable and prudent employer who was properly but not extraordinarily solicitous for his employees' safety, in the light of what he knew, or ought to have known at that time'.

Although the standard of care will vary depending on the circumstances, various judgments have shown that:

- the duty is owed to each employee individually;

- failure to take account of a risk which was so unusual that no one was, or could have been, aware of will not amount to negligence;

- employers will generally be expected to be aware of risks associated with particular types of work, and also aware of Health and Safety Executive (HSE) and other reasonably available safety information on the precautions that should be taken. If a method of protection is practicable and available, it would usually be negligent not to use it. However, according to Murphy: 'Although the employer is obliged to keep himself informed of contemporary knowledge in the field of accident prevention (*Baxter v Harland and Wolff plc*[3]) he is not obliged to adopt all the latest improvements';

- reasonable precautions must be taken – the greater the risk, and the more serious the harm should it occur, the higher the duty to take precautions. A risk must be extremely slight to be ignored and even if the risk is remote, if it could have been easily avoided, it would be negligent not to take the steps required. Where there is risk to life, this will justify great expense and trouble to prevent the event occurring. There may be situations where the danger is so great that work should be stopped altogether;

- the possibility of other people making errors should be considered. Employers should take account of the possibility of mistakes, lapses in concentration, as well as accidental slips;

- individual characteristics should be taken account of. A greater degree of care will be necessary where, for example, children could be injured, or there are inexperienced employees, or employees with low levels of literacy or poor knowledge of English; although the employer will not be liable where they did not know, or could not reasonably be expected to know, of a particular characteristic. Murphy sets out that '... the corollary of this is that in dealing with an experienced employee, the employer may not be under a duty to give warnings about risks which are well known to that employee: *Qualcast Wolverhampton Ltd v Haynes*'[4];

- in determining what is reasonably practicable, a precaution should be taken unless the time, effort and expense of taking it is grossly disproportionate in relation to the risk being combated;

- an employer's resources can be taken into account. But while a higher standard can be expected of organisations with large resources; there are only very limited circumstances when limited resources give rise to a lower standard of care;

- where action is being taken in an emergency, a lower standard of care is demanded;

- while general industry practice influences the standard of care, an employer cannot escape liability simply by showing that other employers are just as negligent;

- there must be a safe system of work for unusual as well as routine operations; and

- statutory duties may influence the common law standard of care, but as the MoJ guidelines (see 3.2) explain, the duties are distinct. Compliance with a statutory duty does not necessarily mean that an employer will not be negligent.

[1]   [1938] AC 57.
[2]   [1984] 1 All ER 881.
[3]   [1990] IRLR 516.
[4]   [1959] AC 743.

**Employers' Liability**

**3.10**   There are two categories of employers' liability:

- *primary liability* – the general duty to take reasonable care for the health and safety of employees (and increasingly other workers who are not strictly employees). This duty cannot be delegated. Even if the employer has delegated performance of the duty to another person he remains liable, so for example, an employer will be liable if an outside contractor causes harm (see *McDermid v Nash Dredging and Reclamation Co Ltd*[1], and 3.17); and

- *vicarious liability* – the employer is also liable for harm caused by his employees. If an employee is negligent while acting in the course of his employment and injures another employee, contractor or member of the public, the employer (rather than the employee) will be liable. There have been numerous cases which have involved asking whether the employee was acting within the course of their employment.

For example, in *Century Insurance Co Ltd v Northern Ireland Road Transport Board*[2], the driver of a petrol tanker caused an explosion by throwing down a match he had used to light a cigarette while delivering petrol. Even though smoking was against the employer's rules, the employer was found to be liable.

In *Smith v Stages*[3] the employer was held to be vicariously liable for the injuries of an employee who was being driven back from work by another employee after they were sent to a job from the Midlands to Wales. In this case, they were being paid for their journey time, even though they had discretion as to how and when they made the journey.

In *Fennelly v Connex South Eastern Ltd*[4] a ticket inspector assaulted a rail passenger after he refused to show the inspector his ticket. The Court of Appeal held that employer was vicariously liable on the basis that the assault was part of the same incident as the request and refusal to provide the ticket – and inspecting tickets was part of the inspector's job.

[1]   [1987] AC 906.
[2]   [1942] AC 509.
[3]   [1989] ICR 272.
[4]   [2001] IRLR 390.

*Employers' defences*

**3.11**   There are two defences available to employers sued for a breach of duties at common law:

- voluntary assumption of risk (or *volenti non fit injuria*) – if successful, this would mean that no damages would be paid. It is generally not successful in work-related injury cases and in any case CMCHA 2007 makes clear that the offence of corporate manslaughter is not subject to this defence;

● contributory negligence – is where the injured employee is partly to blame for the accident. If successful, this would mean that damages would be reduced in a civil case.

## Proof of negligence

**3.12**    Generally it is for the claimant to prove negligence, on the balance of probabilities. But in some cases, the term r*es ipsa loquitur* – the thing speaks for itself – is used and means that it is for the defendant to prove that they were not negligent.

In *Buckley: The Law of Negligence*, Professor Buckley explains that where: '… what occurred was something which would not be expected to occur in the absence of carelessness on the part of those who have control or management of the operation, then a presumption of negligence will be raised in the claimant's favour', and goes on to say that 'If the defendant is able to explain fully and in detail how the accident occurred it will be for the court to decide, applying in the usual way the ordinary principles relating to the evaluation of conduct, whether or not negligence liability should be imposed'.

## Employers' Liability (Defective Equipment) Act 1969

**3.13**    The Employers' Liability (Defective Equipment) Act 1969 (EL(DE)A 1969) means that employers can be liable where an employee is injured at work because of a defect in equipment provided by the employer, even though negligence cannot be established against the employer because the defect was the fault of a third party.

Section 1(1) of EL(DE)A 1969 says that where:

'(a)    an employee suffers personal injury in the course of his employment in consequence of a defect in equipment provided by his employer for the purposes of his employer's business; and

(b)    the defect is attributable wholly or partly to the fault of a third party (whether identified or not),

the injury shall be deemed to be also attributable to negligence on the part of the employer (whether or not he is liable in respect of the injury apart from this subsection) but without prejudice to the law in relation to contributory negligence and to any remedy by way of contribution or in contract or otherwise which is available to the employer in relation to the injury'.

Section 1(2) of EL(DE)A 1969 sets out that any agreement professing to limit liability under s 1(1) will be void. And s 1(3) sets out that equipment includes plant, machinery, vehicles, aircraft and clothing.

## Employers' liability insurance

**3.14**    Most employers are required to take out insurance against claims for an injury or disease to any of their employees. The duties relating to insurance are set out in the Employers' Liability (Compulsory Insurance) Act 1969 and the Employers' Liability (Compulsory Insurance) Regulations 1998, SI 1998/2573. Most employers must:

- insure against liability for injury or disease to an employee arising out of and in the course of their employment in Great Britain. The minimum amount of cover that must be taken out is £5 million;

- display the certificate of insurance prominently at their place of business;

- produce the certificate or send a copy when required to do so by an authorised inspector;

- send the certificate or copy in response to a notice served on behalf of the HSE; and

- permit an authorised inspector to inspect his policy or copy provided that reasonable notice has been given.

Failure to take out and maintain insurance is a criminal offence with a maximum penalty of £2,500 and failure to display a certificate of insurance is also a criminal offence, carrying a maximum penalty of £1,000.

According to guidance from the Health and Safety Executive (HSE) the following employers are exempt:

- most public organisations including government departments and agencies, local authorities, police authorities and nationalised industries;

- health service bodies, including NHS trusts, health authorities, primary care trusts and Scottish Health Boards;

- some other organisations which are financed through public funds, such as passenger transport executives and magistrates' courts committees;

- family businesses – if employees are closely related to the employer (as husband, wife, father, mother, grandfather, grandmother, stepfather, stepmother, son, daughter, grandson, granddaughter, stepson, stepdaughter, brother, sister, half-brother or half-sister). This exemption does not apply to family businesses which are incorporated as limited companies;

- companies employing only their owner where that employee also owns 50 per cent or more of the issued share capital in the company.

The HSE guidance leaflet *Employers' Liability (Compulsory Insurance) Act 1969 A guide for employers* HSE 40 (rev1) revised 01/06 is available on the HSE website at www.hse.gov.uk/pubns/hse40.pdf

Employers' liability insurance is examined in detail by Phil Grace in *Tolley's Health and Safety at Work Handbook* (see *Further Information* below). He advises that employers' liability insurance does not cover claims from, for example, independent contractors or members of the public. This would be covered by a public liability policy, which although not compulsory, is advisable.

Employers' liability is examined in detail by Cressida Murphy is *Tolley's Employment Law* (see *Further Information* below).

## Occupiers' Liability

### The Occupiers' Liability Act 1957 (OLA 1957)

**3.15**    Under the Occupiers' Liability Act 1957 (OLA 1957), a common duty of care is owed to employees and visitors. An occupier is not defined in the Act – instead common law rules apply. A person is an occupier if he has some degree of control over the premises, and there can be more than one occupier in each case – the scope of their duties will depend on the degree of control they have.

In *Wheat v E Lacon & Co Ltd*[1], Lord Denning said:

> 'Wherever a person has a sufficient degree of control over premises that he ought to realise that any failure on his part to use care may result in injury to a person coming lawfully there, then he is an "occupier" and the person coming lawfully there is his "visitor" and the "occupier" is under a duty to his "visitor" to use reasonable control. In order to be an occupier it is not necessary for a person to have entire control over the premises. He need not have exclusive occupation. Suffice it that he has some degree of control with others'.

Premises are fixed or moveable structures, including vessels, vehicles and aircraft.

(From 'Occupiers' Liability' by Jessica Burt in *Tolley's Health and Safety at Work Handbook 2007*).

OLA 1957 defines the duty as 'to take such care as in all the circumstances of the case is reasonable to see that the visitor will be reasonably safe in using the premises for the purposes for which he is invited or permitted by the occupier to be there.' (OLA 1957 s 2(2)).

OLA 1957 s 2(3) provides that:

> 'The circumstances relevant for the present purpose include the degree of care, and of want of care, which would ordinarily be looked for in such a visitor, so that (for example) in proper cases:
>
> (a)    an occupier must be prepared for children to be less careful than adults; and

103

(b)   an occupier may expect that a person, in the exercise of his
calling, will appreciate and guard against any special risks ordinarily incident to it, so far as the occupier leaves him free to do
so.'

Section 2(4)(b) of OLA 1957 sets out that an employer will not be liable
for an accident caused by faulty work on the part of an independent
contractor if it was reasonable to have entrusted the work to them;
reasonable steps had been taken to ensure that the contractor was
competent; and that reasonable steps had been taken to ensure that the
work had been properly carried out.

Section 2(4) provides that:

'Where damage is caused to a visitor by a danger of which he had been
warned by the occupier, the warning is not to be treated without more
as absolving the occupier from liability, unless in all the circumstances
of the case it was enough to enable the visitor to be reasonably safe'.

Under s 2(1) of the Unfair Contract Terms Act 1977, which applies to
business premises: 'A person cannot by reference to any contract term or
to a notice exclude or restrict his liability for death or personal injury
resulting from negligence'.

Solicitor Jessica Burt explains in *Tolley's Health and Safety at Work
Handbook 2007* that this means that explicit notices such as 'Highly
Flammable Liquid Vapours – No Smoking' 'used to absolve an occupier
from liability. Now, however, such notices are ineffective (except in the
case of trespassers) and do not exonerate occupiers ... Such explicit
notices are, however, a defence to an occupier when sued for negligent
injury by a simple trespasser under the OLA 1984' (see 3.16).

Section 3(1) of OLA 1957 sets out that:

'... where an occupier of premises is bound by contact to permit
persons who are strangers to the contract to enter or use the premises,
the duty of care which he owes to them as his visitors cannot be
restricted or excluded by that contract, but (subject to any provision of
the contract to the contrary) shall include the duty to perform his
obligations under the contract, whether undertaken for their protection
or not, in so far as those obligations go beyond the obligations
otherwise involved in that duty'.

Murphy explains:

'The effect of s 3(1) is that not only may the occupier not reduce his
obligations to visitors who are strangers to the contract below the
common law duty of care, but if the contract between himself and, for
example, an independent contractor provided for a higher duty of care
in relation to the independent contractor's use of the premises, then the
independent contractor's employees will be able to avail themselves of
that higher duty'.

The defence that a visitor voluntarily accepted the risk – *volenti non fit injuria* – applies (OLA 1957 s 2(5)) – although Burt says that it has generally not succeeded in industrial injury cases, and it does not of course apply with regard to CMCHA 2007.

OLA 1957 is only concerned with civil liability and does not give rise to criminal liability, so occupiers cannot be prosecuted under the Act.

¹   [1965] 2 All ER 700.

## The Occupiers' Liability Act 1984 (OLA 1984)

**3.16**   OLA 1984 imposes a duty of care to trespassers (as well as people using private rights of way or rights set out in the National Parks and Access to the Countryside Act 1949).

The Act imposes a limited duty of care on occupiers to take reasonable steps to offer protection to trespassers from dangers which should be known to exist on the property.

The duty under OLA 1984 is more restricted than that under the OLA 1957. It only applies where a danger that the occupier knows of (or ought to know of) exists; the occupier knows (or ought to know) that trespassers are likely to come on the land; and that the risk is one which he would be reasonably expected to guard against.

Occupiers' liability is examined in detail in a chapter by Jessica Burt in *Tolley's Health and Safety at Work Handbook* and by Cressida Murphy in a chapter on Employer's Liability in *Tolley's Employment Law*.

## Examples of cases¹

### 3.17

#### *Henderson v Henry E Jenkins & Sons²*

In this case, the brakes on a lorry failed and caused a fatal accident. The cause of the failure was a hole in a pipe carrying brake fluid, but the defect could only have been detected by removing the brakes. This was not recommended by the manufacturers. The company involved had procedures for regularly servicing and inspecting the brakes (without removing them) and it argued that the hole might have developed as a result of a concealed defect which caused the pipe to corrode more quickly than usual. However, the corrosion could have been due to the lorry being used for an unusual use, in which case more detailed inspections should have been carried out. The company did not disclose how the lorry had been used, so its answer as to what had caused the accident was judged to be 'incomplete' and it failed to 'displace the inference of negligence'.

#### *Morris v West Hartlepool Steam Navigation Co Ltd³*

This case involved common practice in an industry. A seaman fell into an unguarded hold of a ship and suffered serious injuries. The general practice was not to guard or cover access to the hold from the inside while the ship was at sea. Although this practice was long established, the nature of the risk and the ease of taking precautions meant that the company had failed to come up to the standard required by a reasonably prudent employer.

## *Paris v Stepney Borough Council*[4]

In this case the employer had not provided goggles to a workman with one eye, and he was blinded in his other eye when a piece of metal entered it. The case showed that employers need to take into account the gravity of harm should it occur. The employer was found to be negligent in not providing goggles, even though the risk of injury was sufficiently small to justify not providing precautions for fully sighted employees.

## *General Cleaning Contractors Ltd v Christmas*[5]

The House of Lords held the employers liable for failing to provide suitable precautions to prevent their employee, a window cleaner, from falling and suffering serious injuries. The window cleaner had been cleaning the windows of a building from the outside, standing on the sill – a method widely used by other window cleaners – as there was nothing to which he could attach a safety harness. A broken sash window fell on his hand, causing him to let go and fall. The judge in the case said:

'Where a practice of ignoring an obvious danger has grown up I do not think that it is reasonable to expect an individual workman to take the initiative in devising and using precautions. It is the duty of the employer to consider the situation, to devise a suitable system, to instruct his men what they must do, and to supply any implements that may be required ...'

In this case the employers should have either given instructions to test each window before cleaning it, or provide equipment to prevent the window closing.

## *Bux v Slough Metals Ltd*[6]

A number of cases have involved protective equipment which has been made available, but employers have not proactively ensured that the equipment has been used or worn. In this case, the employer was aware that goggles provided for use when working near molten metal in a die-casting foundry were not being used, but did not take reasonable steps to ensure that they were worn. The employer should have issued instructions that goggles were to be worn, and enforced the instructions through supervision.

## *Smith v Leech Brain and Co Ltd*[7]

In this case an employee died of cancer as a result of a burn from molten liquid which was spattered on his lip, activating a pre-malignant condition. The accident, which was foreseeable, had happened through the employer's negligence and it was found liable for his death – even though the consequences (because of a latent condition) were more serious than could have been foreseen.

## *Latimer v AEC*[8]

In this case a factory flooded after a heavy storm resulted in the floor in part of the factory becoming slippery as the rainwater mixed with oil. Although the floor was covered with sawdust, because such a large area was affected, there was not enough to cover all of the floor and an employee slipped and was injured. The trial judge held the defendants liable for the injury on the grounds that they should have closed down the factory. However, the Court of Appeal and House of Lords disagreed. Closing the factory was not something that a reasonably careful employer ought to have done.

## McDermid v Nash Dredging and Reclamation Co Ltd[9]

This case involved the employer's non-delegable duty. The employer was held liable for injuries suffered by an employee as a result of the negligence of a tugboat captain, who was not its employee. The injured employee had been instructed to work on a project supervised by the captain, whose method of working was found to be unsafe. Lord Brandon said:

'... it is no defence for the employer to show that he delegated its [the duty to exercise reasonable care] performance to a person, whether his servant, or not his servant, whom he reasonably believed to be competent to perform it. Despite such delegation the employer is liable for the non-performance of the duty'.

## Bolton v Stone[10]

A passer-by was hit and injured by a cricket ball which had been hit out of the ground. Although this was foreseeable, as balls had been hit out of the ground before, the cricket club was not liable because it had only occurred six times in the last 30 years. The risk was therefore one which the reasonable man could choose not to guard against – although the judge said the case was borderline, and that the risk had been extremely small.

Buckley notes: 'The actual degree of probability required is not fixed but necessarily varies from case to case. This is because three other factors are taken into account in assessing the overall risk. These are: the seriousness of the harm if it does actually occur; the overall utility or value of the activity upon which the defendant is engaged; and the extent and cost of effective precautions'.

## Hughes v Lord Advocate[11]

This case involved a child who was injured when he was playing and tripped over a paraffin lamp which had been negligently left near an open manhole by Post Office employees. Paraffin vapour was ignited by the flame of the lamp and exploded, throwing the boy into the manhole where he was severely burnt. Although this precise course of events could not have been foreseen, liability was imposed on the basis that some burning injury to playing children was foreseeable – it was not relevant that the foreseeable harm arose in an unforeseeable manner.

## Ward v Tesco Stores[12]

In this case a customer in a supermarket slipped on some yoghurt which had been spilled on the floor. Although Tesco had a system for clearing up spillages – staff were instructed to look out for spillages and take immediate action and floors were regularly brushed throughout the day. Neither the customer nor Tesco could prove how long the yoghurt had been on the floor before the accidents occurred, and the Court of Appeal ruled that the maxim 'res ipsa loquitur' (see 3.12) applied, and found in favour of the plaintiff. The county court judge had found that the defendants had not taken reasonable care.

---

[1]   These cases are highlighted in *Buckley: The Law of Negligence* Fourth edition (LexisNexis Butterworths, 2005).
[2]   [1970] AC 282.
[3]   [1956] AC 552.
[4]   [1951] AC 367.
[5]   [1953] AC 180.
[6]   [1974] 1 All ER 262.
[7]   [1961] 2 QB 405.
[8]   [1952] 2 All ER 449, HL.
[9]   [1987] AC 906.

¹⁰  [1951] AC 850.
¹¹  [1963] AC 837, [1963] 1 All ER 705, HL.
¹²  [1976] 1 All ER 219, [1976] 1 WLR 810.

## Further Information

**3.18**    As set out above, it is beyond the scope of this publication to provide a detailed description of the law of negligence and the common law duty of care. For further information on this area of the law see (for example):

- Daniel Bennett and Barry Cotter, *Munkman on Employer's Liability* (LexisNexis Butterworths).

- Professor Richard A Buckley, *The Law of Negligence* (LexisNexis Butterworths).

- *Tolley's Employment Law,* ch E60: 'Employers' Liability', written by Cressida Murphy (LexisNexis Butterworths).

- *Tolley's Health and Safety at Work Handbook 2007,* 'Employers' Liabililty Insurance', written by Phil Grace; 'Occupiers' Liability', written by Jessica Burt (LexisNexis Butterworths).

# Chapter 4

# Individual Liability

## Overview

**4.1**

The Corporate Manslaughter and Corporate Homicide Act 2007 (CMCHA 2007) does not impose any new liability on individuals. Indeed, it makes clear that there is no secondary liability for the offence: an individual cannot be guilty of aiding, abetting, counselling or procuring the commission of, or in Scotland, of being art and part of, the offence of corporate manslaughter or corporate homicide (CMCHA 2007 s 18).

However, an individual can still be directly liable for the offence of gross negligence manslaughter, or culpable homicide (in Scotland) if their acts or omissions are judged to be sufficiently serious and have caused a death. In addition, they can also be directly liable for health and safety offences.

This chapter sets out the law on individual liability for gross negligence manslaughter, and for culpable homicide – the latter applies to Scotland.

It looks at the case law in this area, using a briefing on the law on manslaughter provided by the charity and campaign organisation, the Centre for Corporate Accountability (CCA). This includes an examination of the leading case in this area: *R v Adomako*[1], which involved the prosecution of an anaesthetist following the death of a patient.

It also:

• uses the CCA briefing to look at the case law which has developed this test further;

• sets out the Scots criminal law on culpable homicide (again using the CCA briefing);  ➡

109

- provides details of convictions of directors and business owners for gross negligence manslaughter; and

- provides examples of where work-related manslaughter prosecutions have resulted in convictions against managers and other workers.

Finally, it outlines the provisions of ss 7 and 37 of the Health and Safety at Work etc Act 1974 (HSWA 1974) which allow individuals to be prosecuted for health and safety offences.

[1]    [1995] 1 AC 171 (HL).

## Individual Liability for Gross Negligence Manslaughter

**4.2**    Under the common law offence of gross negligence manslaughter, individual officers of a company (including directors and business owners) can be prosecuted for the offence if their own grossly negligent behaviour causes death. The offence is punishable by a maximum of life imprisonment (Offences against the Persons Act 1861 s 5).

The 2000 Home Office paper *Reforming the law on involuntary manslaughter: The government's proposals* sets out that there are two general homicide offences in English law – murder and manslaughter. (In addition, there are specific statutory homicide offences aimed at particular situations, such as causing death by dangerous driving under the Road Traffic Acts – see CHAPTER 10.)

The most serious, murder, requires proof of an intention to kill or cause serious injury. If there are mitigating circumstances, such as provocation or diminished responsibility, the offence is one of manslaughter and this is often referred to as 'voluntary manslaughter'.

'Gross negligence manslaughter' is one of three types of 'involuntary manslaughter', where an individual kills as a result of some blameworthy act on their part but without actually intending to cause death or serious injury – that is without 'malice aforethought':

- unlawful act manslaughter is where the person who caused the death was engaged in a criminal act which carried with it the risk of injury to another person;

- gross negligence manslaughter is where a person causes death through extreme carelessness or incompetence; and

- the third type is where a person is aware that their conduct involves a risk of causing death (or probable serious injury) and unreasonably takes that risk, which has been described as 'manslaughter by subjective recklessness'.

## R v Adomako

**4.3**    The leading case on gross negligence manslaughter is *R v Adomako*[1] which involved the death of a patient who was undergoing an eye operation. The defendant was an anaesthetist who had failed to notice (for some six minutes) that during the operation, the tube from the ventilator supplying oxygen to the patient had become disconnected. The patient suffered a cardiac arrest and subsequently died.

In this case, the House of Lords set down a four stage test for the offence of gross negligence manslaughter:

• did the defendant owe a duty of care towards the victim who has died?

• if so, has the defendant breached that duty of care?

• has such breach caused the victim's death? and

• if so, was that breach of duty so bad as to amount, when viewed objectively, to gross negligence warranting a criminal conviction?

Lord Mackay of Clashfern LC set out what should be the correct approach as follows:

'In my opinion the ordinary principles of the law of negligence apply to ascertain whether or not the defendant has been in breach of a duty of care towards the victim who died. If such a breach of that duty is established the next question is whether that breach of duty caused the death of the victim. If so, the jury must go on to consider whether that breach of duty should be characterised as gross negligence and therefore as a crime. This will depend on the seriousness of the breach of duty committed by the defendant in all the circumstances in which the defendant was placed when it occurred. The jury will have to consider whether the extent to which the defendant's conduct departed from the proper standard of care incumbent upon him, involving as it must have done a risk of death to the patient, was such that it should be judged criminal.

It is true that to a certain extent this involves an element of circularity, but in this branch of the law I do not believe that is fatal to its being correct as a test of how far conduct must depart from accepted standards to be characterised as criminal. This is necessarily a question of degree and an attempt to specify that degree more closely is I think likely to achieve only a spurious precision. The essence of the matter, which is supremely a jury question, is whether, having regard to the risk of death involved, the conduct of the defendant was so bad in all the circumstances as to amount in their judgment to a criminal act or omission.'

[1]    [1995] 1 AC 171 (HL).

## Did the Defendant Owe a Duty of Care towards the Victim who has Died?

**4.4**      According to a briefing on the law of manslaughter by the CCA, which sets out case law developments in this area, there must have been a 'duty of care' relationship between the defendant and the person who died, and in order to determine whether this is the case, the civil law principles of negligence must be considered (see chapter 3).

In an appeal case, *R v Willoughby*[1] (a case which involved arson), it was held that:

'Whether a duty of care exists is a matter for the jury once the judge has decided that there is evidence capable of establishing a duty.'

The briefing points out that while a company may owe a duty of care towards the person who died, it does not necessarily mean that a company director owes one, quoting the judge in the Crown Court ruling in the case of *R v Great Western Railways plc*[2]:

'The fact that an individual is a director of a company does not, of itself, give rise to a duty of care on that person's part to a third party who is injured by the company's activity'.

While this ruling did not set a precedent, the CCA says that the principle does not appear to be in doubt and in *C Evans and Sons Ltd v Spritebrand*[3], the court held that:

'The mere fact that a person is a director or a limited liability company does not itself render him liable for torts[4] committed by the company during the period of his directorship'.

The briefing explains that in law, the conduct of a company director is not seen as the director's own individual conduct, but instead conduct undertaken on behalf of the company. The director's negligent conduct could make the company liable for compensation, but it may not make the director individually liable. Whether there is a duty of care will depend on the facts of the case and whether the director had a personal duty of care.

The briefing advises:

'Issues that are likely to be considered by the court are the specific responsibilities that the director had within the company, whether it is alleged that positive decisions or actions on his or her part was a cause of the death (rather than simply omissions), and whether or not the director had been made aware of the circumstances that created the risk of death. In most cases prosecuted, the issue of whether or not the individual had a duty of care has not been contentious.'

---

[1]   [2004] EWCA Crim 3365.
[2]   (1999) (unreported).
[3]   [1985] 2 All ER 415.
[4]   Negligence is one of three torts, or civil wrongs – see CHAPTER 3 for more detail.

## Has the Defendant Breached the Duty of Care?

**4.5**   Once a duty of care has been shown to exist, it must then be shown that this duty has been breached, again requiring the civil law principles of negligence to be considered.

The defendant would need to have failed to take reasonable care, when judged against the conduct of a reasonable person in that person's position.

The CCA briefing points out that this part of the test is closely connected to whether the breach can be considered to be gross, and is rarely considered separately (see 4.7).

## Has such Breach caused the Victim's Death?

**4.6**   The breach of duty must have caused the death of the victim. An intervening act will only break the chain of causation if it is extraordinary. The CCA briefing sets out case law developments in this area:

The principles set out in *Environment Agency v Empress Car Company Ltd*[1] apply to criminal law cases.

In this case, Empress Car Company had been charged with polluting a river. A diesel tank in a yard which drained directly into the river was surrounded by a bund to contain spillage, but the protection had been overridden by the company. It had fixed an extension pipe to the outlet of the tank in order to connect it to a drum standing outside the bund. An unlocked tap controlled the outlet from the tank and this was opened by an unknown person, allowing the contents of the tank to run into the drum, overflow into the yard and pass down the drain into the river.

The House of Lords held that:

'The fact that a deliberate act of a third party caused the pollution does not in itself mean that the defendants creation of a situation in which the third party could so act did not also cause the pollution'.

The possibility of vandalism of this kind was not an 'extraordinary' event but instead 'a normal and familiar fact of life'.

Lord Hoffman said that it did not break 'the causal connection between the original act of accumulating the polluting substance and its escape.'

In *R v Finlay*[2], which concerned a prosecution where the defendant had given an injection of heroin to the person who died, but did not himself inject it, Buxton LJ summarised the principle in the *Empress* case. He said the court must decide whether the act of a third party:

'... should be regarded as a matter of ordinary occurrence which would not negative the effect of the defendant's act; or something extraordinary, on the other hand which would leave open a finding that the defendant did not cause the criminal act or event.'

In *Finlay* the court said:

'Whether or not the defendant caused heroin to be administered to or taken by the deceased is a question of fact and degree which you have to decide, and you should decide it by applying your common sense and knowledge of the world to the facts that you find to be proved by the evidence. The prosecution do not have to show that what the defendant did or said was a sole cause of the injection of heroin into the deceased. Where the defendant has produced the situation in which there is the possibility for heroin to be administered to or taken by Jasmine Grosvenor, but the actual injection of heroin involves an act on part of another – in this case Jasmine herself – then if the injection of heroin is to be regarded in your view as a normal fact of life, in the situation proved by the evidence, then the act of the other person will not prevent the defendant's deeds or words being a cause, or one of the causes, of that injection. On the other hand, if in the situation proved by the evidence, injection is to be regarded as an extraordinary event, then it would be open to you to conclude that the defendant did not cause heroin to be administered to or taken by the deceased ...'

This principle has most recently been upheld in the case of *R v Kennedy*[3] involving the offence of manslaughter.

The CCA briefing advises:

'The application of this principle has an important bearing on the prosecution of senior company officers – where their conduct is unlikely to be the immediate cause of death. For example, a death of person which was the direct result of the conduct of an untrained and unsupervised worker, could result in the prosecution of a director or senior manager who established a system of work, where the ordinary consequence of that system of work could be lack of supervision and training.'

[1]   [1999] 2 AC 22.
[2]   [2003] EWCA Crim 3868.
[3]   [2005] EWCA Crim 685.

## Was the Breach Gross?

**4.7**      In order to be convicted, the jury must find that the breach of duty by the defendant was 'characterised by gross negligence'. The Health and Safety Executive (HSE) explains in *Report of the public meetings into the legionella outbreak in Barrow-in-Furness* (August 2002) that this last requirement is the most difficult to prove. The courts have repeatedly judged over the years that the level of conduct has to be so severe as to make such negligence a criminal offence. In other words, the court requires that person to have made very serious mistakes or omissions.

The CCA briefing sets out that that courts must consider whether the test set out in the House of Lords decision in *Adomako* is a 'subjective' or an 'objective' one. It explains:

'The distinction between these two tests concern the relevance of the state of mind of the defendant; whether or not it is necessary for the jury to consider whether the defendant was aware of the risk of death arising from the particular set of circumstances. If it was a subjective test – what is often called 'recklessness' – it would be necessary for there to be evidence that the defendant was aware of the risk. If it was an objective test, it would not be required – the focus simply being on the conduct of the person in question.'

Some aspects of *Adomako* appear to show that the 'gross negligence' test consists of both an 'objective' and 'subjective' test.

*Subjective*

**4.8**      Lord Mackay said that 'gross negligence' includes 'recklessness' in the 'ordinary connotation of the word', and supported the different ways that the term was defined in the cases of *R v Stone and Dobinson*[1] and *R v West London Coroner, ex parte Gray*[2]:

● the defendant must be proved to have been indifferent to an obvious risk;

● the defendant had foreseen the risk but was determined nevertheless to run it;

● the defendant had foreseen the risk, had intended to avoid it but had shown in the means adopted to avoid the risk such a high degree of negligence as would justify a conviction.'

[1]  [1977] QB 554.
[2]  [1987] 2 All ER 129.

*Objective*

**4.9**      Lord Mackay also made clear that manslaughter could be provided through an objective test, saying at different points in his judgment:

'The Jury will have to consider whether the extent to which the defendant's conduct departed from the proper standard of care incumbent upon him, involving as it must have done a risk of death ... was such that it should be judged criminal.'

'Whether, having regard to the risk of death involved, the conduct of the defendant was so bad in all the circumstances of the case as to amount in their judgment to a criminal act or omission.'

'... failure to advert a serious risk going beyond mere inadvertence in respect of an obvious and important matter which the defendant's duty demanded he or she should address.'

Since *Adomako* a number of cases have dealt with the question as to whether the test is objective or subjective.

*Attorney-General's Reference (No 2/1999)*[1] resulted from the unsuccessful prosecution of Great Western Railways over the Southall Rail Crash (see chapter 1).

The Attorney-General asked the Court of Appeal to clarify the following: 'can a defendant be properly convicted of manslaughter by gross negligence in the absence of evidence as to that defendant's state of mind?'

The court ruled:

'Although there may be cases where the defendant's state of mind is relevant to the jury's consideration when assessing the grossness and criminality of his conduct, evidence of his state of mind is not a pre-requisite to a conviction for manslaughter by gross negligence. The *Adomako* test is objective, but a defendant who is reckless ... may well be the more readily found to be grossly negligent to a criminal degree.'

*R v DPP ex parte Tim Jones*[2] involved a successful judicial review of a decision by the Crown Prosecution Service (CPS) not to prosecute the managing director of Euromin Ltd, James Martell over the death of Simon Jones (see para 4.10, below).

The court stated:

'If the accused is subjectively reckless, then that may be taken into account by the jury as a strong factor demonstrating that his negligence was criminal, but negligence will still be criminal in the absence of any recklessness if on an objective basis the defendant demonstrated what, for instance, Lord Mackay quoted the Court of Appeal in *Adomako* as describing as: "failing to advert to a serious risk going mere inadvertence in respect of an obvious and important manner in which the defendant's duty demanded he should address" ...'

[1]   [2000] QB 796.
[2]   [2000] IRLR 373.

**4.10**

---

*The death of Simon Jones*

Simon Jones was killed on his first day at work for shipping company Euromin at the dockside at Shoreham by Sea in April 1998. He had been sent by a local employment agency to carry out work involving the unloading of bags of cobble stones from the ➡

---

hold of a ship. He had received no training in this kind of work from the agency, and was not given any formal training by Euromin.

The crane being used to unload the bags was supplied with different attachments: a grab bucket for the lifting of loose material; and a lifting hook for bags. It took around an hour to change from one attachment to the other.

At the time of the accident, the grab bucket was being used to lift the bags of cobble stones, rather than loose material. Although the managing director of Euromin, James Martell, was not on site when Simon was killed, he had initiated an adaptation to be made to the crane: two hooks were fitted within the grab bucket, to which chains could be attached for lifting bags. The presence of chains meant that bags were lifted with the bucket open and also that workers involved in unloading had to stand near, and in some cases immediately under, the open bucket in order to attach the bags to the chain, with the risk that they could be caught in the bucket. Unfortunately, that is what happened to Simon. He was caught in the grab bucket and decapitated.

His death was investigated by the HSE and the police.

The HSE brought charges against Euromin for breaches of s 2 and s 3 of the HSWA 1974. In addition, two weeks after the accident, an improvement notice regarding training and instruction, and two prohibition notices (banning the use of lifting chain attachments within the grab of the excavator and prohibiting the use of the excavator in an area where other people would be at risk) were served.

The police investigated the death for manslaughter and gave the details of their investigation to the Director of Public Prosecutions (DPP) for a decision as to whether bring manslaughter charges.

The DPP found that there were three factors which lead to Simon's death:

- the absence of the usual hatchman and the employment of a casual worker, Mr Kasprzak – he had been given the role of directing the operations of the crane, although he had never done the job before and did not speak English;

- the accidental movement of the lever which closed the mechanical grab on the crane – the lever in the driving cab of the crane operating the closing of the grab bucket was very sensitive, closing the bucket in a second, but the crane operator had not been aware of this; and

- the shortened chains – the crane operator had shortened the chains from their usual eight feet to about six feet, so there was➡

117

less room between the bottom of the chains and the jaws of the clamp, and therefore less room for error.

But in March 1999, the DPP decided not to bring proceedings for manslaughter. Originally, this decision had been based in part on the opinion that it was not possible to show a causative link between the act of fixing hooks on the grab bucket, and the death, in the absence of sufficient evidence as to why the grab had closed.

However, on reconsideration – the DPP delegated this task to a solicitor member of his Casework Directorate – the issue of causation was abandoned and 'the real issue' in the case was identified as being:

'... whether the degree of negligence that could be established against Mr Martell and Euromin was sufficiently serious to provide a realistic prospect that a jury would be satisfied that both were guilty of manslaughter, applying the test in *Adomako* ...'

In the solicitor's opinion:

- Martell held a sufficiently senior position in the company for him to be characterised as the directing mind of Euromin, so if he was guilty of gross negligence in the criminal sense, Euromin would be equally guilty;

- there was a realistic prospect of satisfying a jury that both Martell and the company owed Simon Jones a duty of care, and that there were breaches of the duty of care owed – there had been a failure to provide a safe system of work, and if a safe system of work had been in existence, the death would not have occurred; and

- Martell was negligent in his failure to set in place a safe system of work (sufficient for a prosecution under HSWA 1974).

However, he also outlined that:

'... to establish the offence of manslaughter more is required. I have referred to the *Bateman* test above, which shows that in deciding whether or not there should be a conviction a jury must be satisfied that the defendant, by his negligence showed such disregard for the life and safety of others as to amount to a crime. It is my view that, bearing in mind the factors set out above in particular, the evidence taken as a whole was not sufficient to provide a realistic prospect of satisfying a jury that Mr Martell was guilty of gross negligence sufficient to satisfy the test in *Adomako*.'

The Bateman test he refers was set out in a case involving medical negligence, *Bateman*[1], by Lord Hewart CJ:                                    ➡

'... in order to establish criminal liability the facts must be such that, in the opinion of the jury, the negligence of the accused went beyond a mere matter of compensation between subjects and showed such disregard for the life and safety of others as to amount to a crime against State and conduct deserving punishment'.

In March 2000, in a landmark ruling, two High Court judges overturned the decision in a judicial review of the case brought by Simon Jones's family, *R v Director of Public Prosecutions, ex parte Jones (Timothy)*[2].

In overturning the decision, LJ Buxton questioned the solicitor's interpretation of *Bateman*, pointing out that this is an objective test and that there is no need to show subjective recklessness to secure a manslaughter conviction and ordered the decision to be reconsidered.

The DPP subsequently announced that Euromin and Martell were to be prosecuted. As well as the charge of manslaughter by gross negligence, the company faced three charges under HSWA 1974. Mr Martell faced one charge of manslaughter by gross negligence.

On 29 November 2000, both were cleared of manslaughter by a majority verdict in a trial at the Old Bailey, although the company was found guilty of breaching health and safety law and was fined £50,000 with a further £20,000 costs.

Following the acquittal of Euromin and Martell, the then DPP, David Calvert-Smith, QC, repeated a call for a change in the law:

'I am pleased that the jury had the opportunity to consider all the issues in this case. However, as I have said before, I support the reform of the law recently proposed which would make it easier for the criminal courts to bear down on negligent treatment of employees in the workforce.'

Following Simon's death, a campaign for justice was set up. More information about the case and the campaign is available on the Simon Jones Memorial Campaign website at www.simonjones.org.uk

---

[1]   (1925) Crim App R 8.
[2]   *R v DPP, ex p Jones (Timothy)* (2000) (unreported).

**4.11**   In *R v Alan James Mark Nationwide Heating Services Ltd*[1] the court held that actual awareness of risk is not required for a conviction. The trial judge had correctly directed the jury that:

'... actual foresight or perception of the risk is not a prerequisite of the crime of gross negligence'.

However, other cases indicate that when evidence of the state of mind is available, the jury must at least be allowed to take this into consideration, relying on the sentence in *Adomako* stating that the jury must consider the 'seriousness of the breach of duty committed by the defendant in all the circumstances in which the defendant was placed when it occurred'.

In *R v Misra*[2], the Court of Appeal stated:

'... such evidence [of the state of mind of the defendant] is not irrelevant to the issue of gross negligence. It will often be a critical factor in the decision'.

And referring to *Adomako* went onto say,

'It is therefore clear that the defendant is not to be convicted without fair consideration of all the relevant circumstances in which is breach of duty occurred.'

Here, the Court of Appeal approved the High Court ruling in the case of *R (Rowley) v DPP*[3] which concerned an unsuccessful judicial review of a decision by the CPS not to prosecute following the death of a member of the public in a care home.

In *Rowley*, Lord Justice Kennedy stated that there were five 'ingredients' to the offence of manslaughter, with the first four requiring the application of an objective test – one excluding consideration of the defendant's state of mind. These are:

- whether the defendant owed a 'duty of care';

- whether the defendant was in breach of that duty by not taking the steps that a reasonable person would have done;

- whether that breach caused the death, and

- whether the defendant, in failing to take the steps, created an obvious risk of death.

The final ingredient – which he called 'criminality' or 'badness' – did not require the application of an objective test: the jury must be sure that the defendant's conduct was so bad as in all the circumstances (including the state of mind of the defendant) to amount to a criminal act or omission.

The judge concluded:

'The issue raised in the present case by Mr Hunt [the family barrister] is whether the state of mind of the defendant is a factor which the jury may take into account in the defendant's favour when considering whether his conduct is so bad as to amount to a criminal offence. Mr Hunt submitted that subjective recklessness may help to establish a prosecution case, but that otherwise the state of mind of the proposed defendant is irrelevant.

That seems to us to be an unrealistic approach which the authorities do not require, which no judge would enforce, and which no jury would adopt. Once it can be shown that there was ordinary common law negligence causative of death and a serious risk of death, what remains to be established is criminality of badness. In considering whether there is criminality or badness, Lord Mackay [in the case of *Adomako*] makes it clear that all the circumstances, are to be taken into account.'

[1]   [2004] EWCA Crim 2490.
[2]   [2004] EWCA 2375.
[3]   [2003] EWHC 693.

## Risk of Death

**4.12**    The CCA briefing points out that it is important to note that the relevant risk to be considered by the jury is the risk of death.

In a number of cases (*R v Stone and Dobinson*[1] and *West London Coroner, ex parte Grey*[2]), reference has been made to a broader risk of injury or health and welfare of the person.

However, in *R v Singh (Gurphal)*[3], the Court of Appeal upheld the trial judge's direction that:

'... the circumstances must be such that a reasonably prudent person would have foreseen a serious and obvious risk not merely of injury, even serious injury, but of death.'

This direction was then applied by the Divisional Court in *Lewin v CPS*[4]. And in *R v Misra*[5] the Court of Appeal stated that:

'... as a matter of policy, when making a decision whether to prosecute for this offence in cases like the present, the Director of Public Prosecutions looks for evidence of an obvious risk of death'.

If the risk was limited to the obvious risk of serious injury, prosecution would not follow.

The CCA briefing on the law on manslaughter can be found at: www.corporateaccountability.org/manslaughter/law/main.htm.

[1]   [1977] QB 554.
[2]   [1998] QB 467.
[3]   [1999] CLR 582.
[4]   [2002] EWHC Admin 1049
[5]   [2004] EWCA 2375.

## The Scots Law of Culpable Homicide

**4.13**    The Scottish Executive established an Expert Group to review the law in Scotland on corporate liability for culpable homicide (see CHAPTER 1). This sets out that:

'The crime of culpable homicide applies where the perpetrator might not have intended to kill the victim but nonetheless behaved so recklessly and with such complete disregard or indifference to the potential dangers and possible consequences that the law considers there is responsibility for the death.'

The Law Society of Scotland sets out in a paper submitted to the review that:

'Culpable homicide is a crime at common law which covers "the killing of human beings in all circumstances short of murder, where the criminal law attaches a relevant measure of blame to the person who kills" [Lord Justice General Rodger in *Drury v HMA* 2001 SCCR 583]. The relevant measure of blame will be attributed not only by reference to the conduct involved but also the mental state or *mens rea* of the perpetrator at the time of commission of the alleged offence. In the modern law, homicide in the course of lawful conduct – such as will arise in the area of law under review by the Expert Group – is culpable homicide only where the negligence is gross. In other words, the *mens rea* must amount to criminal recklessness in the sense of total indifference to and disregard for the safety of the public.'

It goes on to say that:

'The application of the common law of culpable homicide and the proof of the *mens rea* involved is largely unproblematic when dealing with an individual accused of the crime. Either evidence of the accused's mental state can be inferred from the facts and circumstances of the case or will be available as a direct result of admissions made.'

And with regard to the application to work-related deaths explains that:

'At common law, directors and senior officers can be prosecuted for culpable homicide if it can be established that the individual committed the act and had sufficient *mens rea* – for the purposes of this offence. *Mens rea* for that offence is criminal recklessness in the sense of total indifference to and disregard for the safety of the public. If he or she had the *mens rea* and was involved in the commission of the offence, albeit not as the principal actor, then he or she could be convicted on an "art and part" basis of the principal offence.'

The CCA briefing on the law of homicide as it applies to individuals sets out case law developments in this area:

The classic definition of involuntary culpable homicide is found in the 1936 case of *Paton v His Majesty's Advocate*[1] which dealt with an appeal against a conviction for culpable homicide arising out a driving incident.

Lord Justice-Clerk Aitchison said:

'It is now necessary to show gross, or wicked, or criminal negligence, something amounting, or at any rate analogous, to a criminal indifference to consequences, before a jury can find culpable homicide proved.'

Although the judge uses the term 'negligence', it appears from comments made in the *Transco* criminal appeal (see CHAPTER 1) that it is not necessary to prove that the defendant owed a 'duty of care', as is required in the English law of manslaughter (see 4.4).

Lord Osborne stated in his ruling that:

'From my consideration of the nature of the common law crime of involuntary culpable homicide, it appears to me to follow that civil common law duties of care, or civil statutory duties of care, can play no direct part in the assessment of guilt, except to the extent that their existence may serve to demonstrate the particular area of responsibility which an individual may carry.'

This potentially broadens the range of defendants that can be prosecuted for the offence, compared to the situation in England.

It also appears from the same case that it is necessary to prove a particular state of mind on the part of the defendant rather than just assessing the conduct of the defendant against an objective standard.

Lord Osborne stated:

'Where there is an issue of involuntary culpable homicide, the resolution of the issue depends, not upon some objective assessment of the conduct of the perpetrator alone, but upon an assessment of "his state of mind at the time of the accident", in other words, an enquiry into whether he possessed the necessary criminal intent at the material time, namely a "complete disregard of potential dangers and of the consequences of his [conduct]".'

And Lord Hamilton stated:

'These authorities make it plain, in my view, that under the law of Scotland the mental element (mens rea) is and remains a necessary and significant element in the crime of "lawful act" culpable homicide. That element may, of course, be proved in various ways, including proof by inference from external facts. But it is, in my view, erroneous to suppose that the actual state of mind of a person accused of culpable homicide of this kind can be ignored and guilt or innocence determined solely on the basis of proof that the conduct in question fell below an objectively set standard.'

This requirement of a mental state is different to the law in England, where it is not necessary to prove a particular state of mind (though it can be taken into account), and makes it more difficult to prove that an individual has committed the offence of culpable homicide than that of manslaughter in England.

The CCA briefing points out that it should be noted that the Scottish approach to proof of a mental state has traditionally been fairly robust and 'objective', tending to draw inferences of a particular state of mind fairly readily from behaviour.

The CCA briefing is at www.corporateaccountability.org/manslaughter/scotland/main.htm#individual.

¹   1936 JC 19; 1936 SLT 298.

# Examples of Cases involving Convictions of Directors and Business Owners for Gross Negligence Manslaughter

**4.14**    According to the Home Affairs and Work and Pensions Committees joint report on the *Draft Corporate Manslaughter Bill*, only 15 directors or business owners were personally convicted of manslaughter by gross negligence between April 1999 and September 2005. The Committee commented: 'the small number of directors successfully prosecuted for individual gross negligence manslaughter shows how difficult it is to prove the individual offence'.

The following sections sets out details of convictions of company directors and business owners convicted of manslaughter:

## Company Directors and Business Owners Convicted of Manslaughter¹

**4.15**

### *Timothy Dighton (Concrete Company Ltd)*

Technician Christopher Meachen was killed in November 2005 as a result of the multiple injuries he sustained after becoming caught in an unguarded slew conveyor which carried aggregate and sand up to hoppers where cement was manufactured at the Concrete Company Ltd plant, Longwater Industrial Estate, Costessey, Norfork.

In June 2007, managing director Timothy Dighton, and area manager Roy Burrows, pleaded guilty to manslaughter at Norwich Crown Court and were convicted and later jailed for 12 months and nine months respectively.

The company, Concrete Company Ltd, was ordered to pay fines and costs totalling £164,000 (£75,000 for breaches of health and safety legislation and £89,000 costs).

The court heard that the company had paid no regard to the safety, livelihood or physical well-being of Christopher, and that his death could have been prevented if guards costing only £2,000 had been fitted to the machine.

According to Norfolk Constabulary, which investigated the death together with the HSE, Christopher had worked for the company since the previous August as a concrete batcher.

Justin McCracken, HSE Deputy Chief Executive, said his death: 'could and should have been avoided by very simple and straightforward safety precautions. HSE inspectors regularly come across examples of poor health and safety standards at workplaces but the inspectors involved in this case were appalled by the total lack of basic health and safety measures at this company's site, which directly led to the fatal incident. This case illustrates how things can go tragically wrong when a company disregards legal standards designed to protect workers. HSE, where appropriate acting with other agencies such as the police, will act decisively to deal with employers who deliberately or negligently flout the law and put their employees' lives at risk.'

## Phillip Wyman (*boat owner*)

Kritztian Takacs was killed in an explosion and fire at a boat yard in Southampton, which also left the boat owner, Philip Wyman, with severe burns. Wyman was charged with gross negligence manslaughter, as well as three health and safety offences, and was found guilty at Winchester Crown count in February 2007 and sentenced to 18 months in prison.

The two men had been carrying out work involving melting lead using propane gas cylinders on the moored boat's hull. A joint investigation by Hampshire Police and the HSE found that there was no regulator on one of the propane gas cylinders being used – gas appliances without regulators can make larger flames but are less controllable.

## Michael Shaw (*Change of Style*)

The director and business owner of a stone-cutting company near Southampton, Michael Shaw, was found guilty of the manslaughter of a 22-year old employee, David Bail, and given a two-year suspended prison sentence at Winchester Crown Court in August 2006. In November 2006, the suspended prison sentence was declared to be too lenient at the Criminal Appeal Court, and was increased to a 15-month jail sentence. The prosecution was brought by Hampshire police who led the investigation. An inquest jury had earlier returned a verdict of unlawful killing.

David died from massive head injuries after he was caught in an automated stone cutting machine. A vital piece of safety equipment – a light sensor system that would have immediately stopped the machine if someone broke a continuous beam – had been deactivated. Hinged guards that would have broken the circuit and stopped the machine if lowered had also been bypassed.

The judge in the case said that although Shaw did not personally disable the safety devices, through his guilty plea, he had acknowledged that safety procedures in his premises were his responsibility.

Shaw and the company were also fined a total of £70,000 for ten breaches of health and safety regulations. Shaw's son, Gavin Shaw was fined £1,500 for one breach, and cleared of manslaughter due to lack of evidence. A manslaughter charge against the firm was ordered to lie on file. Peter Cowley, production manager at the time of the death, had already pleaded guilty to a breach of health and safety legislation and magistrates fined him £600 and £100 costs.

## Mark Connolly (*MAC Machinery Services*)

In March 2006, company director Mark Connolly, of MAC Machinery Services, sub-contractors for Carillion rail, was found guilty on four counts of manslaughter following the deaths of four rail workers at Tebay, Cumbria, in February 2004, and jailed for nine years, (although this was later reduced to seven – see below). He was also found guilty on three counts of breaching health and safety laws.

Roy Kennett, Mark Connolly's crane operator, was also found guilty on four counts of manslaughter and on a single count of breaching health and safety laws and was jailed for two years.

The men, Colin Buckley, Darren Burgess, Chris Walters and Gary Tindall, were among a group of Carillion employees carrying out maintenance work on the West Coast mainline, when they were hit by a runaway trailer, owned by the company. The men were unable to hear the approaching wagon because they were wearing helmets designed to protect against the noise of a generator.

Investigators found that the hydraulic brake system on the three-tonne flatbed trailer had been disconnected. It was also discovered the hydraulic tubes had been filled with ball bearings, rather than brake fluid, to give the impression that everything was above board. Instead, wooden chocks were being used to stop the trailer moving. But the wagon laden with the steel railway track over-ran the wooden chocks, travelling almost four miles down the track before hitting the four workers.

Connolly appealed against the convictions, but although his prison sentence was reduced from nine to seven years, the Appeal court upheld the manslaughter convictions against him and Kennett.

## Wayne Davies (A & E Buildings)

Construction company proprietor Wayne Davies of A & E Buildings, based in Knighton, Powys, was sentenced to an 18-month custodial sentence for manslaughter in January 2006, following a prosecution brought by the CPS. The case, which was heard in Birmingham Crown Court, followed a joint investigation between the police and the HSE into the death of Mark Jones. In May 2006, the Criminal Appeal Court upheld the conviction.

Mark was killed as a result of injuries he received when he fell from a 'home made' basket, suspended from the forks of a telehandler owned by Davies, while installing a barn roof at Hill Farm in Kinver, South Staffordshire, on 28 February 2004. The telehandler tipped over, throwing Mr Jones around 25 feet to the ground. Another employee was also seriously injured as he fell from the telehandler with Mr Jones.

The two men had not been provided with safety harnesses, despite working at heights of up to 30 feet.

Davies was also prosecuted for health and safety offences. The court found that Davies had failed in both his duty to ensure the safety of his employees and in his responsibility to provide safe and suitable means of working at height. He was also found guilty of a breach of HSWA 1974 s 2(1) for failing to ensure the safety of employees in the time before the incident.

In addition, he pleaded guilty to a single charge of providing a telehandler and equipment that was not properly maintained, breaching reg 5 of the Provision and Use of Work Equipment Regulations 1998, SI 1998/2306.

## Paul White (MW White Ltd)

In September 2005, company director Paul White received a 12-month custodial sentence at Norwich Crown Court following the death of an employee at his paper recycling business, MW White Ltd of Ketteringham, Norwich. The custodial sentence followed an earlier guilty plea to manslaughter and health and safety charges. The company was also fined £30,000 with costs of £55,000.

Kevin Arnup was killed after he had climbed into a paper-shredding (or hogger) machine to clear blockages when the machine started. The machine contained a series of hammers projecting 15cm from a shaft, which revolved at high speed.

The investigation, which was carried out jointly by the HSE and detectives from Norfolk Constabulary CID, found that the machine was not securely isolated whilst the unblocking work was being carried out (there was no local electrical isolator provided for the machinery), there was no safe system for such work and the electrical controls for the machine were contaminated with dust.

## Lee Harper (*Harper Building Contractors Ltd*)

Lee Harper, managing director of a building firm pleaded guilty to the manslaughter of employee Daryl Arnold and was jailed for 16 months. He also pleaded guilty to a breach of s 2 of HSWA 1974. At the hearing in December 2004, Mr Harper's company, Harper Building Contractors Ltd, was also charged with an offence of corporate manslaughter and breach of s 2. These charges were ordered to remain on file as the company had gone into liquidation.

Daryl died while working on the roof of a warehouse on the Lynton industrial estate in Salford. The roof was to have been removed and replaced, but no safe system of work had been prepared before the work began and no safety precautions were in place at the time of the incident.

Daryl had never worked on a roof before and he stepped backwards onto a fragile roof light on an adjoining warehouse, which gave way. He fell approximately 6.75m landing on the ground floor directly below and died as a result of his injuries.

Commenting on the case Pam Waldron, HSE's Head of Construction for Scotland and the North West, said:

> '... There was a fundamental failure to recognise that the roof included fragile roof lights that will not bear a man's weight. Moreover, the equipment to prevent people falling through fragile materials is readily available and relatively cheap. A sensible, straightforward approach to health and safety in managing the risks on this job should have prevented this tragic death.'

## Melvyn Spree (*director of Keymark Services*)

In December 2004, director Melvyn Spree and his company, Keymark Services, admitted the manslaughter and unlawful killing of Neil Owen and Benjamin Kwapong. The two men were killed in a crash on the M1 in Northamptonshire in February 2002 when lorry driver Stephen Law, who worked for the company and who was also killed, fell asleep at the wheel and crashed into seven vehicles.

Spree was jailed for seven years. Another director, Lorraine March received a 16-month prison sentence for conspiracy to falsify driving records, and the two directors were banned for life from holding such positions. Company secretary Clare Miller was given 160 hours' community service, for the same charge and the company's 10 full-time drivers were prosecuted for a total of 400 different offences of breaching driving regulations and falsifying vehicle records. Three part-time drivers also received official cautions.

The company was fined £50,000 after pleading guilty to a corporate manslaughter offence and also had its license to operate withdrawn by the Vehicle Inspectorate.

## Alan James Mark (*Director of Nationwide Heating Services Ltd*)

In July 2004, Alan James Mark managing director of Plymouth-based Nationwide Heating Systems Ltd, was convicted of the manslaughter of apprentice Benjamin Pinkham and jailed for 12 months at Exeter Crown Court.

Benjamin died in February 2003 after suffering 90 per cent burns when the storage tank he was cleaning at Princess Yachts International in Plymouth exploded.

Nationwide Heating Systems Ltd was also found guilty of manslaughter. Both Mark and the company had pleaded guilty to three health and safety offences: failing to make a suitable assessment of risks to the company's employees; failure to ensure the health and safety of Mr Pinkham and another apprentice, Jonathan Jarvis, inside the tank; and failure to provide a system of work in a confined space which was safe and without risk to health.

Princess Yachts pleaded guilty at an earlier hearing to two health and safety offences and was fined £90,000 with £10,000 prosecution costs.

## *Peter Pell*

Peter Pell pleaded guilty to the manslaughter of Shaun Cooper, aged 27, who was crushed to death after he was trapped in equipment in a poultry shed in a farm in Wysall, Nottinghamshire in September 2001. He was the second employee working for Pell's poultry shed cleaning company to die in less than six years – Pell was fined £3,000 for health and safety offences in October 1996 after an employee was electrocuted when his tipper truck came into contact with overhead power lines.

The High Court judge in the case, Mr Justice Morland, said that the extreme dangers of modifying farm equipment would not be tolerated and handed down a 12-month prison sentence to Pell. Two charges under HSWA 1974 were left to lie on the file and Pell was also ordered to pay £5,000 costs.

The HSE investigating inspector David Hortop said:

'This sad case was about as bad as it can get. HSE has worked closely with manufacturers of these vehicles to ensure they include safety cages, cut-off systems and other features, and Pell removed all of these as soon as he bought the vehicle so that it could be used in low-roofed chicken sheds, despite there being other vehicles better suited to the job.'

## *Ian Morris (Eng Industrial Services)*

Ian Morris, a sole trader who owned the paint stripping business, Eng Industrial Services, was convicted of the manslaughter of Ghulam Sarwar and Mumtaz Hussain who died after being overcome by dychlormethane chemical fumes which had escaped from the processing area of the factory. He was sentenced to nine months in jail, and also charged under s 2(1) of HSWA 1974 and regulation 6 of the Control of Substances Hazardous to Health Regulations 1999, SI 1999/437.

Mumtaz was an experienced worker at the factory, but his nephew Ghulam had been working at the factory for just two days. The men had been working on the night shift and were found by colleagues the next morning.

## *John Horner (director of Teglgaard Hardwood (UK) Ltd)*

In February 2003, the company and one of its directors, John Horner, pleaded guilty at Hull Crown Court to the manslaughter of labourer 18 year old Christopher Longrigg, who died in April 2000 when a stack of timber fell on him. The timber had been incorrectly stacked and had broken away from its ties. The court was told that the company paid 'scant regard' to even very basic health and safety precautions, and that risk assessments were not carried out.

The HSE principal inspector involved in the case, Barry Clinch, later told *Safety & Health Practitioner* magazine:

'The company was totally indifferent to, and ignorant of, the risks they were running. They had no safety policy, had done no risk assessments, had no safe stacking procedures and did not give training to their staff. It was as though the Health and Safety at Work Act did not exist. They had done absolutely nothing on health and safety.'

The company was fined £25,000 and Horner was also given a 15-month prison sentence, suspended for two years. A charge of manslaughter was also laid against John Horner's son, John, who was a company director. However, criminal charges were not continued against him. The Crown said this was inappropriate as it believed his father to be the main source of company actions.

## Edward Crow and Alistair Crow

In July 2001, Alistair Crow, and his father Edward Crow were found guilty of the manslaughter of Lee Smith, a 16-year-old agricultural student who was working for the Crows on a placement from a local agricultural college. Smith died in November 1999 when the seven tonne JCB Potato Loader he was operating was hit by a lorry on the A49, crushing him to death.

The TUC e-bulletin, *Risks*, reported that sentencing them at Birmingham Crown Court, the judge, Mr Justice McKay, said:

' ... over a period of just over four months both of you knew about, condoned and shut your eyes to a practice whereby this young man was allowed on a regular basis to drive a heavy, powerful and dangerous machine, on the farm and on public roads – a machine on which he had received no training at all.'

## Roger Jackson (Easy Moss Products Ltd)

In March 2000, Roger Jackson, the director of Easy Moss Products Ltd in Dewsbury was convicted of the manslaughter of John Speight, a worker with special needs, who was crushed to death in February 1988. John never regained consciousness after falling from a former British Rail platform trolley which was being used for refuse at the company. It had been lifted six feet into the air by a fork lift truck so that Speight could empty rubbish into a skip. The trolley crashed down on his chest and he died in hospital five days later. The court heard that the trolley was not attached to the fork lift truck and the company's fork lift drivers were untrained.

Jackson received a 12-month sentence, suspended for two years and was convicted of two health and safety offences and fined £10,000 and ordered to pay £25,000 costs.

## Stephen and Julie Bowles (Roy Bowles Transport Ltd)

In 1999, two directors of Roy Bowles Transport Ltd, Stephen Bowles and his sister Julie Bowles, were convicted of the manslaughter of Peter Morgan and Barry Davies, who both died in a seven-vehicle pile up on the M25 in 1997. The accident happened when a lorry driver working for the company, Andrew Cox, fell asleep at the wheel.

Cox and other drivers at the company worked very long hours with the knowledge of the directors. Bowles and Bowles were sentenced to 15 and 12 months' prison sentences respectively, suspended for two years. A company secretary was acquitted of manslaughter.

Cox was convicted of death by dangerous driving on the grounds that he was so exhausted by working excessive hours, he fell asleep at the wheel of the lorry and caused the deaths. He received a two and a half year prison sentence and was disqualified from driving for two years.

## Alan Jackson (director of Jackson Transport (Ossett) Ltd)

In September 1996, the company and its managing (and sole) director, Alan Jackson were convicted for the manslaughter of 21 year old James Hodgson. James died in May 1994 as a result of using steam pressure to clean a valve in a tanker blocked with highly toxic chemicals. He was sprayed in the face with a toxic chemical and later died.

The company was convicted of manslaughter and a range of offences under HSWA 1974. It was fined £22,000 including £15,000 in respect of the manslaughter charge. Mr Jackson was fined £1,500 and imprisoned for a year.

## *Peter Kite (OLL Ltd)*

In a December 1994 judgment, a company specialising in multi-activity holidays, OLL Ltd, and its managing director, Peter Kite, were convicted of gross negligence manslaughter. Kite was sentenced to a term of three years' imprisonment (although this was later reduced to two) and the company fined £60,000 after four students (aged between 16 and 17) were drowned in Lyme Bay. This was the first successful prosecution of a company for gross negligence manslaughter, and the first time a director had received a prison sentence in relation to a work-related death. The Centre's manager Joseph Stoddart was acquitted of manslaughter.

Simon Deane, Clair Langley, Rachel Walker and Dean Sawyer were all students at Southway Comprehensive School and were on a canoeing trip, accompanied by a school teacher and two unqualified instructors, who only had basic proficiency skills in canoeing. The group was swept out to sea and capsized.

## *Norman Holt (David Holt Plastics)*

In December 1989, Norman Holt, director of David Holt Plastics, pleaded guilty to the manslaughter of company employee, George Kenyon, who died in May 1988 after he was dragged into the blades of a plastic crumbing machine. The CPS accepted a 'not guilty' plea from another director, David Holt, although the case was ordered to 'remain on file'. The company was not prosecuted for manslaughter, but the company and directors were fined a total of £47,000 for health and safety offences.

[1]  See Centre for Corporate Accountability (CCA) database on deaths, inquests and prosecutions: www.corporateaccountability.org/prosecutions.htm; news.bbc.co.uk/1/hi/england/2809395.stm; news.bbc.co.uk/hi/england/2795789.stm; news.bbc.co.uk/1/hi/england/4066331.stm; news.bbc.co.uk/1/hi/england/1621825.stm; Health and Safety Executive (HSE) press release 20 January 2006; Staffordshire Police press release 20 January 2006; HSE press release 15 September 2005; Norfolk Constabulary press release 15 September 2005; HSE press release 7 January 2005; Northamptonshire Police Statement re Operation Nuthatch (date unknown); TUC Risks e-bulletin issues 29 24 November 2001 and 113 5 July 2003; Safety & Health Practitioner magazine www.shponline.co.uk; Michael G Welham, *Corporate killing – A managers' guide to legal compliance* (Tolley, 2002).

# Examples of Cases involving Work-related Manslaughter Convictions of managers and other workers

**4.16**     This paragraph sets out examples of cases where there have been work-related manslaughter convictions of managers and others[1].

## *Atalokhia Omo-Bare (landlord)*

Landlord and unqualified handyman Atalokhia Omo-Bare was given a 20-month prison sentence after being found guilty in February 2007 of the manslaughter of Roseline Idugboe, and her two grandchildren, Jeriel Okenchukwu and Jaden Chimaoba Onwegbu-Aguocha. They died after Omo-Bare fitted a faulty boiler with no extractor pipe to their home in east London. He had been a friend of the family and had fitted the boiler as a favour.

## Lin Liang Ren (*gangmaster*)

Gangmaster Lin Liang Ren was found guilty of 21 counts of manslaughter following the deaths of 23 Chinese cockle pickers in Morecambe Bay in February 2004 – two of the bodies were never recovered. He was sentenced to 14 years in prison.

Those killed were Yu Hui, Chen Mu Yu, Guo Nian Zhu, Lin Zhi Fang, Xu Yu Hua, Wu Jia Zhen, Wu Hong Kang, Xie Xiao Wen, Lin Guo Hua, Guo Bing Long, Zhou Xun Chao, Lin Guo Guang, Cao Chao Kun, Guo Chang Mau, Yang Tian Long, Lin Li Shui, Wang Ming Lin, Lin You Xing, Chen Ai Qin, Zhang Xiu Hua and Wang Xiu Yu.

The CPS said they had died because 'their lives were considered less important than the pursuit of profit'.

Lin Liang Ren was also found guilty along with his girlfriend Zhao Xiao Qing of conspiring to pervert the course of justice by trying to conceal who had sent the 23 cockle pickers out to drown in Morecambe Bay.

Lin Liang Ren, his cousin Lin Mu Yong, who was also a gangmaster, and Zhao Xiao Qing were found guilty of facilitating breaches of the Immigration Act by contributing towards illegal immigrants being put to work. Anthony Eden and his son David who owned the company who bought the cockles from the gangmasters were acquitted of the same charges.

## Feda Mulhem (*doctor*)

Mulhem pleaded guilty to the manslaughter of Wayne Jowett, who died a month after the anticancer drug vincristine was injected into his spine. He was given an eight-month prison sentence. Only three days into his first post as a specialist registrar in haematology, he had instructed a junior doctor to inject the drug into the patient's spine, instead of giving an intravenous injection.

An article by barrister Jon Holbrook, 'Criminalisation of fatal medical mistakes', published in *Student BMJ*[2] points out that Mulhem was the latest of several doctors to be prosecuted for gross negligence manslaughter in recent years, and pointed to previous research carried out:

> '... Ferner found that the tendency to prosecute doctors for manslaughter started in about 1990. Between 1867 and 1989 he could find only seven cases. But in the 1990s he identified 13 cases involving 17 doctors. A further article in July last year observed that another six doctors had been tried for gross negligence manslaughter in the two and a half years since Ferner's research.'

These included Rajeev Srivastava and Amir Mizra, both senior house officers, who were convicted of causing the death of a patient after they failed to observe and treat, until it was too late, an unusual side effect of a knee operation they had done. Their 18-month prison sentence was suspended for two years (see also CHAPTER 14).

## Paul Ellis (*teacher*)

Ellis, a teacher from Fleetwood High School, was found guilty of manslaughter in September 2003, following the death of 10 year old Max Palmer in May 2002, and was given a one-year prison sentence. The role of the local education authority, Lancashire County Council, was also investigated, but it was not prosecuted.

Max was accompanying his mother, who was helping with a school trip to the Lake District, which had been organised by Ellis. On the trip, he had led an activity which involved jumping into a natural rock pool – 'plunge pooling'.

The HSE reported that the weather was poor and the water was very cold. There were also serious deficiencies in planning and leading the activity. The plunge pooling session involved jumping four metres into a rock pool in a mountain stream and swimming to an exit point. Ellis jumped in first and said it was alright. Soon afterwards, Max jumped in, but as soon as he surfaced, he was in difficulties and unable to get out. Ellis jumped in to rescue him but, after several minutes, was overcome by the cold. Max's mother, who was accompanying the visit, also attempted a rescue, but she too was gradually overcome by the cold. She was rescued by a pupil who also suffered from hypothermia. Both he and the mother were airlifted to hospital. Max was washed over the weir at the exit to the pool and tumbled down the raging beck. He was pulled out by other pupils, but pronounced dead at the scene.

Ellis was also charged under HSWA 1974 s 7 on the grounds that he had not taken reasonable care of other people who entered the pool (see also CHAPTER 14).

### *Michael Kelly (tourist park manager)*

In August 2003, tourist park manager Michael Kelly, was convicted of the manslaughter of Nathan Pringle who died when he fell into a cesspit while on holiday at a caravan park. Kelly received a one-year suspended prison sentence. The Trevella Caravan Company Ltd, which owned the site and its director, Alan Freear, were also convicted of a health and safety offence and fined £15,000 and £12,000 respectively.

### *Dennis Latham and Barbara Campbell (nurses)*

In February 2003, nursing services manager Latham and his deputy Campbell were jailed for the manslaughter of Marion Dennis, who died several days after being admitted to hospital with septicaemia resulting from pressure sores which had developed while she was a resident in the Ballastowell Gardens nursing home.

### *Barry Ramsey (fairground inspector)*

In 2002, Ramsey was convicted of the manslaughter of Narelle Cozens and Michael Lawrence, who were killed when a car on a fairground ride broke free. He had issued a safety certificate for the ride. He was given an 18-month prison sentence and was also found guilty of two health and safety breaches. The ride owner was cleared of a health and safety offence.

---

1  Further details are available on the Centre for Corporate Accountability (CCA) database on deaths, inquests and prosecutions at www.corporateaccountability.org/prosecutions.htm. See also HSE press releases 24 March 2006; 23 September 2003; HSE education microsite *Glenridding Beck – the facts* (www.hse.gov.uk/schooltrips/index.htm).
2  *Student BMJ* 2004; 12: 1–44 February.

# Individual Liability for Breaches of Health and Safety Law

## Section 7 of HSWA 1974

**4.17**    Employees can be prosecuted under HSWA 1974 s 7 if they contravene the general duties imposed by the section by failing:

- to take reasonable care for someone's health and safety (including their own); or

- to co-operate with their employer, so far as was necessary to enable their employer to comply with a statutory duty or requirement.

The penalty is usually a fine, and has been used in a number of work-related deaths.

> For example, design services manager at Barrow Borough Council, Gillian Beckingham was cleared of manslaughter charges, but prosecuted and fined £15,000 for failing to comply with s 7 following a Legionnaires' disease outbreak at a council arts and leisure centre in 2002, which led to the deaths of seven people. Also, teacher Paul Ellis was convicted of a s 7 offence as well as manslaughter (see 4.16).

## Section 37 of HSWA 1974

**4.18**   Under HSWA 1974, relevant officers of a company can be prosecuted for a health and safety offence which is committed by the company if that offence was the result of the officer's personal 'consent', 'connivance' or 'neglect' (HSWA 1974 s 37):

> 'Where an offence under any of the relevant statutory provisions committed by a body corporate is proved to have been committed with the consent or connivance of, or to have been attributable to any neglect on the part of, any director, manager, secretary or other similar officer of the body corporate or a person who was purporting to act in any such capacity, he as well as the body corporate shall be guilty of that offence and shall be liable to be proceeded against and punished accordingly.'

The punishment is normally a fine, but directors who are found guilty can be disqualified from being a company director for up to two years (Company Directors Disqualification Act 1986 s 2(1)). This sanction has not been used very often. Researchers at the University of Warwick were only able to identify ten directors who had been disqualified for health and safety reasons between the date when the 1986 Act took effect and the end point of their study in 2005 – less than one a year. This compares with more than 1500 company directors disqualified by the courts each year for insolvency or other financial reasons. University of Warwick Professor Alan Neal said, 'We found a marked absence of awareness even of what potential powers may be contained within the 1986 Act.' But this situation is likely to change. The HSC has recognised the need for inspectors to seek greater use by the courts of director disqualification as a penalty, and new instructions on this matter have now been issued to inspectors.

The report, entitled 'A survey of the use and effectiveness of the Company Directors Disqualification Act 1986 as a legal sanction against directors convicted of health and safety offences', by Professor Alan Neal and Professor Frank Wright of the Employment Law Research Unit of the University of Warwick, looked at the use made of powers contained in the Company Directors Disqualification Act 1986 in relation to disqualification orders related to health and safety failures in the management of companies. The full report can be accessed at www.hse.gov.uk/research/rrhtm/rr597.htm.

(CHAPTER 8 looks at ss 7 and 37 of HSWA 1974 in relation to company directors and senior managers in more detail.)

# The Corporate Manslaughter and Corporate Homicide Act 2007

## Overview

**5.1**

> This chapter:
>
> - explains how the Corporate Manslaughter and Corporate Homicide Act 2007 (CMCHA 2007) changes the existing law on corporate manslaughter;
>
> - looks at the reaction to CMCHA 2007 from unions, safety campaigners and employers' organisers;
>
> - summarises the main requirements of CMCHA 2007; and
>
> - examines CMCHA 2007 in detail, with reference to the Ministry of Justice (MoJ) guidance *A guide to the Corporate Manslaughter and Corporate Homicide Act 2007*. This applies throughout the UK, but the MoJ points out that is non-statutory and should not be regarded as providing legal advice, which should be sought if there is any doubt as to the application or interpretation of the legislation; and
>
> - provides commentary on CMCHA 2007, and advice to employers from legal experts in the field.

## Introduction

**5.2**     After many years in the making, CMCHA 2007 will finally come into force on 6 April 2008, after receiving Royal Assent on 26 July 2007 – with the exception of the provisions relating to deaths in custody and publicity orders which will come into effect after the other provisions (see below).

Under the new law, companies, organisations, and government bodies will face an unlimited fine, publicity orders and possibly remedial orders, if they are found to have caused death due to their gross corporate health and safety failures. It is intended that the new offence will be reserved for the very worst cases of corporate mismanagement leading to death.

Prior to this new legislation, a company could be prosecuted for the criminal offence of manslaughter. In order to be guilty of the common law offence of gross negligence manslaughter – generally referred to as 'corporate manslaughter' – a company had to be in gross breach of a duty of care owed to the victim who was killed.

However, it has proved virtually impossible to successfully prosecute a large company for corporate manslaughter where management failures have lead to a death, and instead, prosecutions have nearly always been taken under health and safety legislation. The key problem with the law as it stood was known as the 'identification principle'. Before a company could be prosecuted for corporate manslaughter, a single individual at the top of the company – 'a directing mind' who could be said to embody the company in his or her actions and decisions – had to be shown to be personally guilty of manslaughter. If this could not be shown, the company escaped liability.

In larger companies it has proved extremely difficult to identify an individual who embodies the company and is culpable, as there are often complex management structures and lines of control, and overall responsibilities for safety matters can be unclear.

The MoJ guidelines explain that these difficulties also apply in Northern Ireland and that the extension of the Westminster legislation to Northern Ireland was supported. In Scotland, although the criminal law on culpable homicide differs from the UK law of manslaughter the issues of identifying a directing mind had arisen. Although an expert group established by the Scottish Executive had examined Scots law, it was concluded that its report and the government's Draft Bill were too closely linked to the reserved matters of health and safety and business associations to be within the Scottish Parliament's competence, and the Westminster Act was therefore extended to Scotland (see CHAPTER 1 which explains the background to CMCHA 2007 in detail).

CMCHA 2007 replaces the identification principle with a new test, focusing on how the overall picture of how an organisation's activities are managed by its senior management, rather than focusing on the actions of one individual.

Instead of having to demonstrate that one or more individuals are guilty, liability for the new offence of corporate manslaughter (called corporate homicide in Scotland) depends on a finding of gross negligence in the way in which the activities of the organisation are run. As the explanatory notes to CMCHA 2007 set out:

'In summary, the offence is committed where, in particular circumstances, an organisation owes a duty to take reasonable care for a person's safety and the way in which activities of the organisation have been managed or organised amounts to a gross breach of that duty and causes the person's death. How the activities were managed or organised by senior management must be a substantial element of the gross breach.'

According to the MoJ, CMCHA 2007:

- will make it easier to prosecute companies and other large organisations when gross failures in the management of health and safety lead to the death by delivering a new, more effective basis for corporate liability;

- reforms the law so that a key obstacle to successful prosecutions (that is the identification principle) has now been removed. It means that both small and large companies can be held liable for manslaughter where gross failures in the management of health and safety cause death, not just health and safety breaches;

- complements the current law which individuals can be prosecuted for gross negligence manslaughter and health and safety offences, where there is direct evidence of their culpability; and

- lifts Crown immunity to prosecution. Crown bodies, such as government departments, will be liable for the first time. CMCHA 2007 will apply to companies and other corporate bodies, in the public and private sector, government departments, police forces and certain unincorporated bodies, such as partnerships, where these are employers.

A number of government bodies, and quasi-government bodies, such as government departments, have been able to claim immunity from prosecution because they were said to be acting as a servant or agent of the Crown – know as Crown immunity. In addition, many Crown bodies did not have a separate legal identity for the purposes of a prosecution and the new Act deals with these issues.

CMCHA 2007 will also apply to deaths in custody, which was a key demand of the House of Lords as the Bill progressed through Parliament, although this part of the Act will not come into force on 6 April 2008 – but within three to five years time.

CMCHA 2007 has been generally given a qualified welcome by the trade union movement – it had wanted to see an individual offence included in the Act (also see CHAPTER 1).

TUC General Secretary Brendan Barber said:

'Even though unions wanted the Bill to make individual directors personally liable for safety breaches and penalties against employers

137

committing safety crimes to be tougher, we hope it will mean the start of a change in the safety culture at the top of the UK's companies and organisations.'

And John McClean, National Health and Safety Officer at the general GMB union, said:

'... while the Bill is to be welcomed, GMB feels that it does not go far enough in that individual directors and employers may still be able to evade prosecution for their negligence which results in serious injuries and deaths. GMB sees this Bill as a starting point in the ongoing campaign to make senior managers liable as individuals for negligent behaviour'.

Some safety campaigners have condemned CMCHA 2007. Hilda Palmer, facilitator for Families Against Corporate Killers (FACK) and national Hazards Campaign spokesperson called the passing of the Bill 'a hollow victory', a sentiment echoed by construction union UCATT (see CHAPTER 1). She commented:

'The arguments over whether deaths in custody should be included has obscured the real weaknesses of the Bill. In failing to make those responsible for the way workplaces operate accountable when their failures kill people, in the way as individuals are held accountable and punished with jail sentences, means there will be relatively little deterrent effect'.

But employers' organisations have generally welcomed the new legislation. The Institute of Directors (IoD) Director General Miles Templeman, said:

'After several years of delay, we are glad this legislation is finally on the statute books. The IoD encourages and supports the highest standards of health and safety leadership and performance. We do not condone cavalier attitudes or behaviour over health and safety by any organisation. If and when, sadly, a death has occurred and it is determined to have been corporate manslaughter or corporate homicide, it will be right and proper that the organisation itself can be punished.'

The Construction Confederation also welcomed CMCHA 2007 (see CHAPTER 1).

And many legal experts believe that CMCHA 2007 will have an impact.

Barrister Gerard Forlin specialises in manslaughter, and is widely seen as a leading expert in the field of regulatory crime.

He believes that the Act will make it much easier to successfully prosecute medium and large companies, as well as public sector organisations, for corporate manslaughter because 'it removes the need to pierce the corporate veil and find a directing mind'. Although there are a number of areas that will no doubt be tested in appeal cases in due course, he says that:

'The runway to a conviction will be much easier for the prosecution to find in the future once the Act comes into force.'

Richard Lissack QC, a leading barrister in the field, told a recent Centre for Corporate Accountability (CCA) conference that the effect of the Act will be to make it easier to hold to account an organisation that kills. He told delegates that the Act represents a sea change in the approach to fixing companies with responsibility. 'Once in force, a company may be fixed with responsibility without the need to worry about the doctrine of identification or aggregation', he said. 'It resets common law; whilst the present law is maintained against individuals, against corporations the common law is replaced by the new statutory offence. The key consequence is that corporate liability is no longer parasitic on individual human fault'.

And David Leckie, partner at the law firm Maclay, Murray and Spens told *Health and Safety at Work* magazine:

'Although senior management cannot be prosecuted under the Act, their actions and omissions will be under the microscope as never before and will form a major part of the prosecution's case. For the first time, the question of safety culture – or lack of it – is specifically addressed by the Act and will be a key battleground at trial'.

## Summary of CMCHA 2007

**5.3**    The main requirements set out under CMCHA 2007 are summarised in the box below:

---

- the offence is called corporate manslaughter in England, Wales and Northern Ireland, and corporate homicide in Scotland;

- an organisation is guilty of the offence if the way in which it organises or manages its activities causes a death, and this amounts to a gross breach of a relevant duty of care it owed to the victim;

- an organisation will only be guilty of the offence if the way in which its activities are managed or organised by its senior management is a substantial element of the breach – the senior management test;

- the offence applies where the organisation owed a duty of care to the victim under the law of negligence;

- it will apply to deaths in detention and custody, but this part of CMCHA 2007 will not be enacted on 6 April 2008, but in some three to five years time;

- the offence applies to corporations, government departments (and other bodies listed in a Schedule to CMCHA 2007),➡

---

police forces, partnerships, trade unions and employer associations (where these are employers); but does not apply to corporations sole;

- Crown bodies are not immune from prosecution under CMCHA 2007;

- public policy decisions, exclusively public functions and statutory inspections are excluded from the scope of the offence;

- CMCHA 2007 includes a number of exemptions: for certain military activities and for police and other law enforcement bodies in particular situations (including terrorism and civil unrest); in relation to responding to emergencies; and for statutory functions relating to child protection and probation functions;

- CMCHA 2007 sets out factors for the jury to consider when deciding if there has been a gross breach of a relevant duty of care; it must consider whether health and safety legislation was complied with; and it may consider whether the culture of the organisation tolerated breaches, and any relevant health and safety guidance;

- consent of the Director of Public Prosecutions (DPP) is needed for proceedings for the offence to be instituted;

- there is no secondary liability for the offence – so individuals will not be liable for aiding, abetting, counselling or procuring the commission of, or in Scotland, being art and part of, the offence;

- CMCHA 2007 abolishes the common law offence of gross negligence manslaughter in relation to corporations; and

- an organisation found guilty of corporate manslaughter (or corporate homicide) face an unlimited fine, and the courts will have the power to make remedial orders and publicity orders.

## CMCHA 2007 – A Detailed Examination

**5.4**   This section examines CMCHA 2007 in detail, with reference to MoJ guidelines. It also provides commentary on the new Act, and advice to employers, from legal experts in the field.

### The Offence

**5.5**   The offence is called corporate manslaughter in England, Wales and Northern Ireland, and corporate homicide in Scotland (CMCHA 2007 s 1(5)) and will apply to fatalities caused by gross management failings that occur after the new law comes into force on 6 April 2008.

An organisation is guilty of the offence of corporate manslaughter (or corporate homicide) if the way in which it manages or organises its activities causes a death and this amounts to a gross breach of a relevant duty of care it owed to the victim (CMCHA 2007 s 1(1)). (Relevant duties of care are set out in s 2 – see 5.9).

The MoJ guidance explains that:

'The offence is concerned with the way in which an organisation's activities were managed or organised. Under this test, courts will look at management systems and practices across the organisation, and whether an adequate standard of care was applied to the fatal activity.'

## The Senior Management Test

**5.6**     Although this test is not linked to a particular level of management – instead it considers how an activity was managed within the organisation as a whole – in order to be convicted of the offence, the way in which its activities are managed or organised by its senior management must be a substantial element in the breach (CMCHA 2007 s 1(3)).

Senior management is defined as the people who play a significant role in decision-making in how all, or a substantial part, of the activities are managed or organised; or actually managing or organising all, or a substantial part, of the activities (s 1(4)). Those in the direct chain of management as well as those in strategic or regulatory compliance roles are included in the definition.

The MoJ guidance provides further advice on this:

'These are the people who make significant decisions about the organisation, or substantial parts of it. This includes both those carrying out headquarters functions (for example, central financial or strategic roles or with central responsibility for, for example, health and safety) as well as those in senior operational management roles.

Exactly who is a member of an organisation's senior management will depend on the nature and scale of an organisation's activities. Apart from directors and similar senior management positions, roles likely to be under consideration include regional managers in national organisations and the managers of different operational divisions.'

The offence does not require individual failings by senior managers to be identified. It is sufficient to show that senior management collectively were not taking adequate care and that this was a substantial part of the failure.

The MoJ guidance also makes clear that the offence cannot be avoided by senior management delegating responsibility for health and safety, and inappropriately delegating health and safety matters will leave organisations vulnerable to a charge of corporate manslaughter or homicide. It will consider how responsibility was discharged at different levels of the organisation.

It advises:

'This does not mean that responsibility for managing health and safety cannot be made a matter across the management chain. However, senior management will need to ensure that they have adequate processes for health and safety and risk management in place and are implementing these.'

Here the guidance makes reference to the new guidance on directors' health and safety responsibilities produced by the Health and Safety Executive (HSE) and IoD *Leading health and safety at work – leadership actions for directors and board members* (INDG 417), which is examined in detail in CHAPTER 8.

Lissack says the term is "pretty broad. It doesn't stop at the door of the boardroom. It is aimed deliberately not just at the top end of the organisation, but covers both the formulation of policy and the putting of that policy into effect".

According to James Taylor, senior associate at the law firm Simmons and Simmons[1]:

'What comprises a substantial element will doubtless be the cause of some debate down the line. The Act defines a senior manager as someone who plays a significant role in either making decisions regarding management or actually managing the whole or a substantial part of the organisation's activities. It is a question of fact whether a role is significant or not and this is intended to capture a senior level of responsibility. However, this could lead to some interesting anomalies in the context of multi compartmented organisations. Take, for example, the warehouse managers of a company with two warehouses and a company with twenty. Each warehouse manager is probably doing an identical job, yet the manager in the smaller company would be considered a senior manager and the second one would not.'

And Leckie advises:

'... in order to secure a conviction, the Crown will be required to prove that there was a gross breach of a relevant duty of care and that the way the defendant company's activities were managed by its senior managers was a 'substantial' element in the breach. Organigrams, board and safety committee minutes, emails, internal memos and all other relevant communication will be vital evidence to prove this.'

Mark Tyler, partner at law firm Shook Hardy and Bacon International[2] advises that what is clear is that:

'... the new offence will not apply to deaths due primarily to the negligence of a co-worker or which come about for any reason that cannot be laid at the door of managers with confined-line management responsibilities'.

He predicts that:

'... one indirect effect of the Act will be to cause organisations to concentrate on exactly where safety management responsibilities lie, how they are delegated and monitored, and the provision of high-level training in safety management ... This all stems from the need to ensure that all those who could be classed as senior management personnel are in a position to control risks, and that the organisation can demonstrate the correct 'attitudes, policies and systems' should the need to defend itself ever arise'.

## Gross Breach

In order to amount to a 'gross' breach of duty of care, the conduct of the organisation must have fallen far below what can be reasonably expected in the circumstances (s 1(4)), reflecting the threshold for the common law offence of gross negligence manslaughter. According to Lissack, it is the first time that a statute is attempting to codify what is gross.

Taylor says:

'This test will doubtless develop a body of case law. One issue of concern to practitioners is the emphasis on health and safety guidance when considering a breach by the company. Currently, there are many tiers of health and safety guidance, including Approved Codes of Practice that have particular status when it comes to demonstrating what may have been "reasonably practicable". The Act does not distinguish between such types of guidance and a jury is entitled to consider any guidance (statutory or otherwise) by any authority that is responsible for health and safety enforcement. It is considered that instructing a jury as to what weight to attach to a particular publication will be one of the main arguable points in any corporate manslaughter trial.'

And Leckie points out:

'There will not be many prosecutions each year but some of those which are brought are likely to succeed because the new test is far easier for the Crown to meet. Where there is evidence of a "gross breach" which the prosecution can show falls far below what can reasonably be expected juries are likely to convict.'

(See also 5.15 which sets out the factors a jury must and may consider in deciding whether there has been a gross breach).

**Causation**

The way in which the organisation's activities were managed or organised must have caused the death. The usual principles of causation in criminal law apply – the management failure need not have been the sole cause of death; it need only be a cause. However, it must have made more than a minimal contribution to the death and an intervening act must not have broken the chain of events linking the management failure to the death. An intervening act will only break the chain of causation if it is extraordinary.

The MoJ guidance provides further guidance on causation. It advises that although it will not be necessary for the management failure to have been the sole cause of death, ' "but for" the management failure (including the substantial element attributable to senior management), the death would not have occurred'.

It also sets out that the law does not recognise very remote causes, and in some circumstances, an intervening act may mean that the management failure is not considered to have caused the death.

According to Taylor:

'It should be noted that no express modification is made to the principal of causation and this may continue to be a considerable hurdle in bringing a successful prosecution where multiple events and factors may have contributed to the fatality.'

(See also CHAPTER 4 which sets out case law developments in this area.)

[1] The views of James Taylor are quoted throughout this chapter with his permission. They are expressed in an article, 'Corporate Manslaughter: New Offence Aims to Overcome Current Identification Issues' which first appeared in the October 2006 issue of *Inhouse Lawyer*. It is also published on the Simmons and Simmons free online legal service Elexica at www.elexica.com.
[2] Mark Taylor's opinions are quoted throughout this chapter with his permission. His opinions are set out in an article, 'Corporate Killing: Letter of the Law', first published in the October 2007 issue of *Health and Safety at Work* magazine.

**Which Organisations does the Offence Apply to?**

**5.7**    The offence applies to:

• *corporations* – these are defined as any body corporate, whether incorporated in the United Kingdom or elsewhere. Companies incorporated under companies legislation, and bodies incorporated under statute (as is the case with many non-departmental public bodies and other bodies in the public sector) or by Royal Charter are all covered. But corporations sole[1] which cover a number of individual offices in England and Wales and Northern Ireland are specifically excluded (CMCHA 2007 s 25);

- *government departments and other bodies listed in Schedule 1* – these are Crown bodies which do not have a separate legal personality – s 11 (see 5.18) sets out that there is no Crown immunity under the Act;

- *police forces*; and

- *partnerships, trade union and employers' associations where these are employers* – partnerships within the Partnership Act 1890 and limited partnerships registered under the Limited Partnerships Act 1907 and similar firms and entities come within the scope of the Act (s 25).

(CMCHA 2007 s 1(2)).

The list of organisations to which the offence applies can be further extended by the Secretary of State, for example to further types of unincorporated association. This is subject to approval in both Houses of Parliament before it would come into effect (known as the affirmative resolution procedure) (s 21).

The MoJ guidance provides more guidance on how the offence will apply, or not apply, to organisations in a number of circumstances. It sets out that:

- a parent company cannot be convicted because of failures within a subsidiary: 'Companies within a group structure are all separate legal entities and therefore subject to the offence separately. In practice, the relevant duties of care that underpin the offence are more likely to be owed by a subsidiary than a parent';

- the new offence applies to foreign companies: 'the new offence applies to all companies and other corporate bodies operating in the UK, whether incorporated in the UK or abroad';

- where a company incorporated abroad is operating through a locally registered subsidiary, it is the subsidiary that is likely to be investigated and prosecuted;

- where sub-contractors are involved, whether a particular contractor could be liable for the new offence will firstly depend on whether they owed a relevant duty of care to the victim. The new offence will apply in respect of existing obligations on the main contractor and sub-contractors for the safety of worksites, employees and other workers they supervise;

- the offence applies to charities and voluntary organisations where these have been incorporated, as a company or as a charitable incorporated organisation under the Charities Act 2006, for example. It will also apply where a charity or voluntary organisation operates as any other form of organisation to which the offence applies, such as a partnership with employees;

Tyler says that organisations that are not corporations, particularly in the public sector, are facing a 'fundamental' change: 'These will, for the first time, face collective criminal responsibility for deaths and will be vulnerable to prosecutions for manslaughter'.

And Forlin predicts that in addition to prosecutions taking place in the more dangerous sectors of the economy, such as construction, manufacturing and quarrying, the FTSE 250 companies, and central and local government – particularly government bodies that previously had crown immunity – could well become some of the main targets for prosecutions.

¹   The 2000 report, *Reforming the law on involuntary manslaughter: The government's proposals*, provides the following definition of a corporation sole: '… a corporation constituted in a single person in right of some office or function, which grants that person a special legal capacity to act in certain ways. Examples include many Ministers of the Crown and government officers, for example the Secretary of State for Defence and the Public Trustee and a bishop (but not a Roman Catholic bishop), a vicar, archdeacon, and canon.'

## Fines

**5.8**    An organisation found guilty of corporate manslaughter is liable on conviction on indictment to an unlimited fine (CMCHA 2007 s 1(6)) and the court may also make a remedial order and publicity orders (see 5.16 and 5.17). The offence is triable in the Crown Court in England and Wales and the High Court of Justiciary in Scotland (s 1(7)), both of which involve trials by jury.

The Sentencing Guidelines Council is working on guidelines for courts, which are expected to be finalised by autumn 2008. Proposals for sentencing on corporate manslaughter were published in a consultation document by the Sentencing Advisory Panel (SAP) in November 2007. The proposals are examined in CHAPTER 6. The MoJ says it expects the courts to consider the factors taken into account in health and safety proceedings, that is whether the breach was with a view to profit, the degree of risk and the extent of the danger involved, the objective of achieving a safe environment for the public, and the need to bring that message home. It says there should be additional recognition that an organisation has been found guilty of a homicide offence. It refers to the lead case of *R v Howe and Co (Engineers) Ltd*¹ (for details of this case see CHAPTER 6).

The MoJ also says that in general, fines should reflect the relative size of the offender and the scale of the offence, and points out that the courts have been increasingly willing to impose severe penalties in very serious cases, giving the following examples (which are set out in more detail in CHAPTER 1):

- in 1999, Great Western Trains was fined £1.5 million following the 1997 fatal train crash at Southall;

- in 2003, Thames Trains was fined over £2 million and Network Rail £4 million following the 1999 fatal train crash at Ladbroke Grove;

- in 2005, Transco was fined £15 million following the fatal explosion in Larkhall in 1999; and

- in 2006, the highest ever fines against railway organisations were imposed following the fatal derailment of a train near Hatfield in 2000. Network Rail was fined £3.5million and, after appeal, Balfour Beatty's fine was reduced from £10 million to £7.5million.

The guidance says: 'In appropriate cases, fines on this scale, and even higher, are of the sort that we would expect to see for corporate manslaughter.'

Leckie's view is that '... fines will be significantly higher than those currently imposed under existing health and safety legislation and there is no doubt that, in certain cases, we will see multi million pound fines.'

But he adds: 'Without question, stigma and reputational damage will be the new law's biggest weapon. No organisation will want the opprobrium which will attach to a Corporate Manslaughter conviction or a Publicity Order.'

Taylor also believes that:

'One likely outcome of the new offence will be a distinction in the levels of fines between corporate manslaughter offences and offences under the HSWA with the greater fines that are currently being awarded for fatalities perhaps being reserved for corporate manslaughter convictions.'

But he too sees that the greatest effect of CMCHA 2007 will not, perhaps, be increased prosecutions and fines:

'... but the increased awareness that the potential stigma of manslaughter will create in corporate boardrooms and the calculation of insurance premiums. The potential reputational impact will have a significant effect on many aspects of a company's operations ranging from the level of its insurance premiums to its ability to hire staff and tender for work. It is hoped that this risk will encourage directors to reexamine their policies to make sure they are operating a safe system of work and that risks resulting from their operations are adequately assessed and controlled so that the spectre of fatal accidents need never arise.'

[1]    [1999] 1 All ER 249.

## The Meaning of 'Relevant Duty of Care'

**5.9**    The offence only applies where an organisation owed a duty of care, under the law of negligence, to the person who died, reflecting the common law offence of gross negligence manslaughter. CMCHA 2007 lists the following as a 'relevant duty of care':

- a duty owed to its employees or to other persons working for the organisation or performing services for it;

- a duty owed as occupier of premises;

- a duty owed in connection with—

   o   the supply by the organisation of goods or services (whether for payment or not);

   o   the carrying out by the organisation of any construction or maintenance operations;

   o   the carrying out by the organisation of any other activity on a commercial basis; or

   o   the use or keeping by the organisation of any plant, vehicle or other thing (CMCHA 2007 s 2(1)).

In addition, a relevant duty of care arises where the organisation is responsible for the safety of person in custody or detention (CMCHA 2007 s 2(1), (2)). Various forms of custody and detention are covered, including prisons, the custody area of courts and police stations, immigration detention facilities, prison escort arrangements, secure accommodation for children and young people; and detention under mental health legislation.

There is also provision for the categories of people to whom a duty of care is owed because they are in custody or detention to be extended by the Secretary of State. However, the application of the offence to deaths in custody will not come into effect on 6 April 2008, but at a later date. The government has indicated that this part of the legislation will be enacted within three to five years.

The explanatory notes to the Act give further guidance. The following are 'relevant' duties under CMCHA 2007:

- The duty to provide a safe system of work for employees. The breach of a duty owed to other people whose work the organisation controls or directs, but who are not formally employed, such as contractors, volunteers and secondees, can also trigger the offence.

- Duties to ensure that buildings the organisation occupies are kept in a safe condition.

- Duties owed by organisations to their customers, such as those owed by transport providers to their passengers and by retailers for the safety of their products. It also covers the supply of services by the public sector, such as NHS bodies providing medical treatment.

- The duty of care owed by public sector bodies to ensure that adequate safety precautions are taken, when repairing a road for example, even where duties do not arise because they are not supplying a service or operating commercially.

• The duty of care owed by organisations, such as farming and mining companies, for example, which are carrying out activities on a commercial basis, though not supplying goods and services.

The MoJ guidance explains that statutory duties owed under health and safety law are not 'relevant' duties for the new offence – only a duty of care owed in the law of negligence. It goes on to explain:

'In practice, there is a significant overlap between these types of duty. For example, employers have a responsibility for the safety of their employees under the law of negligence and under health and safety law (see for example section 2 of the Health and Safety at Work etc Act 1974 and article 4 of the Health and Safety at Work (Northern Ireland) Order 1978). Similarly, both statutory duties and common law duties will be owed to members of the public affected by the conduct of an organisation's activities.

The common law offence of gross negligence manslaughter in England and Wales and Northern Ireland is based on the duty of care in the law of negligence, and this has been carried forward to the new offence. In Scotland, the concepts of negligence and duty of care are familiar from the civil law.'

The offence applies where the duty of care owed under the common law of negligence has been superseded by statutory provision (including where this imposes strict liability). For example, the duty of care owed by an occupier, which is now owed under the Occupiers' Liability Acts 1957 and 1984 and the Defective Premises Act 1972 (CMCHA 2007 s 2(4)) is included.

The MoJ guidance sets out that in some cases where a person cannot be sued under the civil law of negligence, the new offence may still apply. For example, this would be the case where a 'no fault' scheme for damages has been introduced.

And the offence is not affected by common law rules precluding liability in the law of negligence where people are jointly engaged in a criminal enterprise ('ex turpi causa non oritur actio') – for example, where there is illegal employment – or because a person has accepted a risk of harm ('volenti non fit injuria') (CMCHA 2007 s 2(6)).

According to Tyler, this slight modification to civil law, whereby CMCHA 2007 disregards the rule that there is normally no duty owed to someone who voluntarily accepts a danger (as in certain sports or adventure activities), 'brings the Act into line with health and safety legislation which concentrates on risk reduction irrespective of whether or not the participants are aware of dangers or signed waivers accepting them'.

Whether a duty of care exists in a particular case is a matter of law for the judge to decide (CMCHA 2007 s 2(5)). Normally in criminal proceedings, questions of law are decided by the judge, whilst questions of fact, and the application of the law to the facts of the case, are for the jury, directed by the judge. However, because of the heavily legal nature of the tests relating to the existence of a duty of care in the law of negligence, CMCHA 2007 sets out that the judge will need to determine some facts, rather than the jury – for example, whether the person killed was an employee of the organisation.

Taylor advises:

'Ultimately the existence of the duty is a matter of law and will be for the judge to decide ... parent and group company structures receive no special status and the determining feature is simply whether a duty exists. If a parent company, as well its subsidiary, owes a duty to the victim, then there is no reason why it too may not be prosecuted where a gross management failure by its senior managers caused death.'

## Public Policy Decisions, Exclusively Public Functions and Statutory Inspections

**5.10**     Public policy decisions, exclusively public functions and statutory functions are excluded from the scope of the offence – any duty of care owed by a public authority in respect of these is not a 'relevant duty of care' (CMCHA 2007 s 3(1)–(3)).

Deaths alleged to have been caused by decisions of public authorities – the definition of which includes Government departments, local councils and other public bodies, are therefore outside the scope of the offence. This would include, for example, strategic decisions made by Health Care Trusts about the funding of particular treatments.

The MoJ guidance sets out that strategic funding decisions and other matters involving competing public interests are exempt, but decisions about how resources were managed are not.

An organisation will not be liable for a breach of any duty of care owed in respect of things done in the exercise of 'exclusively public functions', unless the organisation owes the duty in its capacity as an employer or as an occupier of premises.

Any organisation, not just Crown or other public bodies, performing that particular type of function is excluded, although this does not affect individual liability. These functions will continue to be subject to other forms of accountability such as independent investigations, public inquiries and the accountability of Ministers through Parliament.

Organisations with a duty of care owed in connection with the carrying out of statutory inspections, such as those carried out by health and safety enforcement authorities, will not be liable unless they owe duties as an employer or occupier of premises (CMCHA 2007 s 3(3)).

'Exclusively public functions' are those falling within the prerogative of the Crown, such as providing services in a civil emergency, and activities that require a statutory or prerogative basis and cannot be independently performed by private bodies, such as licensing drugs (CMCHA 2007 s 3(4)).

The MoJ guidance sets out that:

'This does not exempt an activity simply because statute provides an organisation with the power to carry it out (as is the case, for example, with legislation relating to NHS bodies and local authorities). Nor does it exempt an activity because it requires a licence (such as selling alcohol). Rather, the activity must be of a sort that cannot be independently performed by a private body. The type of activity involved must intrinsically require statutory or prerogative authority, such as licensing drugs or conducting international diplomacy.'

It also explains that private companies that carry out public functions are broadly in the same position as public bodies: 'Overall the Act is intended to ensure a broadly level playing field under the new offence for public and private sector bodies when they are in a comparable situation.'

## Military Activities

**5.11**    Certain military activities are exempt in respect of all categories of relevant duty of care (CMCHA 2007 s 4)).

These include peacekeeping operations, operations for dealing with terrorism, civil unrest or serious public disorder, in the course of which members of the armed forces come under attack or face the threat of attack or violent resistance; as well as activities preparing for or supporting these operations. The exemption extends to training involving hazardous activities, and to the activities carried out by members of the special forces.

## Policing and Law Enforcement

**5.12**    Reflecting the existing law of negligence, the police and other law enforcement bodies are exempt in respect of all categories of relevant duty of care, including those as an employer or occupier, with respect to the following circumstances:

- operations dealing with terrorism, civil unrest or serious disorder in which an authority's officers or employees come under attack or the threat of attack; or

- where the authority in question is preparing for or supporting such operations; or

- where it is carrying on training with respect to such operations (CMCHA 2007 s 5(1), (2)).

A wider range of policing and law enforcement activities are excluded from the offence where the pursuit of law enforcement activities has resulted in a fatality to a member of the public, but not in respect of the duty of care owed as an employer or occupier (CMCHA 2007 s 5(3)).

Decisions about and responses to emergency calls, the manner in which particular police operations are conducted, the way in which law enforcement and other coercive powers are exercised, measures taken to protect witnesses, and the arrest and detention of suspects are not, for example, covered by CMCHA 2007.

The exemption is not confined to police forces and extends to other bodies operating similar functions and to other law enforcement activity, such as action by the immigration authorities to arrest, detain, or deport an immigration offender. (Note however, that CMCHA 2007 does not have any bearing on the question of individual liability.)

### Emergencies and the Emergency Services

**5.13**   The offence does not apply to the emergency services when responding to emergencies (CMCHA 2007 s 6(1)). However, the emergency services still have duties as employers and occupiers, so must still provide a safe system of work for their employees and secure the safety of their premises.

Organisations to which the exemption applies are:

- English and Welsh fire and rescue authorities;

- a fire and rescue authority or joint fire and rescue board in Scotland;

- the Northern Ireland Fire and Rescue Service Board;

- any other organisation responding to an emergency either for one of the organisations listed above, or if not, otherwise than operating commercially;

- NHS bodies;

- an organisation providing ambulance services for a relevant NHS body or the Secretary of State or Welsh Ministers;

- an organisation providing services for the transport of organs, blood, equipment or personnel in pursuance of arrangements of the kind mentioned in the paragraph above;

- an organisation providing a rescue service (such as the Coastguard and the Royal National Lifeboat Institution (RNLI);

- the armed forces.

Emergency circumstances are defined as being life-threatening, or causing, or threatening to cause, serious injury or illness or serious harm to the environment or buildings or other property (CMCHA 2007 s 6(7)). Circumstances believed to be emergency circumstances are also covered (CMCHA 2007 s 6(8)).

Medical treatment, and decisions relating to this, other than those to establish the priority for treating patients, is not included in the exemption (CMCHA 2007 s 6(3), (4)). Nor does the exemption apply to duties that do not relate to the way in which a body responds to an emergency – so duties to maintain vehicles in a safe condition, for example, remain.

The MoJ guidance sets out that with regard to NHS trusts (including ambulance trusts) duties of care relating to medical treatment in an emergency, other than triage decisions (which determines the order in which injured people are treated), are not exempt.

## Child Protection and Probation Functions

**5.14**   The offence does not apply in relation to carrying out (or failing to carry out) statutory functions relating to child protection and probation (CMCHA 2007 s 7(1)).

This applies with regard to:

- Parts 4 and 5 of the Children Act 1989;
- Part 2 of the Children (Scotland) Act 1995; or
- Parts 5 and 6 of the Children (Northern Ireland) Order 1995, SI 1995/755.

And it applies to duties owed under:

- Chapter 1 of Part 1 of the Criminal Justice and Court Services Act 2000;
- section 27 of the Social Work (Scotland) Act 1968; or
- Article 4 of the Probation Board (Northern Ireland) Order 1982, SI 1982/713.

However, local authorities and probation services will be covered by the offence with respect to their responsibilities to employees, and as occupiers of premises.

## Factors for the Jury to Consider when Deciding if there has been a 'Gross' Breach

**5.15**   Where it has been established that an organisation owed a relevant duty of care to the victim and it falls to the jury to decide whether there was a gross breach of the duty, the jury must consider whether the evidence shows that the organisation failed to comply with health and safety legislation relating to the breach. If that is the case, it must look at how serious the failure was and how much of a risk of death it posed (CMCHA 2007 s 8(1), (2)).

The jury may also consider the wider context, including cultural issues within the organisation, such as attitudes and accepted practices that tolerated breaches, and it may consider any relevant health and safety guidance.

Health and safety guidance does not provide an authoritative statement of required standards and the jury is therefore not required to consider the extent to which this is not complied with. However, where breaches of relevant health and safety duties are established, health and safety guidance may assist a jury in considering how serious this was.

These factors are not exhaustive, and the jury can also have regard to any other matters they consider relevant (CMCHA 2007 s 8(4)).

The MoJ guidance sets out that relevant health and safety guidance includes statutory Approved Codes of Practice and other guidance published by regulatory authorities that enforce health and safety legislation.

It advises:

> 'Employers do not have to follow guidance and are free to take other action. But guidance from regulatory authorities may be helpful to a jury when considering the extent of any failures to comply with health and safety legislation and whether the organisation's conduct has fallen far below what could reasonably have been expected.'

And it advises companies that in addition to guidance from the HSE (and in Northern Ireland from the Health and Safety Executive Northern Ireland (HSENI)), and local authorities:

> 'There are specific regulatory bodies, and in some cases separate legislation too, for certain sectors of industry (for example, in the various transport sectors: rail, marine, air and roads) and for dealing with particular safety issues (such as food and environmental safety). Further information about the standards that apply in these circumstances should be obtained from the relevant regulatory authority.'

It goes on to say:

> 'Factors that might be considered will range from questions about the systems of work used by employees, their level of training and adequacy of equipment, to issues of immediate supervision and middle management, to questions about the organisation's strategic approach to health and safety and its arrangements for risk assessing, monitoring and auditing its processes.
>
> In doing so, the offence is concerned not just with formal systems for managing an activity within an organisation, but how in practice this was carried out.'

Lissack told delegates to the recent CCA conference that unwritten practice will now be admissible evidence to bring before a jury: 'Organisations with a culture of complacency, those who put profit or productivity before safety, those who turn a blind eye to policy on paper, corner cutters, the health and safety director who never comes to board meetings ...'

And he said the Act means that health and safety guidance is now massively more important.

Law company Martineau Johnson advises in its *Dealpoint* briefing (August 2007):

'... the principal effect of the Act is to shift the emphasis from the scrutinising the role of individual senior officers in the fatality to an assessment of the corporate safety culture and management of the company. It will therefore be important to be able to demonstrate not only that the company has appropriate safety systems in place but also that these are rigorously enforced.

All those involved in decision-making and management will need to be aware that responsibility for health and safety is an integral part of their functions and not a bolt-on that can be left entirely to specified health and safety officers. The company should consider whether their arrangements for health and safety need to be revised in light of the new offence, and may also wish to consider an appropriate awareness-raising campaign amongst those who fall within the definition of "senior management".'

Leckie comments:

'For the first time in health and safety legislation the question of safety culture is specifically addressed. In deciding whether a company is guilty of a gross breach, one of the factors for a jury to consider will be the "attitudes, policies, systems or accepted practices within the organisation that were likely to have encouraged any such failure or to have produced tolerance of it". Safety culture, or lack of it, will therefore become a key battleground at trial and defendant companies will need to establish that they did have in place a positive, trusting and open environment with effective lines of communication between management and workforce.'

And according to Tyler:

'We are likely to see attention focusing on how judges should appropriately direct juries to focus their attention on the evidence relating to management action (or inaction) to control risks, and not simply with the tragic loss of life. Some jurors, faced with a harrowing case, may otherwise find it hard not to infer the defendant must have, in the circumstances, "fallen far below" the standard reasonably expected'.

The advice from law firm Eversheds is:

'Rather than consider the knowledge and motives of senior managers, the risk of death from any failure to comply with legislation will be evaluated in the first instance. Attention will then be given to the attitudes, systems, policies and accepted practices within the organisation that may encourage or tolerate non-compliance with the legislation in order to ascertain how serious the failure was.'

## Remedial Orders

**5.16**    In addition to the power to impose an unlimited fine, an organisation convicted of corporate manslaughter or corporate homicide may also be issued with a remedial order by the court, requiring it to take specific steps to remedy the breach; any matter the court believes to have resulted from the breach and caused the death; and any deficiencies in the organisation's health and safety policies, systems or practices of which the breach appear to be an indication (CMCHA 2007 s 9(1)).

Remedial orders can only be made on an application by the prosecution specifying the terms of the proposed order and after consultation with the health and safety enforcement authority (such as the HSE, Office of Rail Regulation (ORR) or the Food Standards Agency (FSA) or local authority) and there is the opportunity for the convicted organisation to make representations in court (s 9(2), (3)).

The order must specify how long the organisation has to carry out the specified steps, and may require that evidence that the order has been complied with is given to the enforcement authority (s 9(4)). Failure to comply with the order is an offence and liable on conviction to an unlimited fine (s 9(5)). This will be the responsibility of the general prosecuting authorities (the Crown Prosecution Service in England and Wales, the Public Prosecution Service in Northern Ireland and the Procurator Fiscal in Scotland).

The MoJ guidance sets out that remedial orders will be used in relatively rare circumstances, since as Tyler points out below, regulators will have been able to use enforcement powers to address any dangerous practices long before a case comes to court.

Remedial orders are already available under HSWA 1974 s 42 for health and safety offences, but were not previously possible under a manslaughter conviction. However, it has not been used very often – according to the HSE, only five remedial orders have been issued since 1999. According to Tyler, in practice the power to issue them is redundant 'given that by the time matters come to court, defendants have either voluntarily corrected the breaches or have been forced to do so by enforcement notices'.

But other commentators have put forward a different view. For example, Lissack says remedial orders 'are far reaching indeed' and Forlin believes that the courts will use remedial orders. 'For example, they could be used to impose increased fines on companies if they do not comply with directions given to them', he said.

## Publicity Orders

**5.17**   CMCHA 2007 contains a new power to issue publicity orders, although these provisions are not due to come into force until autumn 2008 when supporting sentencing guidelines in England and Wales will be available. The Sentencing Advisory Panel issued a consultation paper (also covering the assessment of fines) with proposals for sentencing for corporate manslaughter in November 2007. Once these have been finalised they will pave the way for publicity orders to be brought into force. (The proposals are examined in CHAPTER 6).

The court, after consulting the enforcing authorities and listening to representations from the prosecution can also require that an organisation convicted of corporate manslaughter or corporate homicide publicises the fact that it has been convicted of the offence; and specify the particulars of the offence, the amount of any fine, and the terms of any remedial order (CMCHA 2007 s 10(1)).

Again the order must specify how long the organisation has to comply, and may require that evidence that the order has been complied is given to the enforcement authority (s 9(4)). Failure to comply with the order is an offence and liable on conviction to an unlimited fine (s 9(5)).

Tyler comments that: 'The power is left remarkably open in terms of the medium of publication and the cost to the defendant.' And Lissack says that publicity orders are very important. 'Death at work has become a part of working life and it is purely serendipitous as to whether it makes the news', he told delegates at the CCA conference. 'Publicity orders will require a company to publicise its failings'.

## Crown Bodies

**5.18**   Crown bodies are not immune from prosecution under CMCHA 2007 (s 11(1)). Crown bodies that are either bodies corporate or are listed in Sch 1 are subject to the offence. A Crown body is to be treated as owing the duties it would owe if it were a corporation that was not a servant or agent of the Crown (s 11(2)). Sections 11(3) and (4) deal with the technicality which means that civil servants in government departments are employed by the Crown rather than the government department they work in, ensuring that the activities and functions of government departments and other Crown bodies can be attributed to the relevant body. Similarly, s 11(5) ensures that the provisions apply to Northern Ireland department in the same way as they apply to bodies listed in Sch 1.

## The Armed Forces

**5.19**    A duty of care is owed to personnel in the armed forces – including the Royal Navy, army and air force – by the Ministry of Defence for the purposes of the offence (CMCHA 2007 s 12).

## Police Forces

**5.20**    Unlike police authorities, which are bodies corporate, police forces are not incorporated bodies. However under CMCHA 2007, a police force is treated as owing the duties of care it would owe if it were a body corporate (CMCHA 2007 s 13). Therefore, police officers, as well as police cadets and police trainees in Northern Ireland, and police officers seconded to the Serious Organised Crime Agency or the National Policing Improvement Agency are treated as the employees of the police force, or other organisation, for which they work and therefore owed the employer's duty of care.

## Partnerships

**5.21**    Partnerships which are not limited liability partnerships – the latter are corporate bodies and so covered by the offence – are not corporations and therefore do not have a distinct legal personality for the purpose of owing a duty of care in the law of negligence. However, in CMCHA 2007, partnerships are treated as though they owed the same duties of care as a corporate body for the purposes of the offence (s 14(1)). Any proceedings will be brought in the name of the partnership rather than any of its members and any fine imposed on conviction must be paid out of the funds of the partnership (s 14(2)).

The MoJ guidance explains further that this approach reflects that taken under other legislation, such as the Companies Act 2006 and means that partnerships will be dealt with in a similar manner to companies and other incorporated defendants.

And it sets out that it has taken a cautious approach in extending the offence to unincorporated associations, since it will represent a new extension of the criminal law to these organisations:

> 'Extending the offence to partnerships will ensure that an important range of employing organisations, already subject to health and safety law, is within the offence and that large firms are not excluded because they have chosen not to incorporate.'

In addition, CMCHA 2007 makes provision for the range of organisations covered by the offence to be extended by secondary legislation (s 21).

## Procedure, Evidence and Sentencing

**5.22**    Any statutory provision that applies in relation to criminal proceedings against a corporation also applies (unless an order made by the Secretary of State has prescribed any adaptations or modifications) to the organisations listed in Schedule 1 to CMCHA 2007 (see 5.29); police forces, partnerships, trade unions and employers' associations. This includes provisions in relation to procedure, evidence and sentencing (s 15).

An order made under section 15 is subject to the negative resolution procedure, which means that it would be laid before Parliament and become law, unless disapproved by Parliament (s 15(4)).

## Transfer of Functions

**5.23**   Where a death has occurred in connection with functions carried out by a government department, one of the bodies listed in CMCHA 2007 Sch 1, incorporated Crown bodies or police forces, and there has been a subsequent transfer of those functions within the public sector, prosecutions will be taken against the body with current responsibility for the relevant function. Where the function has been transferred out of the public sector (in the case of privatisation, for example) proceedings will be taken against the public organisation which last carried out the function (CMCHA 2007 s 16(1)–(3)).

However, in some circumstances it may be appropriate for liability to lie with a different body, for example, where a function transfers between government departments but there is no transfer of personnel. In this case, there is provision for the Secretary of State to make an order specifying that liability rests with a different body. Again an order made under this section is subject to the negative resolution procedure (see 5.22).

## Director of Public Prosecutions Consent for Proceedings

**5.24**   Consent of the Director of Public Prosecutions (DPP) is needed for proceedings for the offence of corporate manslaughter to be instituted. This applies in England, Wales and Northern Ireland. (In Scotland, all proceedings on indictment must already be instigated by the Lord Advocate (CMCHA 2007 s 17).

## No Individual Liability for Corporate Manslaughter or Corporate Homicide

**5.25**   There is no secondary liability for the offence. An individual cannot be guilty of aiding, abetting, counselling or procuring the commission of, or in Scotland of being art and part of, the offence (CMCHA 2007 s 18).

Many safety campaigners and trade unions were very disappointed that CMCHA 2007 does not contain a secondary offence against individuals.

As the Bill was making its way through Parliament, the T&G (now part of the general Unite union) pointed out:

'This Bill's greatest weakness is its complete failure to tackle individual liability. Organisations do not kill people – those who own and run them do. This Bill's failure to legislate for individual as well as corporate liability means that it will not be effective in stimulating the safety culture change required, nor will it deliver justice for those lives lost and damaged through negligence. An effective corporate manslaughter law must do two things – it must prevent fatal accidents by encouraging better management of health and safety; and it must ensure justice for the victims of negligence. In both cases, that requires that guilty individuals, as well as guilty organisations, are held to account under the law. Sadly, this Bill will not achieve this.'

But the MoJ guidance makes clear that although prosecutions will be brought against organisations and not specific individuals, individual directors, managers and employees may be called as witnesses and stand in the dock.

And an individual can still be directly liable for the offence of gross negligence manslaughter, culpable homicide, or health and safety offences. Tyler warns that the absence of an individual offence 'does not mean that directors and senior executives can breath a sign of relief: in practice prosecutors will target them in the same way they would have done before if they are suspected of having committed the offence of common-law manslaughter personally – that is, for gross negligence in the conduct of their management roles', and he goes on to say 'it will remain common for directors and other individuals to appear as co-defendants with their organisations; and, as individuals, they face the extra risk of imprisonment and disqualification from holding directorships.'

Forlin says he expects the Act to be eventually amended and enlarged in order to create an individual offence against those who have a secondary role in any gross management failure.

'More individuals than ever before are being investigated and prosecuted for manslaughter and health and safety offences, and I believe it is only a matter of time before the Act is amended to include a new individual offence carrying a maximum of 14 years imprisonment. There is massive pressure, not only from trade unions and safety campaigners, but also the press and MPs on this issue. Both the Select Committee which scrutinised the draft Bill and the Scottish Expert Group said that there should be an individual offence', he said. 'Senior management, middle management and advisors will all be vulnerable to prosecution if they are seen to have, in effect, aided or abetted the corporate offence'.

## Convictions under CMCHA 2007 and under Health and Safety Legislation

**5.26**   A conviction for corporate manslaughter does not preclude an organisation being convicted for health and safety offences on the same facts (CMCHA 2007 s 19) where this is required in the interests of justice. (An individual can also be convicted on a secondary basis for an offence under HSWA 1974 s 37). Lissack says that this section is important as directors can only be convicted under section 37 if the company is also convicted under the HSWA 1974. A corporate manslaughter conviction alone would mean that there would be no prosecution against a director, unless they were charged with manslaughter as an individual.

## Abolition of Liability of Corporations for Manslaughter at Common Law

**5.27**    The application of the common law offence of gross negligence manslaughter is abolished in relation to corporations, and any application it has to other organisations to which CMCHA 2007 s 1 applies, ie unincorporated associations to which the offence applies (s 20).

However, in Scotland, where the law on culpable homicide differs in certain respects from the law on gross negligence manslaughter, the common law will continue to be in force. The Procurator Fiscal will determine the appropriate charge in light of the circumstances of each individual case.

Where cases occur before 6 April 2008, the MoJ guidance sets out that s 27(4) allows for cases that occur wholly or partly before the new offence comes into force, and prosecutions in those cases will continue to be possible on the basis of existing common law.

## Extent and Territorial Application

**5.28**    CMCHA 2007 applies to England and Wales, Scotland and Northern Ireland, and also applies to other locations where criminal jurisdiction currently applies. For example, it would apply where a death occurred as a result of an incident involving a British ship (or aircraft or hovercraft) but the victim was not on board because they were shipwrecked and drowned.

The MoJ guidance sets out the key areas where the new offence will apply:

'The Act applies across the UK.

- The new offence can be prosecuted if the harm resulting in death occurs:

    o    in the UK

    o    in the UK's territorial waters (for example, in an incident involving commercial shipping or leisure craft)

    o    on a British ship, aircraft or hovercraft

    o    on an oil rig or other offshore installation already covered by UK criminal law.'

And it provides further guidance on jurisdiction:

' "Harm resulting in death" will typically be physical injury that is fatal, and in most cases the injury and death will occur at the same time and in the same location. However, in some cases death may occur some time after the injury or harm takes place. The courts will have jurisdiction in cases where the relevant harm was sustained in the UK, even if the death occurs abroad.'

In the case of fatalities related to ships, aircraft and hovercraft, the offence will apply where the death does not occur on board, as long as it relates to an on-board incident.

CMCHA 2007 does not apply to British companies responsible for deaths abroad. The harm leading to death must occur within the UK or one of the places described above.

The guidance points out that where a death occurs abroad, there are acute practical issues for investigators, since they will not have control over the crime scene or the gathering of evidence relating to the death, while the evidence will be a crucial part of the investigation.

## Schedule 1: List of Government Departments etc

**5.29**

- Assets Recovery Agency[1];

- Attorney-General's Office;

- Cabinet Office;

- Central Office of Information;

- Crown Office and Procurator Fiscal Service;

- Crown Prosecution Service;

- Department for Communities and Local Government;

- Department for Constitutional Affairs (including the Scotland Office and the Wales Office);

- Department for Culture, Media and Sport;

- Department for Education and Skills;

- Department for Environment, Food and Rural Affairs;

- Department for International Development;

- Department for Transport;

- Department for Work and Pensions;

- Department of Health;

- Department of Trade and Industry[2];

- Export Credits Guarantee Department;
- Foreign and Commonwealth Office;
- Forestry Commission;
- General Register Office for Scotland;
- Government Actuary's Department;
- Her Majesty's Land Registry;
- Her Majesty's Revenue and Customs;
- Her Majesty's Treasury;
- Home Office;
- Ministry of Defence;
- National Archives;
- National Archives of Scotland;
- National Audit Office;
- National Savings and Investments;
- National School of Government;
- Northern Ireland Audit Office;
- Northern Ireland Court Service;
- Northern Ireland Office;
- Office for the deputy Prime Minister;
- Office for National Statistics;
- Office of Her Majesty's Chief Inspector of Education and Training in Wales;
- Ordnance Survey;
- Privy Council Office;
- Public Prosecution Service for Northern Ireland;
- Registers of Scotland Executive Agency;
- Revenue and Customs Prosecutions Office;
- Royal Mint;
- Scottish Executive;
- Serious Fraud Office;
- Treasury Solicitor's Department;
- UK Trade and Investment;
- Welsh Assembly Government;

¹  'Assets Recovery Agency' prospectively repealed by the Serious Crime Act 2007
s 74(2)(g), Sch 8 Pt 7 para 178.
²  Now the Department for Business, Enterprise and Regulatory Reform (BERR).

In addition, the MoJ guidance sets out that the offence will also apply to Crown bodies that are incorporated, such as the Northern Ireland departments, Charity Commission, Office of Fair Trading and Postal Services Commission. And it explains that fatalities caused by Executive Agencies come within the scope of the offence. Executive Agencies come under the responsibility of a parent department, which are all covered by the offence.

The Schedule can be amended by an order made by the Secretary of State (CMCHA 2007 s 22).

## Investigation and Prosecution

**5.30**   CMCHA 2007 does not change the current responsibilities of the police to investigate, and the CPS in England and Wales, the Public Prosecution Service in Northern Ireland and the Procurator Fiscal in Scotland to prosecute, corporate manslaughter. The HSE and other health and safety authorities will also continue to use their expertise in investigations in order to look at whether there is liability under more specific legislation, and to provide advice and assistance to the police in investigating corporate manslaughter. The joint approach of the HSE and other enforcement authorities, the police and the CPS is set out in protocols on investigating work-related deaths:

• in England and Wales, the Work-Related Deaths Protocol – the National Liaison Committee on the Work-Related Deaths Protocol has also published an 'Investigators'guide' to improve consistency in its application;

• liaison in Northern Ireland is covered by a separate and broadly equivalent document, Investigation of Work-related Deaths: Northern Ireland Agreement for Liaison; and

• In Scotland, a Protocol on Work-Related Deaths was published in October 2006.

In addition, CMCHA 2007 does not change the role and powers of the independent accident investigation branches which investigate air, marine and rail accidents in order to establish the cause, independently of any criminal investigation.

Eversheds predicts

'The main impact that the Act is likely to have is in relation to the operation of investigations into workplace fatalities. The Health and Safety Executive is already under pressure to achieve more successful prosecutions. As a result, investigations into workplace deaths may be carried out in a more aggressive fashion with the new corporate manslaughter offence in mind.'

And according to Leckie:

'Once the new law comes into force most workplace fatalities will result in a joint Police/Health and Safety Executive corporate manslaughter investigation. If Government predictions are to be believed, such investigations will lead to corporate manslaughter prosecution in only a handful of cases. However, employers will still be subjected to the most demanding of challenges during the investigation stage, which can last for years. Police interviews of personnel, demands for documents, imaging of entire computer systems, adverse publicity and the many other aspects of such investigations will all take a heavy toll on management time and staff morale.'

CHAPTER 6 deals with the enforcement of health and safety law in more detail.

**5.31**

---

*Support for bereaved families*

The MoJ guidelines set out what bereaved families should expect from criminal justice agencies dealing with corporate manslaughter investigations and prosecutions.

In England and Wales, the Code of Practice for Victims of Crime sets out the services victims can expect to receive from criminal justice agencies. It requires a dedicated family liaison police officer to be assigned to bereaved relatives and provides a right to information, including notification.

Family members are entitled to make a personal statement about how a crime has affected them, which will become part of the case papers.

A pilot Victim Advocate Scheme is operating in a number of Crown Courts, allowing families an opportunity to present their family impact statement orally to the court, or to have this done on their behalf.

The CPS Victim Focus Scheme aims to ensure that prosecutors meet with families to explain the charging decision, and possibility of the prosecution reading out in court the impact statement. Family Liaison Officers should be able to provide further advice.

The HSE does not provide a family liaison function, but they and other regulatory bodies should follow the Code of Practice as far as possible when dealing with cases of work-related death that are not➡

---

pursued by the police as manslaughter investigations. Further information about HSE's policy towards victims can be found on the HSE website at www.hse.gov.uk.

In Scotland, the National Standards for Victims of Crime set out what standards victims can expect in their dealings with agencies and voluntary organisations in the criminal justice system.

The relevant Procurator Fiscal enquires into all sudden, suspicious, accidental, unexpected and unexplained deaths. The Victim Information and Advice Service, which is part of the Crown Office and Procurator Fiscal Service, provides a dedicated service to help bereaved next of kin through the criminal justice process by keeping them informed of key developments and identifying other organisations that can offer them practical and emotional support.

A victim statement scheme has been piloted in some parts of Scotland, giving the next of kin of victims of some crimes the right to make a written statement about the emotional, physical and financial impact the crime had on them. Information about the current availability of this scheme can be obtained from the Victim Information and Advice Service (VIA) (further details about local VIAs offices can be obtained from: Victim and Diversity Policy and Development Division, Crown Office, 25 Chambers Street, Edinburgh EH1 1LA; tel: 0131 247 2594.

The Police Service of Northern Ireland assigns specialist Family Liaison Officers to bereaved relatives in homicide cases to provide appropriate support and information about the investigation, and ensure that families are treated appropriately, professionally and with respect for their needs.

**5.32**

---

*Practical advice for employers*

Leckie advises employers:

- audit – now is a good time to conduct a comprehensive audit and review of your safety management system in its entirety;

- in particular, make sure that all of your procedures are properly documented and implemented by all levels of management and staff;

- risk assessment – this cannot be stressed enough. All activities must be risk assessed by a competent person;

- make sure that health and safety responsibilities are clear and in writing at all levels;

- look carefully at the actions of 'senior management'; ➡

- appoint a 'health and safety director' at Board level;
- keep careful records of all meetings where health and safety is on the agenda and make sure it is on the agenda;
- make sure that any action points are completed;
- constantly improve your safety culture – no culture is ever perfect;
- put in place an emergency action plan;
- reputational risk – make sure the PR situation is properly managed and controlled;
- accident investigations – make sure these are carefully managed with legal input. The written conclusions will be one of the prosecution's main exhibits;
- police investigations – have a plan in place for dealing with the police and HSE inspectors. Be aware of their powers;
- don't panic – CMCHA 2007 does not impose any new duties;
- keep up-to-date with the law – it changes constantly; and
- obtain legal advice at all times.

## Ministry of Justice Guidance

**5.33**   The MoJ has produced two guidance documents providing further information about CMCHA 2007 and its implementation.

A general introduction to CMCHA 2007 is provided in a leaflet, *Understanding the Corporate Manslaughter and Corporate Homicide Act 2007*, explaining how the new offence of corporate manslaughter/homicide works, and where it will apply. This is intended to provide fundamental information about the new legislation and is aimed at employers, senior managers and others looking for an overview of the law.

Detailed guidance on the implementation of CMCHA 2007 is provided in *Reforming corporate liability for work-related death: A guide to the Corporate Manslaughter and Corporate Homicide Act 2007*. This explains which organisations are covered, the sort of incident to which it applies, those that are exempt, and the test that will be applied by the court. It is aimed at those who need to know how the new Act will work in some detail, including health and safety managers and professionals.

This more detailed guidance is summarised and referred to throughout this chapter.

Both guides can be downloaded from the MoJ website at www.justice.gov.uk/guidance/manslaughteractguidance.htm, but hard copies of the guidance will not be issued.

## Health and Safety Executive Guidance

**5.34**   The HSE has guidance on CMCHA 2007 on its website at www.hse.gov.uk/corporatemanslaughter/index.htm in the form of Frequently Asked Questions. It also has links to relevant HSE and HSC publications.

# Health and Safety Enforcement and Penalties

## Overview

6.1

> The Corporate Manslaughter and Corporate Homicide Act 2007 does not change the current responsibilities of the police to investigate, and the Crown Prosecution Service (CPS) to prosecute, corporate manslaughter. Nor does it change the role and responsibilities of the Health and Safety Executive (HSE) and other health and safety authorities in investigating and enforcing health and safety laws, and assisting with police manslaughter investigations.
>
> This chapter sets out how breaches of health and safety law (particularly those involving work-related deaths) are investigated and prosecuted and the penalties available to the courts.
>
> It looks at who investigates breaches of health and safety law, describing the role of the HSE, environmental health officers (EHOs) in local authorities, (and local fire and rescue authorities with respect to the enforcement of the Regulatory Reform (Fire Safety) Order 2005, SI 2005/1541).
>
> In addition it:
>
> - describes the powers available to these authorities in carrying out their investigations;
>
> - outlines the HSE's enforcement policy;
>
> - sets out the role of the police and the CPS – and in Scotland, the Crown Office and the Procurator Fiscal Service (COPFS) – in investigating and taking prosecutions for manslaughter in the case of work-related deaths;
>
> - examines the joint protocol for investigating work-related deaths in England and Wales, *Work-related deaths: A protocol*➤

*for liaison* which has been drawn up by the HSE, Office of Rail Regulation (ORR), British Transport Police (BTP), Local Government Association (LGA), Association of Chief Police Officers (ACPO) and the CPS;

- looks at where criminal cases are heard;

- describes the penalties available to the courts where companies and individuals and convicted of health and safety breaches; and

- examines the Sentencing Advisory Panel (SAP) consultation document which contains proposals for sentencing for corporate manslaughter, which was published in November 2007. The final guidelines for judges are expected to be finalised by the Sentencing Guidelines Council by autumn 2008.

Finally, it looks at the debate around alternative sanctions for regulatory breaches, and the provisions of the Regulatory Enforcement and Sanctions Bill, which followed the Hampton review of business-related regulation and enforcement; and the Macrory review of penalties.

Where there are specific enforcement arrangements in particular industries and sectors of the economy these are referred to in the chapters dealing with those sectors.

## Who Enforces Health and Safety Law?

**6.2**   Breaking health and safety law is a criminal offence and therefore enforced by the State's enforcement agencies – mainly the HSE and local authority EHOs.

### Health and Safety Commission and Health and Safety Executive

**6.3**   The Health and Safety Commission (HSC) consists of a chairperson and nine other members who represent employers' organisations, trade union organisations, and other organisations such as local authorities and professional bodies.

Its duties are to take appropriate steps to secure the health, safety and welfare of those at work, to protect the public against risks to health and safety arising from work activities and to control the keeping and use of explosive, highly flammable and other dangerous substances. It is also responsible for carrying out or sponsoring research, promoting training and providing an information and advisory service. It keeps health and safety legislation under review and makes appropriate proposals for new or revised regulations, Approved Codes of Practice and Guidance.

The HSE is the main operational arm of the HSC and has day-to-day responsibility for the enforcement of health and safety legislation. It is divided into several inspectorates. The HSE also provides advice, guidance and information for employers on how to comply with health and safety law. Responsibility for the HSC and HSE lies with the Department for Work and Pensions (DWP).

## Environmental Health Officers (EHOs)

**6.4**    In addition, EHOs, employed by local authority environmental health departments are responsible for enforcing health and safety law in office, shop and warehouse type premises and in some cultural establishments and residential accommodation.

The Health and Safety (Enforcing Authority) Regulations 1998, SI 1998/494, set out which organisation has responsibility for enforcing safety in particular types of premises. This depends on the main activity being carried out:

The HSE regulates health and safety in medium and high-risk premises, including:

• factories and other manufacturing premises, including motor vehicle repair;

• chemical plants and refineries;

• construction;

• mines, quarries and landfill sites;

• farms, agriculture and forestry;

• hospitals, including nursing homes;

• local government, including their offices and facilities run by them;

• schools, colleges and universities;

• domestic gas installation, maintenance or repair;

• utilities, including power generation, water, and waste;

• fairgrounds;

• airports (except terminal buildings, car parks and office buildings);

• police and fire authorities; Crown bodies, including the Ministry of Defence;

• prisons;

• docks;

• nuclear installations;

• offshore gas and oil installations and associated activities, including pipe-laying; and

- barges, and diving support vessels.

Local authorities are responsible for enforcement in lower risk premises, including:

- shops and retailing, including market stalls, coin-operated launderettes, and mobile vendors;

- most office-based activities;

- some wholesale and retail warehouses;

- hotels, guest houses, hostels, caravan and camping sites, restaurants, public houses and other licensed premises;

- leisure and entertainment, including night clubs, cinemas, social clubs, circuses, sports facilities, health clubs, gyms, riding schools, racecourses, pleasure boat hire, motor-racing circuits, museums, theatres, art galleries and exhibition centres;

- places of worship and undertakers;

- animal care, including zoos, livery stables and kennels;

- therapeutic and beauty services, including massage, saunas, solariums, tattooing, skin and body piercing, and hairdressing;

- residential care homes; and

- privately run pre-school child care, e g nurseries.

**Fire and Rescue Authorities**

**6.5**    The local fire and rescue authority (LFRA) enforces fire safety in most workplaces, although the HSE is the enforcement authority for nuclear installations, Crown premises, construction sites and ships, and the local authority enforces fire safety in sports grounds and stands. Fire safety regulation was brought together under a single piece of legislation – the Regulatory Reform (Fire Safety) Order (Fire Safety Order) 2005, SI 2005/1541 (see CHAPTER 2).

The Order provides for the service of an alterations notice where there is a serious risk, or a change (or change of use) to the premises would constitute such a risk. This will specify that there is a risk, or specify what would constitute a risk if a change (or change of use) to the premises was made. When an alterations notice has been served, any change to the premises (including services, fittings or equipment) or use of the premises (including an increase in the quantities of dangerous substances which are present) must be notified to the enforcing authority.

Enforcement notices can also be served where there is non-compliance with the Fire Safety Order which specifies what should be done to remedy the failure within a certain period (of at least 28 days).

A prohibition notice can be served where there is serious risk and use of the premises should be prohibited or restricted. A prohibition may include directions as to the measures that need to be taken to remedy the situation.

Failure to comply with any requirement, prohibition or alterations notice or enforcement notice can result in a fine, or in some cases imprisonment of up to two years.

## Powers of Health and Safety Enforcing Authorities

**6.6**   HSE inspectors and EHOs have the power to:

- enter premises;

- inspect and investigate;

- take measurements, samples and photographs;

- require an area or machine to be left undisturbed;

- seize, render harmless or destroy dangerous items;

- obtain information; and

- take statements.

They also have the power to issue improvement and prohibition notices and can bring prosecutions against any person contravening a relevant statutory provision. In some cases they can revoke or suspend licenses.

### Improvement Notices

**6.7**   Improvement notices direct the employer to take certain actions or make improvements within a given time (not less than 21 days) when a health and safety law has been broken and is likely to be broken again. An employer can appeal to an employment tribunal, in which case the notice is suspended until the appeal is heard.

### Prohibition Notices

**6.8**   A prohibition notice is served where an activity carries an imminent danger or serious personal injury. It forbids the activity until the faults specified in the notice have been rectified. The notice may be deferred, in which case it will come into effect after a specified period. If an appeal is made, the notice remains in effect.

### Prosecutions

**6.9**   Enforcing authorities also have the power to take a prosecution (although not in Scotland – see 6.20).

Prosecutions can arise from non-compliance with an improvement or prohibition notice, or where an employer (or employee) has breached a statutory provision. For example, a prosecution could arise from an accident investigation if the inspector felt that a health and safety offence had been committed.

If an inspector decides to institute court proceedings against an employer, this could result in fines being imposed. The penalty for breaching health and safety law is normally a fine, but it is a breach of criminal law and, therefore, there is provision for prison sentences to be given in certain cases which involve contravening licences and prohibition notices, the illegal use of explosives and the disclosure of confidential information (see 6.24).

## HSC Enforcement Policy Statement

**6.10**    The HSC *Enforcement Policy Statement* (HSC 15) sets out specific criteria for deciding whether to investigate and prosecute breaches of health and safety law.

The policy applies to all Britain's enforcing authorities, including the HSE and all local authorities in England, Scotland and Wales. It makes clear to inspectors, employers, workers and the public what standards are expected when it comes to enforcing health and safety in the workplace.

### Approach to Enforcement

**6.11**    The HSC says that the approach to enforcing health and safety law should be:

- *Proportionate* – enforcing authorities should take account of how far the duty holder has fallen short of what the law requires and the extent of the risks to people arising from the breach. The requirement to control risks so far as is reasonably practicable means that unless there is a gross disproportion between the degree of risk and the cost (in money, time or trouble) in taking measures to avert the risk, the measures must be taken.

- *Targeted* – to activities giving rise to the most serious risks or hazards that are least well controlled. The policy statement also says that when inspectors issue improvement or prohibition notices; withdraw approvals; vary licence conditions or exemptions; issue formal cautions; or prosecute; enforcing authorities should ensure that a senior officer at board level is also notified.

- *Consistent* – in relation to advice given; the use of enforcement notices, and approvals; decisions on whether to prosecute; and in response to incidents. It advises that all enforcing authorities should have arrangements in place to promote consistency in the exercise of discretion, including effective arrangements for liaison with other enforcing authorities.

- *Transparent* – helping duty holders to understand what is (and what is not) expected of them – distinguishing between what is compulsory and what is advisory, and what they should expect from the enforcing authorities. Employees, their representatives, and victims or their families should also be kept informed.

- *Accountable* – Enforcing authorities must have policies against which they can be judged, and an effective, easily accessible mechanism for dealing with comments and handling complaints.

All enforcing authority inspectors are required to issue the HSC leaflet *What to expect when a health and safety inspector calls* (HSC 14) to those they visit (which is available from HSE Books). This sets out that:

- when inspectors offer information or advice, including any warning, they will explain what to do to comply with the law and why. Inspectors will, if asked, write to confirm any advice, and to distinguish legal requirements from best practice advice;

- where an improvement notice is served the inspector will discuss it and where possible resolve points of difference before serving it. The notice will say what needs to be done, why, and by when, and that in the inspector's opinion a breach of the law has been committed;

- where a prohibition notice is served, the inspector will explain why the prohibition is necessary.

## Enforcement Methods and Tools

**6.12**    The *Enforcement Policy Statement* describes the range of enforcement methods or tools that authorities can use:

- giving information and advice – both face-to-face and in writing – including warnings;

- serving improvement and prohibition notices;

- withdrawing approvals;

- varying licence conditions or exemptions;

- issuing formal cautions (in England and Wales); and

- taking prosecutions (or reporting to the Procurator Fiscal with a view to prosecution in Scotland (see 6.20).

The Statement sets out that improvement and prohibition notices and written advice can all be used in court proceedings. And it explains that a formal caution is a statement by an inspector, accepted in writing by the duty holder, that they have committed an offence for which there is a realistic prospect of conviction and is only used where a prosecution could be properly brought. It is not the same as a caution given under the Police and Criminal Evidence Act 1984 by an inspector before questioning a suspect about an alleged offence.

## Investigations

**6.13**   The *Enforcement Policy Statement* sets out the factors that are taken into account in making decisions about whether to investigate a workplace incident. These are:

- the severity and scale of potential or actual harm;

- the seriousness of any potential breach of the law;

- past health and safety performance;

- enforcement priorities;

- the practicality of achieving results; and

- the wider relevance, including serious public concern.

In the case of a reportable work-related death, the enforcing authorities should normally investigate. The exceptions to this are where it is an instance of adult trespass or apparent suicide on the railway, where the police will investigate and advise the HSE if necessary; or there are other specific reasons for not doing so. If this is the case the reasons should be recorded. (See *Work-related deaths – A protocol for liaison*, see 6.21).

## Prosecutions

**6.14**   A prosecution should normally take place in the following circumstances:

- a death has resulted from a breach of the law;

- the gravity of an alleged offence, together with the seriousness of any actual or potential harm, or the general record and approach of the offender warrants it;

- there has been reckless disregard of health and safety;

- there have been repeated breaches giving rise to significant risk, or persistent and significant poor compliance;

- work has been carried out without (or in serious non-compliance with) an appropriate licence or safety case;

- the standard of managing health and safety is far below what is required by health and safety law and is giving rise to significant risk;

- failure to comply with an improvement or prohibition notice; or repetition of a breach that was subject to a formal caution;

- false information has been wilfully supplied, or there has been intent to deceive, in relation to a matter which gives rise to significant risk; or

- inspectors have been intentionally obstructed from carrying out their duties. (If an inspector is assaulted, the enforcing authorities will seek police assistance for a prosecution.)

The Statement explains that health and safety sentencing guidelines regard death resulting from a criminal act as an aggravating feature of the offence. If there is sufficient evidence, such cases should be brought before the court, but there are occasions where a prosecution would not be in the public interest, depending on the nature of the breach and the circumstances of the death.

## Prosecution of Individuals

**6.15**   Enforcing authorities should identify and prosecute or recommend prosecution of individuals if it is warranted. They should consider the management chain and the role played by individual directors and managers, and take action against them where the offence was committed with their consent or connivance, or been attributable to neglect on their part. Where appropriate, directors should be disqualified under the Company Directors Disqualification Act 1986.

Very few directors have been disqualified as a result of health and safety offences, but this may change in the future. Following research carried out at the University of Warwick, which was only able to identify ten directors who had been disqualified for health and safety reasons between the date when the 1986 Act took effect and the end point of their study in 2005, the HSC has recognised the need for inspectors to seek greater use by the courts of director disqualification as a penalty, and new instructions on this matter have now been issued to inspectors (see CHAPTER 4).

## Crown Bodies

**6.16**   Although Crown bodies must comply with health and safety requirements, they are not subject to statutory enforcement of health and safety legislation and so cannot be prosecuted for health and safety offences (although this is not the case in relation to the Corporate Manslaughter and Corporate Homicide Act 2007 – see CHAPTER 5).

Instead, there are non-statutory arrangements which allow the HSE to issue non-statutory improvement and prohibition notices, and the censure of Crown bodies in circumstances where, but for Crown immunity, prosecution would have been justified (See CHAPTER 14.)

## Publicity

**6.17**   The names of all companies and individuals convicted of breaking health and safety law in the previous 12 months should be published annually, and information on these convictions, as well as on improvement and prohibition notices issued should be publicly available.

In addition, media attention should be drawn to factual information about charges laid before the courts, as long as this would not prejudice a fair trial, and consideration should be given to publicising convictions which draw attention to the need to comply with health and safety requirements, or deter the disregard of health and safety duties.

The *Enforcement Policy Statement* is available on the internet at www.gov.uk/pubns/hsc15.pdf and copies of the HSC's Enforcement Policy Statement (HSC15) are also available from HSE Books.

## Police

**6.18**    The police investigate crime in general, and recommend prosecution of offenders to the CPS, and they have a role in establishing the circumstances surrounding a work-related death in order to assist the inquest.

In the case of a work-related death, a CID officer should come to the scene of the death and undertake an 'initial assessment' of whether a full-scale manslaughter investigation should take place. If the officer decides against it, the case is referred to the relevant health and safety authority. An inspector from the enforcement authority should also have attended the scene of the death, in order to determine whether a health and safety offence has been committed. This inspector can refer the case back to the police if there is 'evidence that indicates that manslaughter may have been committed'.

Detective Chief Superintendent Mark Smith of the British Transport Police (BTP) explained to delegates at a Centre for Corporate Accountability (CCA) conference on corporate manslaughter, directors duties and safety enforcement in November 2007, that police investigations into a work-related death can have a considerable impact on an organisation.

In addition to a significant impact on business continuity, they can impact on individuals at all levels. Such investigations involved:

- forensic examination of the scene – this could involve remote scenes, such as a signal box, and the need to control a scene could close down a business for a length of time;
- the use of search warrants and production orders;
- seizure of material – the police often want original documentation, which can affect business activity;
- electronic evidence and digital storage – the police have the power, for example, to take hard drives away;
- interview of witnesses; and
- third party disclosure issues.

(The way the police and HSE work together when investigating work-related deaths is set out at 6.21).

## Crown Prosecution Service (CPS)

**6.19** The function of the CPS is to take over and conduct, on behalf of the Director of Public Prosecutions (DPP) most criminal proceedings in England and Wales. (The DPP is head of the CPS and a government appointed legal officer). (The work of the CPS does not extend to Scotland, where prosecutions are taken by the Procurator Fiscal. And in Northern Ireland, prosecutions are taken by the Public Prosecutions Service for Northern Ireland (PPS)).

The CPS is responsible for:

- advising the police on cases for possible prosecution;

- reviewing cases submitted by the police;

- where the decision is to prosecute, determining the charge in all but minor cases;

- preparing cases for court; and

- presenting cases in court.

When the police have completed their investigation they pass the evidence to the CPS. The CPS will then review the evidence to see what criminal offences may have been committed and, if so, by whom. The CPS is responsible for deciding whether or not there is enough police evidence to undertake a criminal prosecution for a general criminal offence like manslaughter both before, and in some cases after an inquest (see chapter 7), and whether or not a prosecution is in the public interest.

In any criminal case, the CPS reviews the evidence and applies two tests, referred to as the Full Code Test in the *Code for Crown Prosecutors.*

The first test is the Evidential Test, which requires the CPS to be satisfied that there is a realistic prospect of getting a conviction against any potential defendant. This does not require the CPS to be sure of getting a guilty verdict, nor is the degree of certainty of a conviction measured in percentage terms.

If the Evidential Test is passed, it must then consider the Public Interest Test, which is simply deciding whether it is in the public interest to proceed. Even when there is clear evidence that someone is guilty, it is not always in the public interest to prosecute a person or company.

(When other enforcing authorities are taking a decision as to whether to prosecute, they will also take account of the full test set down by the DPP in the *Code for Crown Prosecutors.* No prosecution may go ahead unless the prosecutor finds there is sufficient evidence to provide a realistic prospect of conviction, and decides that prosecution would be in the public interest.)

According to the Work-related deaths Protocol (see 6.21): 'The CPS should always take into account the consequences for the bereaved of the decision whether or not to prosecute, and of any views expressed by them.'

A decision not to prosecute can be challenged through judicial review, although this has only happened twice with regard to a work-related death, in the cases of Simon Jones (see CHAPTER 4) and Daniel Dennis. In December 2006 the High Court ordered the CPS to review its decision not to bring manslaughter charges against Daniel's employer. The 17-year-old was killed in his first week of work after falling through a skylight on the roof of a store. His family was supported in its efforts to have the case reviewed by the GMB, to which his father belonged. In October 2007, Gwent CPS announced that it would be charging his employer with manslaughter. The case was still ongoing as this book went to press.

## Crown Office and Procurator Fiscal

**6.20**   In Scotland, health and safety prosecutions must be made through the Procurator Fiscal office rather than being taken directly to court by HSE or other enforcing authority staff .This may be on the basis of a recommendation by an enforcing authority, although the Procurator Fiscal may investigate the circumstances and institute proceedings independently of an enforcing authority.

Before prosecutions can be instituted, the Procurator Fiscal must be satisfied that there is sufficient evidence and that prosecution is in the public interest. The decision as to proceedings is one for the prosecutor rather than the enforcing authority, although their views will be taken into account.

Responsibility for investigating sudden or suspicious deaths rests also with the Procurator Fiscal. The Procurator Fiscal is required to hold a Fatal Accident Inquiry into the circumstances of a death resulting from a work-related accident ie a death occurring in the course of employment, if the deceased was an employee, or while a person was engaged in their occupation, if the deceased was an employer or self-employed person. However, if a work-related death has resulted in a prosecution, it is unlikely that there will also be a Fatal Accident Inquiry.

An Inquiry may also be held where it appears to be in the public interest on the ground that the death was sudden, suspicious or unexplained, or has occurred in circumstances such as to give rise to serious public concern.

# Work-related Deaths – A Protocol for Liaison

**6.21**    Where a work-related death has occurred, a number of enforcement authorities will work together under an agreed protocol.

The latest version of the Protocol was published in 2003 and sets out agreement for joint working between the police, the HSE, CPS, the LGA and the BTP. It does not take into account co-operation and liaison with the Rail Accident Investigation Branch (RAIB), which had not come into being when the Protocol was written, and the Civil Aviation Authority (CAA) and the Maritime and Coastguard Agency (MCA) are not signatories to this Protocol, although they have agreed to abide by its principles.

It sets down principles for joint working in relation to work-related deaths in England and Wales where the HSE is the health and safety enforcing authority, particularly where manslaughter or corporate manslaughter may have been committed.

A work-related death is defined as a fatality resulting from an incident arising out of, or in connection with work, and will also apply where the victim suffers injuries that are likely to lead to death.

Its underlying principles are as follows:

• decisions concerning prosecution will based be on a sound investigation of the circumstances surrounding work-related deaths;

• there will usually be a joint investigation, with the police investigating where there is an indication of manslaughter (or another serious general criminal offence) and the HSE, local authority (or another enforcing authority if appropriate) investigating health and safety offences. If a joint investigation is not carried out, there will still be liaison and co-operation between investigators;

• the decision to prosecute will be co-ordinated, and made without undue delay;

• the bereaved and witnesses will be kept suitably informed; and

• the parties to the Protocol will maintain effective mechanisms for liaison.

The Protocol sets out in detail how the various agencies should work together when first arriving on the scene, in managing the investigation, and in making decisions about whether to prosecute, and whether the prosecution should be for manslaughter or health and safety offences. It also covers the disclosure of material, including how that material should be shared between different authorities, and it covers special investigations and public inquiries.

It sets out how prosecutions should be managed where the CPS and enforcing authorities are prosecuting offences arising from the same incident, and it sets out procedures where the police or the CPS have notified the coroner that a serious criminal offence arising out of a work-related death (other than a health and safety offence) has been charged (see CHAPTER 7).

*Work-related deaths: A protocol for liaison* (MISC491) (2003) is available from HSE Books or can be downloaded from the HSE website at www.hse.gov.uk/pubns/misc491.pdf.

## The Criminal Courts

**6.22**    A breach of criminal law like health and safety is prosecuted and brought before a court – the magistrates' court or the Crown Court. The charge must be proved 'beyond reasonable doubt' with the burden of proof lying with the prosecution.

Health and safety offences are usually brought before magistrates' courts, with those considered to be more serious going to the Crown Court. Appeals go to the High Court, then the Court of Appeal, and in some cases to the House of Lords and then the European Court of Justice (ECJ).

The magistrates' courts can impose fines of up to £20,000 for breaches of parts of the Health and Safety at Work etc Act 1974 (HSWA 1974), as a result of the Offshore Safety Act 1992, which as well as increasing the maximum amount of fine, also introduced the power to imprison to a maximum of two years (see 6.24 *Penalties*).

A 1999 Court of Appeal decision, in *R v F Howe and Sons (Engineers) Ltd*[1], said that fines being given for health and safety offences were too low. The judgment in the case said that fines must be high enough to make clear to managers and shareholders that they should provide a safe environment for workers and the public.

It said that while in general, fines should not bankrupt a company, some offences were so serious that the defendant should not be in business, and that penalties for a death at work should reflect public opinion about the unnecessary loss of life. Mr Justice Scott Baker said: 'Any fine should reflect not only the gravity of the offence, but also the means of the offender, and this applies just as much to corporate defendants as to any other'. However, the size of the company is not relevant to the standard of care expected of it.

The judge also said that magistrates' courts should consider whether the case should be heard at a higher court where stiffer penalties are available: 'magistrates should always think carefully before accepting jurisdiction in health and safety at work cases, where it is arguable that the fine may exceed the limit of their jurisdiction or where death or serious injury has resulted from the offence'.

He also said that failure to heed warnings, failure to comply with the general duties laid out in HSWA 1974, or deliberate breach of health and safety law in order to maximise profit, should be viewed particularly seriously.

1   [1999] IRLR 434.

## Company Officers

**6.23**     Although prosecutions are normally taken against a company, section 37 of HSWA 1974 allows prosecutions of directors, managers, company secretaries or similar company officers. This applies where an offence alleged against the company is considered to have been committed with the 'consent, connivance of, or to have been attributable to any neglect on the part of' any of those company officers (see CHAPTERS 4, 8).

## Penalties

**6.24**     HSWA 1974 s 33 (as amended) sets out the offences and maximum penalties under health and safety legislation.

When other types of criminal offences are sentenced, the court will be guided by a 'tariff', setting the appropriate level of penalty that should normally apply. There is no tariff in health and safety cases, and instead sentences are fixed on an individual basis for every case and are subject only to statutory ceilings as is set out below.

The court is obliged to take into account a guilty plea and to reduce the sentence according to how early in proceedings the defendant indicated this. The penalties under HSWA 1974 are as follows:

**Failing to comply with an improvement or prohibition notice, or a court remedy order:**

- lower court maximum £20,000 fine and/or 6 months' imprisonment; and

- higher court maximum unlimited fine and/or 2 years' imprisonment.

**Breach of sections 2 to 6 of HSWA 1974:**

- lower court maximum £20;000 fine; and

- higher court maximum unlimited fine.

**Other breaches of HSWA 1974, and breaches of relevant statutory provisions under the Act, which includes all the health and safety regulations:**

- lower court: maximum £5,000 fine; and

- higher court: maximum unlimited fine.

**Contravening licence requirements – these apply to nuclear installations, asbestos removal – or provisions relating to the storage and manufacture of explosives:**

- lower court: maximum £5,000 fine; and

- higher court: maximum unlimited fine and/or 2 years' imprisonment.

Some offences, such as failing to comply with a requirement of an inspector using his or her section 20 powers, or intentionally obstructing an inspector, are triable only in the magistrates' court:

- lower court: maximum £5,000 fine.

In *R v F Howe and Sons* (see 6.22) the court also set down guidance on factors and features to be taken into account when imposing fines:

- Relevant factors are the degree of risk and the extent of danger, the extent of the breach and whether it was an isolated incident or a continuing breach, the defendants resources and the effect of the fine on the business.

- Aggravating factors were set out as being: failure to heed warnings; deliberate breaches with a view to profit; and loss of life.

- Mitigating factors were set out as being: a good safety record; remedial action being taken, early admission of responsibility, and a guilty plea.

In *R v Colthrop Board Mill Ltd*[1], the Court of Appeal said that fines of £500,000 or more for breaches of health and safety law should not be restricted just to major public disasters.

In *R v Friskies Petcare (UK) Ltd*[2], the court provided guidance to the HSE and defendants about how they should prepare and present aggravating and mitigating factors to the court. In this case, an employee was electrocuted in a meat factory and the company had been fined £600,000 in the Crown Court for breaching section 2 of HSWA 1974 and regulation 3 of the Management of Health and Safety at Work Regulations 1999, SI 1999/3242. The company appealed and the fine was reduced to £250,000.

[1]  [2002] 2 Cr App R (S) 80.
[2]  [2000] 2 Cr App R(S) 401.

**Remedial Orders**

**6.25**    Under section 42 of HSWA 1974 a remedial order can be used where a person is convicted of breaching health and safety laws, and it appears to the court that they are in a position to remedy matters in respect of the offence. Remedial orders set out the steps the defendant must take to remedy these matters, together with the time for the order to be complied with.

Remedial orders have not been used very often – a spokesperson for the HSE says that only five remedial orders have been issued since 1999.

## Compensation Orders

**6.26** Magistrates and the Crown Courts can make an order requiring a convicted defendant to pay compensation for any personal injury, loss or damage resulting from the offence; although this power is more restricted if the injury, loss or damage was due to a road traffic accident. If the court does not make a compensation order when it has the power to do so, it must give reasons for its decision.

The maximum sum that can be awarded by magistrates is £5,000 in respect of each offence; but the Crown Court can order an unlimited sum to be paid as compensation. An order can also be made in favour of the relatives and dependants of a deceased person, for bereavement and funeral expenses.

With regard to health and safety cases, the HSE advises that compensation orders may be particularly appropriate where:

- the loss is relatively small and easily quantifiable;

- the injured party is in need of immediate financial help, for example with funeral or other expenses resulting from the offence.

## Community Orders

**6.27** Courts gained the power to make community orders in 2003 (for offences committed after 5 April 2005), although for most health and safety offence the court is likely to consider a fine to be a more appropriate sentence. However, community sentences have been used in relation to manslaughter cases. In September 2006, Gary Collier was given a three-year community probation order after he was found guilty of manslaughter by gross negligence of his two-year old daughter Crystal, after allowing an older child to drive a lorry which crushed her. He had been looking after both children at his business.

## Disqualification Orders

**6.28** The Company Directors Disqualification Act 1986, ss 1 and 2 provide for a disqualification order to be made where a director has been convicted for an indictable offence in connection with the management of a company (including a health and safety offence):

- lower court: maximum 5 years' disqualification;

- higher court: maximum 15 years' disqualification

Again, such orders have not been used very often (see 6.15).

## HSE Prosecutions and Notices Databases

**6.29**    The HSE's prosecutions database was launched in October 2000. It gives details of all successful prosecutions carried out by the HSE and names the convicted defendants. Cases subject to appeal are not published.

Cases involving the prosecution of individuals appear on the database for a period of five years and are then removed from the site (with cases against individuals under the age of 18 removed sooner).

Cases involving the prosecution of corporate bodies are removed from the prosecutions database after five years and placed in the Prosecutions History Database. Details of Crown Censures are available under 'Documents'.

The prosecutions database is accessible at www.hse.gov.uk/prosecutions.

The notices database gives details of all improvement and enforcement notices served by the HSE. Notices appear on the database for a period of five years at www.hse.gov.uk/notices

## Sentencing for corporate manslaughter

**6.30**    Under CMCHA 2007, there are three sanctions available to the court when sentencing for the offence of corporate manslaughter: an unlimited fine, a publicity order and a remedial order.

Proposals for sentencing for corporate manslaughter were set out in a consultation paper by the Sentencing Advisory Panel (SAP) in November 2007, and could mean that companies convicted of corporate manslaughter could face fines running into hundreds of millions of pounds, with fines based on average annual turnover.

The consultation paper looks at sentencing both for corporate manslaughter, and for breaches of health and safety law that result in death. The guidelines being developed will provide guidance for judges when passing sentence in court and are due to be finalised and issued by the Sentencing Guidelines Council in autumn 2008.

The consultation paper sets out that fines imposed on organisations after being convicted of the common law offence of gross negligence manslaughter (which will be abolished by the new Act) and offences under the Health and Safety at Work etc Act (HSWA) 1974 have been criticised as being too low.

Its view is that a fine for a conviction under the CMCHA 2007 should be set at a significantly higher level than for an offence under HSWA and proposes that for an offence of corporate manslaughter, committed by a first time offender pleading not guilty, the starting point should be 5 per cent of annual turnover averaged over the previous three years. Where there are significant mitigating or aggravating factors, this could be reduced to 2.5 per cent or increased to 10 per cent, or more for the worst cases.

With regard to an offence under HSWA 1974 involving death, it proposes a starting point of 2.5 per cent of average annual turnover, with a range of between 1 and 7.5 per cent depending on whether there are aggravating or mitigating factors.

The consultation paper sets out the following aggravating and mitigating factors:

## Aggravating factors increasing the level of harm

**6.31**

● More than one person killed as a result of the offence.

● In addition to death, serious injury caused to others.

## Aggravating factors affecting the degree of culpability

**6.32**

● Failure to act upon advice, cautions or warning from regulatory authorities.

● Failure to heed relevant concerns of employees or others.

● Carrying out operations without an appropriate licence.

● Action, or lack of action, prompted by financial or other inappropriate motives.

● Corporate culture encouraging or producing tolerance of breach of duty.

## Mitigating factor

**6.33**

● Breach due to employee acting outside authority or failing in duties.

## Offender mitigation

**6.34**

● Ready co-operation with authorities.

- Good previous safety record.

According to the TUC health and safety newsletter, *Risks*, the proposals could mean fines running into hundreds of millions of pounds for large companies convicted of corporate manslaughter:

> 'After the Hatfield train derailment that claimed four lives in 2000, health and safety convictions led to maintenance firm Balfour Beatty being fined £7.5 million and Network Rail £3.5 million. If it was fined 10% of its latest annual turnover, Balfour Beatty would have to pay up almost £200 million and Network Rail £600 million.'

The Panel points out that in the case of the record fine of £15 million against Transco, which followed a gas explosion that killed a family of four in their home in Larkhall, South Lanarkshire in December 1999, the fine represented less than 1 per cent of its annual turnover (or 5 per cent of its after-tax profits) and says: 'A fine expressed as a percentage of average annual turnover is designed to have an equal economic impact on all sizes of organisation, in order to reflect the seriousness of the offence even where the offender has large financial resources.'

The consultation paper is also seeking views as to whether it would be appropriate to set a minimum fine both for corporate manslaughter and offences under HSWA 1974 involving death, to ensure that the harm involved in such offences is properly reflected in the sentence, even where the offending company has a very low annual turnover.

The Centre for Corporate Accountability (CCA), has said that the proposed fines are inadequate when compared with fines for breaking competition law. It says: 'Organisations convicted of killing people should face the threat of far larger fines than those organisations who are found to have been involved in breaking European competition law – which currently attracts a maximum "administrative" fine of 10% of the annual global turnover of the organisation.'

The consultation paper also sets out proposals regarding publicity orders and remedial orders.

The Panel suggest that publicity orders could take the following forms:

- publication on television/radio and/or in a local/national/trade newspaper, including relevant broadcaster/newspaper websites;

- publication on the organisation's website and in its annual report, informing (potential) customers and those who might be interested in investing in the organisation;

- notice to shareholders; and

- letters to customers and/or suppliers of the organisation.

Although it will not be issuing detailed guidance on the extent of publicity, the SAP may set down minimum standards, such as requiring publication in the local media where the conviction involves a local organisation; but publication in national media where a large, national organisation is convicted. In both these cases, the SAP says a notice in relevant trade journals should be required, shareholders should be notified, and publication in the annual report should always be required.

On remedial orders, the proposals sets out that the order is rehabilitative rather than punitive, and is intended to provide an additional safeguard for a limited number of cases where the organisation has failed to respond to other interventions. In most cases, by the time the case has come to court, other enforcement action is likely to have been taken by the regulatory authorities. The Panel says that the costs of complying with an order should not be taken into account in setting the fine for the same offence.

The employers' organisation CBI was due to examine the proposals in mid-December before making its response, and the Construction Confederation will also be consulting its members before submitting a formal response. However, a spokesperson for the Confederation said he anticipated that there could be concern about fines based on turnover in a sector which traditionally has low margins. 'Turnover does not necessarily reflect ability to pay and there is a risk that fines based on turnover could be disproportionate', he said.

Trade unions, like the CWU, have indicated that they will be pushing for action to be taken against individual directors, including disqualification, following convictions for serious health and safety offences in connection with major injury and death.

Copies of the consultation paper are available from: Gareth Sweny, Sentencing Guidelines Secretariat, 4th floor, 8–10 Great George Street, London SW1P 3AE; www.sentencing-guidelines.gov.uk.

Responses to the consultation should be sent to Mrs Lesley Dix, Secretary to the Panel, at the Sentencing Guidelines Secretariat at the address above or email info@sentencing-guidelines.gsi.gov.uk by 7 February 2008.

Following the consultation, the Panel will submit its recommendations to the Sentencing Guidelines Council, which will draw up the final guidelines for judges.

## Alternative Sanctions – the Draft Regulatory Enforcement and Sanctions Bill

**6.35** The government's draft Regulatory Enforcement and Sanctions Bill would allow regulators to use alternative penalties. The draft Bill implements the recommendations of the Hampton review of regulation and enforcement, *Reducing administrative burdens: Effective inspection and enforcement*, published in 2005, and the Macrory review of penalties, *Regulatory justice: Making sanctions effective,* (November 2006). The 2005 Hampton Report found that penalty regimes are cumbersome and ineffective and recommended a comprehensive review of regulators' penalty regimes. The Minister for the Cabinet Office then commissioned Professor Richard Macrory to investigate the area and his report was accepted in full by the government.

The Bill is set out in two parts:

*Part 1* will establish the Local Better Regulation Office as a statutory corporation with statutory powers to promote better communication between local authorities, and between them and central government; and

*Part 2* will provide an 'extended sanctioning toolkit' for regulators, consisting of: monetary penalties, fixed and variable; discretionary requirements; cessation notices and enforcement undertakings. These sanctions would be used in combination with each other and alongside existing sanctions available to regulators.

The Bill will provide Ministers with delegated powers to 'draw down' appropriate sanctioning options for the regulators they have responsibility for through secondary legislation. This will be done once the regulator has been agreed as working to the Regulators' Compliance Code. The government is also separately consulting on a Statutory Code of Practice which will place statutory obligations on regulators.

## Fixed Monetary Penalties

**6.36**   These are relatively low fixed fines for low level, minor or multiple instances of non-compliance which would be imposed directly by a regulator without the involvement of the criminal courts.

The level of penalties would be predetermined by legislation and there would be a right of appeal.

The regulator would issue a penalty notice to the defaulter, which would include information on the circumstances of the alleged offence, state the consequences of non-payment, state the amount of the fixed penalty and how the penalty can be paid. Regulators would be able to impose late payment penalties and offer early payment discounts.

## Discretionary Requirements

**6.37**   These allow the regulator to require the defaulter to:

- pay a **variable monetary penalty** – this would be an appropriate level of penalty, applied to more serious offences and would take into account aggravating and mitigating circumstances;

- take such steps as the notice may specify, within a deadline, to make sure that the non-compliance does not continue or recur by issuing a **compliance notice**; and/or

- take such steps as the notice may specify, within a deadline, to restore the position, so far as possible, to what it would have been if the regulatory non-compliance had not happened by issuing a **restoration notice**.

## Cessation Notices

**6.38**    These are notices requiring that the activity giving rise to the non-compliance is ceased. They may be used with discretionary requirements and other sanctions and could be temporary or permanent.

## Preventative Notices

**6.39**    The government also asked for views on preventative notices which would require a defaulter to take steps where an offence is highly likely to occur and which presents a significant risk of serious harm to human health and the environment.

## Enforcement Undertakings

**6.40**    These are promises made by the defaulter to the regulator to take specific actions related to the non-compliance and would present an alternative to enforcement action. Regulators would be able to accept undertakings from defaulter in a formal way; monitor the compliance with those undertakings; and certify the completion of the undertakings.

The defaulter would be immune from prosecution or other sanction for that instance of regulatory non-compliance unless they fail to comply with the undertakings.

## Other Alternative Sanctions Proposed

**6.41**    In addition to providing alternative sanctions for regulators, there have also been calls for the criminal courts to have access to a wider range of penalties and sanctions.

Macrory said 'we can improve the effectiveness of criminal courts in dealing with regulatory non-compliance by having access to more imaginative sentencing options when dealing with businesses than the simple imposition of fines'.

His report recommended that the government should consider introducing restorative justice pilot schemes which could be used as a pre-court diversion, instead of a monetary administrative penalty; and within the criminal justice system – as both a pre- or post-sentencing option.

And he said it should consider introducing the following alternative sentencing in the criminal courts:

- profit orders – where the profits made from regulatory non-compliance are clear, the criminal courts have access to profit orders, requiring the payment of such profits, distinct from any fine that the court may impose;

- corporate rehabilitation orders – In sentencing a business for regulatory non-compliance, criminal courts have on application by the prosecutor, access to a corporate rehabilitation order (CRO) in addition to or in place of any fine that may be imposed;

- publicity orders – in sentencing a business for regulatory non-compliance, criminal courts have the power to impose a publicity order, in addition to or in place of any other sentence.

## Calls for Higher Penalties and Sanctions for Corporate Manslaughter Convictions

**6.42**   Within the Corporate Manslaughter and Corporate Homicide Act 2007 itself, there is provision for unlimited fines, remedial orders and publicity orders. But there have been calls for other sanctions to be imposed on companies convicted of corporate manslaughter.

The House of Commons Home Affairs and Work and Pensions Committees, which scrutinised the government's draft Corporate Manslaughter Bill (see CHAPTER 1), reported that suggestions for alternative corporate sanctions presented in evidence included:

- corporate probation orders or corporate death sentence (ie mandatory dissolution);

- naming and shaming organisations through the HSE's Public Register of Conviction and/or publicity in the media, by notice or in the company's annual report;

- confiscation of assets associated with the offending and prohibition of the corporation from business activities associated with the offending;

- cessation from any activity in the company or company branch until an acceptable plan of action is introduced or the revocation of any relevant licence or statutory authorisation allowing the organisation to undertake its respective business activity;

- equity fines to require an organisation to create shares up to a particular value which would either be taken by the government, or go into a victims' fund. Such fines would reduce the value of shares in a company;

- punitive damages to be paid to relatives of the victims. Section 130 of the Powers of Criminal Courts (Sentencing) Act 2000 allows the criminal courts to award compensation following conviction for an offence, but the Act only applies to an offender who is an individual, and therefore does not apply to organisations; also, the Committee heard evidence criticising the levels of compensation currently available, particularly where the victim was over 18 with no dependents; Eileen Dallaglio, whose daughter was killed in the Marchioness river disaster (see CHAPTER 1) received compensation totalling just £310.46[1];

- the power to order the seizure of dangerous or defective equipment prior to conviction or the forfeiture and destruction of such equipment after conviction;

- restorative justice mechanisms; and

- ensuring that conviction affects a company's Comprehensive Performance Assessment or leads to an Audit Commission inquiry.

The trade unions have also called for higher penalties in health and safety cases generally, and in corporate manslaughter cases particularly.

The Amicus section of the general Unite union says in its *Health and Safety Penalties and Sanctions Brief*, which was prepared in advance of the Bill gaining Royal Assent:

'... all current fines coming out of health and safety cases are too low. Recent cases taken by health and safety inspectors, under existing health and safety law, have seen fines in the region of only £100,000, where workers have been killed. No individual manslaughter or corporate manslaughter charges have been brought in these cases. This puts a very low value on loss of life, and many fines have been much lower than this.'

It goes on to say that corporate manslaughter must be millions of pounds rather than tens of thousands of pounds, pointing out that even a million pound fine may be a relatively small amount to a large organisation.

It points out that the Financial Services Authority can impose fines of up to 10 per cent of the gross turnover of a company for breaches of financial legislation, which it says might be closer to the appropriate level of fines for corporate manslaughter offences. It also supports the use of equity fines (see above).

However, the union recognises the problem of fining a public company, asking 'What is the point in Government money being paid back to the Government?' and arguing that it points to the need for other forms of sentencing, including:

- corporate probation – which would give the court the power to place conditions on an organisation, including setting periods of time during which the organisation must deliver identified, good health and safety practices. The court could require companies to employ additional safety advice, or train managers for example; and

- corporate community service orders – requiring organisations to provide health and safety services to workers or to the local community. This would mean putting something back into a community, or to families, or to workers, that have been affected by a workplace death or deaths.

[1]   House of Commons Home Affairs and Work and Pensions Committees Draft Corporate Manslaughter Bill, First Joint Report of Session 2005–06 Volume III, Q319.

**6.43**

---

*Corporation probation*

In its briefing paper prepared in November 2006 while the Bill was still progressing through Parliament, *Corporate Manslaughter and Corporate Homicide Bill: Impact on major rail disaster cases*, Thompsons solicitors set out how corporate probation could be used by the courts.

It explains that corporate probation is a supervision order imposed by a court on a company that has committed a criminal offence and can require a company and its officers and directors to alter their conduct in a particular way.

In the case of a company convicted of corporate manslaughter, the aim of any penalties imposed by the court will be to penalise the company for the offence, deter future offences and instigate a change in culture, procedure, organisation or activity so that such future deaths and injuries do not occur.

Under corporate probation a company would be placed under supervision of the court. The court would have the option, for example, of suspending half the fine pending satisfactory completion of the probationary period.

And it explains:

'The terms of the probation order might be that the company has to review its safety policy, its safety procedures, initiate a training programme for directors and senior management or others, require a reduction in accidents etc. If after completion of the probationary period the company has satisfied the terms of the order, that is the end of the matter. If the company fails to co-operate or comply, the suspended sentence could be invoked and further penalties could be imposed, including, if felt desirable, the disqualification of directors.'                                ➡

---

A probation order would probably involve the court appointing an expert or body such as the HSE to supervise the company and report back to the court, and the order and penalties would be recorded at Companies house, so details would be kept on the company's records.

Thompsons says this type of sentencing 'gives the court the power to set terms which will suit the companies own situation and achieve a positive change in the way in which the company operates. It provides a flexibility which other penalties do not and has as its objective, achieving a positive and long term change in company behaviour.'

The briefing sets out that corporate probation has been introduced in the USA and Canada:

In the USA, it can be imposed on corporations that commit criminal offences, with the main objective appearing to be forcing companies to pay restitution, preventing them from hiding assets or subverting payment of restitution. However, the US Sentencing Council gave courts the power to introduce 'any probationary conditions related to the nature and circumstances of the entire case and the purposes of sentencing'.

In Canada, the purpose is to improve occupational safety, and the introduction of corporate probation arose from the 1992 Westray Mine Disaster in which 26 people died. Prosecution of the company failed because of the need to identify a controlling mind or directing mind, similar to problems faced in similar UK prosecutions.

The Canadian law created a criminal code duty on '*every one who undertakes, or has the authority, to direct how another person does work or performs a task ... to take reasonable steps to prevent bodily harm to that person, or any other person, arising from that work or task*'.

And it provides for probation orders which could be useful in directly influencing the future conduct of organisations convicted of offences.

The briefing sets out that the optional probation conditions available include:

- 'making restitution;

- establishing policies, standards, and procedures to reduce the likelihood of subsequent offences (however, the court must first consider whether it would be more appropriate for another regulatory body to supervise the development of implementation of such policies, standards and procedures); ➡

- communicating those policies, standards, and procedures to its representatives;

- reporting to the court on the implementation of those policies, standards and procedures;

- identifying the senior officer responsible for compliance with those policies standards and procedures; and

- providing, in the manner specified by the court, the following information to the public, (i) the offence of which the organisation was convicted, (ii) the sentence imposed, and (iii) any measures taken by the organisation to reduce the likelihood of its committing further offences, and (iv) complying with any other reasonable conditions considered desirable by the court in preventing subsequent offences by the organisation or to remedy the harm caused by the offence.'

The report was published by the RMT rail union.

**6.44**

---

*Concern about enforcement agency resources*

In July 2007, the union representing HSE inspectors, Prospect, claimed that the 2006–07 statistics for work-related deaths, which showed an 11 per cent increase on the previous year, confirmed that HSE's reaction to its shrinking budget and reduced workforce has been to cut the amount of investigation and enforcement.

It said the HSE had lost more than 1000 posts since 2002, including 250 jobs since April 2006, and was facing a further 100 job losses in the remaining half of the 2007/08 financial year. It said the organisation was also facing a 15 per cent budget cut by 2011 to meet Treasury efficiency targets: the DWP, HSE's parent department, had accepted cuts of 15 per cent below the rate of inflation for the three years from 2008–11. If transferred to the HSE, the union says that this level of cuts would result in over 500 more job losses.

Steve Sumner, National Health and Safety Policy Advisor at the employers' organisation Local Government Employers (LGE) said that local authority inspectors will also require greater resources where they are involved in investigations that could lead to corporate manslaughter convictions.

# Chapter 7

# Inquests and Public Inquiries

## Overview

### 7.1

> This chapter looks at coroners' inquests (and their equivalent in Scotland – fatal accident inquires) which are held after there has been a work-related death:
>
> - it outlines when an inquest is held, the role of the inquest, the role of the coroner, the procedure at an inquest, the possible verdicts and what happens where manslaughter or health and safety investigations are also taking place; and
>
> - it examines the government's proposals for reforming the coroners system.
>
> It also looks at the system for holding public inquiries, explaining the different types of public inquiry that have been held and their purpose.

## Inquests

### 7.2

'Coroners have a vital task, giving certainty and re-assurance to bereaved people, and meeting the public interest by determining the facts of deaths which are reported to them. These deaths may be violent, or unnatural, or of unknown cause. The coroner, supported by his or her staff, will investigate these cases and conclude with a formal inquest. That will give an official finding of the facts, and can identify lessons for preventing future deaths.'

(From the foreword to *Coroners Reform: The Government's Draft Bill – Improving Death Investigation in England and Wales* (June 2006).)

**When is an Inquest Held?**

**7.3**    According to *Coroners Reform: The Government's Draft Bill – Improving Death Investigation in England and Wales*, in 2005 coroners in England and Wales were notified of some 230,000 deaths, representing nearly 45 per cent of all deaths, but only around 10 per cent of those reported result in an inquest.

Deaths in a disaster and work-related deaths are usually followed by an inquest as they are mandatory where there is reasonable cause to suspect a 'violent or unnatural death'.

A work-related death is one that takes place as a result of an incident at work or the result of other people carrying out their work. It covers:

• the death of a worker during (or after in the case of an industrial disease) the course of his or her employment;

• the death of a member of the public from work activities; and

• the death of a member of the public in an incident like a train crash.

Some deaths in road traffic incidents will also be work-related – for example, if an incident involved a commercial vehicle with defective brakes, or a driver had worked very long hours.

The Coroners Act 1988 requires that the inquest must be held in front of a jury, where:

• the death was caused by an accident, poisoning or disease, notice of which is required to be given under any Act to a government department, or to any inspector or other officer of a government department or to an inspector appointed under section 19 of the Health and Safety at Work etc Act 1974; or

• the death occurred in circumstances, the continuance or possible recurrence of which is prejudicial to the health or safety of the public or any section of the public (Coroners Act 1988 s 8(3)).

The Reporting of Injuries, Diseases and Dangerous Occurrences Regulations 1995, SI 1995/3163, (see CHAPTER 2) require that all work-related deaths are reported, and therefore there will be a jury in these cases.

**What is the Role of the Inquest?**

**7.4**    The inquest is not like an ordinary court of law – it is purely a fact-finding mission. The coroner is prohibited from deciding any issues of civil or criminal liability on the part of a named individual.

Its role is rather to:

• to find out the medical cause of death;

- to draw attention to the existence of circumstances which, if nothing is done, might lead to further deaths;

- to advance medical knowledge; and

- to preserve the legal interests of the deceased person's family or other interested parties.

The inquest will determine:

- who the deceased was and how, when and where they came by their death; and

- to find the information required to register the death, such as the cause of death.

## Who Conducts the Inquest?

**7.5**    The coroner presides over the inquest and is the State's official certifier of cause of death. Coroners are appointed by the local authority where the court is located and are people who have been solicitors, barristers and/or qualified medical practitioners for at least five years.

Coroners' officers are usually former police officers who are responsible for investigating on behalf of the coroner. This normally involves their taking written statements – 'depositions' – from witnesses, which are given to the coroner before the inquest.

The powers and duties of the coroners' office are set down in the Coroners Act 1988 and the Coroners Rules 1984, SI 1984/552.

The coroner is responsible for deciding on the scope or ambit of the inquest and must ensure that the relevant facts are fully and fairly investigated and are the subject of public scrutiny during the inquest hearing. *R v N Humberside & Scunthorpe Coroner, ex parte Jamieson*[2] established that it is for the coroner to decide what is relevant to the discharge of his statutory duty.

[1]    [1994] 3 All ER 972.

## Procedure at the Inquest

**7.6**    The coroner will begin the inquest and, in the case of a work-related death, swear in the jury and outline to them what their duties are. He or she will explain to the jury that they are there to establish the answer to the questions: who the person was, where they died, when they died and how they came by their death.

The coroner will also usually explain the Coroners Rules 1984, rr 36 and 42: that the inquest is not held to establish any criminal or civil liability and cannot blame anyone for the death; and that the coroner and/or the jury must not name anyone in delivering their verdict.

The coroner will then call the witnesses. A witness may either be asked to attend the inquest or receive a formal summons to do so. She/he will usually begin by questioning the witnesses and by taking them through the witness statement they will have given. There is then the opportunity for barristers representing any 'properly interested person' (such as the family of the deceased) to also question the witnesses.

The following people can question witnesses:

- a parent, child, spouse and any personal representative of the deceased;

- any beneficiary of an insurance policy issued on the life of the deceased;

- the life insurer;

- any person whose act or omission, or that of his agent or servant (including an employer) may in the opinion of the coroner have caused or contributed to the death;

- any person appointed by a trade union to which the deceased belonged (where the death was caused by an injury (or industrial disease) received during the course of their employment;

- an inspector appointed by, or representative of, an enforcement authority, or any person appointed by a government department to attend the inquest;

- the chief police officer; and

- any other properly interested person (in the opinion of the coroner).

In some cases, the coroner will warn the witnesses that they do not have to answer questions if they feel their answer might incriminate them in a criminal offence.

Once all the evidence has been heard, any barristers and/or legal representatives for 'properly interested persons' may request the opportunity to address the coroner on the law in relation to possible verdicts to leave to the jury. The jury will be asked to leave the court until the legal submissions have been made.

After all the witnesses have been questioned, the coroner sums up the evidence, but barristers do not have the right to sum up.

The coroner then addresses the jury on possible verdicts open to them and following this the coroner will address the court on the verdict or the jury will retire and consider their verdicts (see 7.7).

## Verdicts

**7.7**   The verdicts that can be left to a jury, if the evidence supports it, after a workplace death inquest are:

• unlawful killing – where a worker died as a result of conduct on the part of some individual considered to be 'grossly negligent';

• death due to industrial disease;

• accidental death – which covers a large range of situations, from a mishap to a death caused by conduct which would be considered to be negligent but is not so negligent that a verdict of unlawful killing is appropriate; or

• open verdict – when the evidence given does not disclose enough about how a worker died, eg there was no eyewitness.

If a verdict of unlawful killing is returned the case will be referred to the Crown Prosecution Service (CPS) for it to consider whether or not to prosecute for manslaughter. However, the CPS points out that the burden of proof for an unlawful killing verdict at an inquest is not the same as that for a criminal trial. The criminal standard requires that a jury is 'sure' while the civil standard requires that it is 'probable'.

If there is not a verdict of unlawful killing, the Health and Safety Executive (HSE) or local authority will decide whether or not to prosecute a company or individual for a health and safety offence.

Under rule 43 of the Coroners Rules 1984, after the verdict the coroner may announce that he or she will write to the person or authority that has the power to take action to prevent the recurrence of similar fatalities. This is often referred to as recommendations. The coroner is the only person entitled to make any comment in court after the verdict. The jury cannot make any recommendations, but they can write 'a narrative verdict' incorporating their concerns, as long as they do not criticise anyone in person.

According to Michael Appleby and Gerard Forlin in *A guide to health and safety prosecutions*[1], 'The trend nowadays in work-related incident inquests is for the jury to return a narrative verdict giving a detailed analysis of the circumstances of the death'.

The inquest ends with the coroner and jury signing a document (Form 22) – the inquisition – giving the result of the inquest. This records the answers to the questions: who the person was, where they died, when they died and how, ie the medical cause of death.

After the inquest, the coroner sends any details required by the registrar of deaths. She/he will also write to the relevant authorities under rule 43 if deemed appropriate.

An inquest verdict can be overturned or amended if it appears that the coroner has made an error in interpreting the law, by judicial review. This is a legal procedure where a judge can review decisions made by the coroner and decide whether they are appropriate and/or correct and held in the divisional court. Judicial reviews have been taken in cases where it was felt that there was insufficient inquiry into the death, or failure to call relevant witnesses. It must be done as soon as possible after the verdict has been given and within three months. It should be undertaken by a person with sufficient interest, e g the family of the deceased, or a person who might be charged with causing the death.

A verdict can also be overturned or amended if new evidence is found that was not available at the original inquest by applying to the Attorney-General for his permission (a process similar to a judicial review.

¹   Published by Thomas Telford (www.thomastelford.com/books).

## Inquests and other Investigations

**7.8**   Coroners are required to adjourn any inquest pending police investigations of any possible homicide charges (which includes manslaughter), and any inquest held after a trial cannot record a verdict inconsistent with the findings of the trial.

If a manslaughter investigation is taking place, a full inquest will be delayed until it has been concluded. If the CPS decides not to press any manslaughter charges, the inquest can take place.

If a prosecution does take place, the inquest will again be postponed until it has been completed and it is then up to the coroner to decide after the trial whether there will be an inquest. It is extremely unusual for there to be an inquest after trial.

If there is no manslaughter investigation, and instead the HSE is investigating the death with regard to health and safety offences, the inquest will take place prior to the HSE deciding whether or not to prosecute. This is usually three or four months after the death.

According to the campaign group, the Centre for Corporate Accountability (CCA) in its submission to the Constitutional Affairs Committee consultation on the Coroners Reform Draft Bill of June 2006 (see 7.9):

'While very few work related deaths lead to a manslaughter prosecution, increasingly the police and CPS do a lengthy investigation to determine whether manslaughter prosecution is warranted. HSE investigations into fatalities are also becoming more lengthy.'

As a result, many inquests do not take place until years after the death has occurred, partly due to the length of manslaughter investigations, but also because of a problem with a lack of capacity in the coroner's service.

Once a case is ready for the coroner, it can take many months for the inquest to be scheduled, and even then the date can then be postponed.

If there is a public inquiry, the inquest will usually await any inquiry (see 7.11).

As most work-related deaths do not result in a prosecution by the HSE or other regulatory body (65 per cent) and of those cases prosecuted, most result in a guilty plea by the company, there is usually no trial. The CCA has pointed out that for many families, the inquest is usually the only forum for them to hear about the circumstances surrounding the death of a relative or loved one at work.

The charity and campaign organisation Inquest, which provides advice for bereaved people and professionals on contentious deaths and their investigation has published a pack providing information on the inquest system: *Inquests – An information pack for families, friends and advisors.* It can be purchased for £10 from: Inquest, 89–93 Fonthill Road, London N4 3JH; www.inquest.org.uk (free download).

## Coroners Reform: The Government's Draft Bill

**7.9**    The government says that at present, the coroners system is 'fragmented, non-accountable, variable in its processes and its quality, ineffective in part, archaic in its statutory basis', and it put forward a Draft Bill to reform the system in June 2006. The *Coroners Reform: The Government's Draft Bill – Improving Death Investigation in England and Wales* (June 2006) was scheduled to begin its passage through Parliament in order to become an Act during the 2007/08 Parliamentary session. However, it was not included in the Queen's speech, which means that the reforms, while the government says it remains committed to them, have been delayed.

The Draft Bill sets out the following five key reforms to the coroners system.

1.   Bereaved people will have a clear legal standing in the investigation and processes, with new righs of appeal. There will be a coroners' charter setting out guidelines and standards to make clear what service they can expect, and to promote better understanding between them and the coroner and coroner's staff.

2.   A chief coroner, who will be accountable to Parliament through the Lord Chancellor, will provide national leadership, with the help of support staff and an advisory Coronial Council, and will be responsible for:

   •   developing national standards and guidance;

   •   supporting coroners and advising government; and

- considering appeals against coroners' decisions and responding to complaints.

3. Coroners will continue to operate as a local service, appointed and funded by local authorities, and supported by coroners' officers and other staff provided by the local police or local authority, and they will work closely with local heath authorities.

4. A service consisting of full-time coroners will be established, and there will be new powers for Ministers to determine the size and boundaries of coroners' areas to ensure effective operation and coordination with other statutory services.

5. The processes for coroners' investigations and inquests will be modernised, and coroners will be given new powers to obtain the evidence they need for investigations and to impose reporting restrictions in cases where no public interest would be served by the publicising the details.

In addition to the proposals in the Bill, the government says that it will also provide coroners with significant new medical expertise to help inform their decision making. There will be a new chief medical adviser to the coroner service who will advise on strategic medical issues, and each coroner will be funded to buy in medical support, in consultation with the local authority.

The Bill replaces the whole of the Coroners Act 1988, and although some of the clauses are a reworking of the 1988 Act using contemporary language, most are new, creating a governance structure and giving coroners powers aimed at improving the effectiveness of investigations.

The legislative changes proposed in the Bill are part of a package of reforms aimed at addressing some of the weaknesses in the present coroner system, identified in the 2003 reports of the Fundamental Review of Death Certification and Investigation, and the Shipman Inquiry (which looked at the failings allowing GP Harold Shipman to murder elderly patients).

## Scotland – Fatal Accident Inquiries

**7.10**   There is a different system in Scotland, where Fatal Accident Inquiries, conducted by a sherriff, take place rather than coroners' inquests and these are governed by the Fatal Accident and Sudden Deaths (Scotland) Act 1976.

The Law Society for Scotland explains that:

'The lower court in Scotland is the Sheriff Court. Each Sheriffdom (of which there are six) has a Sheriff Principal, with Sheriffs sitting in each main town. This court has both civil and criminal jurisdictions. Appeals in civil cases go first to the Sheriff Principal, or the Court of

Session, and then the House of Lords. Only the most serious criminal matters are outwith the Sheriff's jurisdiction. There is no appeal from Sheriff to Sheriff Principal in criminal cases, the appeal lies with the Court of Criminal Appeal.'

The decision as to whether an inquiry into a work-related death is held is taken by the head of the Procurator Fiscal Office, the Lord Advocate. Any death that appears suspicious, and this can include work-related deaths are investigated.

But according to the CCA, if the work-related death, involving an employee or a member of the public, has resulted in a prosecution, it is unlikely that there will be any Fatal Accident Inquiry. It says that when inquiries do take place, they tend to be more wide ranging than inquests.

Scottish law requires the sheriff to hear sufficient evidence to allow him to make a 'determination' on the 'cause or causes' of the death, whether there were any 'reasonable precautions' that could have been taken would have avoided that death, and whether there were any 'defects' in the system of work operating at the time. There is no jury and no verdict at Fatal Accident Inquiries.

## Public Inquiries

**7.11**　In cases involving multiple fatalities, a public inquiry may be held. In *Corporations and criminal responsibility*[1], Celia Wells set out that there are a number of different types of public inquiry, and they have a number of functions and purposes:

The main purpose of a public inquiry is to establish the facts, survey causes and identify any culpability, and there are two main types, technical investigations and judicial inquiries.

Technical investigations have to be held following certain types of accident. There are statutory systems for mandatory inquiries following rail, air and shipping accidents and these are often conducted in private by an inspector. In general, a report of the inquiry will be published.

Wells explains that in the case of judicial inquiries, many statutes which provide for mandatory technical inquiries also give discretion for a more formal investigation in the form of a public inquiry. For example, a Formal Investigation was ordered by the Minister of Transport under Merchant Shipping legislation following the sinking of the *Herald of Free Enterprise* which resulted in the Sheen Report 1987 (see CHAPTER 1); while a formal investigation was set up under the regulation of the Railways Act 1871 following the Kings Cross underground station fire, resulting in the Fennell Report 1988 (see CHAPTER 1).

Ad hoc inquiries have been set up where there is no specific provision for accident investigation. For example, after the Hillsborough football stadium disaster, the Home Secretary appointed Lord Justice Taylor to hold a public inquiry, which resulted in the 1990 Taylor Report (see CHAPTER 14). Earlier an inquiry into the 1985 Bradford Football Stadium Fire resulted in the 1986 Popplewell Inquiry.

Wells sets out that there is also a special type of discretionary judicial inquiry which has been set up under the Tribunals of Inquiry Act 1921. For example, the Cullen Inquiry set up after primary school children were killed in a shooting in Dunblane was established under this Act, and they have been subsequently used to examine child abuse in North Wales' children's homes and the events leading to the conviction of Dr Harold Shipman. This type of inquiry requires the authorisation of both Houses of Parliament that the matter is of urgent public importance and they are always chaired by a senior judge, with High Court powers being exercised.

In the case of the Laming Inquiry which was held into the Shipman murders of his elderly patients, the initial decision to hold a departmental rather than public judicial inquiry was successfully challenged in a judicial review.

Tribunals of Inquiry under the 1921 Act and many judicial inquiries set up under specific Acts of Parliament provide powers to compel witnesses, compel the production of documents, require evidence to be given on oath, whereas Departmental and discretionary inquiries do not.

Wells says:

'It can be difficult to predict the procedure which will be adopted since even the same type of inquiry may be conducted differently according to the circumstances, including the personal style of the judge'.

And she sets out that inquiries do not give rights to legal representation, cross-examination or of appeal:

'It is not a trial, with an allegation, or a statement of claim, with a burden of proof, and with a determination at the end that one side has made out the case. The inquiry itself is responsible for gathering evidence, questioning witnesses, and determining the progress and direction of the proceedings'.

The Health and Safety Commission may, with the consent of the Secretary of State, direct that a public inquiry be held under section 14 of the Health and Safety at Work etc Act 1974. Such an inquiry is held in accordance with the Health and Safety Inquiries (Procedures) Regulations 1975, and the purpose is to reveal the underlying causes and to learn lessons for the future.

The public inquiry into the Stockline explosion in Glasgow (see CHAPTER 12) will be the first to be held under the UK Inquiries Act 2005 in mainland Britain.

¹   Second edition (2001) Oxford University Press.

# Chapter 8

# Wider Corporate Accountability – Directors and Senior Managers

## Overview

### 8.1

The Corporate Manslaughter and Corporate Homicide Act 2007 does not contain any new duties – rather it changes the basis for manslaughter convictions against organisations.

Some safety campaigners and trade unions had wanted the Act to contain specific duties on directors with regard to health and safety, to make them more accountable, but this was rejected by the government. The Health and Safety Executive (HSE) and the Institute of Directors (IoD) have recently published guidance outlining directors' responsibilities on health and safety, but the TUC has said that it will continue to campaign for specific legal duties on employers.

This chapter:

- provides an outline of the current legal position with regard to directors' health and safety duties, using a briefing produced by the charity and campaign group, the Centre for Corporate Accountability (CCA);

- summarises the advice set out for directors, and their equivalents in the public and voluntary sectors, in HSE and IoD new guidance: *Leading health and safety at work – leadership actions for directors and board members* (INDG 417);

- outlines HSE guidance on reporting on health and safety in annual reports;

- refers to the HSE's voluntary web-based tools for measuring corporate performance on health and safety: the Corporate Health and Safety Performance Indicator (CHaPSI) and Health and Safety Performance Indicator; ➡

- outlines guidance for directors from the safety organisations Royal Society for the Prevention of Accidents (RoSPA) and the Institution of Occupational Safety and Health (IOSH);

- sets out trade union demands for specific legal duties for directors of companies with responsibility for health and safety, including an outline of the latest private members' bill, the Health and Safety (Directors Duties) Bill, which sought to introduce legislation in this area in 2005; and

- finally, looks at the wider context of corporate governance and corporate social responsibility.

## Directors' Duties – the Current Legal Situation

**8.2**

'Directors are responsible for how companies operate. It is directors who set a company's policy on health and safety, and it is they who decide how high health and safety is on the agenda in comparison with other matters. It is they who determine the resources, including management resources, which a company allocates to health and safety. It is they who decide how health and safety is monitored in the company, whether accidents are properly investigated and what preventative action is taken for the future …'

(Ross Cranston, QC, MP introducing a private members' Bill to require companies to appoint a director as the health and safety director; and to impose duties on this director and on other directors of companies in relation to health and safety (Hansard, 25 March 2003).)

The Corporate Manslaughter and Corporate Homicide Act 2007 does not impose new duties on directors, or amend company law, and under existing legislation, it is perhaps surprising to find, bearing in mind the quote above, that directors have no positive obligations to ensure that their companies are compliant with health and safety legislation, according to guidance in this area produced by the Centre for Corporate Accountability (CCA), which is campaigning for a change to the law (see 8.3 for a more detailed explanation of the legal position with regard to directors' duties).

**8.3**

*Centre for Corporate Accountability (CCA) guidance on directors' health and safety duties – the legal position*

In health and safety law, the general duties fall upon employers (or manufacturers, employees, suppliers, occupiers and so on). While duties are therefore placed on the company as the employer, general duties are not imposed on directors by health and safety law). ➡

However, the CCA guidance[1] on directors' duties says that ss 37 and 7 of the Health and Safety at Work etc Act 1974 (HSWA 1974) 'may impose some form of obligations on company directors.

*Section 37*

The guidance explains that s 37 allows company directors and other company officers to be prosecuted if an offence by the company has resulted from the directors' 'consent', 'connivance' or 'neglect':

> 'Where an offence under any of the relevant statutory provisions committed by a body corporate is proved to have been committed with the consent or connivance of, or to have been attributable to any neglect on the part of any director, manager, secretary or other similar officer of the body corporate or a person who was purporting to act in any such capacity, he as well as the body corporate shall be guilty of that offence and shall be liable to be proceeded against and punished accordingly.'

*Consenting* to an offence is where a person is aware that an offence is going on and agrees to it in some way (ie turning a blind eye or turning the other cheek of an individual).

*Conniving* in an offence is where two or more persons are aware that an offence is going on and do nothing about it (ie conniving together to perpetuate a risky situation and or a statutory breach).

The section does not impose any explicit duties on directors, but it does allow a prosecution to take place if particular conduct exists.

The guidance explains:

> '... the section does appear to impose an *implicit duty* that if a director is *aware* that an offence is being committed by the company, the director has a duty to stop it continuing. This is an implicit duty because although the section does not state it, a failure by a director to take action to stop his company omitting an offence, once s/he is aware of it, can result in him/her committing an offence. It should be noted that it is an offence by a director whether or not s/he is aware that the particular conduct in question is or is not an offence.'

*Neglect* – directors (and other company officers) can be prosecuted under s 37 for 'neglect' even though s 37 does not impose any legal duty for directors to do something, and ordinarily a person can only act with 'neglect' if there is a failure to comply with a legal duty imposed upon that person to do something; ie a risk is highlighted to a responsible director or manager, who thereafter neglects to take commensurate control actions.

However, the courts have stated that, for the purposes of this section, it is *not* necessary for a duty to be 'legal' in order for a ➡

prosecution to take place: any imposed duty – legal or not – is sufficient. Whether or not prosecution can take place for neglect depends on whether the company has imposed duties upon the director concerned.

Some 28 directors were prosecuted between 2002 and 2005, according to CCA figures, and most, if not all of these prosecutions related to offences under HSWA 1974 s 37. In addition, the HSE has recently changed its guidance to inspectors suggesting that consideration be given to prosecuting directors under s 37 (see 8.4).

*Section 7*

Section 7 of HSWA 1974 places a duty upon all 'employees' to 'take reasonable care for the health and safety of himself and of other persons who may be affected by his acts of omissions at work'. Technically it covers 'executive directors' – that is to say directors who are employed (through a contract of employment). However, it is unlikely that these duties extend to the conduct of the directors when they act as 'officers of the company' rather than 'employees'. Some lawyers also argue that the courts would not allow a prosecution of a director for a breach of section 7 as this would against the intention of Parliament (which intended directors to be prosecuted under section 37).

[1] See www.corporateaccountability.org/directors/duties/law.htm.

**8.4** However, there is no doubt that there is increasing attention being paid to the role of directors in health and safety.

According to RoSPA:

'In the decade it has taken to secure the introduction of the new offence of Corporate Manslaughter, there has been a growing focus on the health and safety responsibilities of directors and senior managers in all organisations. Increasingly health and safety is now accepted as a board level corporate performance issue, an important dimension of Corporate Social Responsibility on which organisations should report to their stakeholders. The Health and Safety Executive have continued to focus on the business benefits of effective health and safety management while continuing to bear down on poor performers. In future, in the event of accidents resulting in death, prosecution of organisations for the offence of corporate manslaughter cannot be ruled out. And where prosecutions are taken under health and safety law the enforcing authorities will also be looking to see if directors or senior managers can be prosecuted as well the organisation ... No business, however outstanding, can afford to delay reviewing their corporate governance of health and safety. Directors need to be able to show that they have taken all reasonable steps to manage risks, and have effective health and safety management systems in place, including arrangements for involving their workforce.'

In addition, Errol Taylor, Deputy Chief Executive at RoSPA drew attention to changes to the HSE's Enforcement Policy Statement, which he says have not been widely publicised, but which make clear that in future the HSE will always consider prosecuting directors when their companies are being dealt with under health and safety law (see CHAPTER 6).

'With revised guidance prepared jointly by the Institute of Directors and the HSE on the health and safety responsibilities of directors, it would be wise to expect more prosecutions against individuals, as well as organisations, under existing health and safety laws. Directors are clearly therefore much more under the health and safety spotlight than hitherto', commented Taylor. The IoD and HSE guidance (which has now been published) is examined in the following section.

## HSE and IoD Guidance on Directors' Responsibilities on Health and Safety

**8.5** The Health and Safety Commission (HSC) announced in May 2006 that it would not pursue the development of statutory duties for directors and would instead be publishing revised guidance.

In October 2007, the HSE and the IoD guidance on directors' responsibilities on health and safety, *Leading health and safety at work – leadership actions for directors and board members* (INDG 417) was launched. This guidance is summarised below.

It is addressed to directors (and their equivalents) of corporate bodies and organisations in the public and voluntary sectors – including governors, trustees and officers. In addition, the HSE has produced additional guidance for small businesses and major hazard industries (see below).

Although the guidance is not obligatory, the Corporate Manslaughter and Corporate Homicide Act 2007 requires a jury to consider any breaches of health and safety legislation and it can have regard to any health and safety guidance. In addition to other health and safety guidance, the HSE and IoD advise that this guidance could be a relevant consideration for a jury depending on the circumstances of the particular case.

The guidance sets out that directors can be personally liable for breaches of health and safety law, and that members of the board have both collective and individual responsibility for health and safety.

It advises that health and safety must be led by the board, and that health and safety must be included as a key business risk in board decisions, and sets out three essential principles which underpin the guidance:

**Strong and active leadership** – with visible, active commitment from the board; effective 'downward' communication systems and management structures; and the integration of good health and safety and business decisions;

**Worker involvement** – in promoting and achieving a safe and healthy workplace; effective 'upward' communication; and the provision of high quality training; and

**Assessment and review** – identifying and managing health and safety risks; accessing and following competent advice; and monitoring, reporting and reviewing performance.

The guidance then sets out what boards and board members are legally obliged to do – which it terms core actions; and it sets out ways of giving these core actions practical effect through good practice guidelines:

### Plan the Direction for Health and Safety

**8.6**     The guidance says that the board should set the direction for effective health and safety management and that board members need to establish a health and safety policy that is not just a document, but an integral part of the organisation's culture, values and performance standards.

In sentencing Barrow Borough Council for health and safety offences following the outbreak of Legionnaires' disease, which killed seven people, Mr Justice Burnton made the following remarks[1]:

'Health and safety, as we have heard, was not an agenda item for senior management. The result of that was that health and safety was not, and the necessary precautions were not, monitored by senior officers. There was a written policy on health and safety, which as a matter of drafting was a thing of, as I said, some beauty. If it had existed beyond its existence on paper, it would have very substantially mitigated the blameworthiness of those representing the Borough, so far as this outbreak is concerned. But there was no evidence that that policy existed otherwise than simply on paper.'

The guidance says that all board members should take the lead in ensuring that health and safety duties and benefits are communicated throughout the organisation, and that executive directors must develop policies to avoid health and safety problems and respond quickly where difficulties arise or new risks are introduced. Non-executives must ensure that health and safety is properly addressed.

---

[1]     *Report of the public meetings into the legionella outbreak in Barrow-in-Furness, August 2002*, HSE, 2007.

**Core actions**

* in agreeing a policy, boards must be aware of the significant risks faced by their organisation;

* the policy should set out the role of the board and that of individual board members in leading the health and safety of its organisation;

* it should require the board to 'own' and understand the key issues involved; and decide how best to communicate, promote and champion health and safety; and

* the health and safety policy should evolve over time, including when there is major organisational change such as restructuring or a significant acquisition.

**Good practice**

* health and safety should appear regularly on board meeting agendas;

* although the Chief Executive Officer (CEO) can give the clearest visibility of leadership, the board should consider naming a member as health and safety 'champion';

* a health and safety director on the board shows the issue is being taken seriously and that its strategic importance is understood;

* the board should set targets; and

* a non-executive director acting as scrutineer to ensure that there are robust processes to support boards facing significant health and safety risks.

Giving a presentation to the 2006 Health and Safety Lawyers Association (HSLA) conference, *Director responsibility for health and safety – new policy directions*, Professor Frank Wright, Professor of Law at Warwick School of Law pointed out that while 70 per cent of accidents are due to management failure:

'... one in 6 organisations fails to appoint an individual director to have responsibility for the management of health and safety, and that many boards do not collectively provide the necessary leadership to ensure that risks to health and safety are properly controlled.'

## Deliver Health and Safety

**8.7**    The guidance says that there must be an effective management system to ensure, so far as is reasonably practicable, the health and safety of employees, customers and members of the public.

**Core actions**

* members of the board must ensure that:

    ○    health and safety arrangements are adequately resourced;

○   they obtain competent health and safety advice;

○   health and safety is a factor when making senior management appointments;

○   risk assessments are carried out; and

○   employees or their representatives are involved in decisions that affect their health and safety;

• the board should consider the health and safety implications of introducing new processes, new working practices or new personnel, dedicating adequate resources and seeking advice where necessary;

• boardroom decisions must be made in the context of the organisation's health and safety policy and health and safety must be 'designed-in' when implementing change.

**Good practice**

• leadership is more effective if visible – board members should be seen on the 'shop floor' following all safety measures themselves and immediately addressing any breaches;

• procurement standards for goods, equipment and services should prevent the introduction of health and safety hazards;

• the health and safety arrangements of partners, key suppliers and contractors, should be assessed;

• a separate risk management or health and safety sub-committee, chaired by a senior executive, should ensure that key issues are addressed;

• health and safety training should be given to board members to promote understanding and knowledge of the key issues in the organisation;

• the guidance says that going beyond the legal duty to consult worker representatives and supporting worker involvement improves participation and helps prove the organisations commitment to health and safety.

**Monitor Health and Safety**

**8.8**      Management systems must allow the board to receive specific (e g incident-led) and routine reports on health and safety performance.

**Core actions**

The board should ensure that:

• preventive information, for example on, training and maintenance programmes, should be reported as well as incident data, such as accident and sickness absence rates;

- regular audits of the effectiveness of management structures and risk controls should be carried out;

- the impact of changes such as the introduction of new procedures, work processes or products, or any major health and safety failure, is reported to the board as soon as possible; and

- there are procedures to implement new and amended legal requirements and to consider other external developments and events.

**Good practice**

- sickness absence and workplace health monitoring to alert the board to underlying problems;

- collection of workplace health and safety data to allow the board to benchmark its performance against others in its sector;

- appraisals of senior managers to assess their contribution to health and safety performance;

- receipt of regular reports on the health and safety performance and actions of contractors by the board; and

- involving workers in monitoring to achieve greater support for health and safety.

## Review Health and Safety

**8.9**   A formal boardroom review of health and safety performance is essential to establish whether the health and safety principles outlined above have been embedded in the organisation.

**Core actions**

The board should review health and safety performance at least once a year and this should:

- examine whether the health and safety policy reflects the organisation's current priorities, plans and targets;

- examine whether risk management and other health and safety structures have been effectively reported to the board;

- report health and safety shortcomings, and the effect of all relevant board and management decisions;

- decide what measures are needed to address any weaknesses and monitor their implementation; and

- consider immediate reviews in the light of major shortcomings or events.

**Good Practice**

- report health and safety and wellbeing performance in annual reports to investors and stakeholders (see 8.13);

- extra 'shop floor' visits by board to gather information for the formal review; and

- celebration of good health and safety performance at central and local level.

## Auditing and Reporting

**8.10**    Larger public and private-sector organisations should have formal procedures for auditing and reporting health and safety performance.

The board should ensure that any audit is perceived as a positive management and boardroom tool.

It should have unrestricted access to both external and internal auditors, keeping their cost-effectiveness, independence and objectivity under review.

**8.11**

---

*Health and safety leadership checklist[1]*

- How do you demonstrate the board's commitment to health and safety?

- What do you do to ensure appropriate board-level review of health and safety?

- What have you done to ensure your organisation, at all levels including the board, receives competent health and safety advice?

- How are you ensuring all staff – including the board – are sufficiently trained and competent in their health and safety responsibilities?

- How confident are you that your workforce, particularly safety representatives, are consulted properly on health and safety matters, and that their concerns are reaching the appropriate level including, as necessary, the board?

- What systems are in place to ensure your organisation's risks are assessed, and that sensible control measures are established and maintained?

- How well do you know what is happening on the ground, and what audits or assessments are undertaken to inform you about what your organisation and contractors actually do?

- What information does the board receive regularly about health and safety, e g performance data and reports on injuries and work-related ill health?                                              ➡

---

- What targets have you set to improve health and safety and do you benchmark your performance against others in your sector or beyond?

- Where changes in working arrangements have significant implications for health and safety, how are these brought to the attention of the board?

1 *Leading health and safety at work – leadership actions for directors and board members* (INDG 417), HSE and IoD.

**8.12**    A list of key resources is provided in the guidance, which can be found at www.hse.gov.uk/leadership.

## HSC Guidance on Reporting on Health and Safety in Annual Reports

**8.13**    Although every company must have a health and safety policy by law, it is not currently a legal requirement that companies include health and safety in their annual reports. However, HSC guidance in this area sets out the minimum standards for what annual reports should say about health and safety. This includes:

- outlining the company's health and safety policy, significant risks faced by employees/others and the strategies and systems in place for controlling those risks;

- the company's health and safety goals/targets, which should be measurable and relate to the health and safety policy;

- details of progress towards achieving goals/targets;

- plans for the forthcoming period; and

- arrangements for consulting employees and involving safety representatives.

The report should also include data on the company's health and safety performance, including:

- the number of injuries, illnesses and dangerous occurrences, reportable under the Reporting of Injuries, Diseases and Dangerous Occurrences Regulations 1995, SI 1995/3163;

- details of any fatalities and remedial action taken;

- the number of physical or mental work-induced health problems reported for the first time during that period;

- the number of employee days lost through work-related illness or injury;

- the number of health and safety enforcement or prohibition notices served on the company, with brief details;

219

- the number and nature of health and safety convictions for the period in question, including fines imposed and remedial action taken; and

- the total cost to the company of work-related injuries and illness suffered by staff over the reporting period.

The guidance is available online at: www.hse.gov.uk/revital/annual.htm and from the HSE.

See also the IOSH guide on *Reporting performance* at www.iosh.co.uk/ technical (see 8.16).

## Corporate Health and Safety Performance Indicator

**8.14**    The HSE Corporate Health and Safety Performance Indicator (CHaSPI) is a voluntary, web-based tool to assist large organisations with over 250 employees (both public and private) to:

- measure the effectiveness of their internal controls over health and safety; and

- benchmark their performance against their own targets and the performance of their peers.

It asks a series of questions on, for example, health and safety management, occupational health risk management and sickness absence rates. A score out of 10 is then calculated. The overall results are made publicly available. It aims to encourage and help organisations to improve their health and safety and go beyond the legal minimum standards, and is also aimed at small and medium sized enterprises (SMEs), and includes a number of director leadership case studies.

CHaSPI can be found on the internet through HSE's website at: www.h-se.gov.uk. The full text of the case studies on director leadership on health and safety and previous case studies published in February and May 2005 can be accessed on the HSE website at: www.hse.gov.uk/ corporateresponsibility/casestudies.

In addition, a web-based tool to assist small-to-medium-sized enterprises (SMEs) track and assess how well they are managing their own health and safety performance, the Health and Safety Performance Indicator ('the indicator') can be accessed at: www.hspi.info-exchange.com. It was developed to help SMEs regularly assess their health and safety performance, for example from one year to the next. It is also intended to help companies tell their insurers how well they are managing health and safety so they can more accurately calculate insurance premiums based on individual performance.

# Other Guidance for Directors

## RoSPA Director Action on Safety and Health (DASH) Initiative

**8.15** This initiative aims to raise awareness of the need for effective board level and senior management leadership of health and safety management and create a clearer expectation that boards should set targets, review progress and report periodically on corporate health and safety performance, recognising the business benefits which high health and safety standards can contribute to commercial success. RoSPA believes that senior managers must lead health and safety management by personal example.

The following are all accessible on RoSPA's website at www.rospa.com:

- *DASH – Measuring and reporting on corporate health and safety performance – Towards best practice* (2001) – presents consensus and best practice advice on measuring and accounting for corporate health and safety performance. It takes account of responses and follow up interviews with 'key players' in relation to a series of questions raised in a consultation document issued by RoSPA in March 2000 as contribution to the HSE's strategic focus on board level leadership of health and safety management.

- *Targets for change* – follows on from DASH and explores good practice in setting corporate health and safety improvement targets.

- *GoPOP – Going public on performance* – encourages all organisations to report on their health and safety performance in an open and transparent way. GoPOP 'Going Public on Performance' is a corporate performance web portal.

- *Back to the floor (BTTF): Report and case studies*, by Dr Sara Lumley – looks at director involvement in workplace health and safety and good practice.

- *Partners in progress* – an initiative to involve high performing organisations in its membership to help shape the occupational safety and health agenda.

## IOSH Guidance

**8.16** IOSH has also produced guidance for directors. *Questioning performance: The director's essential guide to health, safety and the environment* by David Eves and the Rt Hon John Gummer aims to help senior people gain assurance and discharge their responsibilities properly by enabling them to ask the right questions, understand the answers and see that they and their board take the best decisions about managing health, safety and environmental risks. It explains what needs to be done to comply with the law and provides examples of best practice.

Other IOSH guides available (see: www.iosh.co.uk/technical) include: *Reporting performance, systems focus*; and *Business risk management*.

## Demands for Specific Legal Duties for Directors of Companies with Responsibility for Health and Safety

**8.17**   The government set out in its 2000 strategy document, *Revitalising Health and Safety*, that it would impose statutory duties on directors, and in 2004 a Work and Pensions Select Committee which examined the work of the HSC/E recommended that the government fulfil this promise to impose statutory duties on directors.

The government responded saying it had no immediate plans to legislate in this way, and that it believed there was an appropriate balance of legislative and voluntary responsibilities on directors for occupational health and safety, although it asked the HSC to 'undertake further evaluation to assess the effectiveness and progress of the current measures in place, legislative and voluntary, and to report its findings'.

The HSC confirmed in May 2006 that it would not pursue the development of statutory duties for directors, and instead revised guidance was published in October 2007 (see 8.5).

But safety campaigners and trade unions have said that they will continue to campaign for specific health and safety duties for directors so that senior officials can be held directly accountable for deaths that have occurred due to their gross negligence.

Mick Antoniw, a partner at Thompsons Solicitors said:

'After a ten-year battle at long last the families of the victims of corporate manslaughter, and the trade unions, have succeeded in achieving a law which will play a key part in improving health and safety and reducing deaths at work. The next part of the campaign is for legal duties to be imposed on directors of companies with responsibility for health and safety.'

The TUC and its affiliate unions want to see specific health and safety duties placed upon directors and senior managers. The Amicus section of the general Unite union points out that the duties under of HSWA 1974 s 2 concern employers as corporate entitities (see 8.3).

It is demanding a general health and safety duty on directors to take all reasonable steps to ensure health and safety, supported by more specific duties including the following:

- to ensure that health and safety risks arising from their organisations' activities are properly managed;

- to accept their responsibility, individually and collectively, to provide health and safety leadership;

- to ensure, individually and collectively, that all board decisions reflect its health and safety intentions as articulated in the health and safety policy statement;

- to recognise their role, individually and collectively, in engaging the active participation of workers in improving health and safety; and

- to ensure, individually and collectively, they are kept informed of and alert to relevant health and safety risk management issues.

Unite Amicus also says that current penalties under HSWA 1974 do not, in effect, provide for imprisonment. It is only breach of a licensing requirement or breach of a notice by an inspector that could lead to imprisonment. It wants to see this changed so that the sanction of imprisonment can be applied against directors for the most serious breaches.

The communications union CWU announced in November 2007 that it had been told by the Health and Safety Minister Lord MacKenzie: 'The issue of new legal health and safety duties for directors is still on the table and the ball is firmly in their court. If they don't deliver better behaviours and good practice in line with the newly published HSE/Institute of Directors guidance, then the government will look again at the case for further legislative change'.

**8.18**

---

*Health and Safety (Director Duties) Bill*

There have been attempts to introduce directors' duties through private members' Bills, most recently in January 2005 when Stephen Hepburn, MP for Jarrow, supported by the construction unions T&G (now part of Unite) and UCATT, put forward the Health and Safety (Director Duties) Bill, which sought to amend HSWA 1974 and the Companies Act 1985 in order to:

- place a general duty on all company directors to take all reasonable steps to ensure that the company acts in accordance with the obligations imposed on it by applicable law relating to health and safety;

- impose a duty on all companies, other than those that are defined as small or medium under the Companies Act 1985, to appoint one of its directors as the health and safety director and to put that person's name in their annual return;

- require the nominated health and safety director to take all reasonable steps to comply with the statutory duties set out in the Bill. These are outlined in detail below; and

- put legal obligations on the board to ensure that there are adequate arrangements to provide the nominated health and safety director with the information necessary to carry out his or her duties and to take into account the information provided by that nominated director. ➡

---

*General duty on all directors*

Clause 2 of the Bill set out a general duty on all company directors to take all reasonable steps to ensure that the company acts in accordance with the requirements of health and safety legislation – the key duty currently absent in law.

The Bill did not prescribe the 'reasonable steps' required, instead giving the HSC the power to draft an Approved Code of Practice that would set out the details of those steps.

*Nominated health and safety directors*

Clause 1 of the Bill required the nominated health and safety director to take all reasonable steps to comply with the duties laid out in the Bill. These duties are concerned with ensuring that the board of directors has all the appropriate information that will allow them to comply with health and safety law.

The specific duties are:

(a)    To inform the other directors not less than four times a year of:

- how the company's activities are affecting the health and safety of its employees and other persons not in the company's employment; and

- the adequacy of the measures taken by the company to ensure it complies with any law relating to health and safety and any further measures that may be necessary for this purpose.

(b)    To inform other directors promptly on:

- any significant health and safety failure by the company and the steps that have been taken, or will be necessary, to rectify it;

- details of any deaths, injuries or other incidents that the company has a duty to report under law;

- details of any notice served on the company or on one of its employees under relevant statutory provisions; and

- details of any proceedings brought against the company for an offence relating to health and safety or for any offence arising out of a death.

(c)    To inform the board on the health and safety implications of its decisions.

The Bill fell in March 2005.

# Health and Safety and Corporate Governance

**8.19**   In addition to health and safety legislation and guidance, the IoD and HSC guidance above states:

'For many organisations, health and safety is a corporate governance issue. The board should integrate health and safety into the main governance structures, including board subcommittees, such as risk, remuneration and audit.

The Turnbull guidance on the *Combined Code on Corporate Governance* requires listed companies to have robust systems of internal control, covering not just "narrow" financial risks but also risks relating to the environment, business reputation and health and safety.'

The Turnbull guidance is centred upon the financial aspects of a company, but is linked to corporate losses in the wider context, including health and safety. It requires organisations to establish a risk management strategy. The guidance was adopted by the London Stock Exchange and obliges listed companies to publish an annual risk management report as part of their annual reporting arrangements. Further details are available on the Institute of Chartered Accountants England and Wales (ICAEW) website at www.icaew.com

According to Lawrence Waterman, writing in the introduction to Tolley's *Health and Safety at Work Handbook 2007*:

'This has prompted many large businesses to adopt formal plan-do-check-act management systems to achieve the level of assurance required for directors to sign such reports.'

Guidance has also been produced for the public sector by the Audit Commission: *Worth the risk: An introduction to risk management and its benefits*; and by the Charities Commission: *Accounting reporting by charities: Statement of recommended practice*.

Waterman says:

'Across the public and private sectors, therefore, the development of corporate governance is linked to and integrated with risk management – all organisations are asked to identify what could blow them off course, resulting in a diminution of services, a loss of profitability, the development of an unsustainable approach to their work. Health and safety is an important part of the matrix of risks identified in any such exercise, and the management and control of the health and safety risks has become part of what the board of directors or trustees have to achieve and assure.'

A detailed examination of corporate governance in relation to health and safety can be found in *Managing risk – The health and safety contribution* by John Stevens, Lawrence Bamber and Elvis Cotena (www.tottelpublishing.com).

## Corporate Social Responsibility and the Companies Act 2006

**8.20**    Increased interest in the ethical behaviour of companies, including their health and safety practice, and many companies already produce an annual corporate responsibility or corporate social responsibility report, setting out how their performance with regard to their environmental impact, the way they treat their employees, social and community issues and so on, and many already include information about their health and safety performance in these reports.

The Companies Act 2006 came into force on 1 October 2007 (although not all its provisions have been enacted). It will affect all UK companies, and requires that they consider their impacts on the community, employees and the environment.

According to a briefing on the 2006 Act by the campaign groups Corporate Responsibility Coalition (CORE) and the Trade Justice Movement (TJM), *Act Now! A campaigner's guide to the Companies Act 2006,* two key sections highlight the links between a company's financial performance and its social and environmental impacts:

- **Section 172** on directors' duties sets out that company directors have a responsibility to consider their company's impacts on a range of social and environmental matters, recognising that violating social and environmental standards can present financial risks to the company. Case law will establish over time how the duty is applied in practice.

- **Section 417** on transparency requires that publicly listed UK companies, that is mainly those that are listed on the main market of the London Stock Exchange, produce an annual 'business review', including information about their social and environmental impacts where these may have a bearing on the financial performance of the company. The requirement for companies to produce a Business Review came into force in October 2007, and the government will review in 2009 how successful social and environmental reporting by companies has been.

The Core Coalition website is at www.corporate-responsibility.org.

# Chapter 9

# Construction

## Overview

### 9.1

> This chapter looks at work-related deaths in the construction sector, where the highest number of workers are killed.
>
> It also looks at views of how the Corporate Manslaughter and Corporate Homicide Act 2007 (CMCHA 2007) is likely to impact on the sector.
>
> It provides examples of cases involving corporate manslaughter convictions in the industry, together with examples of health and safety prosecutions in construction that have been highlighted by the Health and Safety Executive (HSE), and it sets out health and safety legislation applying specifically to construction: the Construction (Design and Management) Regulations 2007.
>
> Finally, it looks at action to address the high rate of fatalities in the industry, agreed by the Strategic Safety Forum which was convened by the Secretary of State for Work and Pensions (DWP) in September 2007.

## Fatalities in Construction

**9.2**     Although only around 7 per cent of the workforce is employed in the construction industry, a quarter of all worker fatalities occur there, and the Health and Safety Executive (HSE) says that this means that there is more than one death every week on Britain's building sites. And the number of fatalities is increasing – in 2006/07, 77 building workers were killed, an increase of 31 per cent on the previous year.

An HSE analysis of fatal accident statistics over the last 10 years show that falls from a height accounted for around half of all fatalities in the industry mainly involving roofs, ladders, scaffolds and raised platforms.

In 2006/07, there were 23 fatal injuries to workers in the construction industry due to falling from a height, and 19 of these were as a result of falling from a height of more than 2m. There were 16 fatalities due to being hit by a moving or falling object, and 10 from contact with electricity.

## Employer, Union and Legal Expert Views of CMCHA 2007

**9.3**      There are different views about what the impact of the Corporate Manslaughter and Corporate Homicide Act 2007 (CMCHA 2007) will be on the industry when it comes into effect on 6 April 2008. It has been welcomed by the employers' organisation the Construction Confederation, particularly its application to the public sector. It said:

'We welcome the Corporate Manslaughter Act as a useful addition to existing provision and a proportionate response which rightly focuses on joint responsibility rather than targeting individuals ...

'The decision to lift Crown immunity and extend the offence to cover the public sector is welcome in that it should encourage public sector clients to take into account a contractor's health and safety performance when awarding contracts.'

But the construction union UCATT said it:

'... was a severe disappointment for UCATT as it failed to include clauses which would have allowed the imprisonment of company directors, if their negligence had led to the death of a worker.

'Without such clauses ... UCATT have argued there will not be a step change in safety in the construction industry, the most dangerous industrial sector in Britain.'

But Sam Nichols, senior associate in the Construction and Engineering team at law firm Taylor Wessing says:

'I think the new law will make a difference. Although it does not introduce new legal duties for corporations – the offence is effectively a re-badging of existing obligations – fear of a prosecution and the ensuing publicity, damage to reputation and stigma this will bring will drive corporations to take their health and safety responsibilities seriously. Prosecutions under health and safety legislation are not generally publicised in the way that corporate manslaughter convictions will be.

'I don't expect there to be a flood of prosecutions. The intention is to name and shame a limited number of companies – the Home Office anticipates between 10 and 13 additional convictions a year – but some of these are likely to be construction companies. They have featured in high profile incidents including recent rail disasters.'

And although historically corporate manslaughter prosecutions have only been successful against sole traders and small companies, he predicts that:

'The new legislation should make it easier to prosecute medium-sized and large companies than under the common law, under which it is easier to show a "controlling mind" in small organisations. The yardstick now is shared responsibility among senior management, and there should be no reason why large companies cannot be prosecuted.'

However, he says that there are several grey areas which are relevant to the construction industry (and in general):

'There are likely to be problems defining the boundaries of senior management. For example, is a site manager a senior manager? The test is whether they manage a substantial part of the companies' activities, and could be relevant to the size of the company.

'Also in what circumstances is it legitimate to delegate health and safety responsibility to junior managers? If junior managers are not properly equipped to take on these responsibilities, the organisation will be potentially culpable.'

Nichols advises:

'Employers in construction would be advised to:

- Review the health and safety guidance in construction – particularly with regard to the Health and Safety at Work etc Act 1974 and the Construction (Design and Management) Regulations 2007;

- Establish what industry standards apply;

- Compare policy and procedure documents with what is actually happening in the organisation and ensure that procedures are being implemented;

- Evaluate and where necessary improve corporate culture regarding health and safety and ensure that there is an active process of review in place;

- Ensure that risk assessments are up to date;

- Critically, be clear about who senior management are and ensure that they are aware of their responsibilities. Under the new legislation it is senior management that is culpable;

- Make sure that senior managers are competent, and are allocated sufficient time and resources to enable them to exercise their health and safety responsibilities properly. They may need additional training;

- Carry out a board-level review of health and safety compliance; and

- Review insurance cover to ensure that it will meet the costs of defending a case (although the risk of the fines themselves are not likely to be insurable).'

# Health and Safety Prosecutions in the Construction Industry

**9.4**     Many construction companies have been prosecuted following fatalities in the industry under health and safety law (see 9.13). There have also been cases involving individual and corporate manslaughter convictions following work-related deaths in the industry, even though these are generally rare (see 9.5). As in other industries these have involved small companies and sole traders.

**9.5**     The following are examples of cases involving work-related deaths and corporate manslaughter or individual manslaughter convictions in the construction sector.

In August 2001 English Brothers Ltd pleaded guilty to the manslaughter of Bill Larkman, a gang foreman, who died in June 1999 when he fell more than eight metres through a fragile roof to his death. The company was fined £25,000.

Company proprietor Wayne Davies of A & E Buildings was sentenced to an 18-month custodial sentence for manslaughter in January 2006, following the death of Mark Jones, who was killed as a result of injuries he received when he fell from a 'home made' basket, suspended from the forks of a telehandler while installing a barn roof.

Lee Harper, managing director of Harper Building Contractors Ltd pleaded guilty to the manslaughter of employee Daryl Arnold and was jailed for 16 months. Daryl died while working on the roof of a warehouse.

These cases are set out in more detail in CHAPTERS 2, 4.

# Construction Health and Safety Legislation

**9.6**     Under CMCHA 2007, in considering whether there has been a 'gross' breach of a relevant duty of care (see CHAPTER 5) the jury must consider whether the evidence shows that the organisation failed to comply with health and safety legislation relating to the breach. If that is the case, it must look at how serious the failure was and how much of a risk of death it posed (s 8(1), (2)).

The jury may also consider the wider context, including cultural issues within the organisation, such as attitudes and accepted practices that tolerated breaches, and it may consider any relevant health and safety guidance.

In addition to CMCHA 2007 and the health and safety legislation that applies across different sectors, including the Health and Safety at Work etc Act 1974 (HSWA 1974) and the Management of Health and Safety at Work Regulations 1999, SI 1999/3242, (see CHAPTER 2) construction employers also need to know about the Construction (Design and Management) Regulations 2007, SI 2007/320, which came into effect in April 2007. SI 2007/320 is examined in detail below.

# Construction (Design and Management) Regulations 2007

**9.7**    In 2007, new legislation came into force in an attempt to address the high fatality rate in the industry.

The Construction (Design and Management) Regulations 2007, SI 2007/320, came into force in April 2007, consolidating and revising the main pieces of construction health and safety at work legislation: the Construction (Design and Management) Regulations 1994, SI 1994/3140, and the Construction (Health, Safety and Welfare) Regulations 1996, SI 1996/1592. There is now a single, simplified set of construction safety regulations.

The HSE says that SI 2007/320:

- clarify construction client responsibilities when they are exercising their influence over the health and safety standards on their projects;

- replace the role of planning supervisor in the Construction (Design and Management) Regulations 1994 with a new role of CDM co-ordinator; the co-ordinator acts as the client's key advisor on health and safety issues for the project,

- emphasise the importance of competence at **all** levels in securing health and safety, and simplify the assessment of competence;

- cut down on health and safety paperwork, which should be project-specific, relevant, proportionate to the risk, and help to manage the risk; and

- simplify when projects are notifiable and formal plans and appointments are required: if they will last more than 30 days or will involve more than 500 person days of construction work. Projects for a domestic client are not notifiable. Formal plans and appointments are only required for notifiable projects.

## Who is a Duty Holder?

**9.8**    SI 2007/320 sets out the duty holders under the regulations, and guidance from the HSE[1] explains that under SI 2007/320, these are as follows:

- **Clients** – A client is anyone having construction or building work carried out as part of their business. This could be an individual, partnership or company and includes property developers or management companies for domestic properties.

- **CDM co-ordinators** – A CDM co-ordinator has to be appointed to advise the client on projects that last more than 30 days or involve 500 person days of construction work. The CDM co-ordinator's role is to advise the client on health and safety issues during the design and planning phases of construction work.

- **Designers** – The term designer has a broad meaning and relates to the function performed, rather than the profession or job title. Designers are those who, as part of their work, prepare design drawings, specifications, bills of quantities and the specification of articles and substances. This could include architects, engineers and quantity surveyors.

- **Principal contractors** – A principal contractor has to be appointed for projects which last more than 30 days or involve 500 person days of construction work. The principal contractor's role is to plan, manage and co-ordinate health and safety while construction work is being undertaken. The principal contractor is usually the main or managing contractor for the work.

- **Contractors** – A contractor is a business who is involved in construction, alteration, maintenance or demolition work. This could involve building, civil engineering, mechanical, electrical, demolition and maintenance companies, partnerships and the self-employed.

- **Workers**—A worker is anyone who carries out work during the construction, alteration, maintenance or demoliton of a building or structure. A worker could be, for example, a plumber, electrician, scaffolder, painter, decorator, steel erector, as well as those supervising the work, such as foreman and chargehands.

[1]   See www.hse.gov.uk/construction/cdm/summary.htm.

## The CDM Regulations in Detail

**9.9**   SI 2007/320 is divided into five parts:

- Part 1 deals with the application of the regulations and definitions;

- Part 2 covers general duties that apply to **all** construction projects;

- Part 3 contains additional duties that **only** apply to notifiable construction projects, ie those lasting more that 30 days or involving more than 500 person days of construction work;

- Part 4 contains practical requirements that apply to **all** construction sites; and

- Part 5 contains the transitional arrangements and revocations.

A summary of the main requirements under the regulations is provided below.

*Part 2: General management duties applying to construction projects*

**9.10**   Regulation 4 requires that CDM co-ordinators, designers, principal contractors, contractors and workers must be competent, or in the case of workers, under the supervision of a competent person, to perform any requirement and avoid contravening any prohibition imposed by the relevent statutory provisions.

Every person involved in a project and placed under a duty by the regulations must co-operate with others working on the same or an adjoining site as far as is necessary to perform any duty or function under the regulations. Those working under the control of another person must report anything he or she is aware of that could endanger the health and safety of themselves or others (SI 2007/320 reg 5).

Regulation 6 sets out that activities must be co-ordinated in order to ensure the health and safety of those carrying out, and those affected by, construction work.

The general principles of prevention (as specified in Schedule 1 to SI 1999/3242) must be taken account of in the design, planning and preparation of a project, and in carrying out the construction work (SI 2007/320 reg 7).

Regulation 8 allows for clients to elect in writing to be treated for the purpose of the Regulations as the only client or clients, where there is more than one client in relation to a project.

Every client must take reasonable steps to ensure that the arrangements made for managing the project, including the allocation of sufficient time and other resources) by persons with a duty under the regulations (including the client) are suitable to ensure that:

- the construction work can be carried out, so far as is reasonably practicable, without risks to health and safety;

- the requirements of Schedule 2 (which concerns welfare facilities) are complied with; and

- any structure designed for use as a workplace has been designed taking into account the provisions of the Workplace (Health, Safety and Welfare) Regulations 1992, SI 1992/3004, that relate to the design of, and materials used in, the structure (SI 2007/320 reg 9).

Regulation 10 is concerned with the client's duty in relation to information and requires that they ensure that those designing the structure and contractors are promptly provided with pre-construction information in the clients possession (or reasonably obtainable), including:

- any information about or affecting the site of the construction work;

- any information concerning the proposed use of the structure as a workplace;

- the minimum amount of time before the construction phase (defined as the period of time starting when the construction work in any project starts and ending when construction work in that project is completed) which will be allowed for planning and preparation; and

- any information in the health and safety file.

The information should be relevant to the person to whom the client provides it for the purposes of ensuring the health and safety of people carrying out construction work, or affected by the way in which it is carried out, or who will use the structure as a workplace, and should assist them to perform their duties under the regulations and determine the resources which are to be allocated for managing the project.

The duties of designers are set out in reg 11. No designer shall commence work in relation to a project unless any client for the project is aware of his duties under the regulations. So far as is reasonably practicable, taking due account of other relevant design consideration, designers must, in preparing or modifiying a design which may be used in construction work in Great Britain, avoid foreseeable risks to the health and safety of those:

- carrying out construction work,

- liable to be affected by such work,

- cleaning windows or any translucent or transparent wall, celing or roof in or on a structure;

- maintaining the permanent fixtures and fittings of a structure; or

- using a structure as a workplace.

In complying with this duty, designers must eliminate hazards which may give rise to risks and reduce the risks from any remaining hazards, and in doing so give priority to collective over individual measures.

The provisions of SI 1992/3004 which relate to the design of, and materials used in the structure must be taken account of where it will be used as a workplace.

Reasonable steps must be taken to provide sufficient information about aspects of the design of the structure or its construction or maintenance to assist clients, other designers and contractors comply with their duties under the regulations.

Regulation 12 deals with designs prepared or modified outside Great Britain and requires that the person who commissions it, if based within Great Britain, or if not any client for the project must ensure that reg 11 is complied with.

The duties of contractors are set out in reg 13. Contractors must not carry out construction work unless clients for the project are aware of their duties under the regulations. Contractors must plan, manage and monitor construction work, so far as is reasonably practicable in order to ensure that it is without risks to health and safety, and any contractors appointed or engaged must be informed of the minimum amount of time allowed for planning and preparation before the work begins.

Every worker carrying out construction work under the control of the contractor must be provided with health and safety information and training including:

- site induction (where not provided by the principal contractor);

- information on health and safety risks identified by the risk assessment carried out under SI 1999/3242, or arising from the activities of another contractor of his undertaking, of which he is, or ought reasonably to be aware;

- the measures identified by the risk assessment as necessary to be taken;

- any site rules;

- procedures to be followed in the event of serious and imminent danger; and

- the identity of the persons nominated to implement those procedures.

Construction work should not begin until reasonable steps have been taken to prevent access to unauthorised persons to the site; and contractors should ensure that the requirements concerning the provision of welfare facilities (set out in SI 2007/320 Sch 2) are complied with.

*Part 3: Additional duties where the project is notifiable*

**9.11**    Regulation 14 requires that where a project is notifiable, a CDM co-ordinator must be appointed by the client as soon as practicable after initial design work or other preparation for construction work has begun. After the appointment of the CDM co-ordinator, a principal contractor must be appointed as soon as practicable after enough is known about a project to ensure the client can select a suitable person.

There must be a CDM co-ordinator and principal contractor throughout the construction phase, and the client shall be deemed to have been appointed to these positions in the absence of another appointment. Appointments must be in writing.

Regulation 15 requires that the client must promptly provide the CDM co-ordinator with preconstruction information (as described in reg 10). And reg 16 requires the client to ensure that the construction phase does not start unless the principal contractor has prepared a construction phase plan, and welfare facilities are provided.

The client must provide the CDM co-ordinator with all the health and safety information in their possession which is likely to need to be included in the health and safety file, including information regarding the location of any asbestos (SI 2007/320 reg 17).

Regulation 18 concerns additional duties of designers and requires that designers should not commence work (other than initial design work) unless a CDM co-ordinator has been appointed for the project. The designer must provide with the design sufficient information about aspects of the design of the structure, or its construction or maintenance, to assist the CDM co-ordinator to comply with their duties under the regulations.

Contractors must not carry out construction work unless they have been provided with the names of the CDM co-ordinator and principal contractor, given access to relevant parts of the construction phase plan, and notice of the project has been given to the HSE or Office of Rail Regulation (ORR) (reg 19).

Contractors must provide the principal contractor with any information which might affect health and safety or justify a review of the construction phase plan, or been identified for inclusion in the health and safety file.

They must promptly identify any contractor appointed or engaged by them to the principal contractor; comply with any health and safety directions of the principal contractor and any site rules, and promptly provide details of any death, injury, condition or dangerous occurrence notifiable under the Reporting of Injuries, Diseases and Dangerous Occurrences Regulations 1995, SI 1995/3163.

Contractors must ensure that construction work is carried out in accordance with the construction phase plan; take appropriate action to ensure health and safety where it is not possible to to comply with the construction phase plan, and notify the principal contractor of any significant finding which requires the construction phase plan to be changed.

Regulation 20 sets out the duties of CDM co-ordinators. They shall:

- give suitable and sufficient advice and assistance regarding the measures the client needs to take to comply with the regulations;

- ensure there is co-operation and co-ordination on health and safety during planning and preparation for the construction phase, and that the general principles of prevention are applied;

- liaise with the principal contractor regarding the contents of the health and safety file, the information needed to prepare the construction phase plan, and any design development which may affect planning and management of the construction work;

- take reasonable steps to identify and collect pre-construction information and promptly provide relevant information to designers and contractors;

- take reasonable steps to ensure that designers comply with their duties;

- take reasonable steps to ensure co-operation between designers and the principal contractor regarding any design changes;

- prepare (or review and update) the health and safety file which contains information likely to be needed to ensure health and safety. This must be passed to the client at the end of the construction phase.

The CDM co-ordinator must notify to the HSE (or ORR) the particulars set out in Schedule 1, which include dates of the construction, location of the site, contact details, and number of workers (SI 2007/320 reg 21).

Regulation 22 sets out the duties of principal contractors. They must:

- plan, manage and monitor the construction phase to ensure it is carried out without risks to health and safety, including facilitating co-ordination and co-operation and the application of the general principals of prevention;

- liaise with the CDM co-ordinator;

- ensure that there are sufficient welfare facilities;

- draw up site rules where necessary for health and safety;

- give reasonable directions to any contractor to enable compliance with their duties under the regulations;

- ensure that contractors are informed of the minimum amount of time allowed for planning and preparation before the construction work begins;

- consult a contractor where necessary before finalising the construction phase plan;

- ensure access to relevant parts of the construction phase plan to contractors in good time before construction work begins;

- ensure that contractors are given sufficient time to prepare for construction work before it begins in order to provide sufficient welfare facilities and carry out the work safely;

- identify to contractors information likely to be needed by the CDM co-ordinator for the health and safety file, and ensure that the information is promptly provided;

- ensure that the particulars specified in Schedule 1 are displayed and can be read by construction workers;

- take reasonable steps to prevent unauthorised persons to the site; and

- ensure that every construction worker is provided with a suitable site induction, and health and safety information and training.

Regulation 23 requires that the principal contractor prepare a construction phase plan before the start of construction which is sufficient to ensure that the construction phase is planned, managed and monitored to ensure the work is carried out safely. The plan must be reviewed and revised as necessary and it must be implemented. The plan should identify the risks to health and safety arising from the construction work and include measures to address such risks, including any site rules.

The principal contractor also has a duty to ensure that there is co-operation and consultation with workers carrying out construction work (SI 2007/320 reg 24).

*Part 4: Duties relating to health and safety on construction sites*

**9.12**    Part 4 applies to every person who controls the way in which any construction work is carried out by a person at work, other than a contractor carrying out construction work.

It sets out requirements regarding:

- **Safe places of work**: There must be suitable and sufficient safe access and eggress which is properly maintained, the place of work must be made and kept safe, and there should be sufficient working space (SI 2007/320 reg 26);

- **Good order and site security**: Construction sites must be kept in good order and in a reasonable state of cleanliness and where necessary the perimeter should be indicated by signs or fenced off, or both. No timber with projecting nails should be used (reg 27);

- **Stability of structures**: Reasonable steps should be taken to ensure that any structure which may become unstable does not collapse. Any buttress, temporary support or temporary structure must be designed, installed and maintained in order to withstand any foreseeable loads and must only be used for the purposes it was designed for. Structures must not be unsafely loaded (reg 28);

- **Demolition or dismantling**: This must be planned and carried out in a way that prevents danger, or reduces the danger to as low a level as reasonably practicable. The arrangements must be recorded in writing in advance (reg 29);

- **Explosives**: shall be stored, transported and used safely and securely, and explosive charges shall only be used where suitable and sufficient steps have been taken to ensure that the risk of injury from the explosion or projected or flying material has been prevented (reg 30);

- **Excavations**: Steps should be taken to prevent the collapse of any (or part of any) excavation, the dislodging or falling of material, and to prevent anyone being buried or trapped by falling material. Where supports or batterings are necessary, construction work should only be carried out in the excavation after it has been inspected by a competent person (at the start of the shift, after an event likely to have affected the strength or stability of the excavation, and after any material has unintentionally fallen or is dislodged (reg 31);

- **Cofferdams and caissons**: These should be of suitable design and construction, equipped with suitable shelter or escape routes, and properly maintained. They should only be used to carry out construction work after inspection by a competent person at the start of the shift or after an event likely to have affected strength or stability shows that it can be carried out safely (reg 32);

- **Reports of inspections**: Where the person who carries out the inspections above is not satisfied that the work can be carried out safely, a report including the particulars set out in Schedule 3 to the Regulations must be prepared and sent to the person on whose behalf the report was prepared. The report should include details of the risks to health and safety, the action taken as a result of the risks identified and details of any further action considered necessary and it should be kept available for inspection by the person on whose behalf it was prepared (reg 33);

- **Energy distribution installations**: These should be suitably located, checked and clearly indicated where necessary to prevent danger. Where there is a risk from electric power cables, they should be directed away from the area of risk or the power should be isolated and earthed where necessary. If it is not reasonably practicable to do this, suitable warning notices and barriers, suspended protections or measures providing an equivalent level of safety should be used (reg 34);

- **Prevention of drowning**: Where there is a risk of falling into water or other liquid with a risk of drowning, measures must be taken to prevent, or minimise the risk of drowning, and suitable rescue equipment must be provided, maintained and used where necessary. Where people are taken to work by water they must be transported safely, and vessels must not be overcrowded or overloaded (reg 35).

- **Traffic routes**: Construction sites must be organised so that pedestrians and vehicles can move safely, with a suitable number of traffic routes of sufficient size in suitable positions provided (reg 36).

- **Vehicles**: The unintended movement of vehicles must be prevented or controlled. Warnings should be given if there is a risk from movement of vehicles, vehicles should be operated and loaded safely, and people should only travel on vehicles, or remain on a vehicle while loading or unloading, in a safe place provided for that purpose. Steps should be taken to prevent vehicles falling into any excavation or pit, or overunning the edge of any embankment or earthwork (reg 37).

- **Prevention from risk of fire, explosion, flooding or asphyxiation**: Injuries arising from any of these risks should be prevented, so far as is reasonably practicable (reg 38);

- **Emergency procedures**: Where necessary, there should be suitable and sufficient arrangements for dealing with any foreseeable emergency, including evacuation procedures. Everyone to whom these arrangements extend should be familiar with them, and they should be tested at suitable intervals (reg 39);

- **Emergency routes and exits**: Where necessary, there should be a sufficient number of suitable emergency routes and exits, indicated by suitable signs, to enable people to reach an identified safe area quickly in the event of danger (reg 40);

- **Fire detection and fire-fighting**: Suitably located fire-fighting equipment and fire detection and alarm systems should be provided where necessary, examined and tested at suitable intervals and properly maintained (reg 41);

- **Fresh air**: There should be sufficient fresh or purified air, and any plant used for ensuring this should give visible or audible warning of failure (reg 42);

- **Temperature and weather protection**: The temperature in indoor workplaces should be reasonable during working hours, and where work is outdoors, there should be protective clothing or work equipment provided to protect against adverse weather (reg 43); and

- **Lighting**: Every place of work, as well as approaches and traffic routes, should be provided with suitable and sufficient lighting, which is natural light where reasonably practicable. Secondary lighting should be provided where necessary for health and safety in the event of failure of primary artificial lighting (reg 44).

Schedule 2 details the welfare facilities to be provided under regs 9, 13 and 22. These are:

- suitable and sufficient sanitary conveniences;

- suitable and sufficient washing facilities;

- an adequate supply of drinking water;

- suitable and sufficient changing rooms and lockers; and

- rest facilities.

HSE guidance on SI 2007/320 is available in an Approved Code of Practice: *Managing health and safety in construction* from HSE Books.

# Health and Safety Prosecutions following Work-related Deaths in the Construction Industry highlighted by the HSE

**9.13**     The HSE has highlighted the following prosecutions following work-related deaths in the construction industry, together with HSE guidance on preventing death and injury, over the last 12 months:

## *Dawson-Wam Ltd[1]*

In October 2007, Dawson-Wam Ltd, a Bedfordshire company, was fined £100,000 and ordered to pay more than £76,000 costs after it was prosecuted over the death of employee John Walsh, who was killed when the auger drive unit of a piling rig he was attempting to dismantle flew off its stand and struck him. The company pleaded guilty to section 2(1) of HSWA 1974.

The case lead to the HSE warning construction companies of the dangers of using improvised procedures when dismantling heavy machinery.

HSE inspector Alec Ferguson said:

'Employers need to ensure that where circumstances prevent the use of standard methods of work, then the risks arising from any method subsequently adopted should be very carefully assessed. In particular, employers who are even considering departure from manufacturer's guidance in respect of specialist equipment should assess the risks which may result very carefully indeed before proceeding. Attempting to dismantle heavy equipment in a way not recommended by its manufacturer is likely to be a very risky enterprise which should only be embarked on when absolutely necessary and, even then, only following very careful planning of a truly safe system of work.'

Dawson-Wam Ltd accepted that it failed to suitably assess the risk from dismantling the piling rig in a different method from the manufacture's operators manual, and that it failed to provide adequate instruction and information to its employees for dismantling the drive unit from the carrier in such circumstances.

The company was also prosecuted in April 2007 when it was fined £75,000 and ordered to pay costs of £34,425 after pleading guilty to a charge under HSWA 1974 following the death of another worker.

Piling rig operator Peter Roberts died in May 2004 after trying to clear a blocked concrete pump with compressed air.

The process involved drilling a hole into the ground with the auger of a piling rig, pumping concrete into the hole as the auger was withdrawn and finally inserting reinforcement bars.

On the day of the accident there was a delay in the delivery of concrete to Mr Robert's piling rig and concrete which remained in the flexible rubber hose used to connect a concrete pump to the rig began to harden, leading to a blockage.

After attempts to clear the blockage failed, it was decided to try using compressed air. The flexible hose was broken up into individual sections and at least two of these were blown out with compressed air without their ends being restrained. During the unblocking of the last section, the end of the hose whipped upwards and struck Mr Roberts on the head, causing fatal injuries.

The HSE prosecuted the company, arguing that despite the company being aware that this was a high risk operation, they had failed to carry out a formal risk assessment of the cleaning and unblocking of the rig, which meant there was no safe system of working.

HSE inspector Robert Hodkinson commented:

'Cleaning out or unblocking piling rigs and associated equipment, such as concrete pumps and pipe work, with compressed air is a very high risk activity and should therefore have been formally assessed. A risk assessment is the starting point for developing a formal safe system of work for such operations. Once developed, clear instruction and training should then be given to those carrying out the work.

'Whilst no charges were brought directly in relation to selecting compressed air as a method for this particular operation, a safer alternative to clean out such equipment would be to use water. Indeed, the British Concrete Pumping Group Code of Practice states that using compressed air to clean out a pipeline should only be done when there is no practical alternative. The operation must be carried out under the close supervision of a suitably trained person.

'I recommend that all piling companies and others who use concrete pumps and associated equipment reassess their cleaning and unblocking operations to ensure that they have safe systems of work in place, and that employees carrying out such activities have received clear instruction and training'.

## Permanent Flooring Ltd and RL Davies and Son Ltd[2]

In June 2007, two construction companies were fined for breaches of the HSWA 1974 following the death of 19-year old Miall Roberts who was electrocuted after the concrete pump he was working on came into contact with an overhead power line. Another worker on the site, Darren Gittins, received an electric shock but was uninjured.

Permanent Flooring Ltd of Bagillt, Flintshire, pleaded guilty to breaching HSWA 1974 s 3(1) and to a charge under s 2(1) for putting Mr Gittins at risk. They were fined £6,000 and ordered to pay a contribution towards costs of £12,000.

RL Davies and Son Ltd of Llysfaen, Conwy pleaded guilty to breaching s 3(1) and was fined £25,000 and ordered to pay costs of over £15,000.

Mr Roberts was employed by a third party, who were acting as a labour supplier to the two defendant companies in this case.

The HSE has warned construction companies of the consequences that can result from the failure to carry out proper risk assessments where there are overhead power lines close to work activities.

HSE inspector Chris Wilcox said:

'... it is imperative that employers ensure their staff and contractors are protected by carrying out a full risk assessment of the site before work starts.

'Household voltages are enough to kill, but in this case the voltage involved was nearly 50 times greater. Overhead power lines can be switched off if the operators are given sufficient notice, but if this isn't possible, they should be consulted on safe systems of work.'

## McDonald and Ross Ltd and Ron Boyd Trading[3]

In May 2007, steel fabrication company, McDonald and Ross Ltd, and a road haulage sole trader, Ron Boyd Trading, were fined a total of £37,500 at Edinburgh Sheriff Court. Driver Nicholas McKellar died after a steel beam weighing almost 1000kg fell from a vehicle as it was being unloaded. Both companies had pleaded guilty to breaches of HSWA 1974.

HSE inspector Isabelle Martin commented after the case:

'It is entirely foreseeable that a load on a vehicle will move during transit on the road. It is therefore important that the load is placed onto the vehicle in its most stable orientation and that appropriate measures are taken to ensure that it cannot fall from the vehicle at any time. It is also important that the stability of the load is assessed prior to beginning to unload it.

'This incident could, therefore, easily have been prevented. The beam that fell from the vehicle was one of three identical beams placed on the vehicle. Each of these beams could have been placed on their side therefore making it very unlikely that they could fall.'

McDonald and Ross Ltd were contracted by a residential developer to fabricate, deliver and erect a steel framed building, but were unable to deliver the steel to the construction site themselves and therefore subcontracted delivery to The Ron Boyd Group.

The HSE investigation revealed that McDonald and Ross Ltd had failed to assess the risks involved in loading and unloading steel. They also failed to ensure that the steel was correctly placed upon the timber bearers on the vehicle. Ron Boyd had failed to ensure that his employees involved in loading, unloading and transporting steel to site had been properly trained.

The HSE said that contractors should have made arrangements for the safe delivery and unloading of materials to their sites. A number of simple steps can prevent this type of accident occurring. The British Constructional Steel Association (www.steelconstruc-tion.org) has a range of publications including a *Guide to Work at Height during the Loading and Unloading of Steelwork.*

## Unichem plc, Telford Tower & Scaffolding Ltd, Pochin (Contractors) Ltd, David Isherwood, and Ian McCann[4]

In April 2007, fines totalling £68,000 and more than £40,000 costs were imposed on three companies and two individuals following the death of scaffolder Darren Brownbill, who died after falling through a fragile roof light while working on an extension to a warehouse operated by Unichem plc.

The HSE said that everybody involved in planning and carrying out construction work has some responsibility for ensuring the health and safety of the workers. The following were charged:

• Darren Brownbill's employer, Telford Tower & Scaffolding Ltd, pleaded guilty to a charge under HSWA 1974 s 2(1) . The company was fined £35,000 and ordered to pay £20,000 costs;

• the main contractors, Pochin (Contractors) Ltd, pleaded guilty to a charge under s 3(1). The company was fined £25,000 and ordered to pay £15,000 costs;

• the clients, Unichem plc, pleaded guilty of a charge under the reg 11 of the Construction (Design and Management) Regulations 1994, SI 1994/3140 (now superceded by SI 2007/320). The company was fined £3,000 and ordered to pay £2.407 costs;

• project designer, David Isherwood, a partner in the firm of Isherwood McCann pleaded guilty to a charge under SI 1994/3140 reg 13(2)(a)(i). He was fined £2,500 and ordered to pay £1,500 costs

• Planning supervisor, Ian McCann, a partner in the firm of Isherwood McCann pleaded guilty to a charge under SI 1994/3140 reg 15(1). He was fined £2,500 and ordered to pay £1,500 costs.

1 See HSE Press Releases 25 April 2007 and 2 October 2007.
2 See HSE Press Release 18 June 2007.
3 See HSE Press Release 11May 2007.

## Future Developments: Strategic Safety Forum and the Framework of Action for Improving Construction Safety

**9.14**    The government has recognised that more needs to be done to address the high rate of fatalities in the industry. In September 2007, the HSE published figures showing that nearly one in three construction refurbishment sites it inspected put the lives of workers at risk, and that work was stopped immediately at 244 of the sites.

On 17 September 2007, a Strategic Safety Forum was convened by Peter Hain, the Secretary of State for the Department of Work and Pensions (DWP), at which an action plan to cut workplace deaths and improve health and safety standards was agreed by representatives of the construction industry and the trades unions.

Key areas for action agreed include:

• sharing best practice – working together to agree standards of health and safety to be achieved on housebuilding and domestic repair/refurbishment projects;

• raising levels of competence – extending the requirement for all site workers in the housebuilding sector to carry a Construction Skills Certification Scheme (CSCS) card or be able to demonstrate their occupational and health and safety competence to the same or better standard; and ensuring all workers receive induction training before they start work on a new site;

• encouraging worker involvement – ensuring that all projects include trade unions and worker representatives;

• integrated working – ensuring that site specific planning and induction is provided to all those in control of tower crane erection, operation and dismantling, with an emphasis on appropriate risk assessment; and

• steps to drive out the informal economy in the sector, which can impact health and safety.

UCATT welcomed the Forum as an important first step and said:

'For the first time UCATT was able to win Government recognition that high levels of bogus self-employment in the construction industry massively decreases workplace safety. Self- employed workers having no employment rights and therefore no union safety representatives.'

The union has also called for a large rise in inspection numbers and for the government to renew the Workplace Safety Advisor scheme (which provided specially trained safety advisers to workplaces without safety representatives). And it has raised the issue of contract compliance, calling for clients not to abdicate their safety responsibilities 'once the ink is dry on the contract'.

In the report it submitted to the Forum, *Critical safety issues and necessary improvements in the construction industry*, the union sets out that:

- achieving more safety on sites starts from a directly employed workforce – the union says that around 50 per cent of construction workers in the UK are self-employed and many of these are 'bogus' self-employed when all employment tests reveal they should be directly employed. The union says that self-employment deprives workers of basic employment rights and massively diminishes the level of safety on sites. And it says that bogus self-employment and sub-contracting leads to fragmentation of the working structures, with safety imperatives getting weakened or lost in the process of being passed down the hierarchy. It argues that self-employed workers lack essential safety training, and that building sites without a directly employed workforce often do not have union representation, which is known to bring vast safety improvements. In summary, it argues that self-employed workers are exposed to a higher risk of being injured or killed on site;

- the number of HSE inspectors in the construction division, as well as the number of inspections, investigations, enforcement notices and prosecutions must be increased, and it outlines its concerns about cuts in HSE resources (see CHAPTER 6);

- efforts must be made to reverse the dramatic rise in fatalities in the housebuilding sector;

- migrant workers are particularly vulnerable as regards their working conditions and their safety on site;

- the Gangmasters Licensing Act 2004 should be extended to include the construction industry, which would lead to the elimination of the worst agencies in the sector (see CHAPTER 11). It wants to see on-site, understandable safety inductions for migrant workers before they start a job, understandable safety signage on construction sites, and employers providing language training to equip workers with a better level of the English language;

- legislative changes that implement the provision of directors' duties (see CHAPTER 8);

- increased rights for safety representatives; and

- a continuation of the Worker Safety Advisor scheme.

éy?cs

## Public sector procurement

The Construction Confederation has called on government and other public sector clients to do more to help improve health and safety performance in construction by showing greater leadership, following the results of a survey it carried out in 2005 to find out the extent health and safety management plays a role in the awarding of public sector contracts.

It found that:

- only 52 per cent of respondents were always required to undergo a health and safety assessment during the bidding process;

- 13 per cent said their health and safety performance was never a significant factor;

- only 48 per cent thought public sector clients considered health and safety performance to be a very important factor when awarding contracts;

- nearly 60 per cent said they were never made aware of the Office of Government Commerce procurement guidance note No 10 on health and safety during the bidding process;

- only 13 per cent of respondents were always asked to make specific provisions for occupational health; and

- just over a third said that post-completion health and safety reviews were never carried out.

Construction Confederation Chief Executive Stephen Ratcliffe commented:

'Companies who perform best at health and safety should also get a commercial return in that they are more able to compete for work. Sadly we are not there yet.

Government, as the industry's biggest single client, is in a tremendous position of influence to encourage employers with good health and safety management practices.

We need our public sector clients to show leadership by ensuring that it only puts on its select lists those suppliers who can demonstrate good health and safety practice, who look after their workforce and who improve quality. These are the real measures of best value.'

The HSE has also recently published research showing that the public sector could do more to meet its health and safety obligations when procuring building projects. According to a report in the➡

safety journal Health and Safety Bulletin (HSB) (issue 360 July 2007) public sector clients commission about 40 per cent of the UK construction industry's total input, with an average annual death toll of 17.

*Health and safety in public sector construction procurement* is available on the HSE website at www.hse.gov.uk/research/rrpdf/rr556.pdf.

*Chapter 10*

# Transport

## Overview

### 10.1

> This chapter looks at work-related deaths in transport and at the
> likely impact of the Corporate Manslaughter and Corporate Homi-
> cide Act 2007 (CMCHA 2007), when it comes into effect on 6 April
> 2008, in relation to deaths on the road, and in the rail, maritime and
> aviation industries. In particular:
>
> - it looks at the issue of work-related road safety since this
>   affects a huge number of employers, and has been described as
>   the most dangerous work-related activity performed by most
>   people in the UK;
>
> - it provides information about manslaughter and health and
>   safety prosecutions that have followed work-related deaths in
>   road accidents;
>
> - it outlines guidance from the Health and Safety Executive
>   (HSE) and the Royal Society for the Prevention of Accidents
>   (RoSPA) on occupational road risk; and
>
> - it looks specifically at road haulage agencies.
>
> In addition:
>
> - it looks at fatalities in the rail, maritime, and aviation indus-
>   tries and refers to specific safety legislation in these sectors;
>   and
>
> - finally, it briefly outlines the role of the air, marine and rail
>   accident investigation branches, which undertake investigation
>   to establish the cause, examine the consequences and identify
>   safety lessons that can be learned from accidents, independent
>   of any criminal investigation, in these sectors.

249

## Work-related Road Safety

**10.2**    According to the HSE it is estimated that up to a third of all road traffic accidents involve somebody who is at work at the time, which may account for over 20 fatalities and 250 serious injuries every week. Research it commissioned estimates that between a third and half of all road traffic incidents involve someone at work. Some 127 professional drivers die each year in road accidents, and a further 116 commercial vehicle drivers are killed.

Occupational Road Risk (ORR) is something that RoSPA has made a top priority. In an article in *Freight Transport Review*[1], Roger Bibbings, occupational safety advisor at RoSPA, wrote:

'The Department for Transport recently released the first breakdown of UK road accident figures to show what victims were doing at the time of a collision. The figures, which showed that one in four road accidents involve someone at or on their way to or from work, are likely to be a serious underestimate of the real position, but they confirm what we have always suspected: driving for work is the most dangerous work-related activity performed by most people in the UK.'

Michael Appleby, partner at law firm Fisher Scoggins, told a 2006 RoSPA seminar on road death and corporate manslaughter:

'Not that long ago the police would have been content to focus their attention on frontline workers who were directly involved in the incident – ie in a work related road accident, the driver. They would be the people most likely to be arrested and interviewed under caution. However not anymore: these days the management chain will also come under scrutiny as well. As the HSE's *Successful health and safety management* (HSG 65) says:

"Accidents, ill health and incidents are seldom random events. They generally arise from failures of control and involve multiple con-tributory elements. The immediate cause may be a human or technical failure, but they usually arise from organisational failings which are the responsibility of management."

'Just because the fleet manager was sitting in his office miles away from where the road crash happened does not mean the police will not come knocking on his door.'

And in *A guide to health and safety prosecutions* Appleby and barrister Gerard Forlin[2] say that ORR 'is something that is fast rising up the safety agenda' and that 'Criminal investigations of road traffic accidents as work-related incidents are on the increase'.

In his presentation to the RoSPA seminar, Ian Brooks, then Chief Inspector at the Metropolitan Police set out that the police investigate all incidents as unlawful killing until the contrary is proved. He also described a pilot scheme in operation in London under the Freight

Operator Recognition Scheme (FORS) initiative. In order to establish compliance with road traffic laws and health and safety legislation, freight operators were asked about:

- driver – driving license checks, assessment, high-risk drivers, seat belts, mobile phones and the use of private vehicles;

- vehicle – daily checks, defect reporting and maintenance records; and

- journey – depot movements, schedules and congestion.

Employers would also be asked whether their health and safety policy specifically includes 'work-related road risks'.

A new version of the *Road Death Investigation Manual*, which will include guidance on corporate manslaughter, was due to be published in November 2007 by the National Police Improvement Agency (NPIA).

1  Issue 13 (2007).
2  Michael Appleby and Gerard Forlin, *A guide to health and safety prosecutions*, published by Thomas Telford (2007) (www.thomastelford.com/books).

## Manslaughter and Health and Safety Prosecutions following Fatal Road Traffic Accidents

**10.3**    There have been relatively few cases involving corporate manslaughter convictions, or manslaughter convictions of company directors, but a number have followed fatal road traffic accidents as the examples below show.

*Cases involving manslaughter convictions following work-related deaths on the road*

**10.4**

### Keymark Services and Melvyn Spree[1]

In December 2004, director Melvyn Spree and his company, Keymark Services, admitted the manslaughter and unlawful killing of Neil Owen and Benjamin Kwapong. The two men were killed in a crash on the M1 in Northamptonshire in February 2002 when lorry driver Stephen Law, who worked for the company and who was also killed, fell asleep at the wheel and crashed into seven vehicles. Spree was jailed for seven years and banned for life from holding such positions. (See CHAPTER 1 for details of the case.)

### Stephen and Julie Bowles (Roy Bowles Transport Ltd)[2]

In 1999, two directors of Roy Bowles Transport Ltd, Stephen Bowles and his sister Julie Bowles, were convicted of the manslaughter of Peter Morgan and Barry Davies, who both died in a seven vehicle pile up on the M25 in 1997. The accident happened when a lorry driver working for the company, Andrew Cox, fell asleep at the wheel. (See CHAPTER 4 for details of the case.)

1  See news.bbc.co.uk/1/hi/england/4066331.stm.

2   *R v Roy Bowles Transport Ltd* (1999) (unreported).

## Examples of health and safety prosecutions for work-related road deaths

**10.5**   The HSE has also prosecuted a number of employers following fatal road traffic accidents under health and safety legislation, including the following (see also 10.11 on Raymond Knapman and Robert Legg)[1].

### The Produce Connection

In July 2006 potato distribution firm The Produce Connection was fined £30,000 and ordered to pay £24,000 costs following the death of a 'chronically fatigued' employee, Mark Fiebig. His car drifted into the path of an oncoming lorry as he drove home on the A10 near Ely in Cambridgeshire in 2002 after working three consecutive 19-hour shifts. The judge in the case said that the firm had failed to monitor the hours employees worked.

Roger Bibbings, Occupational Safety Adviser at the Royal Society for the Prevention of Accidents (RoSPA) commented on the case in an article in *Freight Transport Review*[1]:

> 'The case was thought to be the first of its kind in the UK because The Produce Connection admitted breaching health and safety legislation even though Mr Fiebig died outside working hours.'

### Royal Mail[2]

In 1997, Royal Mail was prosecuted after a 16-year-old postal worker was killed when he was knocked off his motorbike. Although it was accepted that the accident was caused by the driver of the other vehicle involved, it was argued that a significant contributory factor was the failure of Royal Mail to have appropriate health and safety procedures in place.

Royal Mail was fined £15,300 and ordered to pay £14,514 for breaches of section 2 of the Health and Safety at Work etc Act 1974 (HSWA 1974).

According to Bibbings, more directors and senior managers could be prosecuted under road traffic law for 'cause and permit' offences, in relation to mobile phone use for example.

1   Issue 13 (2007).
2   See *A guide to health and safety prosecutions* by Michael Appleby and Gerard Forlin.

## Work-related Road Safety Task Group Guidance on Preventing Deaths on the Road

**10.6**   The government set up the independent Work-related Road Safety Task Group to propose ways to reduce at-work traffic accidents following a commitment given in its road safety strategy, *Tomorrow's roads – Safer for everyone.*

Its report, *Reducing at-work road traffic incidents,* said that deaths and injuries on the road could be reduced by applying existing safety management systems to occupational road activities and it made 18 recommendations, including the following:

- more rigorously applied health and safety law with regard to on-the-road work;

- activities (no new law necessary);

- HSE guidance to help employers manage at-work road safety; and

- mechanisms for closer working between enforcing authorities.

The report proposed that employers should do more to assess, and take proportionate action to reduce risks, and that where they fail, appropriate action should be taken against them.

*Reducing at-work road traffic incidents* can be accessed online at www.hse.gov.uk/roadsafety/report.htm.

Following the report, the HSE and DfT produced guidance, which is examined below.

## HSE Guidance: Driving at Work: Managing Work-related Road Safety

**10.7**    The HSE and Department for Transport (DfT) guidance *Driving at Work: Managing work-related road safety* is aimed at any employer, manager or supervisor with staff who drive or ride a motorcycle or bicycle at work.

In it, the HSE clearly sets out that health and safety law – including the Health and Safety at Work etc Act 1974 (HSWA 1974) and the Management of Health and Safety at Work Regulations 1999, SI 1999/3242, which applies to on-the-road work activities as it does to other work activities, and that employers have a responsibility to ensure that others are not put at risk by these activities. Employers must therefore assess the risks involved in work-related driving activities, and put in place all 'reasonably practicable' measures to manage those risks.

It says that:

'Some employers believe, incorrectly, that provided they comply with certain road traffic law requirements, e g company vehicles have a valid MOT certificate, and that drivers hold a valid licence, this is enough to ensure the safety of their employees, and others, when they are on the road. However, health and safety law applies to on-the-road work activities as to all work activities, and the risks should be effectively managed within a health and safety management system.'

The HSE guidance makes clear that health and safety legislation applies in addition to duties under road traffic law, such as the Road Traffic Act and Road Vehicle (Construction and Use) Regulations, which are administered by the police and other agencies such as the Vehicle and Operator Services Agency (VOSA), and legislative requirements which companies with large goods vehicles (LGV) or passenger service vehicles (PSV) may also be subject to.

Risk assessments for any work-related driving activity should follow the same principles as risk assessments for any other work activity (see 10.8).

**10.8**

---

*HSE advice on risk assessments for work-related driving activities*

Step 1 – Look for hazards that may result in harm when driving on public roads. Consult employees or their representatives and seek the views of those who drive extensively, as well as those that only use the roads occasionally. The main areas to consider are the driver, the vehicle and the journey.

Step 2 – Decide who might be harmed. This will usually be the driver, but could be passengers, other road users or pedestrians. Consider groups who could be particularly at risk, such as young or newly qualified drivers and those driving long distances.

Step 3 – Evaluate the risk and decide whether existing precautions are adequate or more should be done. Consider how likely it is that each hazard will cause harm. Can the hazard be eliminated, for example by holding a telephone- or video-conference instead of holding a meeting to which people have to travel.

If the hazard cannot be eliminated, it will need to be controlled by working through a hierarchy of control measures:

- Consider whether policy on the allocation of company cars actively encourages employees to drive rather than consider alternative means of transport.

- Consider an alternative to driving, eg going at least part of the way by train.

- Try to avoid situations where employees feel under pressure, eg avoid making unrealistic claims about delivery schedules and attendance which may encourage drivers to drive too fast for the conditions, or exceed speed limits.

- Organise maintenance work to reduce the risk of vehicle failure, eg ensure there are maintenance schedules and that vehicles are regularly checked by a competent person to ensure they are safe.                                               ➡

---

• Ensure that drivers and passengers are adequately protected in the event of an incident, eg ensure that seatbelts, and where installed airbags, are correctly fitted, work properly and are used. For those who ride motorcycles and other two-wheeled vehicles, crash helmets and protective clothing should be of the appropriate standard.

Ensure that company policy covers the important aspects of the Highway Code such as not exceeding speed limits.

Step 4 – Record your findings (employers with five or more employees are required to record the significant findings of the risk assessment), and tell employees about what has been done.

Step 5 – Monitor and review the assessment and revise it if necessary – for example if there are new routes, new equipment or a change in vehicle specification, seeking the views of employees and safety representatives. There should be a system for gathering, recording and analysing information about road incidents and recording details of driver and vehicle history.

*Source*: Summary of the advice given in HSE/Department for Transport (DfT) publication, *Driving at work: Managing work-related road safety* (INDG382).

**10.9**    The guidance also advises employers to ask themselves:

• Does the health and safety policy statement cover work-related road safety?

• Is there top-level commitment to work-related road safety in the organisation and is responsibility clearly defined? Does the person who is responsible for it have sufficient authority to exert influence and does everyone understand what is expected of them?

• Are there adequate systems to manage work-related road safety effectively? For example, are vehicles regularly inspected and serviced in accordance with manufacturers' recommendations?

• Is performance monitored to ensure that the work-related road safety policy is effective? Are employees encouraged to report all work-related road incidents without fear that punitive action will be taken against them? Is sufficient information collected to allow informed decisions to be taken about the effectiveness of existing policy and the need for changes?

And it sets out a range of questions employers need to ask when evaluating whether work-related road safety is being effectively managed under the following headings:

*Drivers*

Competency: Are you satisfied that your drivers are competent and capable of doing their work in a way that is safe for them and other people?

Training: Are you satisfied that your drivers are properly trained?

Fitness and health: Are you satisfied that your drivers are sufficiently fit and healthy to drive safely and not put themselves or others at risk?

*Vehicles*

Suitability: Are you satisfied that vehicles are fit for the purpose for which they are used?

Condition: Are you satisfied that vehicles are maintained in a safe and fit condition?

Safety equipment: Are you satisfied that safety equipment is properly fitted and maintained?

Safety critical information: Are you satisfied that drivers have access to information that will help them reduce risks?

Ergonomic considerations: Are you satisfied that drivers' health, and possibly safety, is not being put at risk, eg from inappropriate seating position or driving posture?

*The journey*

Routes: Do you plan routes thoroughly?

Scheduling: Are work schedules realistic?

Time: Are you satisfied that sufficient time is allowed to complete journeys safely?

Distance: Are you satisfied that drivers will not be put at risk from fatigue caused by driving excessive distances without appropriate breaks?

Weather conditions: Are you satisfied that sufficient consideration is given to adverse weather conditions, such as snow or high winds, when planning journeys?

The guidance has been produced in partnership with the DfT and alerts employers and the self-employed to the fact that their responsibilities under current health and safety law extend to driving at work. It contains generic advice on managing work-related road safety effectively and on integrating it into existing health and safety arrangements.

Copies of *Driving at Work: Managing work-related road safety* (INDG382), are available free of charge from HSE Books. Copies can also be downloaded free from the HSE website at: www.hse.gov.uk/pubns/ indg382.pdf.

## RoSPA guidance on occupational road risk (ORR) – Managing Occupational Road Risk (MORR) in a Nutshell

**10.10** RoSPA's guidance, *Managing occupational road risk (MORR) in a nutshell*, is summarised below:

- ensure safe journey planning – top of the list of possible risk reduction measures is 'meeting without moving' using videoconferencing, or the next best, going by train or plane;

- ensure that vehicles are fit-for-purpose, properly maintained and have additional safety features where necessary;

- avoid systems of work which cause people to speed (such as 'just in time' delivery, payment by number of calls made, 'job and finish', and unrealistic guaranteed call-out or delivery times;

- avoid asking staff to drive while tired and at times of day when falling asleep at the wheel is more likely. Address employees' sleep deprivation (caused by looking after sick children or dependants for example) and avoid introducing distractions like making and receiving mobile phone calls while driving, even 'hands free' (No mobile while mobile![1]). Managers need to consider potential health impairments, driver fitness issues, and issues such as alcohol and drugs which can affect their people's ability to drive safely;

- always plan the safest routes, avoiding congestion, crash sites and adverse weather. If a journey at the start of day is excessively long, staff should go the night before. Managers should consider the effects of stress and fatigue and poor worklife balance;

- assess drivers' attitudes and driving competence, follow their crash and penalty points histories and analyse and learn from their crashes and 'near-misses'. Driver assessment should be used to target training at those with greatest needs; and

- above all, train line managers, consult safety reps, require senior managers to lead by example and recognise, celebrate and reward safe driving achievement. A good approach is to set up a multi-disciplinary team, with driver and safety rep involvement, to develop an action plan with clear targets.

More on RoSPA's guidance on MORR can be accessed online at www.rospa.com/roadsafety/resources/employers.htm. For information about RoSPA's MORR auditing, training for managers and drivers visit www.morr.org.uk.

¹ The Road Vehicles (Construction and Use) (Amendment) (No 4) Regulations 2003 (SI 2003/2695) made it a specific offence to use a hand-held phone or similar device when driving a motor vehicle. There are exemptions for two-way radios used by the emergency services and taxi drivers, and when making 999 or 112 emergency calls. The legislation also means that employers cannot require employees to use a hand-held phone while driving.
The Road Safety Act 2006 came into effect in 2007, introducing a new offence of 'causing death by careless or inconsiderate driving' and increasing the penalties for offences including driving while using a hand-held mobile phone.

## Road Hauliers, HGV Drivers and the Employment Agencies and Employment Businesses Regulations 2003

**10.11**    The private recruitment industry has grown significantly in recent year, according to the Department for Business, Enterprise and Regulatory Reform (BERR) and it estimates that there are around 1,700 employment agencies and employment businesses in the UK, and an estimated one million temporary and contract workers.

In February 2007, a consultation on measures to protect vulnerable agency workers, *Success at work*, was launched. This sets out proposals for the Conduct of Employment Agencies and Employment Businesses (Amendment) Regulations 2007 which were due to be debated in Parliament in October 2007, made in December 2007 and come into force in April 2008. Guidance on the amendments was due early in 2008.

*Success at work* included an examination of the issue of HGV drivers seeking to gain employment through agencies without proper driving qualifications and seeking to work longer hours driving than is legal.

Regulation 20 of the Conduct of Employment Agencies and Employment Businesses Regulations 2003, SI 2003/3319, (Conduct Regulations) requires agencies and employment businesses (before introducing or supplying a worker) to: 'take all such steps, as are reasonably practicable, to ensure that the work-seeker and the hirer are each aware of any requirements imposed by law, or by any professional body, which must be satisfied by the hirer or the work-seeker to enable the work-seeker to work for the hirer in the position which the hirer seeks to fill'.

The Conduct Regulations also require that 'when the business has information indicating actual or potential unsuitability of worker, it must either end supply of worker or take further steps to establish suitability'.

*Success at work* does not propose amending the regulations with regard to the employment of HGV drivers, but instead proposes amending and publicising guidance on reg 20 to make clear to agencies employing drivers that they would breach the Conduct Regulations if they failed to abide by other applicable legislation in force in the UK governing drivers.

Clearer guidance for agencies and the companies that use them is to be developed by BERR. This will include material warning agencies of the consequences of coercing or colluding with drivers to work excessive hours and spelling out that such practices breach agency legislation.

In addition, BERR, in partnership with other transport bodies and the Association of Chief Police Officers (ACPO), is developing a protocol to provide a framework for information sharing between all the organisations to help prevent crime and take more effective action against rogue operators who break the law.

*Success at work* says that:

'It is doubtful whether those agencies seeking to cut corners illegally are aware that if they encourage drivers to work excessive hours and this results in a fatal accident, they will be liable to a prosecution for manslaughter.'

BERR says that it will use its powers under the Conduct Regulations to seek to ban those who have demonstrated themselves to be unsuitable from running a driver or any other agency.

In April 2007, the main provisions of a new EU Regulation on drivers' hours[1] came into force, placing an automatic liability on transport operators for infringements committed by their drivers, and introducing co-liability for driver employment agencies that fail to ensure that contractually agreed transport time schedules respect the new EU Regulation.

The DfT provides guidance for both goods and passenger vehicles on the 'Drivers' hours and tachograph rules in the UK and Europe'. In addition, the DfT also provides guidance on the application of the Road Transport (Working Time) Regulations 2005, SI 2005/639, which apply to mobile workers (basically drivers and crew) operating on vehicles subject to the EU drivers' hours rules.

As this book went to press, the DfT was reviewing its drivers' hours and working time guidance and as part of this process was considering whether to produce targeted guidance for drivers. In addition to this VOSA produces the 'Safe Operators Guide' for both goods and passenger vehicles on the 'Drivers hours and tachograph rules in the UK and Europe' which will be distributed to all vehicle operators to ensure there is little excuse for failing to have a copy when inspected. These guides will refer to appropriate agency guidance and legislation.

*R&B, Raymond Knapman and Robert Legg*[2]

Knapman and Legg were partners in an agency, R&B, which supplied drivers to haulage operators. In 2005, they were acquitted of manslaughter, after two lorry drivers, Mark Chadbourne and Anthony Best, were killed when Mr Chadbourne's lorry crossed the road into the path of Mr Best's lorry on the A303 in Wiltshire and the two vehicles collided. Mark Chadbourne, who had been supplied by R&B, had exceeded his legal driving hours when he ran into the other lorry.

Although the two escaped manslaughter convictions, Knapman was later given a two and a half year prison sentence at Winchester Crown Court after he had pleaded guilty at an earlier hearing to eight charges of deception relating to supplying drivers to the safety of persons not in his employment.

He also admitted one health and safety offence, although no separate penalty was imposed for this.

Legg was fined £1,000 with £1,500 costs by the court after he pleaded guilty to a health and safety charge.

Hauliers Langdon Transport, who Mr Chadbourne was delivering for when he was killed also admitted that they had failed to ensure the safety of their employees and others employed by them under HSWA 1974 and was fined £17,500 with £1,500 costs.

In May 2007, an employment tribunal banned Knapman and Legg from running any employment agency or employment business – Knapman for the maximum terms of 10 years; and Legg for five years.

The Employment Agencies Act 1973, s 3A allows a tribunal to issue an order prohibiting a person from running an employment agency or business for a specified time if it is satisfied that the person is unsuitable to do so. The Department for Trade and Industry (now BERR) applied for the ban in this case.

According to the road safety campaign group, Brake, a director of a haulage company who is found to have asked his drivers to break tachograph regulations, and one of his tired drivers subsequently killed, could be charged with aiding and abetting death by dangerous driving and sentenced to a maximum of 14 years.

[1]    Council Regulation (EC) 561/2006 (OJ L 102, 11.04.2006, p 1).
[2]    Health and Safety Bulletin Issue 360 (July 2007).

*Further information*

**10.12**    The DfT website has information on road safety, including safety when driving for work: www.thinkroadsafety.gov.uk.

The Highway Code is available from the Stationary Office or can be accessed at www.highwaycode.gov.uk.

Drivers' hours and tachographs rules for goods vehicles in the UK and Europe are set out on the Department for Transport (DfT) website at www.dft.gov.uk/stellent/groups/dft_freight/documents/page/dft_freight_504543.hcsp.

Drivers' hours and tachograph rules for road passenger vehicles in the UK and Europe are set out at the DfT website at www.dft.gov.uk/stellent/groups/dft_rdsafety/documents/page/dft_rdsafety_504544.hcsp.

The Driving Standards Agency deals with driver training and testing: www.dsa.gov.uk.

The Vehicle Inspectorate deals with vehicle testing: www.via.gov.uk/vehicle_testing/index.htm.

The VOSA regulates operators of large goods vehicles (LGV) and passenger services vehicles (PSV): www.vosa.gov.uk/vosa.

Information about the road safety charity Brake can be found on its website at www.brake.org.uk.

Information about the charity for road crash victims, Roadpeace can be found on its website at www.roadpeace.org.

# Railways Industry

## Fatalities on the Railways

**10.13** The Office of Rail Regulation (ORR) reported 341 fatalities in the industry in its *Railway Safety Statistical Report 2006* although the vast majority of these fatalities occurred as a result of trespass or suicide (321):

- 4 employees and contractors were killed, compared to six in 2005;

- 8 passengers were killed;

- 10 pedestrians were killed at level crossings, compared with 16 in 2005; and

- there was one fatal train accident involving a car; and another incident in which a car driver died as a result of suicide.

In recent years, train crashes involving loss of life, particularly those at Clapham, Southall, Ladbroke Grove, Hatfield and Potters Bar have put railway safety in the spotlight, and it was partly because of these accidents, and the subsequent failure to prosecute any of the companies involved for manslaughter, that CMCHA 2007 will be enacted. Details of what caused these train crashes, and the subsequent prosecutions are set out in CHAPTER 1).

Rail passengers were also killed in the following incidents[1]:

- In March 1989, a train travelling from Horsham to London was hit by another travelling from Littlehampton to London at Purley in south London. Five people were killed and another 90 were injured. The driver, Robert Morgan, was convicted of manslaughter and sentenced to 18 months in jail, of which 12 were suspended, after he admitted passing a red signal, but in December 2007, his conviction was overturned (see below).

- Also in March 1989, two electric trains collided near Bellgrove station in east Glasgow, killing two people and injuring 52 more.

The cause of the crash was identified as a single-track system introduced by British Rail, which confused the train drivers.

• In January 1999, a commuter train ran into the buffers at Cannon Street station in London, killing two passengers and injuring another 240. The cause of the accident was identified as the driver failing to brake in time, but no charges were brought.

• In October 1994, two trains collided on a single track at Cowden in Kent after one of the trains passed through a red signal. Five people died and 11 people were injured.

• In August 1996, two trains collided at Watford Junction, killing one person and injuring another 69 injured. One of the drivers had passed through a red signal, but was cleared of manslaughter charges.

The rail union RMT points out that although high profile train crashes in which members of the public have been killed have attracted media attention, the deaths of railway workers tend to attract less attention. In its 2005 submission to the Home Affairs and Work and Pensions Committee which scrutinised the draft Corporate Manslaughter Bill (see CHAPTER 1), it highlighted the following:

In just one year (2004) eight railway workers were killed in four separate incidents, including that which occurred at Tebay in February 2004, when four workers were killed and three more injured when a runaway rail wagon came loose at a yard and ran four miles away down the hill on the track near Tebay before ploughing into the men working on the track.

The inquiry into the incident found that due to inadequate planning, a rail wagon had to be hired at extremely short notice and therefore there was little choice but to use a supplier who was relatively new and had not been thoroughly assessed. The rail wagon hired had brakes which were not functional, no test was carried out and the consequences were fatal.

In September 2004, two more workers were killed between Cannock and Hednesford. A road rail vehicle (RRV) being used to reposition rail as unloading and relaying of rail was taking place, reversed back up the track and struck the two men working on the relaying of rail. The union says that inadequate planning was to blame. A detailed work plan was not produced in time for the job, and insufficient planning had taken place in respect of an inspection of the site, so details were not safely recorded in the method statement produced for the work. Labour supply organisations were being used and sufficient notice should have been given of the job and the intended duties so that an assessment could be undertaken by the contractor of the necessary competence of the personnel required. This was not done and safe systems of work were not planned to take account of the multiple activities and vehicles being used on the worksite.

1   See *Tolley's Corporate killing – A managers' guide to legal compliance*, by Michael G Welham.

## Trade Union Views of CMCHA 2007

**10.14**   The RMT is extremely disappointed that CMCHA 2007 will not contain individual sanctions when it comes into force on 6 April 2008. RMT health and safety officer Paul Clyndes said:

'The union is extremely disappointed that the Act does not contain provision for custodial sentences.'

In November 2006 the union published a report by solicitors Thompsons, *Corporate Manslaughter and Corporate Homicide Bill: Impact on major rail disaster cases*, and says that this still represents the union's position with regard to the impact of the Act itself.

The report says that:

'In respect of the railway disasters which are the subject of this paper, from Southall in 1997 to Potters Bar in 2002, the Bill as currently drafted would make no difference in terms of sanctions. Bereaved families and injury victims are unlikely to consider it adequate that the only positive outcome of the Bill would be the ability to secure a manslaughter conviction and attach that label to companies guilty of gross corporate negligence.'

It also criticises the government for performing a U-turn from its 2000 position when it said:

'The Government considers that there is no good reason why an individual should not be convicted for aiding, abetting, counselling or procuring an offence of corporate killing'.

The report also says that there is a 'glaring loophole' whereby companies can establish complex corporate structures using subsidiary companies to avoid any liability on the parent – the report explains that the courts have not ruled that parent companies have a duty of care in relation to the activities of their subsidiaries. And it says that the 'senior management' test will continue to cause difficulties.

However, while the report argues that the new legislation would make no difference in terms of sanctions, it sets out that had the law been in place when the rail disasters highlighted in the report occurred:

'In respect of Southall, bearing in mind the history of near accidents which had not been acted upon, charges may have been brought under the new legislation had it been in force at the time.

'In connection with Paddington, it is likely that Railtrack would have been successfully prosecuted under the new law.

'Similarly, following Hatfield, it is likely that prosecutions under the new law would have succeeded.

'Applying the terms of the Bill to Potters Bar, prosecutions would probably have succeeded against Jarvis and Network Rail.'

The train drivers' union ASLEF is a little more positive. It believes that it is unfair that individual directors will not be liable under CMCHA 2007: 'If train drivers cause an accident they can go to prison – yet the bosses who provide them with equipment which may be faulty and cause an accident will get off scot-free.' But it concedes:

'Nevertheless, there are positive aspects to the Act. The reputation damage which a corporate manslaughter conviction will cause should ensure that safety is clearly on the radar. Hopefully even though management cannot be prosecuted as individuals, their actions will fall increasingly under the microscope.'

## Examples of cases involving manslaughter convictions following work-related deaths in the Railway Industry

**10.15**   While manslaughter prosecutions against large companies involved in rail disasters have all collapsed (see chapter 1), there have been cases involving manslaughter convictions of individuals in the industry.

### Mark Connolly and Roy Kennett (*MAC Machinery Services*)[1]

In March 2006, company director Mark Connolly, of MAC Machinery Services, sub-contractors for Carillion rail, was found guilty on four counts of manslaughter following the deaths of four rail workers at Tebay, Cumbria, in February 2004, and jailed for nine years, (although this was later reduced to seven). He was also found guilty on three counts of breaching health and safety laws.

Roy Kennett, Mark Connolly's crane operator, was also found guilty on four counts of manslaughter and on a single count of breaching health and safety laws and was jailed for two years.

### Robert Morgan (*train driver*)

Train driver Robert Morgan was jailed after he pleaded guilty to manslaughter following the Purley train crash (see 10.13), but he was recently cleared on appeal. His union, the train drivers union Aslef, said that the original conviction had not taken into proper account the fact that the signal involved was dangerous. It had been passed at danger on four previous occasions – by different drivers – between 16 October 1984 and the Purley tragedy. At the trial neither the prosecution nor the defence were aware that signal T168 was a 'multi-SPAD' (regularly passed at danger) signal. After his conviction was overturned, the union said: 'Today a signal with this history would be immediately assessed for risk and action would be taken to remedy the danger. This did not happen in 1989.'

Aslef has also pointed out that manslaughter prosecutions were also taken against drivers involved in the Southall and Watford train crashes (see 10.13) but these failed.

[1]   See (2006) 156 NLJ 1789 and CHAPTER 4.

## Railway Safety Legislation

**10.16**    Railway safety legislation is extremely complex and there are several Acts and sets of Regulations laying down safety standards in the rail industry.

The ORR summarises the legislation relating to railways on its website at www.rail-reg.gov.uk:

- the Railways Act 1993 (RA 1993) contains most of ORR's functions including, but not limited to, licensing, access agreements, review of access charges and enforcement. It also contains its statutory duties which it must take into account in exercising its functions. RA 1993 brought about the privatisation of the railways;

- the Railways Act 2005 largely amends RA 1993, transfering safety in relation to the railways from the HSE to ORR and most of the Strategic Rail Authority's functions to the DfT;

- the Railway and Transport Safety Act 2003 abolished the Rail Regulator and created the Office of Rail Regulation: Schedule 1 sets out the legal framework of ORR. It also established the Rail Accident Investigation Branch, which investigates railway accidents;

- the Transport Act 2000 has been largely repealed by the Railways Act 2005. It made some amendments to RA 1993, including the introduction of the regime in section 16A which enables ORR in certain circumstances to require the operators of railway facilities to provide new facilities, or facility owners to improve existing facilities; and

- the Railways and Other Guided Transport Systems (Safety) Regulations 2006, SI 2006/599, came into force on 10 April 2006 and replaced:

    o    the Railways (Safety Case) Regulations 2000, SI 2000/2688;

    o    the Railways (Safety Critical Work) Regulations 1994, SI 1994/299; and

    o    the Railways and Other Transport Systems (Approval of Works, Plant and Equipment) Regulations 1994, SI 1994/157.

Under SI 2006/599, which implements requirements in the Railway Safety Directive, railway operators and railway infrastructure managers on the mainline railway must maintain a Safety Management System (SMS); and hold a safety certificate (or 'authorisation' for infrastructure managers) showing that the SMS has been accepted by the safety authority before they are allowed to operate.

Tramways and heritage operators running trains at less than 40 km an hour will not require certification/authorisation, but do need to have and maintain a SMS.

Transport operators who require a safety certificate or authorisation must prepare an annual safety report.

SI 2006/599 also combines national provisions for non-mainline railways to maintain a SMS and to ensure the safe design of new and altered vehicles and infrastructure, through a process of safety verification. Safety verification replaces SI 1994/157 and controls initial integrity risks arising from the introduction of new or altered vehicles and infrastructure which introduce a significant and novel risk to the operation.

In addition, SI 1994/157 implements recommendations from Lord Cullen's Public Inquiry into the railway collision at Ladbroke Grove, on the control of safety critical work – this relates to the management of workers with regard to competence, fatigue and fitness. (See also CHAPTER 1 on the Working Time Regulations 1998, SI 1998/1833.

There are transitional arrangements which mean that the holder of an accepted railway safety case under the Railways (Safety Case) Regulations 2000, SI 2000/2688, is deemed to comply with the requirement to obtain a safety certificate and/or safety authorisation until a specified date, after which they will need to have obtained a full certificate and/or authorisation under SI 2006/599. This date depends on the date that their Railway Safety Case periodic review would have fallen due. Full certificate/authorisations are required by 1 October 2008 at the latest.

Other rail safety legislation includes:

- the Railways (Interoperability) Regulations 2006, SI 2006/397, which deal with the requirements of the high speed European rail network;

- the Transport and Works Act 1992, which contains offences regarding the consumption of alcohol and drugs by transport workers (which are enforced by the police); and it sets down general safety provisions concerning, for example, rail crossings and signs and barriers at crossings, approval of works, plant and equipment and directions limiting speeds and loads; and

- the Carriage of Dangerous Goods and Use of Transportable Pressure Equipment Regulations 2007, SI 2007/1573, which came into force on 1 July 2007. These consolidated the regulations relating to the carriage of all dangerous goods including radioactive materials.

ORR also publishes a number of safety publications, which can be downloaded from its website:

- *Guidance on minor railways* (September 2007);

- *Safety critical tasks – Clarification of ROGS regulations requirements* (August 2007);

- *Safe movement of trains* (May 2007);

- *Guidance on tramways* (November 2006);

- *Developing and maintaining staff competence* (March 2007);

- *Railway safety principles and guidance* is intended to give guidance and advice to those involved in the design and construction of new and altered works, plant and equipment (which includes trains and other rail mounted vehicles) capable of affecting the safety of railways, tramways or other guided transport systems, which require approval. The guidance is published in several parts and represents good practice at the time it was written:

  o *Railway safety principles and guidance Part 1* (1996);

  o *Railway safety principles and guidance Part 2A – Guidance on infrastructure* (1996);

  o *Railway safety principles and guidance Part 2B – Guidance on stations* (1996);

  o *Railway safety principles and guidance Part 2C – Guidance on electric traction systems* (1996);

  o *Railway safety principles and guidance Part 2D – Guidance on signalling* (1996);

  o *Railway safety principles and guidance Part 2E – Guidance on level crossings* (1996);

  o *Railway safety principles and guidance Part 2F – Guidance on trains* (1996);

  o *The management of steam locomotive boilers* (revised 2005);

  o *The provision of welfare facilities at transient railway infrastructure* (2005).

## Enforcement of Rail Safety Legislation

**10.17**  The Health and Safety (Enforcing Authority for Railways and Other Guided Transport Systems) Regulations 2006, SI 2006/557, make the ORR an enforcing authority for the purposes of HSWA 1974, giving the ORR powers to serve enforcement notices, and prosecute for breaches health and safety law affecting the railways (see 10.18). They also set out the areas of responsibility of the ORR and the HSE.

The memorandum of understanding between the HSE and ORR (April 2006) sets out that:

'The Railways Act 2005 (Amendment) Regulations 2006 remove "guided bus systems" and 'trolley vehicle systems' from the definition of "railway safety purposes", so these systems remain with HSE. The amendment regulations also make it clear that "transport system" does not include fairground equipment as defined in section 53 of the HSWA.'

## Office of Rail Regulation (ORR)

**10.18**    The ORR came into being in 2004, but in April 2006 it took over responsibility for health and safety regulation of the rail industry from the HSE. It is an independent statutory body led by a Board. The Secretary of State for Transport makes appointments to the Board for a fixed term of up to five years (and can also make dismissals).

Its key roles are:

- to ensure that Network Rail, which owns and operates the track and signalling (the national railway infrastructure) manages the network efficiently and in a way that meets the needs of its users;

- to encourage continuous improvement in health and safety performance;

- to secure compliance with relevant health and safety law, including taking enforcement action as necessary;

- to develop policy and enhance relevant railway health and safety legislation; and

- licensing operators.

In addition to giving advice and information, and giving warnings, ORR inspectors – HM Rail Inspectorate (HMRI) – serve improvement and prohibition notices, vary exemption conditions, issue formal cautions in England and Wales only, and prosecute (or report to the Procurator Fiscal with a view to prosecution in Scotland). (A formal caution is a statement by an inspector, accepted in writing by the duty holder that they have committed an offence for which there is a realistic prospect of conviction. A formal caution is only be used where a prosecution could be properly brought. Formal cautions are entirely distinct from a caution given under the Police and Criminal Evidence Act 1984 by an inspector before questioning a suspect about an alleged offence.)

In 2006/07 HMRI issued 28 enforcement notices: 23 improvement notices and four prohibition notices. It also took six prosecutions, resulting in fines totalling £943,000 and costs of £132,770.

## British Transport Police (BTP)

**10.19**    The BTP enforces law and order on the railway, including London Underground, Docklands Light Railway and Croydon Tramlink and is also responsible for pursuing any possible criminal prosecutions, including manslaughter, following a rail accident (see also CHAPTER 6).

# Maritime Safety

**10.20**    This section covers work on water-borne transport – including shipping, fishing, and craft on inland waterways.

Statistics on deaths at sea and on inland waterways are published in the annual report of the Marine Accident Investigation Branch (MAIB) annual report. According to the most recent report, there were 56 deaths as a result of UK vessel accidents:

Six of these deaths occurred on merchant vessels 100 gross tonnes (gt) and over, five on merchant vessels under 100 gt, 28 on non-commercial pleasure craft, which include craft from inflatable dinghies and canoes, to sailing yachts and jet skis.

There were 17 deaths on fishing vessels and the MAIB says that fishing is the most dangerous to be, by many orders of magnitude, the most dangerous occupation in the UK.

In addition, a further seven deaths occurred on non-UK commercial vessels in UK waters.

New research for the Maritime and Coastguard Agency (MCA) and DfT by Dr Stephen Roberts and Judy Williams at Swansea University School of Medicine, *Update of mortality for workers in the UK merchant shipping and fishing sectors,* demonstrates how dangerous merchant shipping, and particularly fishing, continues to be.

The research shows that there were 32 deaths from accidents in the UK merchant shipping industry between 1996 and 2005. The report says that the fatal accident rate in UK merchant shipping during this period was 12 times higher than in the general workforce of Great Britain. It was also 2.5 times higher than in the construction industry and 8.5 times higher than in manufacturing.

During the same period there were a total of 160 deaths from accidents identified in the UK fishing industry. The fatal accident rate in the UK fishing industry over this time was 115 times higher than that in the general workforce of Great Britain. The fatal accident rate in fishing was also 24 times higher than in the construction industry and 81 times higher than in manufacturing

Two maritime accidents in particular, the *Herald of Free Enterprise* disaster and the *Marchioness* disaster – and the subsequent inquiries, failed prosecutions and campaigning by the families of those killed – were influential in the eventual reform of the law and the passing of CMCHA 2007 (see CHAPTER 1 for details).

## Trade Union Views of CMCHA 2007 and its Impact on Maritime Safety

**10.21**  Andrew Linington, head of Campaigns and Communications at maritime union Nautilus UK says that CMCHA 2007 should help to ensure that corporations are held to account rather than its members, a number of whom have found themselves in court charged with man-slaughter following fatal accidents at sea. He says:

'The problem for our members at present is that the captain of the ship is legally responsible for safety, but in many cases they do not have the ability to influence safety issues, since these are dealt with and set by onshore managers. Very often they cannot govern what happens on their ship, because crucial issues such as the determination of budgets is done onshore.'

The RMT represents merchant seafarers and it set out in its submission to the Home Affairs and Work and Pensions Committees (see 10.13) that it wanted to see CMCHA 2007 give protection to seafarers in the same way as shore based workers.

General Secretary Bob Crow said:

'RMT believe that the failure to make individual Directors directly accountable under the legislation represents a lost opportunity. How-ever we welcome the fact that the Act will cover all ships in UK territorial waters, and all UK registered ships wherever they may be.'

According to the Ministry of Justice (MoJ), CMCHA 2007 applies to deaths on foreign flagged vessels in UK waters and to deaths on UK flagged vessels (ie British ships) outside UK waters.

A MoJ spokesperson said:

'This represents no change in the law: UK criminal law already extends to territorial waters and British vessels (and indeed the other areas cited in section 28 of the Act, like oil rigs). An example of British vessel aspect of this in practice is the Herald of Free Enterprise. There, a British ship capsized just outside the port of Zeebrugge but it was still possible to bring a prosecution in the courts here.'

**10.22** Examples of manslaughter prosecutions and convictions with regard to work-related deaths at sea or inland waterways are rare; although a spokesperson for the MCA said there are cases against individuals are currently in the pipeline.

## Maritime Safety Legislation

**10.23** The legislation applying to health and safety at sea and on inland waterways is very complex. A Memorandum of Understanding between the HSE, MCA and the MAIB for health and safety enforcement activities etc at the water margin and offshore sets out the roles and powers of these organisations.

The MCA enforces marine safety. It's statutory powers and responsibili-ties derive primarily from the Coastguard Act 1925, the Merchant Ship-ping Act 1995 and the Merchant Shipping and Maritime Security Act 1997 and associated secondary legislation. It is an agency of the DfT. Its website is at www.mgca.gov.uk

The Memorandum of Understanding also sets out the domestic legislation that applies: the Merchant Shipping Act 1995 and several merchant shipping, and merchant shipping and fishing vessels regulations, which set out specific health and safety requirements ranging from lifting operations and lifting equipment, to manual handling, to the employment of young workers. There are regulations covering docks and harbours: the Docks Regulations 1988, SI 1988/1655, and the Dangerous Substances in Harbour Areas Regulations 1987, SI 1987/37, and specific regulations with regard to the offshore industry (see CHAPTER 13). The Adventure Activities (Enforcing Authorities and Licensing Amendment) Regulations 1996, SI 1996/1647, include sailing for schools and young people under the age of 18.

Inland waterways are also subject to specific safety rules. For example, the RMT union is currently campaigning against government proposals that would reduce the training standards for boatmasters skippering passenger and cargo vessels on the Thames. These were introduced after the *Marchioness* tragedy and the union says that the introduction of a new generic boatmaster's licence as proposed need not undermine the specific arrangements for boatmasters for the River Thames in this way. Under an EU directive on harmonising boatmasters' licences there is provision for the application of higher standards for the Thames.

Linington explains that because shipping is an international industry, UK legislation is often derived from European directives, and ultimately from the International Maritime Organisation (IMO), fundamentally the main safety regulator, and to some extent the International Labour Organisation (ILO).

He says it is important to note that the International Safety Management Code – which was introduced by the IMO in response to incidents such as the *Herald of Free Enterprise* disaster – requires that there is a designated person within management onshore with responsibility for health and safety issues, who is ultimately accountable and responsible for safety on ships.

As with other sectors, if a manslaughter charge is brought, this is done by the police (although there will be a joint investigation with the HSE or MCA).

*Memorandum of Understanding between the Health and Safety Executive, the Maritime and Coastguard Agency and the Marine Accident Investigation Branch for health and safety enforcement activities etc. at the water margin and offshore* is available on the HSE's website at: www.hse.gov.uk.

## Aviation Safety

**10.24**   The Civil Aviation Authority's (CAA) Safety Regulation Group (SRG) publishes details of fatalities in UK aeroplanes, helicopters and general aviation (see below) on an annual basis. According to its *Safety Plan Update* published in April 2007 and based on provisional data for 2006:

- none of the nine accidents involving UK large public transport aeroplanes were fatal. The last fatal accident involving this category of aircraft was in 2001, where a Shorts SD360, on a cargo flight, suffered a double engine flameout shortly after take-off from Edinburgh and crashed into the Firth of Forth, killing the two people on board. When considering passenger flights involving UK large public transport aeroplanes, the last fatal accident occurred in 1999, where a Boeing 757 crashed on landing at Gerona, Spain and one person suffered injuries that subsequently proved fatal;

- in 2006, UK small public transport aeroplanes were not involved in any accidents. The annual average for the last 10 years has been two accidents. The last fatal accident involving this category of aircraft was in 2005, where an Islander crashed on approach to Campbeltown while on an ambulance flight and two people suffered fatal injuries;

- there were five accidents involving UK large public transport helicopters in 2006, compared with the annual average of the previous five years which is two accidents. One of these five accidents resulted in fatalities: A SA365 Dauphin crashed into the sea in Morecambe Bay in December 2006, resulting in fatal injuries to all seven people on board (five oil platform workers and two crew). The Air Accident Investigation Branch (AAIB) investigation is ongoing; and

- UK general aviation aeroplanes and helicopters were involved in 176 accidents in 2006, seven of which were fatal. There were three fatal microlight accidents and one fatal gyroplane accidents. The British Gliding Association reported that during the 2005/06 gliding year there were three fatal accidents.

The CAA is not planning to produce separate guidance on CMCHA 2007 and a spokesperson for the pilots' union BALPA says that the 2007 Act has not been raised in discussions in the industry. The CAA says that it is not aware of any manslaughter charges being brought in the industry.

### Aviation Safety Legislation

**10.25**   Aviation safety is covered by a vast array of legislation. The CAA's SRG publishes a document setting out UK domestic aviation safety legislation: CAP 393: Air Navigation: The Order and the Regulations, which can be accessed at www.caa.co.uk/docs/33/CAP393.pdf. This runs to some 438 pages, and is published for the use of those concerned with air navigation (but is not to be treated as authoritative).

In addition, the European Aviation Safety Agency (EASA) is the rule-making and standard setting organisation for aviation safety regulation on behalf of member states. The Agency has taken over aircraft and product certification, responsibility for rules related to the design and maintenance of aircraft products and parts, and standard setting for organisations involved in the design, production and maintenance of these products and parts. Over time, its rulemaking role will include aircraft operations, flight crew licensing and air traffic management matters. It website is at www.easa.eu.int.

In addition, the International Civil Aviation Organisation sets the international context for safety, see www.icao.int.

## The Role of the Air, Marine and Rail Accident Investigation Branches

**10.26** These organisations are concerned with the determining the circumstances and causes of accidents, in order to preserve life and avoid accidents in the future, not to apportion blame or liability. They do not enforce the law or carry out prosecutions.

The MAIB investigates marine accidents to or on board UK ships worldwide, and other ships in UK territorial waters.

The Rail Accident Investigation Branch (RAIB) is the independent railway accident investigation organisation for the UK. It investigates railway accidents and incidents on the UK's railways to improve safety.

The UK Air Accidents Investigation Branch (AAIB) is part of the DfT and is responsible for the investigation of civil aircraft accidents and serious incidents within the UK.

# Chapter 11

# Agriculture

## Overview

### 11.1

> This chapter looks at fatalities in agriculture, and provides examples
> of cases involving manslaughter convictions following work-related
> deaths, as well as health and safety prosecutions highlighted by the
> Health and Safety Executive (HSE).
>
> It looks at the National Farmers' Union view of the impact of the
> Corporate Manslaughter and Corporate Homicide Act 2007
> (CMCHA 2007), together with that of the T&G Section of the
> general Unite union, and it sets out legislation applying to the
> agricultural sector, in addition to the general health and safety
> legislation set out in CHAPTER 2, including the Gangmasters Licens-
> ing Act 2004.
>
> Finally, it refers to the TUC's publication on the safety of migrant
> workers, and the T&G section of the general Unite union campaign
> to improve the safety of children on farms.

## Fatalities in Agriculture

**11.2**    Farming has one of the highest accident rates in the country,
second only to construction. There were 34 fatalities in 2006/07, 10 of
which resulted from being injured by an animal. Heath and Safety
Commission (HSC) statistics show that over the 11-year period from
1996/97 to 2006/07, nearly three quarters of all fatal injuries in these
industries were due to:

- being struck by a moving vehicle (22 per cent) – the vehicles
  commonly involved are tractors, forklift trucks and all terrain
  vehicles;

- falling from a height (17 per cent);

- being struck by a moving/falling object (17 per cent);

- contact with moving machinery (10 per cent); and
- being trapped by something collapsing/overturning (7 per cent).

## National Farmers' Union (NFU) and T&G Section of Unite Views of CMCHA 2007

**11.3**     The National Farmers' Union (NFU) view is that the structure of the farming industry, which is made up largely of small and micro-businesses, means that the Corporate Manslaughter and Corporate Homicide Act 2007 (CHCHA 2007) is unlikely to have a major impact in terms of the way that prosecutions for work-related deaths in the industry are taken when it comes into effect on 6 April 2008. It says that it is likely that farmers who are found to be responsible for a death as a result of their work activities will continue to be prosecuted for breaches of health and safety legislation (and in rare cases for the individual offence of gross negligence manslaughter) because the nature of farming means that in most cases there is not a corporate entity to prosecute.

Chris Kaufman, National Secretary for the Rural Agricultural and Allied Workers (RAAW) Group of T&G (Unite) said:

> 'No union official who has ever sat with a grieving family who said goodbye in the morning to a husband and father – never to see them alive again – can possibly forget the pain.

> 'Agriculture has a truly appalling health and safety record for occupational death, injury and disease – and that's not even taking into account the massive under-reporting of 'accidents' and illness in the industry or the huge numbers of casual, mostly migrant workers who have boosted the employed ranks of late (estimated at over a quarter of a million).

> 'UNITE/T&G thinks that real change will only come with the shock of the first clang of the closing prison door. Employers cannot wash their hands of corporate responsibility, even if many, by virtue of their size, are able to duck under the Act's radar from April 2008. There are many big companies operating in horticulture, dairy and arable and many partnerships which formed limited companies who would be candidates for prosecution – especially where the union's solicitors were instructed to pursue a member's case.'

## Examples of cases involving manslaughter convictions following work-related deaths in agriculture

**11.4**     There have been many prosecutions taken against farmers and other agricultural business owners following fatalities, and also a number of cases have included manslaughter convictions.

**11.5**

*Peter Pell*

In December 2003, Peter Pell was sentenced to a year's imprisonment after pleading guilty to the manslaughter of employee, Shaun Cooper, who was killed as he cleaned chicken sheds at a farm in Nottinghamshire while working for Pell's poultry shed cleaning company. On top of the manslaughter conviction, two charges under section 2 and section 8 of the Health and Safety at Work etc. Act 1974 (HSWA 1974) were left to lie on file, and Pell was ordered to pay £5,000 costs. Cooper was found crushed on a skid steer vehicle which Pell had removed all the safety features from (see CHAPTER 4 for full details of the case).

*Alistair and Edward Crow*

In July 2001, Alistair Crow, and his father Edward Crow were found guilty of the manslaughter of Lee Smith, a 16-year old agricultural student who was working for the Crows on a placement from a local agricultural college. Smith died in November 1999 when the seven tonne JCB Potato Loader he was operating was hit by a lorry on the A49, crushing him to death (See CHAPTER 4 for full details of the case).

# Health and Safety Legislation Applying to the Agricultural Sector

## Gangmasters

**11.6**     Following the Morecambe Bay tragedy (see CHAPTER 4) the Gangmasters Licensing Act 2004 was introduced.

The Gangmasters Licensing Act 2004 applies to the whole of the UK and covers agricultural and horticultural work, shellfish gathering and the processing or packaging of any products from these industries or sectors.

A gangmaster is defined as anyone employing, supplying and or supervising a worker to do work in the sectors above; whether based in the UK or offshore. The Act covers all forms of sub-contracting.

Employment agencies and employment business (as defined by the Employment Agencies Act 1973) come within the ambit of this Act if they are engaged in activities for which a licence is required.

The Act established the Gangmasters Licensing Authority which investigates and enforces the Act. It sets the conditions of the licence; processes licence applications; sets and collects licence fees; maintains a public register of licensed gangmasters; and has the power to modify, suspend or revoke licences.

There are four specific offences:

● operating without a licence;

● obtaining or possessing a false licence or false documentation which is likely to cause another person to believe that a person acting as a gangmaster is licensed;

● using an unlicensed gangmaster (subject to a reasonable steps/due diligence defence); and

- obstruction of enforcement officers/compliance officers exercising their functions under the Act.

The Act also amended the Proceeds of Crime Act 2002 to enable the assets of convicted gangmasters to be seized, and the Police and Criminal Evidence Act 1984 to make operating without a licence and/or possession of a false licence or false documentation arrestable offences.

The Gangmasters Licensing (Exclusions) Regulations 2006, SI 2006/658, set out exclusions and the Gangmasters (Appeals) Regulations 2006, SI 2006/662, set out the appeals procedure.

Licensing started on 6 April 2006 for gangmasters supplying workers to the agriculture, horticulture and fish processing industries. From 1 December 2006, it has been illegal to hire workers from an unlicensed gangmaster in these industries. Licensing for shellfish gathering has a separate timescale: issuing began on 1 October 2006, and became mandatory on 1 April 2007.

Anyone found to be operating without a valid licence will be fined up to £5,000 or imprisoned for up to 10 years – the Act contains provision for higher sentences for repeat offences – if convicted of operating without a licence or possessing a false licence/documents. Gangmasters are charged between £250 and £4,000 for each licence.

There are trade union demands for legislation to be extended to the construction sector (see chapter 9 Construction).

## Other Agriculture Legislation

**11.7**    Other legislation applying specifically to agriculture includes regulations made under the Agriculture (Safety, Health and Welfare Provisions) Act 1956, such as the Prevention of Accidents to Children in Agricultural Regulations 1998, SI 1998/3262, and the Agriculture (Tractor Cabs) Regulations 1974, SI 1974/2034, although much of this older legislation has been revoked as a result of more modern legislation which applies across industrial and service sectors (see CHAPTER 2).

# Cases involving Health and Safety Prosecutions following Work-Related Deaths Highlighted by the HSE

**11.8**

*Peter Pell[1]*

Peter Pell (who was found guilty of manslaughter – see 11.4) had previously been fined for health and safety offences in October 1996 after an employee was electrocuted when his tipper truck came into contact with overhead power lines. Skegness magistrates found Pell guilty of breaching section 2(1) of HSWA 1974, the Management of Health and

278

Safety at Work Regulations1992, SI 1992/2051, reg 3, and the Electricity at Work Regulations 1989, SI 1989/635, reg 14 and he was fined a total of £3,000 and ordered to pay £1,453 costs.

The HSE guidance *Shock horror – Safe working near overhead power lines in agriculture* highlights the dangers of working near high voltage power lines. When tall machinery like combines, tipping trailers or long irrigation pipes, are used too close to power lines then the consequences can be fatal for nearby workers and those who go to assist.

If a piece of equipment gets too close or comes into contact with an overhead line, the electricity will be conducted and it can pass through anyone who is on the equipment or touching it. A jet of water, liquid slurry or a fishing rod can also cause a discharge of electricity and a high risk of a fatal or severe shock.

One of the biggest problems is that people do not notice overhead power lines. Lines which are obvious can blend in to the scenery. The guidance leaflet sets out minimum clearance distances from different sorts of pylons and lines.

It also aims to provide a trainee's summary guide and is aimed at agricultural college students and farm workers. It is supported by a video showing reconstructions of the type of events that typically lead to accidents. The video and leaflet are intended to provide resource material for college lecturers and trainers.

The overall message for anyone working in agriculture is to remember to 'Look out – Look up' for overhead power lines.

Copies of *Shock horror – Safe working near overhead power lines in agriculture* (INDG389) are available from HSE Books.

*Shock horror: The dangers of electrocution by overhead power lines* video is available from HSE Books.

[1] See HSE Press Release 22 December 2003.

## 11.9

### Hillcrest EM Ltd[1]

In November 2006, Hillcrest EM Ltd of Normanton, pleaded guilty to breaches of health and safety law and was fined £4,000 with costs of £2,232 awarded, following the death of David Willott, who died from multiple injuries he sustained while using a pump driven by a tractor power take off (PTO) to unblock a blocked slurry tanker. There was no power input connection guard and his clothing caught on the shaft and he became entangled, which resulted in the amputation of his arm

The company pleaded guilty to breaches of reg 1(1) of the Provision and Use of Work Equipment Regulations 1998, SI 1998/2306, for not ensuring that measures were taken to prevent access to a dangerous part of machinery November 2006. It also pleaded guilty to a breach of reg 3(1) of the Management of Health and Safety at Work Regulations 1999, SI 1999/3242, for not carrying out a suitable and sufficient risk assessment. Magistrates fined the company £4,000 and awarded costs of £2,232.

The prosecution prompted a warning from the HSE to the farming community to ensure all farm equipment is properly guarded. Every year people are killed or seriously injured in accidents involving tractor PTOs and PTO drive shafts, most of which could be prevented by the PTO and PTO drive shaft being fitted with guards of good design which are properly used and maintained.

The HSE previously highlighted an incident in which a 12-year-old child was killed when he became entangled on an unguarded PTO shaft connecting a tractor to a roller mill. It appears that he approached or was in the vicinity of a roller milling machine whilst the machine was being operated and became entangled on the power input connection stub on the PTO drive shaft.

It advises that simple points to remember are:

● broken, damaged or badly fitting guards can be just as dangerous as no guard at all;

● protect the tractor PTO with a shield covering the top and both sides of the PTO so that it stops anyone making contact with it;

● guard PTO drive shafts by enclosing them along their full length;

● when buying a guard with a PTO drive shaft, make sure it has the CE mark on it and has a Declaration of Conformity, also check it has been made and tested to the appropriate standard and make sure it's the correct size and length;

● check all guards regularly, eg daily when in use, for wear and damage;

● ensure no one is in danger before engaging the PTO drive;

● do not wear scarves, loose or damaged clothing which could be caught in moving parts;

● never try to clear blockages from a PTO-driven machine while it is moving. Always: disengage the power drive, stop the tractor engine, ensure the controls are in neutral and the hand brake is applied, remove the engine key, wait for all movements to cease before attempting to clear any blockage and use a tool to clear the blockage.

[1]  See HSE Press Release 8 November 2006.

**11.10**

*Enidvale Ltd, trading as BK Grain Handling Engineers and Mansel Raymond, trading as Raymond Bros[1]*

In June 2007, the HSE prosecuted Enidvale Ltd trading as BK Grain Handling Engineers, of Marlborough, Wiltshire, and Mansel Raymond, trading as Raymond Bros of Jordanston Hall, Letterston, Pembrokeshire following the death of Alan Ellison in June 2004. He was helping to install a new grain drying system at Mr Raymond's farm when he fell around 8m through a fragile roof onto a concrete floor below.

His employer, Enidvale Ltd pleaded guilty to breaching regs 3(1) and 7(1) of SI 1999/3242 and was fined £20,000 and ordered to pay costs in excess of £8,000.

Raymond Bros was found guilty of breaching s 2(1) of HSWA 1974, in relation to risks to safety of their employees, and was fined £10,000 and order to pay costs of £15,000.

HSE inspector Wayne Williams commented:

'Working at height is extremely dangerous, as this case has so tragically demonstrated, and it is imperative that employers carry out proper risk assessments, and ensure their staff are adequately trained to work at height.'

A 'black spot' report highlighting the dangers of falls from heights in the agricultural industry was produced by the HSE after analysing accident statistics over a 10-year period to 2002. Falls from height claimed 80 lives and it remains the second largest cause of fatalities in the agricultural sector.

The report, *Why fall for it? Preventing falls in agriculture*, shows that falls have occurred because risks were not properly assessed and little, or no, safety equipment was used. Many accidents occur during roof work and involve falls through roof sheets and roof lights.

It says that the fragile nature of many roofing materials is constantly ignored as farmers appear to take chances, risking serious injury and even death. The booklet highlights the importance of selecting and using the correct equipment for carrying out safely any work at height.

Some fatal accidents and many serious injuries occur because the wrong equipment is used. For example, accidents happen when ladders are used for work which could be done more safely from alternative access equipment such as a scaffold tower or a work platform on a materials handler.

Copies of *Why fall for it? Preventing falls in agriculture'* (INDG369), are available free from HSE Books.

[1] See HSE Press Release 28 June 2007.

**11.11**

*Harry Hall, Mark Hall, Hall Hunter Partnership (Farming) Ltd and Aventis Services Ltd[1]*

Berkshire fruit farming company Hall Hunter Partneship (Farming) Ltd was prosecuted in July 2005 following an HSE investigation into the deaths of two young Polish workers who became entangled in farm machinery used to coil rope.

Hall Hunter specialises in commercial cultivation of strawberries and raspberries, which involves the erection and dismantling of 'polytunnels', secured with long lengths of rope.

Adam Borowik and Sebastian Skorupski died after they became entangled between rope and a rotating shaft. They were using a tractor-mounted fleece winder machine, which was not suitable for rope winding as it did not have an automatic cut off in the event of entanglement. In addition, they had not been adequately trained, nor made aware of the dangers posed by the task.

The judge, Jonathan Playford QC, said:

'In relation to Hall Hunter Partnership, no adequate risk assessment had been carried out and it was particular to the partnership to address this problem because they had 300 workers, many of whom were students and many from abroad who may not have had full understanding of safe working practices.'

Hall Hunter Partnership (Farming) Ltd, directors Harry Hall and Mark Hall and the company contracted to erect and dismantle polytunnels, Aventis Services Ltd, were fined a total of £80,000.

Harry Hall, Mark Hall and Hall Hunter Partnership (Farming) Ltd all pleaded guilty to breaching section 2(1) of HSWA 1974 and reg 3(1)(a) of SI 1999/3242.

Aventis Services Ltd pleaded guilty to breaching s 3 (1) of the HSW Act 1974 and reg 3(1)(b) of SI 1999/3242. All four defendants were fined £10,000 for each count and ordered to pay costs of £15,516.25.

The HSE says that farmers must ensure they take into account how machines should be operated when deciding safe working practices and if they want to use a machine for a purpose for which it was not designed, they should check with the manufacturer before doing so.

Farmers must also ensure that workers are trained for the tasks they are asked to do and made aware of any dangers. It says that this case also highlights the necessity of carrying out a proper risk assessment, which would have shown the serious risk of entanglement.

The HSE has developed software to help farmers carry out a comprehensive health and safety assessment of their farms and this is available free from the HSE website at www.hse.gov.uk/agriculture/assessment/index.htm.

[1] See HSE Press Release 19 July 2005.

**Safety of Migrant Workers**

**11.12** Guidance on the safety of migrant workers from the TUC aimed at employers as well as safety representatives says that since the deaths in

Morecambe Bay (see CHAPTER 4), there have been further individual tragedies involving migrant workers, mainly in agriculture and construction.

It points out that while many migrant workers face no, or very little, increased risk, since they speak fluent English, may have worked in the UK for many years and have the same working conditions and security as non-migrant workers, 'there is no doubt that migrant workers with low English language skills or with vulnerable employment or residency status are at greater risk'. The guidance concentrates on this latter group of workers.

In 2006, the HSE published research based on interviews with 200 migrant workers and reported findings including the following:

- a third had received no health and safety training and most of the rest only had a short induction session;

- many migrant workers worked over 60 hours a week, particularly in agriculture, catering and processing and packaging;

- undocumented or unauthorised workers who worked under greater fear of dismissal and deportation had less information about their health and safety rights; and

- around half of these interviewed had difficulties with English, although many tried to hide it from their employer for fear of not getting work.

The TUC says that lack of protective clothing is also an issue in many cases – the guide says:

'Often migrant workers are asked to provide their own protective clothing, not told about the need for protective clothing or issued with inappropriate or inadequate protective clothing and equipment. Often protective clothing is second hand, and there is little training in how to use it.'

It also states that:

'... few migrant workers report knowing of a risk assessment having been done for their job and it is quite clear that, in many industries where migrant workers are concentrated, risk assessments are rare. Even where a risk assessment has been done, it is unlikely that it has covered many of the issues that might be specific to migrant workers, such as cultural differences or language problems.'

It advises:

'For most employers the HSC guidance "Five steps to risk assessment" (see CHAPTER 2) is the best starting point, although the risk assessment should also specifically address the presence of migrant workers, in particular issues around previous work experience, perceptions of risks, language and literary skills, the applicability of current training and safety materials, and whether training methods need to be tailored to different groups of workers.'

The TUC wants to see more enforcement activity. It says that the main reason that many migrant workers face increased risks to their health, safety and welfare is simply the lack of adequate enforcement of existing regulations and is calling for much greater resources to be put into enforcement of those areas where migrant workers are concentrated.

*Safety and migrant workers – a guide for safety representatives* can be downloaded from the TUC website at www.tuc.org.uk.

**11.13**

---

*T&G (Unite) Children on Farms Campaign*

In the 10-year period between 1993 to 2003, 45 children were killed on farms and half of all farmyard fatalities are children. A survey carried out by HSE inspector Mike Walters, seconded to the T&G (now part of the general Unite union) found that half of the accidents involved children being run over or struck by moving vehicles, and that the second most common cause of death was drowning in slurry or dirty water lagoons and in moving grain.

The key objectives of the campaign are to prevent children under 16 years old from working on farms; and to bring about a cultural shift in the rural and farming community to stop farms being regarded as an extension of the home and, by association, a fit place for children to be. Specifically, the union wants:

- a ban on children under 16 driving or operating farmyard equipment such as tractors and criminal penalties for adults who allow under-16s to drive farm vehicles;

- ratification, without exclusions, of International Labour Organisation (ILO) Article 16 which states that children under 16 are prevented from working in hazardous circumstances; and

- a government strategy for improving health and safety on farms, embracing improved monitoring and enforcement, written risk assessments and an awareness raising campaign.

WT Banks and Co (Farming) Ltd[1] was prosecuted following the death of a child in October 2003. A fork-lift truck being driven by the farm director caused the death of his nephew when the child either fell from the moving machine or was reversed over. The company was fined £17,500 and costs of £2,779 were awarded.

---

[1] See HSE Prosecutions Database.

# Chapter 12

# Manufacturing

## Overview

**12.1**

This chapter looks at work-related deaths, and prosecutions following deaths, in the manufacturing sector, which covers a very wide
and diverse range of work activities: including engineering, shipbuilding and repair, motor vehicle repair, textiles, printing, wood
working, paper, rubber, plastics, metals, foundries, ceramics, quarries, glass, concrete, cement, waste recycling and the food industry.
The Health and Safety Executive (HSE) estimates that some four
million people are employed in manufacturing. In particular, the
chapter:

- looks at the fatality rate in the sector;

- describes cases involving manslaughter convictions resulting
  from work-related deaths in manufacturing; and

- looks at cases involving health and safety prosecutions arising
  from work-related deaths in manufacturing that have been
  highlighted by the HSE.

## Fatalities in Manufacturing

**12.2**    According to the Health and Safety Commission (HSC) and
National Statistics report, *Statistics of Fatal Injuries 2006/07*, 35 workers
were killed in manufacturing industries last year, compared with 45 in the
previous year.

Those manufacturing industries with the highest rate of fatal injury are:
recycling of scrap and waste; manufacture of wood and products of
wood; manufacture of other non-metallic mineral products; and manufacture of basic metals.

Around two-thirds of all fatal injuries in manufacturing during the
10-year period 1997/98 to 2006/07 were due to:

- being struck by a moving/falling object (23 per cent of all fatalities);
- contact with moving machinery (19 per cent);
- falling from a height (15 per cent); and
- being struck by a moving vehicle (15 per cent) with fork-lift trucks killing five people.

## Cases involving Manslaughter Convictions in Manufacturing

**12.3** A number of cases involving work-related deaths in the manufacturing industry have resulted in manslaughter convictions of companies and individuals:

### *John Horner and Teglgaard Hardwood (UK) Ltd*

In February 2003, Teglgaard Hardwood (UK) and one of its directors, John Horner, pleaded guilty at Hull Crown Court to the manslaughter of labourer Christopher Longrigg, who died in April 2000 when a stack of timber fell on him. The company was fined £25,000 and Horner was also given a 15-month prison sentence, suspended for two years.

### *Timothy Dighton (Concrete Company Ltd)*

In June 2007, managing director Timothy Dighton, and area manager Roy Burrows, pleaded guilty to manslaughter at Norwich Crown Court and were convicted and later jailed for 12 months and 9 months respectively, following the death of technician Christopher Meachen. The company, Concrete Company Ltd, was ordered to pay fines and costs totalling £164,000 (£75,000 for breaches of health and safety legislation and £89,000 costs).

Christopher was killed in November 2005 as a result of the multiple injuries he sustained after becoming caught in an unguarded slew conveyor at the company's plant on the Longwater Industrial Estate, Costessey, Norfork. He had been cleaning the pit of the conveyor while the conveyor belt was still running.

### *Michael Shaw (Change of Style)*

The director and business owner of a stone-cutting company near Southampton, Michael Shaw, was found guilty of the manslaughter of a 22-year-old employee, David Bail, and given a two-year suspended prison sentence at Winchester Crown Court in August 2006. In November 2006, the suspended prison sentence was declared to be too lenient at the Criminal Appeal Court, and was increased to a 15-month jail sentence. The prosecution was brought by Hampshire police who led the investigation into David's death. He died from massive head injuries after he was caught in an automated stone cutting machine on which safety features had been de-activated.

### *Paul White (director of MW White Ltd)*

Company director, Paul White received a 12-month custodial sentence (six months' imprisonment and the remaining time released under a supervision order) at Norwich Crown Court following the death of employee Kevin Arnup[1] at his paper recycling business, MW White Ltd of Ketteringham, Norwich in December 2003. The custodial sentence followed Mr White's earlier guilty plea to manslaughter and health and safety charges. His company was also fined £30,000 with costs of £55,000 for offences under s 2(1) and s 37(1) of the Health and Safety at Work etc Act 1974 (HSWA 1974).

### Ian Morris (*Eng Industrial Services*)

Ian Morris, a sole trader who owned the paint stripping business, Eng Industrial Services, was convicted of the manslaughter of Ghulam Sarwar and Mumtaz Hussain who died after being overcome by dychlormethane chemical fumes which had escaped from the processing area of the factory. He was sentenced to nine months in jail, and also charged under s 2(1) of HSWA 1974 and regulation 6 of the Control of Substances Hazardous to Health Regulations 1999, SI 1999/437.

### Roger Jackson (*Easy Moss Products Ltd*)

In March 2000, Roger Jackson, the director of Easy Moss Products Ltd in Dewsbury, which made linings for hanging baskets, was convicted of the manslaughter of John Speight, a worker with special needs, who was crushed to death in February 1988. John never regained consciousness after falling from a former British Rail platform trolley which was being used for refuse at the company. It had been lifted six feet into the air by a forklift truck so that Speight could empty rubbish into a skip. The trolley crashed down on his chest and he died in hospital five days later.

Jackson received a 12-month sentence, suspended for two years and was convicted of two health and safety offences and fined £10,000 and ordered to pay £25,000 costs.

### Norman Holt (*David Holt Plastics*)

In December 1989, Norman Holt, director of David Holt Plastics, pleaded guilty to the manslaughter of employee George Kenyon, who died in May 1988 after he was dragged into the blades of a plastic crumbing machine. The Crown Prosecution Service (CPS) accepted a 'not guilty' plea from another director, David Holt, although the case was ordered to 'remain on file'. The company and directors were fined a total of £47,000 for health and safety offences.

Further details of all these cases can be found in CHAPTER 4, and CHAPTER 1 contains further details of the prosecution against Teglgaard Hardwood (UK) Ltd.

¹   See also *Arnup and anor v MW White Ltd* [2007] EWHC 601 (QB); [2007] All ER (D) 521 (Mar).

## Health and Safety Legislation applying to Manufacturing

**12.4**   Most industry specific legislation has now been replaced by the Workplaces (Health, Safety and Welfare) Regulations 1992, SI 1992/3004. However, a few provisions of the Factories Act 1961 remain in force and although SI 1992/3004 has replaced and revoked much of the Non-Ferrous Metals (Melting and Founding) Regulations 1962, SI 1962/1667, some provisions still apply. Similarly, the Shipbuilding and Ship-Repairing Regulations 1960, SI 1960/1932, still apply to certain operations in shipyards, harbours and wet docks.

# Cases involving Work-related Deaths and Health and Safety Prosecutions highlighted by the HSE

## 12.5

### *Corus UK[1]*

Steelmaker Corus UK Ltd was fined £1,333,000 and ordered to pay costs of almost £1.75 million in December 2006 following charges brought by the HSE after three workers died in 2001 from a blast furnace explosion at the company's Port Talbot site. The explosion was caused by water in the furnace coming into sudden contact with hot material. As water turned into steam it expanded rapidly, creating pressure, and blew a confined vessel apart.

Stephen Galsworthy, Andrew Hutin and Leonard Radford were fatally injured in a massive explosion which occurred within Blast Furnace no 5 at the Corus works on 8 November 2001. In December 2006, the company pleaded guilty before Swansea Crown Court to two charges of failing to ensure the safety of their employees and others brought by HSE under s 2(1) and 3(1) of HSWA 1974.

In a statement at the conclusion of the case, HSE Director for Wales, Terry Rose said:

'This was systematic corporate management failure at the Port Talbot works. Proper management attention may have broken the chain which led to the explosion. I hope Corus, and indeed the iron and steel industry worldwide, learn from Port Talbot and make sure that those lessons are put into practice in their management systems, and maintained. This must be a wake up call for the industry. The process is centuries old but the risks need to be managed to the highest modern standards.'

Rose went on to say:

'As far as we can establish an explosion of this magnitude is unprecedented in any blast furnace anywhere in the world.

'The proper design, maintenance and operation of the water cooling system are vital to the safe operation of the furnace and the ability to detect, and stop, water leaking into the furnace in quantity is very important. Corus failed to do this in relation to Blast Furnace 5. Those failings were spread over many years, with many different people involved. That is why HSE prosecuted the company, rather than any individuals.'

### *Pin Croft Dyeing and Printing Co Ltd[2]*

A Chorley company was fined £100,000 and ordered to pay £18,895 costs after pleading guilty in November 2006 to three criminal charges brought by the HSE following the death of employee Daryl Lloyd, in a tow tractor incident.

Rosemary Leese Weller, the HSE inspector who investigated the case, said:

'Daryl's death was entirely preventable by simple health and safety precautions such as provision of a well maintained vehicle, properly maintained floor surface and by ensuring sufficient training in its use.'

Pin Croft Dyeing and Printing Co Ltd was fined a total of £100,000 after pleading guilty to three charges:

- under HSWA 1974 s 2(1) in that it failed to ensure the safety of its employee;

- under the Management of Health and Safety at Work Regulations 1999, SI 1999/3242, reg 3(1)(a) in that it failed to make a suitable assessment of the risks to Daryl's health and safety; and

288

- under the Provision and Use of Work Equipment Regulations 1998, SI 1998/2306, reg 5(1) in that it failed to ensure that the tow tractor being driven by Daryl was maintained in efficient working order.

## World's End Waste (Investments) Ltd[3]

A London-based waste transfer company, World's End Waste (Investments) Ltd, was fined £100,000 at the Old Bailey in May 2005. The prosecution, brought by the HSE, followed its investigation into the death of Sam Boothman at a waste transfer site at Pensbury Place in Wandsworth on 1 June 2004.

The tipper truck driver was working for World's End Waste Ltd at its Wandsworth site. He had discharged his load at the transfer shed and had moved the truck to another part of the site to secure its tailgate, when he was hit from behind by the bucket of a shovel truck driven by another employee. He suffered severe multiple crushing injuries and died shortly after. World's End Waste Ltd pleaded guilty to a charge that it had failed to ensure the safety of its employees, including Mr Boothman, so far as reasonably practicable.

Speaking after the case, HSE principal inspector Margaret Pretty, said:

'The case shows everyone in the waste transfer industry the importance of planning for workplace transport and having safe systems of work in place. A one-way traffic system, the use of a banksman and designated pedestrian walkways, all of which were subsequently introduced by the company, may have prevented this fatality.'

World's End Waste (Investments) Ltd pleaded guilty to a charge of breaching section 2(1) of HSWA 1974 at the City Magistrates' Court on 4 April 2005. The company was sentenced at the Central Criminal Court, Old Bailey on 27 May 2005 and fined £100,000 and ordered to pay £4,982 costs.

## Bill Briggs-Price[4]

Newark scrapyard owner Bill Briggs-Price was fined £50,000 at Nottingham Crown Court in April 2005.

At a previous hearing at Newark Magistrates' Court, Mr Briggs-Price admitted breaching HSWA 1974 s 2(1) in failing to ensure the safety of employees and SI 1999/3242 reg 3(1) in failing to complete a suitable and sufficient risk assessment. He was fined £40,000 on the first charge and £10,000 on the second. He was also ordered to pay £6,749 costs.

The HSE prosecution followed an investigation into the death of Simon Teece at Briggs Metal in Newark, on 10 January 2004. Simon died after a metal shearing machine sliced through him while he was attempting to change one of the blades. Mr Teece had a hand held remote unit that controlled the machine in his possession at the time of the incident. However, its emergency stop device was broken.

After the sentencing hearing, HSE inspector Giles Hyder said:

'Employees were exposed to high and entirely preventable risks and this horrific incident could have been easily avoided if a few very simple precautions had been taken. Properly isolating the machine while the work was being carried out and keeping the machine in general good repair could have prevented this incident.'

## Leadmaster Ltd[5]

Nottingham paint shop Leadmaster Ltd was fined £20,000 at Newark Magistrates' Court in April 2005.

The HSE prosecution followed an investigation into the circumstances surrounding the death of Robert Fountain, who had been spray-painting a 300kg fabricated steel grid hanging from a forklift truck in the company's Newark paint shop (trading as Parsons) on 17 June 2004. He was found by his son Jason, trapped against a steel table by the grid, which had fallen on him.

The company admitted one charge under HSWA 1974 s 2(1). It was fined £20,000, the maximum at a magistrates' court, and ordered to pay costs of £2,922.

HSE inspector David Appleton said:

'This was a tragic incident to a newly recruited employee. It would have been simple and cheap to prevent this death by using a rope or strap to secure the fabrication, or by placing it on trestles for painting.

The incident underlines the need for a safe system of work to be devised for all tasks and for everybody involved to understand how to do the job safely.'

## Environmental Tyre Disposals Ltd (ETD) and MIDCO Waste Management Ltd (MIDCO)[6]

Two waste management companies were fined a total of £140,000 at the Old Bailey in March 2005. The fine followed a prosecution brought by the HSE after an investigation the death of Thomas Akwasi Aseidu-Ampofoh, who was crushed to death under a telescopic reach truck.

The incident took place at Environmental Tyre Disposals Ltd's (ETD) tyre recycling site at Stonehill Business Park, Edmonton, London on 1 July 2001, where MIDCO Waste Management Ltd (MIDCO) also operate a tyre shredding business. Thomas, who was employed by ETD, was instructed to support MIDCO staff in shredding tyres. It was during this operation, whilst he was driving a telescopic reach truck using it to push tyres towards the shredder (to be placed in the shredder by a crane operated by a MIDCO employee) that it toppled over crushing him between the side of the truck and the ground.

The investigation found that both companies failed to take adequate measures to prevent or control risks arising from the use of the truck by untrained operators.

Simon Hester, HSE investigating inspector commented:

'Mr Aseidu was employed by ETD primarily as a tyre checker. He was not trained to operate the loader which was the task he undertook on that day and which cost him his life ... A risk assessment, adequate supervision and suitable training were all absent in this case. This left the level of safety provided by both companies far below the required standard. Both companies have now addressed these shortcomings but I am convinced that if these simple steps had been taken, Mr Aseidu's death would have been prevented.'

Environmental Tyre Disposals Ltd of Taplow, Maidenhead, Berks pleaded guilty to a charge under HSWA 1974 s 2(1) and was fined £70,000.

MIDCO Waste Management Ltd of Hinckley, Leicestershire pleaded guilty to charges of breaching HSWA 1974 ss 2(1) and 3(1) and was fined £70,000.

ETD and MIDCO were ordered to pay HSE's costs of £29,982 together with a compensation award of £3,492 to Mr Aseidu's brother for funeral expenses and a bereavement order made to his widow of £7,500.

The HSE also issued a safety alert to the waste and recycling industry following nine reported fatalities in an eight week period, seven of whom were killed by being struck by a vehicle.

Commenting on the figures, Paul Harvey, principal inspector of HSE's Waste and Recycling Section said:

'The tragedy of these incidents must act as a stimulus for the industry to review its procedures, making sure that vehicle risks are properly controlled. Wherever possible pedestrians and vehicles should be segregated, paying special attention to transfer stations and sorting areas. Street collection activities need to address the risks to collection staff and other road and pavement users.

'Using reversing aids such as mirrors, CCTV, detectors and beacons do reduce the risks. In most public access areas you will usually need to provide reversing assistants, their job being to help the driver and prevent or warn pedestrians entering manoeuvring areas when the risks cannot be controlled adequately by other means.'

## Howard Hawkins[7]

In March 2005, the HSE and Sussex Police warned motor vehicle repair garages about the importance of having a safe system in place for handling and storing petrol after the owner of a Sussex garage, Howard Hawkins, was found guilty of breaching section 2(1) of HSWA 1974. He was sentenced at Lewes Crown Court receiving a fine of £10,000 with costs of £15,000. The prosecution followed the death of an apprentice mechanic, Lewis Murphy, who died four days after becoming engulfed in flames in an explosion at the Anchor garage, Peacehaven, Sussex on 19 February 2004

HSE inspector Joanna Teasdale said:

'HSE issues simple guidance for petrol handling and storage in garages and we are always happy to advise on these matters. Most of the hazards of fuel removal can be mitigated by the use of a proprietary fuel retriever; providing a suitable container; eliminating static electricity; and capturing any petrol vapour displaced. This case is particularly distressing as Mr Murphy was learning the trade and so was heavily reliant on the duty of care owed to him by his employer. This was sadly absent.'

*Health and safety in motor vehicle repair'* (HSG67) provides practical advice on how to organise health and safety in garages and explains which laws apply to motor vehicle repair and how to comply with them. HSE free leaflet/poster *Safe use of petrol in garages* (INDG331) represents best practice and gives general guidance on petrol and fuel retrieval. Both are available from HSE Books and the free leaflet can be downloaded from the HSE website.

## British Sugar plc and VM Plant Ltd[8]

Fines totalling £650,000 were imposed on two companies following the death of a woman at a British Sugar plc factory.

The HSE prosecuted British Sugar plc and contractor VM Plant Ltd at Bury St Edmunds Crown Court in February 2005 after dispatch clerk Lorraine Waspe was killed on 5 February 2003. The 40-year-old British Sugar employee was run-over by a shovelling vehicle at the firm's factory in Bury St Edmunds, Suffolk.

British Sugar admitted failing to ensure that Lorraine Waspe and other workers were not exposed to risks to their safety and thereby breaching HSWA 1974 ss 2(1) and 3(1) and was fined £300,000.

The company was also fined £100,000 for failing to ensure that workplace transport was operated safely at the site. In particular, it failed to segregate pedestrians from areas where vehicles were in operation adequately and ordered to pay £31,457 costs.

Cambridge-based contractor VM Plant Ltd, which owned and operated the shovelling vehicle involved in the accident was found guilty and fined £250,000 for failing to ensure the health and safety of employees and people not in its employment. The firm was also ordered to pay prosecution costs of £13,739.

Commenting on the case, investigating HSE inspector Frank Sykes said:

'The court has recognised the importance of preventing accidents by ensuring that all workplace transport is conducted to suitable standards. The level of fine reflects the seriousness of this incident and the very tragic loss of life.'

## Sovereign Rubber Ltd[9]

Sovereign Rubber Ltd of Stockport was fined a total of £175,000 plus £20,000 costs after pleading guilty at Manchester Minshull Street Crown Court in May 2004 to three charges arising from two incidents at their premises in Carrington Field Street, Stockport in October 2001.

Company employee Malcolm France, a maintenance engineer, died while attempting to clear a blockage on a Carter Mk 3 rubber mixing machine. Nearly three weeks earlier, his colleague Lee Williams had suffered severe lacerations to his hand while dealing with the same machine but this accident was not reported to the HSE.

The fines related to two charges under s 2(1) of HSWA 1974 and one charge of reg 3(2) of the Reporting of Injuries, Diseases and Dangerous Occurrences Regulations 1995, SI 1995/3163.

## Ford Motor Co[10]

Ford Motor Co was fined a total of £300,000 at Winchester Crown Court in June 2003 for breaching health and safety legislation after Christopher Shute died at a Ford factory in Southampton when he fell into an emulsion paint overspray capture tank, used to collect excess paint from spray booths on the transit van production line.

Ford was fined £250,000 for breaches of s 3(1) and £50,000 for breaching s 2(1) of HSWA 1974 and ordered to pay an additional £46,688 towards the costs of bringing the prosecutions.

The HSE said that the fine sent out a clear message regarding the legal requirement to ensure proper control of contracted companies.

Paul MacKenzie, Director, Philip Services (Europe) Ltd and Peter Preston, Field Services Manager, Philip Services (Europe) Ltd pleaded guilty to separate breaches of duties under HSWA 1974 s 37 and were fined £5,000 each.

[1]   See HSE Press Release 15 December 2006.
[2]   See HSE Press Release 29 November 2006.
[3]   See HSE Press Release 31 May 2005.
[4]   See HSE Press Release 11 April 2005.
[5]   See HSE Press Release 19 April 2005.
[6]   See HSE Press Release 30 March 2005.
[7]   See HSE Press Release 11 March 2005.
[8]   See HSE Press Release 22 February 2005.
[9]   See HSE Press Release 12 May 2004.
[10]  See HSE Press Release 17 June 2003.

**12.6**

---

*The explosion at Stockline plastics factory, Maryhill, Glasgow*

On 11 May 2004, an explosion at the Stockline plastics factory in Maryhill Glasgow, which was occupied by ICL Plastics Ltd and ICL Tech Ltd, killed 9 employees and seriously injured 40 others including a member of the public. Those who died were Peter Ferguson, Thomas McAulay, Stewart McColl, Margaret Brownlie, Annette Doyle, Tracey McErlane, Timothy Smith, Ann Trench and Kenneth Murray.

It was described as the worst health and safety incident in Scotland since Piper Alpha (see CHAPTER 1), and the worst on mainland Scotland since the 1960s, in a report by the Universities of Strathclyde and Stirling, *The ICL/Stockline disaster – an independent report into working conditions prior to the explosion* (August 2007).

A joint investgation involving the HSE and Health and Safety Laboratory (HSL), Strathclyde Police and Crown Office and the Procurator Fiscal Service (COPFS) identified the cause of the explosion as a leak from a corroded pipe carrying Liquefied Petroleum Gas (LPG). The leaked LPG accumulated in an unventilated room, and ignition of the gas caused an explosion of such force that it caused the building to collapse. Most of those who died were working in a second floor office.

The HSE submitted a report of its investigation to the Procurator Fiscal in 2005 and prosecutions under health and safety legislation were taken. (In Scotland health and safety prosecutions must be made through the Procurator Fiscal office rather than being taken directly to court by HSE staff.)

ICL Plastics Ltd was fined £200,000 at the High Court at Glasgow, after pleading guilty to a breach of HSWA 1974 ss 2 and 4. The company had failed to ensure the safety of its employees and others by not carrying out a suitable and sufficient risk assessment or having a proper system to inspect and maintain the LPG pipe.

Its associate company ICL Tech Ltd was fined £200,000 after pleading guilty to a breach of sections 2 and 3 of HSWA 1974 for the same failings.

The joint Strathclyde and Stirling report questioned why the prosecution opted for charges under HSWA 1974, as opposed to a prosecution for the common law offence of corporate homicide, concluding:                                                                      ➡

293

'It is likely that this decision was influenced by the general pessimism in the Scottish legal profession about such prosecutions following the successful appeal against Transco's prosecution for corporate homicide in June 2003 ... the cost of the prosecution of Transco, combined with the crown's failure to secure a prosecution created a climate in government and in the wider legal profession that undermined support for the prosecution of such cases.'

No director or company has ever been convicted of a homicide offence following a work-related death in Scotland and the *Transco* case remains the single case where such a prosecution was attempted, even though the legal test that must be met is less strict in Scotland, compared with England and Wales (see CHAPTER 4). In the *Transco* appeal the court ruled that although the offence of corporate homicide was admissible in Scotland, in the case of *Transco* such a charge was inadmissible (see CHAPTER 1).

The report called for a full-scale public inquiry to investigate how decisions are made to prosecute corporations for committing the most serious offences, and on 1 October 2007 it was announced by the Lord Advocate, Elish Anglioni QC, and the Secretary of State for Work and Pensions, Peter Hain MP, that a public inquiry will take place. It is the first public inquiry under the UK Inquiries Act 2005 in mainland Britain.

The Lord Advocate commented:

'As health and safety legislation is reserved to the United Kingdom Parliament, and the investigation of deaths in Scotland fall solely under my jurisdiction as the Lord Advocate, only a joint inquiry could truly address all of the issues which arise as a result of this case.'

Mr Hain said:

'The findings of the inquiry are likely to have significance across the United Kingdom. It is vital for both the United Kingdom and Scottish Governments to work together to establish a full inquiry into the events leading to the explosion and the lessons which we can learn for the future.

'When talking to the families they told me their key concerns are to establish the facts, provide an explanation of why this happened, explain where the failures were and ensure we do not allow this to happen again. They also raised particular concerns over the qualifications of the pipe installers, the approach to risk assessment and the availability of advice on these matters – all these issues can and should be examined.

'They have also made it clear to me that they want to see the role that the Health and Safety Executive (HSE) played in regulating➡

these premises prior to the incident is fully investigated. I fully support them on this point. No issue relevant to the circumstances should be out of bounds.'

In December 2007 it was announced that Lord Gill, the Lord Justice Clerk and Scotland's second most senior judge, was appointed Chairman of the Inquiry, and that the terms of reference are:

- to inquire into the circumstances leading up to the incident on 11 May 2004 at the premises occupied by the ICL group of companies, Grovepark Mills, Maryhill, Glasgow;

- to consider the safety and related issues arising from such an inquiry, including the regulation of the activities at Grovepark Mills;

- to make recommendations in the light of the lessons identified from the causation and circumstances leading up to the incident; and

- to report as soon as practicable.

# Chapter 13

# Energy and Utility Supply

## Overview

### 13.1

> This chapter looks at where work-related deaths have occurred in the energy and utility supply industries, focusing particularly on the extractive industry element of the sector, where there is a higher than average fatality rate.
>
> It refers to specific legislation applying to this sector; and it sets out prosecutions following work-related deaths that have been highlighted by the Health and Safety Executive (HSE).

## Fatalities in the Extractive and Utility Supply Industry

**13.2**    The latest report on work-related deaths from the Health and Safety Commission (HSC) and National Statistics, *Statistics of fatal injuries 2006/07* shows that although there are a relatively small number of fatalities, the rate of fatal injury in what is termed the 'extractive and utility supply' sector is higher than the national average, mainly as a result of the extractive industry element of the sector (which includes mining and quarrying).

There have been 88 fatal injuries to workers in the 10 years from 1997/98 to 2006/07 in the extractive and utility supply industries. Of these:

- 16 involved being struck by a moving/falling object;

- 14 resulted from falls from a height;

- 11 involved contact with electricity; and

- a further 8 were from being struck by a moving vehicle.

In 2006/07, 10 workers were killed – five were coal mining operatives, two were quarry workers and three were from 'other' occupations.

There are some 137 coal mining sites operating within Great Britain including 26 licenced underground coal mines employing around 5,598 people and 31 opencast coal sites. The HSE confirms that: 'Mines can be hazardous environments and the possibility of fire, flood, explosion and collapse has the potential to simultaneously affect a large number of people', although fatal accidents in the mining industry have, over the previous four years, averaged less than one.

According to the HSE, the quarry industry fatality rate averaged three times that of construction. In the 10-year period 1991/92 to 2000/01 there were 19 fatal injuries. But it reported that since the launch of the industry's Hard Target Initiative in June 2000, a 52 per cent reduction in accidents has been achieved.

The HSE defines a quarry as including, 'all surface mining: ie opencast coal, industrial minerals, kaolin, ball clay, brick clay, barytes, gypsum, silica sands, fluorspar, china stone, slate, fullers' earth, limestone, dolomite, basalt, and aggregates. Thus defined, the industry consists of some 25,000 direct employees, 25,000 contractors and daily 35–40,000 lorry drivers.'

The initiative included education and training initiatives to improve competence and health and safety performance; working with key groups such as chief executive officers (CEOs) and employee representatives to ensure effective control of high-risk plant, such as vehicles and conveyors, and high-risk processes such as explosives and geotechnics; and highlighting particular safety concerns such as falls from height, tip and excavation rules, provision and use of seatbelts, stability of tips and excavations, and quarry design.

The current phase, *Target zero – a world class industry: working towards sustainability* aims to achieve a further 50 per cent reduction in injuries by 2010 and zero incidents by 2015.

With regard to the offshore industry, the HSE says that: 'Although there have been improvements in health and safety offshore since the Piper Alpha disaster in 1988, the risks are ever present – fire, explosion, release of gas and structural failure all have the potential to cause major loss of life.' Two workers were killed in the industry in 2006/07, the same figure as for 2005/06.

In addition, offshore workers have been killed in accidents at sea and in air accidents, which are recorded separately by the Marine Accident Investigation Branch (MAIB) and the Civil Aviation Authority (CCA), respectively.

For example, in December 2006, seven people were killed when a SA365 Dauphin helicopter crashed into the sea in Morecambe Bay as it was taking oil workers to the North Morecambe gas platform, killing the two crew and five oil workers on board. The accident is currently being investigated by the Air Accident Investigation Branch (AAIB).

And in September 2007, three men died after an accident on the gas rig standby vessel Viking Islay in the North Sea, off the East Yorkshire coast. The emergency response and rescue vessel was supporting the Ensco 92 drilling rig on BP's Amethyst field when the accident happened as the men were securing an anchor on the bow of the vessel. The accident is currently being investigated by the MAIB.

In November 2007, the HSE published the results of a three-year study, which had inspected and investigated 100 offshore installations, and said that the message for those in the board rooms of the oil and gas offshore companies was: 'there is still much more to do and those in a position of leadership must ensure that systems, procedures and best practice is adopted to achieve the goal of the UK continental shelf becoming the safest offshore sector by 2010'.

A copy of the report is available on the HSE website on http://www.hse.gov.uk/offshore/programme.htm.

## Union and Employer Views of the Corporate Manslaughter and Corporate Homicide Act 2007

**13.3**    The representative organisation for UK offshore oil and gas industry companies licensed by the Government to explore for and produce oil and gas in UK waters and those who form any part of the industry's supply chain, Oil and Gas UK, issued a statement with regard to the forthcoming Act in April 2006:

'The UK's offshore oil and gas industry takes its responsibilities towards the safety of its workforce very seriously, and a great deal of effort is being made across the sector to help make the offshore workplace a safe environment for all. Significant improvements have been made in the industry's safety performance over the past ten years, but more work needs to be done if the UK is to reach its goal of becoming the safest oil and gas region in the world by the year 2010. It should also be noted that the Health and Safety at Work Act already provides a framework for unlimited fines and the possibility to prosecute individual Directors.'

Jake Molloy, general secretary of the OILC trade union, which was set up in the aftermath of the Piper Alpha disaster, said that the union was disappointed with the Act. It had wanted to see more 'innovative sentencing options'.

It produced a report in September 2005, Beyond Inadvertance – An OILC Discussion Paper on Corporate Killing, which said:

'This legislation is an opportunity not to be missed to develop innovative sentencing options. Corporate probation is one such. A company could agree to a programme of internal reform, management re-education and external oversight and in exchange would earn a discount on its fine when the external auditor assured the court that the necessary corporate remedies had been achieved. Other possibilities include suspension without pay of senior managers, prohibition of director's bonuses and share options etc.'

The report also called for the Government to use the supply chain to induce good practice:

'The Government has signalled its intention that, for all major procurement contracts, it will set a good example and buy only from suppliers who have proved that they comply with health and safety legislation and who have in place satisfactory health and safety procedures and practices. Presumably, doing business with a firm with a criminal conviction for unlawful killing will be out of the question until such times as rehabilitation is satisfactorily completed. The potential for loss of business on this scale may frighten the board more than the prospect of a peppercorn fine such as the £900,000 paid by Shell earlier this year for the deaths of two men on the Brent Bravo platform [see para below]. The fine sounds impressive until it is realised that it is the equivalent of a few pence to someone on an average salary.'

## Specific Health and Safety Legislation

### Offshore Oil Platforms

**13.4**    There is specific legislation applying to the sector to deal with the hazards arising from the operation of fixed/mobile installations, wells and pipelines, supported by legislation linked to generic industrial hazards, as follows.

The Offshore Installations (Safety Case) Regulations 2005, SI 2005/3117, require that all offshore installations have a safety case accepted in writing by HSE before they start operating in UK waters. Those parts of an installation that are identified as critical for the safety of the installation must be verified as suitable by independent and competent people.

A safety case is the means by which a dutyholder shows that:

* the management system is adequate to ensure compliance with relevant statutory provisions;

* the management system ensures satisfactory management of arrangements with contractors and sub- contractors;

* adequate arrangements for audits and reporting have been established;

- all hazards with the potential to cause a major accident have been identified and evaluated; and

- all major accident risks have been evaluated and measures have been, or will be, taken to control the risks to ensure that relevant statutory provisions will be complied with.

Other legislation includes the following.

- The Offshore Installations (Safety Representatives and Safety Committees) Regulations 1989, SI 1989/971, which require consultation with safety representatives when reviewing and revising a safety case, as well as preparing one.

- The Offshore Installations and Pipeline Works (Management and Administration) Regulations 1995, SI 1995/738, which set out requirements for the safe management and administration of offshore installations, including the use of permit to work systems. The regulations require owners (or operators) to appoint a competent manager to be in charge of the installation; and ensure the safety of the helideck and helideck operations and appoint a competent person to control all helideck operations.

- The Offshore Installations (Prevention of Fire and Explosion, and Emergency Response) Regulations 1995, SI 1995/743, provide for the protection of people from fire and explosion, and for securing effective emergency response. The regulations require operators (or owners) to take measures to prevent fires and explosions and provide protection from any which do occur; and provide effective emergency response arrangements.

- The Offshore Installations and Wells (Design and Construction, etc) Regulations 1996, SI 1996/913, are aimed at ensuring the integrity of installations, the safety of offshore and onshore wells, and the safety of the workplace environment offshore. The Regulations require operators (and owners) to ensure the installation is structurally sound, stable and, if necessary, buoyant; provide, maintain and keep clean accommodation, washing and toilet facilities; and ensure that workplaces are, clean, well ventilated, of a reasonable temperature and not overcrowded.

The Health and Safety at Work etc Act 1974 (Application outside Great Britain) Order 2001, SI 2001/2127, extended the Health and Safety at Work etc Act 1974 (HSWA 1974) offshore. As a result:

- HSWA 1974 applies to diving to examine or carry out remedial work on the sea bed immediately following the removal of an installation;

- the definition of 'offshore installation' includes supplementary units providing power and other support services to installations; and

- HSWA 1974 applies to the use and operation of all buildings and structures within the territorial seas (ie the 12 mile limit), including so-called 'energy structures' to generate wind/wave power, and any cables connecting them to the National Grid onshore.

In addition, merchant shipping legislation applies to vessels. A leaflet for offshore and marine support workers explaining the roles of the different organisations which look after health and safety, *Regulating health and safety in the UK offshore oil and gas fields – Who does what?*, has been published by the HSE, the Maritime and Coastguard Agency (MCA) and the Marine Accident Investigation Branch (MAIB) of the Department for Transport. The guidance is available on the HSE website and from HSE Books.

More advice on HSE's Offshore Division, is available on the HSE website at www.hse.gov.uk/offshore/index.htm. A number of publications can be downloaded from the site, including: *Planning to do business in the UK offshore oil and gas industry? What you should know about health and safety*, which contains a summary of health and safety legislation applying offshore.

## Mines

**13.5**    The Management and Administration of Safety and Health at Mines Regulations 1993, SI 1993/1897, apply to coal and non-coal mines. These set out the duties of mine owners, employers and employees and provide for the appointment, authority and duty of mine managers. *Redgrave's Health and Safety*[1] set out the regulations, which require that:

- the mine owner must make financial and other provision to ensure, so far as is reasonably practicable, that the mine is managed and worked in accordance with relevant statutory provisions;

- the HSE must be sent notification of the intention to begin working at a mine;

- the mine owner must appoint a suitably qualified and competent manager to manage, command and control the mine. In addition, a substitute must be appointed to hold the authority and perform the duties of the manager in their absence;

- a suitable management structure must be established, and must be set down in writing, to ensure that the mine is worked safely and those working below ground are under thorough supervision at all times;

- the manager must ensure, so far as is reasonably practicable, that all plant and equipment is safely installed and systematically inspected, examined, tested and maintained by suitably qualified and competent people; and

- the manager must ensure that arrangements are in place to ensure that there is adequate inspection of all parts of the mine by a suitably qualified and competent person.

The regulations also set out requirements regarding qualifications and training, the appointment of suitably qualified and competent surveyors to ensure that suitable accurate plans and sections of the mine are prepared and maintained; as well as records, notification of certain information to the HSE and the provision and display of information.

Other legislation includes:

- the Coal Mines (Owners' Operating Rules) Regulations 1993, SI 1993/2331, which resulted from the privatisation of British Coal;

- the Mines Miscellaneous Health and Safety Provisions Regulations 1995, SI 1995/2005, which implemented the European 'Boreholes' Directive; and

- the Boreholes, Sites and Operations Regulations 1995, SI 1995/2038, protect those involved in onshore drilling operations; and

- the Escape and Rescue From Mines Regulations 1995, SI 1995/2870.

Regulations to control the level of inhalable and respirable dust in coal mines, the Coal Mines (Control of Inhalable Dust) Regulations 2007, SI 2007/1894, came into force in October 2007. The measures do not derive from EU legislation, but take account of the Chemical Agents Directive and maintain implementation of the Extractive Industries (Mines and Quarries) Directive.

The HSE microsite on mining is at www.hse.gov.uk/mining/index.htm.

[1] Michael Ford and Jonathan Clarke, *Redgrave's Health and Safety*, fifth edition, LexisNexis Butterworths (2007).

## Quarries

**13.6**    The Quarries Regulations 1999, SI 1999/2024, cover all quarries specific health and safety issues. The Regulations cover risk control, use of explosives, safety of excavations and tips, involving the workforce in health and safety, and duties of employers and people at work.

Under the regulations, no person can undertake any work in a quarry unless he or she is competent to do so (or is acquiring such competence through training and supervision). The HSE says that a lack of competence has shown itself in the historically poor accident and ill health history of the industry.

The regulations are workplace rather than employer-based, so contractors and hauliers, for example, who work daily on quarry sites, are covered, since the legislation applies to:

- those employed directly by the operator;

- those on contract or agency workers; and

- those who drive lorries into and out of quarries.

The HSE document *Do you work in a quarry? A simple guide to the Quarries Regulations 1999* sets out the following:

The regulations cover mineral extraction; crushing, screening, washing, drying, bagging and similar work; transport around a site and to (but not on) public roadways; and tips (including stockpiles) of any kind.

Most duties under the regulations are placed on the operator – generally the company running the quarry.

The operator must ensure that the quarry is designed, staffed and equiped so that it can be run safely and must consider the following:

**Planning and preparation**

- consider the site geology;

- decide what plant is required;

- decide on site layout including haul roads and the siting and building of tips;

- take into account the presence of roadways, streams, electricity lines etc;

- appoint a suitable overall quarry manager and management team, setting out their responsibilities;

- assess the risks and ensure a plan is prepared and revised as required, including risks to health and safety from materials and equipment;

- set up lock-off and permit-to-work systems for particularly hazardous tasks;

- develop a health and safety document and site rules and ensure that everyone understands them; and

- notify the HSE about the quarry and any hazardous excavations or tips.

**Day-to-day work**

- ensure there are enough suitable employees and contractors to do the work;

- ensure that all employees and contractors are competent, and have had adequate training, including proper induction, for the work they have to do. They must be properly trained and have the experience and knowledge to work safely and some need formal qualifications, e g explosives supervisors, geotechnical specialists and shotfirers. Induction should include a site tour explaining relevant hazards and how they are dealt with and also the first-aid and other emergency arrangements. In addition, training or coaching will often be required for people taking on new responsibilities or using new equipment or systems of work;

- encourage the workforce to be actively involved in health and safety;

- ensure that the work is properly co-ordinated and that contractors co-operate with each other;

- report accidents, dangerous occurrences and cases of ill health to HSE as required by the Reporting of Injuries, Diseases and Dangerous Occurrences Regulations 1995, SI 1995/3163, (see CHAPTER 2).

**Monitor and review**

Monitor and review physical safeguards, eg guards, interlocks and visibility aids and safety procedures:

- routinely;

- after accidents or near misses; and

- when working practices change significantly

in order to:

- ensure safeguards and safety procedures are satisfactory and appropriate and work in practice;

- explain the findings to everyone affected; and

- put any required changes into practice.

**Health and safety document**

All operators are required to prepare a health and safety document demonstrating that the risks at the quarry have been identified and are properly controlled. This must set out in writing:

- what the risks are;

- the measures taken to control those risks;

- how the quarry is managed; and

- how the work of everyone, including contractors, is co-ordinated.

The health and safety document must be kept under the review and must be available to every employer and person at work at the quarry.

**Other provisions**

The guidance also sets out that:

- quarries must be properly inspected and maintained to safeguard people's health and safety, and guidelines should set out what should be inspected, how often, in what detail and who should do the inspections;

- areas of the quarry where there are particular health or safety hazards need to be marked and treated as danger areas. Unauthorised people must be excluded from such areas, for example, by erecting warning signs and barriers. People should only enter a danger area if it is essential and when appropriate safeguards are in place. There should be barriers that clearly identify the boundary of the danger area and make entry impossible without a conscious effort; and

- suitable barriers must be provided around the quarry if members of the public are likely to trespass on to the site.

The Regulations also set out specific requirements regarding benches and haul roads, vehicles, escape and rescue facilities, permits to work, safety drills, fire and explosion hazards, control of harmful and explosive atmospheres, lighting, explosives, excavations and tips and record keeping.

The HSE microsite on quarrying is at www.hse.gov.uk/quarries/index.htm

### Nuclear Industry

**13.7**    Legislation regulating safety in the nuclear industry covers health, safety and radioactive waste management at nuclear sites, which aims to protect both the public and workers. In addition, there is also legislation to protect nuclear and radioactive materials on licensed civil nuclear sites, sensitive nuclear information and those employed in the civil nuclear industry, against 'criminal or malevolent acts that threaten national security, the environment or public safety'.

### *The Nuclear Installations Act 1965*

**13.8**    The Nuclear Installations Act 1965 (NIA 1965), as amended, requires that a site cannot have nuclear plant on it unless a site licence has been granted by the HSE. NIA 1965 stipulates that only a corporate body, that is, a legally united body that can act as one individual, such as a registered company or a public body, can hold such a licence. The Act requires the HSE to attach conditions to nuclear site licences. There are 36 standard conditions set out in the HSE document *Nuclear site license conditions* and cover safety issues including:

- preventing unauthorised access to the site (or parts of the site);

- controlling the introduction and storage of nuclear matter on the site to ensure safety;

- recording where nuclear matter is sent so that HSE/Nuclear Installations Inspectorate (NII) can be sure that there are adequate arrangements for safely handling such material at the destination, and to ensure that licensable activities are not carried out on non-licensed sites;

• keeping adequate records for a suitable period to ensure that the safety case for operation is available at all times, that design and construction information is available for decommissioning, that operational records are available to assist investigations in the event of an accident or incident and operational records are available for the statutory number of years after the cessation of operations for the purpose of assisting any claims of damage to health as a result of exposure to ionising radiation;

• ensuring that there are adequate arrangements to deal with incidents that may occur on the site;

• providing warning notices to advise what to do in the event of a fire or other emergency;

• providing adequate instructions to people allowed on the site to ensure that they are aware of the risks and hazards associated with the plant and its operations, the precautions that must be taken to minimise the risk to themselves and others and the actions to be taken in the event of an accident or emergency;

• providing adequate training (and keep records) for people carrying out activities during the design, construction, manufacture, commissioning, operation or decommissioning of a nuclear installation which may affect safety;

• ensuring that only suitably qualified and experienced people perform duties which may affect safety;

• setting up a senior level committee to consider and advise the licensee on matters which affect the safe design, construction, commissioning, operation and decommissioning of any installations on its licensed site and any other matter relevant to safety;

• making arrangements for the preparation and assessment of safety-related documentation used to justify safety during the design, construction, manufacture, commissioning, operation and decommissioning;

• periodically carrying out a review of the safety case;

• indicating, using a site plan, all buildings and plant or areas which might affect safety and providing a schedule, updated as necessary, giving details of each building and its associated operations;

• applying quality assurance to all activities associated with the design, construction, manufacture, commissioning, operation and decommissioning of the installations on the site including the preparation and review of safety documentation;

• assessing the average effective dose for any class or classes of workers the executive specifies and notifying the HSE if the dose exceeds a specified level;

- providing and implementing adequate control over the construction and installation of new plant which may affect safety, through planning the design and construction of any safety related plant. There are also conditions concerning the modification and commissioning of plant and equipment;

- producing a safety case to justify the operation of the installation. The purpose of this condition is to ensure that the licensee produces such a safety case and that it identifies all the necessary conditions and limits that ensure that the plant is kept within parameters which ensure the safety of the plant during normal operation and fault and accident conditions.

- ensuring that all operations which may affect safety are carried out in accordance with written instructions – referred to as operating instructions;

- keeping adequate records regarding the operation, inspection and maintenance of any safety-related plant;

- ensuring that safety-related operations are carried out only under the control and supervision of suitably qualified and experienced personnel;

- ensuring that there are always sufficient and operable safety mechanisms, devices and circuits;

- ensuring regular and systematic examination, inspection maintenance and testing, by and under the control of suitably qualified personnel and keeping records of maintenance activities; and

- carrying out tests, inspections and examinations.

There are also conditions regarding the periodic shutdown of plant and processes and of specified operations; the accumulation, disposal and leakage and escape of radioactive waste; decommissioning; and the control of organisational change.

*Ionising Radiations Regulations 1999*

**13.9**    In addition, the Ionising Radiations Regulations 1999, SI 1999/3232, provide for protection of workers in all industries from ionising radiations.

The regulations set a limit on the dose of radiation to the whole body (effective dose) to which workers aged 18 and over can be exposed: 20 millisieverts (mSv) in a calendar year. However, in special cases, a dose limit of 100mSv in five years may apply, with no more than 50mSv in a single year, subject to strict conditions.

For trainees the limit is 6mSv in a calendar year, and for any other person, including members of the public, the limit is 1mSv a year. The limit for the skin applies to doses averaged over an area not exceeding 1cm$^1$.

The Nuclear Industries Security Regulations 2003, SI 2003/403, require an approved security plan for each nuclear premises; deal with the security of transport of nuclear material, requiring that only approved carriers transport certain categories of nuclear material; and provide for the security of sensitive nuclear information through the maintenance of adequate secuirty standards, including the vetting of nuclear industry personnel with access to sensitive nuclear material or information. The Nuclear Directorate's Office for Civil Nuclear Security (OCNS) regulates security of the UK's civil nuclear industry.

The HSE's microsite on nuclear safety is at www.hse.gov.uk/nuclear/index.htm.

¹  See SI 2001/2975.

## Gas Supply

**13.10**   There is specific health and safety legislation affecting those involved with the transmission, distribution and storage of natural gas.

### *Gas Safety (Management) Regulations 1996*

**13.11**   The Gas Safety (Management) Regulations 1996, SI 1996/551, set out that a person must not convey gas in a network unless a safety case has been prepared and accepted by the HSE, and that where another person is conveying gas in a network, there must be a sole network emergency coordinator for the network.

A network emergency co-ordinator is a person who has prepared a safety case and had it accepted by the HSE.

A safety case sets out the significant findings of the risk assessment required under the Management of Health and Safety at Work Regulations 1999, SI 1999/3242, reg 3 together with the arrangements taken in pursuance of reg 4 (see CHAPTER 2). It also sets out the safety management system, arrangements for ensuring that employees are competent, arrangments to ensure that there is co-operation between suppliers, procedures regarding gas escapes and investigations, ensuring that the content and characteristics of gas supply comply with the regulations, ensuring continuity of supply, and supply emergencies.

The safety case must be revised as appropriate, and reviewed at least every three years. The procedures and arrangements set out in the safety case must be followed, and there is a duty on every person conveying gas to co-operate with other suppliers.

The regulations also require that there is a continuously-manned telephone service to receive reports of gas escapes, and that gas escapes are investigated, and the regulations contain requirements concerning the content and characteristics of the gas conveyed, and record keeping requirements.

## Pipelines Safety Regulations 1996

**13.12**    The Pipelines Safety Regulations 1996, SI 1996/825, (which also apply offshore) set out :

- that a pipeline be designed to withstand expected strains and processes, be capable of being examined and maintained safely, be constructed of suitable materials and constructed and installed so that it is sound and fit for purpose;

- the provision of safety systems necessary for health and safety;

- that work on a pipeline is carried out in such a way that its integrity will not be prejudiced;

- that the safe operating limits of a pipeline be established and not exceeded, save for testing;

- that adequate arrangements be made for dealing with incidents and emergencies involving a pipeline;

- that a pipeline be maintained in good repair;

- that a disused pipeline be left in a safe condition; and that work for that purpose be performed safely;

- that no person cause such damage to a pipeline as may give rise to danger;

- that reasonable steps are taken to draw attention to the presence of a pipeline; and

- that operators of different parts of a pipeline co-operate with each other so far as necessary to enable them to comply with these Regulations.

In the case of a 'major accident hazard pipeline' (which conveys a dangerous fluid) the Regulations also require:

- an emergency shut-down valve, where it is connected to an offshore oil or gas installation;

- specified information to be notified to the HSE in specified circumstances;

- a document to be prepared containing specified information, setting out arrangements and procedures which must be followed;

- procedures to be followed in an emergency; and

- a local authority to prepare a plan to cope with an emergency from such pipeline in its area.

The HSE's gas supply microsite is at: www.hse.gov.uk/gas/supply/index.htm.

## Cases involving Prosecutions following Work-related Deaths highlighted by the HSE

**13.13** As far as research for this publication has been able to ascertain, manslaughter prosecutions following work-related deaths have not taken place in the energy and utility supply sectors (at least in recent years), with the exception of the failed prosecution against Transco, which is outlined in CHAPTER 1.

Following the Piper Alpha explosion (see CHAPTER 1), in which 167 people lost their lives, there was no prosecution of Occidental Petroleum or any of its senior officers for manslaughter or health and safety offences.

The following health and safety prosecutions following work-related deaths in the industry have been highlighted by the HSE:

*Shell Expro[1]*

Shell UK Ltd, trading as Shell UK Exploration and Production (Shell Expro), were fined a total of £900,000 at Stonehaven Sheriff Court in April 2005 following the deaths of two workers on Shell Expro's Brent Bravo offshore production platform on 11 September 2003.

Sean McCue and Keith Moncrieff were inspecting pipework in the utility leg of the installation, located some 180 miles east of the Shetland Isles, when they were overcome by a large release of hydrocarbon gas.

Shell Expro admitted breaching HSWA 1974 ss 2(1) and 3(1) by failing to ensure the health and safety of employees and people not in their employment, and reg 3(1) of the Management of Health and Safety at Work Regulations 1999, SI 1999/3242, by failing to complete a suitable and sufficient risk assessment. The company admitted that there were fundamental failures in health and safety management on Brent Bravo.

After the hearing, Tom McLaren, a principal inspector with HSE's Offshore Division, said:

'Essential barriers to the unplanned release of hydrocarbon gas that should have been in place were not – even though these were not high-cost items for an offshore operator. As a direct consequence of these failures, two men died.'

He also set out:

'This incident had very serious underlying causes: failure to maintain known defective equipment properly and a failure to assess potential consequences. HSE believes that the circumstances on Brent Bravo which led to these two deaths could have occurred on other offshore installations if maintenance had been neglected and continuation of production allowed to take priority over safety, notwithstanding the fact that this approach is senselessly short-sighted. The message to the oil industry is clear: they should critically examine their own maintenance systems to make an honest assessment of how much confidence their senior management can have in the safety and integrity of their installations.'

*Aberdeen-based offshore operator Well Ops (UK) Ltd, formerly Cal Dive International Ltd*[2]

Aberdeen-based offshore operator Well Ops (UK) Ltd, formerly Cal Dive International Ltd, were fined a total of £110,000 at Aberdeen Sheriff Court following the death of Derrick Love who died after being struck by a 12 m long well intervention tool weighing 370 kg (800 lbs) on the offshore multi service vessel, MSV Seawell, in February 2006.

The deck operator was part of the team on the deck floor. He was employed by TDM International Ltd an Aberdeen based contractor who provided labour to Well Ops (UK) Ltd.

The tool was being lifted in what is known as a slick line operation involving a single wire and multiple sheave (pulley) and winch arrangement. The tool parted when it came into contact with one of the sheaves and fell 12 m, striking Derrick. The assembly was approximately 12 m long and weighed 370 kgs (800 lbs).

The HSE warned offshore operating companies of the importance of having properly secured heavy loads. HSE principal inspector Ken Staples commented after the case:

'This case has highlighted the importance of companies with duties under the law to ensure that they have robust management systems in place to identify the hazards associated with lifting operations and suitable and sufficient measures in place to reduce the risks to those engaged in such operations.'

Well Ops (UK) Ltd was charged with a single breach of HSWA 1974 s 3(1).

*Transco plc*[3]

Following a failed corporate homicide prosecution (see CHAPTER 2 for details of the prosecution) Transco plc was fined a total of £15m at the High Court of Justiciary in Edinburgh, under HSWA 1974 s 3 after a six-month trial. On 22 December 1999, a massive explosion destroyed the house at 42 Carlisle Road, Larkhall, killing Andrew and Janette Findlay and their two children Stacey and Daryl.

John Sumner, Head of the HSE's Chemicals Unit in Scotland, said:

'With regard to pipeline safety, it should be noted that HSE served an improvement notice in September 2000 to accelerate Transco's mains replacement programme. This resulted in the replacement of all known sections of the sort of main that ruptured at Larkhall in the three years after the accident. In other words, some 2,500 km of ductile iron medium pressure gas mains were replaced by plastic pipeline.

'The conviction sends a message not just to Transco but to all operators of hazardous plant of the need to keep accurate records, operate effective management systems and properly maintain pipelines and equipment.'

*Lyons Landfill Ltd and Francis Michael Lyons (trading as Frank Lyons Plant Services)*[4]

The HSE warned companies to be aware of the serious risks involved from contact with or working in close proximity to overhead power lines following the sentencing in November 2006 at St Albans Crown Court, of Lyons Landfill Ltd and Francis Michael Lyons (trading as Frank Lyons Plant Services) of Felstead, Essex.

Both the company and Mr Lyons were fined £80,000 each, and each ordered to pay £35,000 prosecutions costs. HSE's prosecution follows a joint investigation with Hertfordshire Police into the death of a self-employed lorry driver, Nathaniel Hugh Scollan

312

(also known as Hugh Breffni), who was visiting a combined quarry and landfill site at Hollingson Meads Quarry, Pole Hole, Gilston, Harlow, on 10 September 2003.

Lyons Landfill Ltd was convicted of an offence under HSWA 1974 s 3(1) and Francis Lyons (trading as Frank Lyons Staff Services) was convicted of an offence under s 3(2). Francis Lyons was acquitted of an offence under s 37 relating to his activities as a director of Lyons Landfill Ltd.

He was electrocuted when the grab of the crane mounted on his lorry came into contact with overhead power lines. The investigation found that Mr Scollan parked beneath the overhead lines when waiting for a load of ballast from the quarry. He apparently raised the lorry-mounted crane and sustained fatal injuries from the subsequent electric shock. The site was poorly laid out with stockpiles encroaching near the overhead lines, inadequate signs, poorly designed crossing points and inadequate measures taken to keep plant clear of the lines. Help and advice to put in place safe procedures for working near overhead power lines is available in the HSE's guidance note *GS 6 Avoidance of danger from overhead electric power lines* (3rd edition). Where vehicles must work around live overhead power lines then barriers can prevent close approach and there should be carefully designed and defined passageways for plant to pass under the lines where this is essential.

Guidance on electricity in quarries and a leaflet about safe working near overhead power lines in agriculture is available on the HSE website at www.hse.gov.uk.

1   See HSE Press Release 27 April 2005.
2   See HSE Press Release 24 May 2007.
3   See HSE Press Release 26 August 2007.
4   See HSE Press Release 7 November 2006.

# Chapter 14

# Public Services

## Overview
### 14.1

The Corporate Manslaughter and Corporate Homicide Act 2007 (CMCHA 2007), when it comes into force on 6 April 2008, will apply to corporations; departments and other body listed in Schedule 1; police forces; partnerships; and trade unions or employers' associations that are employers. CHAPTER 5 sets out the 2007 Act in detail together with the Ministry of Justice (MoJ) guidance to the Act, *A guide to the Corporate Manslaughter and Corporate Homicide Act 2007,* and commentary from legal experts.

The MoJ guidance makes clear that the new offence of corporate manslaughter (corporate homicide in Scotland) applies to a number of public sector bodies:

CMCHA 2007 applies to:

- companies incorporated under companies legislation or overseas;

- other corporations including:

  o   public bodies incorporated by statute such as local authorities, NHS bodies and a wide range of non-departmental public bodies;

  o   organisations incorporated by Royal Charter;

- limited liability partnerships;

- all other partnerships, and trade unions and employer's associations, if the organisation concerned is an employer;

- Crown bodies such as government departments; and

- police forces.

This chapter: ➡

- looks at how CMCHA 2007 will impact on public sector workplaces, setting out in particular how it is likely to apply in local authorities, the health service, and the civil service;

- sets out the exemptions from the offence of corporate manslaughter or corporate homicide that CMCHA 2007 sets out for different parts of the public sector;

- highlights cases involving manslaughter and health and safety prosecutions that have been brought against public sector organisations, and individuals working in public sector organisations (including schools and police forces) following work-related deaths; and

- provides guidance for employers from employers' organisations, legal experts and trades unions.

It also looks at the issue of deaths in detention and custody, which proved to be such a controversial part of the Act.

## Application of CMCHA 2007 to the Public Sector

### Exemptions

**14.2**   The MoJ guidance on CMCHA 2007 sets out the exemptions in ss 3 to 7 of the Act, which mean that the offence of corporate manslaughter or corporate homicide will not apply to deaths connected with the management of particular activities.

It explains that there are two types of exemption:

**Comprehensive exemptions** – which mean that the new offence does not apply in respect of any duty of care an organisation owes. These apply to:

- *public policy decisions* (s 3(1)) – strategic funding decisions and other matters involving competing public interests, for example, but not decisions about how resources were managed;

- *military combat operations* (s 4) – potentially violent peacekeeping operations and dealing with terrorism and violent disorder are included in this exemption, as are related support and preparatory activities, and hazardous training.

- *police operations dealing with terrorism and violent disorder* (s 5(1), (2) – which also extends to support and preparatory activities and hazardous training.

**Partial exemptions** – which mean that the new offence does not apply unless the death relates to the organisation's responsibility as employer (or to others working for the organisation) or as an occupier of premises. These apply to:

- *policing and law enforcement activities* (s 5(2)) – where the comprehensive exemption described above does not apply;

- *the emergency response* of fire authorities and other emergency response organisations; NHS trusts (including ambulance trusts) – but duties of care relating to medical treatment in an emergency, other than triage decisions (determining the order in which injured people are treated) are not exempt; the Coastguard, Royal National Lifeboat Institution and other rescue bodies; and the armed forces;

- *carrying out statutory inspection work* (s 3(3)) *child-protection functions* or *probation activities* (s 7);

- *the exercise of 'exclusively public functions'* (s 3(2)) – which covers functions:

  o   carried out by the government using prerogative powers, such as acting in a civil emergency; and

  o   that, by their nature, require statutory (or prerogative) authority. To be exempt, the activity must be of a sort that cannot be independently performed by a private body. It must intrinsically require statutory or prerogative authority, such as licensing drugs or conducting international diplomacy.

## Local Government

### Fatalities caused by the Work-activities of Local Authorities

**14.3**     Although deaths arising from the work activities of local authorities are rare, they do occur. In the three-year period from 2000 to 2003, for example, there were a total of 17 deaths notified under the Reporting of Injuries, Diseases and Dangerous Occurences Regulations 1995, SI 1995/3163, (see CHAPTER 2).

Steve Sumner, Local Government Employers (LGE) National Health and Safety Policy Adviser said:

'Local authorities owe a relevant duty of care to many people and are therefore exposed to the risk of a charge of corporate manslaughter in the event of a death. Firstly as an employer, local authorities employ around 2.2 million people some of whom are engaged in hazardous activities. Local government activities provide a diverse risk environment with employees up trees and down sewers and everywhere in between. Local authorities also owe a duty of care to clients, other service users and the public. Therefore the death of a client in a residential care home or a member of the public killed by a refuse vehicle on its grounds could result in an investigation for corporate manslaughter. Clearly where multiple deaths occur such as in the Barrow legionnaires disease outbreak, then depending on the evidence a conviction for corporate manslaughter under the new test will be a very real possibility.'

Barrow in Furness Borough Council became the first local authority to be charged with corporate manslaughter following an outbreak of Legionnaires' disease in 2002, which killed seven people (see 14.7). With the collapse of the case, it appeared that a local authority could probably not be convicted for corporate manslaughter. A briefing on corporate manslaughter and local authorities by the law firm Eversheds[1] reported that the police conducted manslaughter investigations into five local authorities in 2005 following fatal road traffic accidents, but no prosecutions followed.

Although the trial judge in the Barrow Borough Council case expressed doubt that even the chief executive officer of the Council could be considered to be the directing mind of a local authority, the reform of the law through CMCHA 2007 means that local authorities can now be prosecuted for corporate manslaughter (or corporate homicide in Scotland).

[1]   *Local Government Briefing Note 52/2006 2 November 2006 Corporate Manslaughter and Corporate Homicide Bill.* The briefing was updated in August 2007 following the Bill gaining Royal Assent.

## Advice from Local Government Employers (LGE) and Legal Experts

**14.4**   The employers' organisation Local Government Employers (LGE) has produced guidance on the CMCHA 2007 for local authorities: *Ten things to know about the Corporate Manslaughter and Corporate Homicide Act 2007.*

This sets out that local authorities are clearly within the scope of CMCHA 2007 since they are corporate bodies by virtue of section 2 of the Local Government Act 1972. It advises that they owe a duty of care to employees as employers, and to clients and services users as occupiers of land and suppliers of services and as such 'their exposure is significant'.

It also sets out the following activities carried out by local authorities which do not carry a relevant duty of care.

- CMCHA 2007 specifically refers to public policy decisions that do not carry with them a 'relevant duty of care'. The specific example used is the 'allocation of public resources or the weighting of competing public interests'. (Note however that Chris Green, Partner at law firm Weightmans warns: 'This exemption may not be widely interpreted and would not extend to a duty which was not met simply because the level of resources allocated to the discharge of a particular given function was not sufficient').

- Undertaking statutory inspections do not carry with them a 'relevant duty of care'.

- There are additional exemptions in the provision of child protection and probation functions that are not considered to a 'relevant duty of care'.

(See CHAPTER 5 which examines the Act in detail).

The advice points out that while very few employees, clients or service users are killed each year, local authorities should not be complacent. It predicts that the Act will mean that where there is a fatality, there are likely to be more police investigations, and more convictions:

'Under the new arrangements it is likely that there will be more police investigations into work related deaths for possible Corporate Manslaughter charges. Even if charges are not brought, the investigation will be unsettling and many senior managers may find the experience uncomfortable. There may also be an expectation that where a charge of Corporate Manslaughter is not laid that health and safety charges will be. This may place greater pressure on the Health and Safety Executive. It is likely that there will be more convictions as they will be easier to obtain.'

An organisation is guilty of the offence of corporate manslaughter (or corporate homicide) if the way in which it manages or organises its activities causes a death and this amounts to a gross breach of a relevant duty of care it owed to the victim. In order to be convicted of the offence, the way in which its activities are managed or organised by its senior management must be a substantial element in the breach.

## The senior management test

**14.5** The LGE advice on this 'senior management test' is as follows:

'For Local Authorities this appears to suggest that senior managers would be the corporate management team who set in place the strategic agenda in terms of the organisations management and operational managers that are engaged in actually managing the authority's activities.

'Further, the definition of senior managers does not exclude elected members; they may therefore be considered senior managers within the authority. They must understand that they may become part of a Corporate Manslaughter investigation if a death occurs.

'It has been suggested that senior managers can avoid liability for the organisation by delegating their role to junior managers. This is not practical as strategic decisions about how the organisation or substantial parts of it are managed or organised cannot be delegated. This would paralyse the organisation. Further strategic managers, line managers and individual employees have health and safety responsibilities that cannot be delegated.'

Eversheds' Briefing Note on CMCHA 2007, *Briefing Note 50/2007 – Corporate Manslaughter and Corporate Homicide Act 2007*, says that the definition of 'senior manager' seems to extend to encompass operational managers alongside strategic decision-makers.

It also notes:

'... the actions of senior management below director level can still be deemed to be the actions of the organisation. Management failings can be aggregated together between an organisation's senior managers, without the need for a specific individual having to be the directing mind to be guilty of gross negligence manslaughter.'

In the opinion of Chris Green, 'senior management' would 'probably include directors and assistant directors of service but is arguably wider, so as to include anyone with strategic or senior operational responsibility within its remit.'

*Avoiding a coroporate manslaughter or corporate homicide conviction*

**14.6**    With regard to an actual conviction, the LGE says that although the fines are likely to be very high, judges have been sympathetic when imposing sentences on local authorities convicted of health and safety offences, because of the problem that a fine has the effect of recycling public money back into the Treasury and away from local services. But like other commentators (see CHAPTER 5), it warns that a conviction would mean significant image and reputation issues, as well as political issues which will be explored by council tax payers and the local and national media.

Its advice with regard to avoiding a corporate manslaughter conviction is as follows:

'The simple answer is to ensure that no one is killed as a result of the way that you manage or organise your activities. Therefore, authorities should not be distracted from their primary aim of compliance with the Health and Safety at Work etc Act 1974.'

There are a number of simple steps to take, these should not be expensive, CMCHA 2007 does not impose new duties, but introduces a new offence and you should therefore be doing the following already:

- ensure that the authority has in place an effective health and safety management system (see *Successful health and safety management* (HSG 65) – available from the HSE at www.hse.gov.uk);

- as part of the management system, ensure that a robust health and safety policy is in place. Within that policy all health and safety roles and responsibilities should be articulated;

- job descriptions of staff should reflect their role in health and safety management, particularly at a senior level;

- reflect upon the competencies of existing senior managers with respect to health and safety management. Provide additional developmental opportunities to address any deficiencies;

- strategic managers should be trained to ensure they understand their role in the effective management of health and safety;

- line managers should receive training to enable them to manage health and safety within the part of the organisation for which they are responsible;

- elected members should receive training on their role and responsibilities within the health and safety system. This is particularly important for portfolio holders/cabinet members and chairs of scrutiny committees;

- Ensure that health and safety performance is regularly considered at board level, to ensure adequate representation of these issues appoint a Director responsible for health and safety; and

- Mainstream health and safety into decision-making processes and ensure proper scrutiny of the health and safety implications of policy decisions.

In short, if the authority complies with its duties under the Health and Safety at Work etc Act 1974 (HSWA 1974), it should have little to fear from this new offence.

Eversheds' advice is that in the light of the high-risk areas in which authorities operate, such as highways, housing, leisure and social care, which means that deaths do inevitably occur, and potential manslaughter charges will be in the minds of the investigating authorities: 'the time is ripe for health and safety management systems to be scrutinised and overhauled.'[1]

It also advises local authorities to have realistic, achievable health and safety policies:

'The whole ethos of the new law is to emphasise the importance of compliance with existing health and safety law and guidance. Statements in policy documents need to be clearly evidenced in practice and not exceed legal thresholds. If a statement of intent is unachievable, and a fatality occurs, the organisation will be held accountable to its own declared standard rather than the legal minimum.

'In this context, many local authorities make impressive declarations of intent towards their employees and stakeholders, but these declarations, if not deliverable, should be re-evaluated.

'Local authorities need to spend time carefully reviewing health and safety policies, systems and accepted practices now. Senior managers

321

need to appraise themselves of any tolerated but unsafe habits that may have permeated the working environment and take action to root these out.'

It provides a suggested checklist for local authorities to review their procedures in order to assess their potential risk of exposure to prosecutions for corporate manslaughter:

- assess your organisational structure to determine who could be considered a 'senior manager' within the definition of CMCHA 2007 (potentially covering all heads of service and some operational managers below that level) – these individuals should be appropriately trained and competent for their role;

- job titles and descriptions should be reviewed to ensure that they represent the seniority of the post holder's position in a health and safety context;

- senior managers (and members) may require updated training on their health and safety responsibilities;

- review all health and safety policies to ensure that statements made and standards set are achievable and do not exceed legal obligations, unless there are good reasons;

- check that your insurance cover includes legal protection in the event of criminal charges for corporate manslaughter; discuss the matter with your insurance officer or broker;

- review the authority's health and safety culture to promote a safer environment for your employees and the public;

- revisit your disaster management plan and ensure that there is a protocol for dealing with the authorities and calling your lawyers when any fatality occurs; and

- consider insurance and indemnity policies for staff and members who may need legal support during the period of any investigation, which could cover expenses where they are not personally found guilty of such offences.

And Chris Green say that councils would be well advised to look now at their safety culture and how far their strategic instructions are actually carried out in practice.

[1]   Briefing note 50/2007 – Corporate Manslaughter and Corporate Homicide Act 2007.

**14.7**

---

*The Barrow legionnella case[1]*

*The outbreak and investigation*                                             ➡

---

In August 2002, seven people died and a further 180 people became ill as a result of an outbreak of legionella, the source of which was traced to the air conditioning unit at the council-owned arts and leisure centre, Forum 28, in Barrow-in-Furness, Cumbria. Those who died were: Richard Macauley, Wendy Milburn, Georgina Sommerville, Harriet Low, Elizabeth Dixon, June Miles and Christina Merewood.

An investigation into the outbreak was led by the Barrow division of Cumbria Police, working with the HSE and environmental health officers from the local authority.

The HSE report, *Report of the public meetings into the legionella outbreak in Barrow-in-Furness, August 2002*, summarised the events that lead to the outbreak.

Until March 2001 the water treatment on the cooling towers at Forum 28 was under contract and appropriate control, as part of a wider heating and ventilation contract.

But in late 2000, because of call out delays being experienced, alternative contractors were sourced. The Forum 28 building manager cancelled the contract, but resigned the following day with the associated loss of knowledge and continuity.

The report says that the Design Services Group (DSG) at Barrow Borough Council, was involved in procuring a replacement contract, as it had expertise in contract management and had procured the previous providers. It also undertook the contract negotiations with the replacement contractor.

The DSG manager, Gillian Beckingham, made a significant error in the recording of the minutes of a meeting in July 2001, when the issue of water treatment was being discussed – recording 'checking/ dosing to be omitted'. The purpose of the discussion was to explore removing the weekly dip slide test, part of the overall biological monitoring of the cooling tower water system. It was not the prosecution case that the intention had been to remove the dosing. However, the error was carried forward during the procurement of the replacement contract by DSG.

The technical manager at Forum 28 was asked to obtain a quote for an updated cost for water treatment and heating and ventilation maintenance from the previous contractor who had provided a comprehensive service up until April 2001. This quote, which included water treatment service, was significantly more expensive than the replacement contract, which quoted just for heating and ventilation maintenance. The cheaper contract was accepted. DSG did not compare or contrast the contract specifications or question➡

the price difference. Neither did it establish the necessary competencies of the contractor to undertake the work.

The outcome was that only heating and ventilation maintenance and cleaning and chlorination of the cooling towers was provided for, and not water management. There was therefore no:

- chemical treatment;

- microbiological monitoring; or

- system checks.

According to the report, the contract documentation was largely inadequate, ambiguous and of little value. There was no adequate contract specification, which meant neither party had sufficient knowledge of the arrangements in place. No risk assessments had been asked for or provided for the contract. Although the contractor provided a less than professional service, none of its direct activities had placed anyone at significant risk. By their own admission they probably should have undertaken at least one clean and chlorination of the system, but that would not have prevented the outbreak.

External auditors engaged by the Council had identified the lack of health and safety risk assessments before the outbreak and had recorded this finding in the audit report to the Council.

The HSE said:

'On receipt of the audit report, leaders at Barrow Borough Council should have constructed an action plan to complete the risk assessments, with an allocated timescale, and appointed individuals whose responsibility was to ensure the plan was put into effect and completed on time.'

On two separate occasions, a heating and ventilation engineer brought his concerns about the lack of water treatment to the attention of the DSG Manager, but no effective remedial action was taken either time. On one occasion he was informed the water treatment was being carried out in-house and on the other he was left to progress a quote for the service but, unfortunately, he left the company shortly after, again with the associated loss of knowledge and continuity.

Ms Beckingham acknowledged his concerns but failed to communicate these to other officers at the Council or to managers at Forum 28, or to take effective remedial action. The HSE commented that:

'The deficiencies identified may have been addressed if the contractor's concerns had been formally recorded and communicated to the responsible person and also made known to the leaders of the organisation.'

➡️

*Legal proceedings*

The HSE report also sets out the legal proceedings and their outcome:

The HSE advised the Crown Prosecution Service (CPS) on the level of health and safety and management standards it would expect to find in a reasonably well-run organisation, ie the benchmark standard as described in the statutory guidance on control of legionella, *Legionnaires' disease: The control of legionella bacteria in water systems: Approved Code of Practice and guidance* (L8). The CPS compared that benchmark to the actual situation and took the view that it was 'so far below' as to be gross, and therefore criminal (see CHAPTER 4).

Manslaughter prosecutions were then taken against Barrow Borough Council and their Design Services Manager. It was the first time that a manslaughter prosecution was undertaken against a corporation that was not a limited company. Both were also charged with offences under the Health and Safety at Work etc Act 1974.

The first trial started in February 2005. Barrow Borough Council entered a guilty plea to the charge under HSWA 1974 s 3 and was fined £125,000 with £90,000 costs. Sentencing the local authority, the judge commented that if the Council had been a commercial organisation with a multimillion-pound turnover, the fine would have exceeded £1m.

He further commented on the lack of a health and safety 'ethos' at the local authority:

'In my judgement, the prosecution submission that the ethos within Barrow was inimical to a proper concern for heath and safety, and the taking of proper, easily taken, precautions for health and safety is entirely justified on the evidence. And in my judgment the failings were not only at the lowest levels, or even at the level of Ms Beckingham, those failings went all the way, I am afraid to say, to the top of the Council in terms of its serving officers. It is likely they went beyond the officers to the councillors because there is no evidence that there was proper attention given to health and safety within the Borough. The result of that, it seems to me, was an ethos where insufficient attention was given to the requirements of health and safety. And that is one reason why, within the Design Services Group, it was not given the attention and consideration it required, and it was for similar reasons that within Forum 28 the attention to health and safety was not what was required.'

However, the manslaughter case against the local authority was dismissed on the grounds that Ms Beckingham was not at a➡

sufficiently senior level within the Council to embody the corporation and was not a 'directing mind' of the Council.

The jury found Beckingham guilty of an offence under HSWA 1974 s 7, but were unable to agree whether she was guilty of manslaughter. She appealed against her conviction and in March 2006 her appeal was upheld by the Court of Appeal and her conviction under HSWA 1974 s 7 was overturned.

She was then tried again for manslaughter and the health and safety charge and the second jury acquitted her of manslaughter, but convicted her again under HSWA 1974. She was ordered to pay £15,000 in fines, but was not asked to pay any additional costs. (The option of a community penalty was not yet available.)

## Health and Safety Prosecutions following Fatalities as a Result of Local Authority Activities

**14.8**    While Barrow Borough Council may be the only local authority to have faced a corporate manslaughter charge, they are certainly not the only one to have been prosecuted for health and safety offences following a work-related death.

For example, in 2007 the London Borough of Newham[1] was fined £125,000 and ordered to pay costs of £6,000 after 13-year old Ryan Dean died after falling backwards down a stairwell that had been allowed to remain in an unsafe condition for over six months. The adjoining wall of the stairwell was only two bricks high in some places after being damaged by vandalism.

The Council had previously pleaded guilty to a charge brought by the HSE of failing to maintain adequately the communal areas of a council owned and maintained parade of shops and flats – a breach of section 3 of HSWA 1974.

Commenting on the case, the HSE investigating inspector, Dominic Long, said:

'Local Authorities have a legal obligation to ensure that tenants and other members of the public are not placed at unnecessary risk arising from poor procedures for repairing damage to buildings. This case should serve as a reminder to Councillors and Chief Executives of the importance of effective maintenance systems to ensure repairs are carried out quickly and to appropriate standards. Had such a system been in place, Ryan Dean's death might have been prevented.'

The Council had been informed about the initial damage to the wall at Easter and over the next few months tried, on five occasions, to repair the wall. Each time the job either was not found or the wrong type of maintenance employee was sent. The job remained unfinished.

The Council has since changed its procedures so that such repairs are flagged up as health and safety emergencies and dealt with within eight hours. A check visit is also carried out to ensure that the job has been completed.

The Council also reviewed its policy relating to decanting buildings (emptying them of tenants, shopkeepers etc. prior to demolition) as it seems that because the parade was in the process of being decanted the caretakers and estates staff overlooked it and regular inspections were not carried out.

According to Sumner, local authorities should focus not on CMCHA 2007, but think about HSWA 1974: 'If local authorities are complying with the Health and Safety at Work Act and managing health and safety properly, they significantly reduce the risk of anyone getting killed,' he said. 'Nevertheless, the Corporate Manslaughter and Corporate Homicide Act should serve as a catalyst to act – a reality check to review health and safety policies and leadership on health and safety'.

And he warns that if a local authority were to be convicted of corporate manslaughter, it would cause 'irrevocable damage' to its reputation and its relationship with council tax payers.

[1] See HSE Press Release 3 May 2007.

## Prosecutions following the Deaths of School Students and Children
## 14.9

### *Peter Kite and OLL Ltd*

This case is an example of the first successful corporate manslaughter conviction following the deaths of four school students on a school trip. In a December 1994 judgment, a company specialising in multi-activity holidays, OLL Limited, and its managing director, Peter Kite, were convicted of gross negligence manslaughter. Simon Deane, Clair Langley, Rachel Walker and Dean Sawyer were all students at Southway Comprehensive School and were on a canoeing trip, accompanied by a school teacher and two unqualified instructors, who only had basic proficiency skills in canoeing. The group was swept out to sea and capsized.

(Details of the case against the company and the director are set out in more detail in CHAPTERS 1, 4.)

### *Paul Ellis[1]*

Teacher Paul Ellis, from Fleetwood High School, was found guilty of manslaughter in September 2003, following the death of 10-year-old Max Palmer in May 2002, and was jailed for a year. Max was accompanying his mother, who was helping with a school trip to the Lake District, which had been organised by Ellis. On the trip, he had led an activity which involved jumping into a natural rock pool – 'plunge pooling'.

Ellis was also charged under HSWA 1974 s 7 on the grounds that he had not taken reasonable care of other people who entered the pool. The role of the local education authority, Lancashire County Council, was also investigated, but it was not prosecuted. (details of the case are set out in CHAPTER 6).

As a result of Max's death, the HSE has a specific area on its website containing information about school trips: www.hse.gov.uk/schooltrips/index.htm. This sets out that the overwhelming majority of educational visits are carried out safely and responsibly by teachers who take the time and effort to get things right and that the benefits of such trips to pupils can be immense. But it warns that the risks must be properly managed.

### James Porter[2]

Headteacher and proprietor James Porter, of the private Hillgrove School in Bangor, Gwynedd, was fined £12,500 and ordered to pay £7,500 costs for breaching s 3(1) of HSWA 1974 in September 2007. Three-year-old Kian Williams died just over a month after falling down steps at the school in July 2004. Porter was prosecuted because, as proprietor for the school, he was also the employer and had primary responsible for health and safety matters.

The HSE's investigation into Kian's death identified shortfalls in the levels of supervision for pre-school aged children at the school, which resulted in Kian being able to enter an area which was off limits.

HSE principal inspector Steve Scott commented on the case saying:

'On the day of the incident there was one member of staff supervising 59 pupils with an age range of three to eleven. This was well out of line with accepted ratios found elsewhere. It was not possible for the teacher on duty that day to see all parts of the split-level playground. Some areas were simply out of sight.'

Guidance on supervisory ratios for pre-school aged children (*Children Act 1989: Guidance and Regulations*, Vol 2) suggests that 2:26 is an appropriate ratio for supervising adults to children.

¹   See HSE Press Releases 23 September 2003 and 9 March 2005 and HSE website at www.hse.gov.uk/schooltrips/index.htm.
²   See HSE Press Release 28 September 2007.

# NHS

## Views on the Impact of CMCHA 2007 on the NHS

### The employer view

**14.10**    A spokesperson for NHS Employers said that it does not expect CMCHA 2007 to be a major issue for NHS trusts, and that it expects that cases like the one at Southampton University Hospitals NHS Trust, which involved the death of a patient as a result of medical negligence on the part of two doctors (see 14.12), would continue to be taken by the HSE under health and safety legislation.

### The view of medical and legal experts

An editorial in the British Medical Journal (BMJ)[1] by Ash Samanta, consultant rheumatologist at the University Hospitals of Leicester NHS Trust, and Jo Samanta, Lecturer in Law at De Montford Univesity, looked at the implications of the Southampton case for the NHS as the Corporate Manslaughter Bill was making its way through Parliament, and advised senior medical and managerial staff in the NHS to take note of the case in order to prepare themselves for the implications of an indictment for corporate killing. They set out:

'The indictment in the case at Southampton General Hospital was based on a failure of the trust to ensure that patients were not exposed to risk in health and safety, take up references for clinical staff, supervise adequately the working of junior doctors, implement protocols for handover of the care of patients, and develop lines of communication for nursing staff to report concerns. By the trust pleading guilty to an amended charge of failing to adequately manage and supervise the doctors in this case, the other issues have not been subject to scrutiny by the court. These could have relevance in similar actions for other NHS trusts in the future. In response to the Southampton case, the lead clinical coordinator for the National Confidential Enquiry into Patient Outcomes and Death said that these problems cannot be tackled by individual doctors but require careful planning by clinical teams, trusts, and, in some cases, strategic health authorities.

'Senior medical and managerial staff in the NHS would do well to take note of this, to give high priority to complying with health and safety law, and to prepare themselves for the implications of an indictment of corporate killing. Directors and managers may be personally indicted for breaches under section 37 of the Health and Safety at Work Act 1974.

'Senior healthcare professionals and managers of trusts might find themselves in the dock charged with corporate manslaughter. Health and safety risk management should be integrated into all activities of NHS trusts, with a particular emphasis on the supervision of junior doctors and other staff in training grades. Policy documents should be drafted carefully, and schemes for delegation to junior medical staff must be underpinned by a robust system of training and review.'

David Firth, partner at Capsticks Solicitors also thinks that NHS Trusts need to take action to ensure that they are not vulnerable to a corporate manslaughter conviction:

'The process of investigation and prosecution is going to be very uncomfortable and could mean board members in the witness box facing questions without the right to remain silent. Such an investigation could damage individual and corporate reputation', he said.

He advises NHS Trusts to use the short period before CMCHA 2007 comes into force in April 2008 to review how non-clinical and clinical risks are managed; and examine policy documents to see how the organisation would be perceived if investigated in the context of a corporate manslaughter charge.

He also advises that NHS Trusts need to ensure that health and safety is not just an item on the job description of 'senior managers' in the organisation – but that they really have responsibilities for health and safety, with proper resources allocated to them, and that health and safety matters are brought to the attention of the Board. And Trusts need to look beyond their core areas of health care, to estates management and catering, for example.

'You need to be complying with health and safety law and showing that you do', he advises.

Writing in the 6 September 2007 issue of *Health Service Journal*, Jill Mason partner at the law firm Mills and Reeve advises in an article, 'Corporate Manslaughter Act – do or die':

> '... most activities of an NHS body will fall within the Act. Executive directors, non-executive directors and senior managers are all affected. They need to be aware of the impact this Act has on them. While they will not be prosecuted, they could be called to give evidence.'

> 'Guidance issued by the Department of Health, professional bodies and the Health and Safety Executive take on even more importance. If they have not been followed, there will need to be a good reason why. The actions of senior management, the existence of policies, systems, practices, procedures and attitudes will be intensively investigated. Unlimited fines can be imposed. Other key issues for NHS bodies will be the negative publicity, the stress on staff involved in a prosecution and the time which will be taken up.

> 'Governance should be at the top of the agenda for NHS bodies in any event. However, we recommend that all NHS bodies should review their risk management, quality and safety assurance policies and procedures. You must ensure that all staff who need to be trained are trained and supervised and that changes in practices are communicated and acted on.'

Andrew Hopkins, associate lawyer at law firm Browne Jacobson advises that hospitals should have in place comprehensive and well-documented health and safety management systems, which could include:

- a clear and focused health and safety policy for the hospital;

- a thorough awareness of HSE guidance regarding health and safety management;

- an audit trail showing how and where this guidance has been applied; and

- an audit trail to show how systems and procedures recommended by HSE guidance or adopted following risk assessments are implemented, supervised, monitored and reviewed.

'Trusts need to focus not just upon the clinical risks to which patients are vulnerable, but also the management of patient care to avoid the consequences, both financial and in terms of publicity, which inevitably follow a criminal prosecution,' he says.

¹  BMJ Vol 332, 17 June 2006 (see bmj.com).

## *The Medical Defence Union view*

**14.11**    The Medical Defence Union (MDU), which advises members on criminal matters which might arise from their clinical duties, has warned hospital doctors that they may face more investigations into their conduct when the law comes into effect, with all the uncertainty, disruption to their professional and personal lives and considerable stress that this will involve.

MDU solicitor, Ian Barker said:

'The MDU cannot be sure of the practical effects of any new legislation, until it has been in operation for some time but we hope the Corporate Manslaughter Act will not lead to individuals being unfairly blamed for adverse incidents.'

He went on to say:

'We are concerned that more healthcare professionals may be subjected to the disruption and demands of a police investigation. Relatives of patients who have died in hospital may understandably demand that the death is investigated to determine whether the new corporate offence might have been committed, while coroners may feel obliged to pass more cases to the police from a similar concern. As a result, more doctors and nurses could be investigated and interviewed under caution as police try to distinguish between an individual error and corporate responsibility.

'We also have a concern that the new offence of corporate manslaughter may set employer against employee. A memorandum of understanding – *Investigating patient safety incidents involving unexpected death or serious untoward harm: a protocol for liaison and effective communications between the National Health Service, Association of Chief Police Officers and Health & Safety Executive*, February 2006 – means that trusts are now encouraged to liaise more closely with the police and HSE following unexpected deaths or serious untoward harm in the NHS. It would be profoundly regrettable, in the context of the new Act, if trusts used such an opportunity to downplay their own responsibility, perhaps by highlighting individuals' mistakes within systems failures.'

# Cases involving Health and Safety Prosecutions of NHS Trusts following Work-related Deaths highlighted by the HSE
## 14.12

### Southampton University Hospitals NHS Trust[1]

In April 2006, in what has been described as a landmark case, Southampton University Hospitals NHS Trust was prosecuted and fined £100,000 at Winchester Crown Court for breaching s 3 of HSWA 1974 (although the fine was later reduced to £40,000 on appeal).

The prosecution followed the death of Shaun Phillips, a patient who developed a bacterial infection following a routine knee operation at the hospital and subsequently died of staphylococcal toxic shock syndrome.

Two doctors, Rajeev Srivastava and Amir Mizra, both senior house officers, were earlier convicted of gross negligence manslaughter in April 2003. They had responded inadequately to the patient's obvious signs of infection, such as his raised temperature and pulse rate, and failed to chase up blood test results that should have led to antibiotics being administered. Their 18-month prison sentence was suspended for two years.

### South West London and St George's Mental Health Trust[2]

The Trust was fined £7,500 with £3,694 costs for breaching HSWA 1974 after an elderly visitor, William Durrant died after falling as he was leaving the grounds of Springfield Hospital. He fell, fracturing his hip and wrist and although he was immediately taken to hospital, he died a month later.

The HSE inspector commented:

'This case is a sad reminder to the NHS of the importance of applying a properly thought out and effective maintenance regime for its properties, to ensure the safety of staff, patients and the visiting public alike.'

The Trust was also fined £28,000 with £14,000 costs at the Central Criminal Court in May 2005, following a prosecution brought against it by the HSE for breaching HSWA 1974 s 2 after a nurse was killed by a psychiatric patient in June 2003.

According to the HSE, healthcare assistant Mamade Eshan Chattun was a junior member of staff working alone, at the John Meyer Ward of Springfield University Hospital, without clear procedures, and with inadequate measures in place to check on his safety. He died after suffering multiple injuries in the attack.

Brian Etheridge, HSE's Field Operations Director for London commented:

'By pleading guilty the Trust has acknowledged that it has fallen short of the standards required. Health and safety is not an unnecessary extra, nor should it be a burden on employers. We simply ask for a sensible approach to the identification and management of risks. In this case such an approach would have prevented a tragic and unnecessary loss of a young father, who was simply doing his job as a health care assistant. We want to send a strong message to other hospital trusts and organisations who have to manage potential violence at work.'

The HSE said that St Georges NHS Mental Trust had not implemented risk assessments until after the tragedy.

## Other cases[3]

### Mid-Essex NHS Hospital Trust

In 2006, Mid-Essex NHS Hospital Trust was prosecuted and fined £30,000 and ordered to pay £10,000 costs following the death of a patient, nine-year old Tony Clowes, who died during what should have been a routine operation. A document setting out the case is available on the Trust's website at www.meht.nhs.uk/trust/documents/PartI-Item11-HSEreportMarch2006.pdf.

### Welsh Ambulance Service and Cardiff and Vale NHS Trust

The Welsh Ambulance Service and Cardiff and Vale NHS Trust were fined a total of £27,500 after a 93-year-old woman who had been dropped off at the wrong house by an ambulance crew died in August 2003.

[1]  Reported in *A guide to health and safety prosecutions* by Michael Appleby and Gerard Forlin (Thomas Telford www.thomastelford.com/books) and an article by John Holbrook, *Criminalisation of Fatal Medical Mistakes*, published in the Student BMJ (2004) 12:1–44 February (see student.bmj.com).
[2]  See HSE Press Release 5 May 2005 and HSE (London) Press Release 5 March 2007.
[3]  See HSE Prosecutions Database (www.hse.gov.uk/prosecutions).

**14.13**

## Hospital infections

In October 2007, a report by the Healthcare Commission into a major outbreak of the hospital superbug *Clostridium difficile* (*C difficile*) (which causes severe diarrhoea) at Maidstone and Tunbridge Wells NHS Trust's three hospitals, said that some 90 patients definitely or probably died as a result of the infection. The Commission's investigation looked at the trust's control of infection and the quality of care for patients with *C difficile* between April 2004 and September 2006 and its report detailed significant failings in infection control. The investigation found that the Trust had not put in place appropriate measures to manage and prevent infection, despite having high rates of *C difficile* over several years.

It said that the Board did not address problems that were consistently raised by patients and staff. These included the shortage of nurses, poor care for patients and poor processes for managing the movement of patients from one ward to another, all of which contributed to the risk of spreading the infection.

It issued recommendations for national action, sending a message to all NHS Trusts that Boards must provide strong leadership in preventing and managing infection. The Commission calls for *C difficile* to be managed as a serious medical condition in its own right, not just a clinical complication.

Anna Walker, the Commission's Chief Executive, said that the tragedy had clear implications for the whole NHS and that:  ➡

'Trust boards have a critical role to play with regards to leadership and creating a culture of safety. They must understand and monitor what is happening in their trust and ensure that quality of care and patients' safety are their priorities.

'Infection control is complex. Cleanliness is an important part, but there are other relevant factors such as the appropriate use of antibiotics, availability of isolation facilities, regular training of staff, adequate levels of staff and high standards of nursing care.

'One thing this report really highlights again is the importance of leadership. Our inspections suggest infection control is not always prominent enough on the radar of some boards. Everybody – from managers to clinicians and cleaners – must understand their role. This will not happen effectively without commitment from the top.'

Kent Police and the HSE were reviewing the evidence to see if any criminal charges should be brought as this book went to press.

A spokesperson for the MoJ said that under the new CMCHA 2007, NHS Trusts could be charged with corporate manslaughter in connection with deaths as a result of hospital infections. Debating the Corporate Manslaughter and Corporate Homicide Bill earlier this year, Conservative MP John Redwood said that 5,890 people died of MRSA and *C difficile* in 2005 (*Hansard*, 5 June 2007).

# Civil Service

## Crown Immunity and Crown Censures Served after Work-related Fatalities

**14.14**   Crown bodies, which are organisations that act on behalf of the Queen (such as government departments and the Royal Mint) are obliged to comply with health and safety law, but cannot be prosecuted for offences under HSWA 1974. This is known as Crown immunity. Instead of taking prosecutions, the HSE can only serve Crown censures. According to the HSE notices database, between May 1999 and June 2005, only 17 Crown censures were served – five of could be identified as being related to fatalities from the information available on the database.

At present therefore, Crown immunity is still in force with regard to health and safety, but will not apply to the offence of corporate manslaughter when the CMCHA 2007 comes into effect in April 2008.

Phil Madelin, health and safety officer at the Public and Commercial Services Union (PCS) said:

'It has been accepted by government that Crown immunity has to go – the issue is how and when. There is no justification for being able to maintain Crown immunity for health and safety and this is also the view of government'.

He expects Crown immunity to be lifted by the time CMCHA 2007 comes into force, and says the union is 'extremely pleased' that the new Act does not include any form of Crown immunity.

If Crown immunity is not lifted, Madelin says there will be a ridiculous situation where if, for example, there were to be a legionella outbreak which killed people or caused serious illness, families of those who died would have redress, but no enforcement action would be possible under health and safety legislation where people were made seriously ill.

He said that government departments should be accountable in law as any other employer, and he believes that health and safety will be taken more seriously 'when there is a Permanent Secretary in the dock, as happened in the police service when Metropolitan Police Commissioners found themselves being prosecuted by the HSE after the Police Safety Act 1997 deemed police officers employees for the purposes of the Health and Safety at Work etc Act 1974' (see 14.17).

## Public and Commercial Services (PCS) Union View of the Impact of CMCHA 2007 on the Civil Service

**14.15**   Madelin believes that the biggest impact of CMCHA 2007 is likely to be felt in the Ministry of Defence (MOD), even with the exclusions that apply (see 14.2).

Most Crown censures issued by the HSE which can be identified as being taken as a result of fatalities from the information available on the HSE Notices database have involved the MOD[1]:

- in May 2006, the MOD and Royal Air Force were censured for failing to ensure that risks to the safety of employees were adequately controlled following the death of an employee who fell while climbing Lockwood's Chimney, during the conduct of 'adventurous training' at the Resource Initiative Training Centre at Fairbourne;

- in November 2004, the MOD was censured after a contract electrician came into contact with live terminals and died as a result of an electrical explosion – another contractor was injured; MOD employees had failed to make 11000 volt switchgear safe for contractors to maintain; they did not recognise live terminals and failed to lock the shutter in the closed (protective) position. In addition, safety programmes for previous years contained similar errors but were not detected by the auditing process;

**14.16**   *Public Services*

- in April 2003, the MOD was censured after it re-surfaced a road with an unsuitable limestone macadam that became dangerously slippery over time; two fatal accidents occured in 1997 and 1998, although by this time the road had been adopted by the Highway Authority and MOD were no longer responsible for it; and

- in July 2000, a cadet was killed when she was run over by a vehicle during a night exercise; there was poor planning and the risks were not properly identified and controlled.

The only censure that can be identified as involving a fatality, but not involving the MOD, was issued against the Royal Mint. An employee was killed when a 6.5 tonne furnace fell from an overhead crane during a routine operation and hit him. The furnace was not properly located on the crane hook at the start of the operation, a safety device designed to confirm that the hook was fully engaged was not functioning properly at the time of the accident, and employees were not aware of its purpose. In addition, the Royal Mint had not conducted a suitable and sufficient risk assessment.

In March 2007, the HSE called the MOD to its headquarters to answer two Crown censures, both arising from fatalities involving the use of workplace transport. It said that detailed investigations of the incidents had brought to light significant systemic shortcomings in the corporate arrangements for assessing transport risks in the MOD. The MOD was censured under HSWA 1974 s 2(1).

Corporal Thomas Eirian Rees died on 22 May 2003 after being crushed between two armoured personnel carriers being unloaded from a low loader at Teesport, Middlesbrough, Cleveland.

On 1 May 2004, Lance-Bombardier Robert Wilson died on 1 May 2004 after being crushed between a multiple launch rocket system vehicle and a large lift truck at Albemarle Barracks, Northumberland.

Both soldiers were on duty at the time of these incidents and the activities were subject to the full application of HSWA 1974 as they took place in Great Britain.

---

[1]   See HSE Prosecutions Database: Crown censures taken by HSE since 1 April 1999 at www.hse.gov.uk/prosecutions/documents/crowncensures.htm.

## Police Forces

**14.16**   Under the CMCHA 2007, the offence of corporate manslaughter will not apply to police operations dealing with terrorism and violent disorder. And in other circumstances, it will only apply to the police as employers and occupiers of premises – not in relation to policing and law enforcement activities.

But under existing law, there have been manslaughter prosecutions brought against individual officers, and police forces have also been prosecuted under health and safety legislation, following the deaths of police officers and members of the public – most recently in relation to the shooting dead of the Brazilian man, Jean Charles de Menezez, who was mistaken for a suicide bomber in the wake of the fatal tube and bus bombings in London in July 2005, and the failed bombings two weeks later.

## Examples of Cases involving Manslaughter and Health and Safety Investigations and Prosecutions brought against Police Officers and Police Forces

**14.17**

---

*Hillsborough disaster April 1989*

*The events leading to the disaster*

Individual officers of South Yorkshire police faced manslaughter charges following the Hillsborough Disaster in April 1989 when 96 Liverpool Football Club fans were crushed to death at Sheffield Wednesday's ground.

Liverpool FC were to play Nottingham Forest FC in an FA cup semi-final at Hillsborough, but shortly before the match was due to start, more than 2,000 Liverpool fans were still outside the stadium. The senior police officer outside the ground was concerned about the pressure of numbers of supporters trying to get into the stadium, and the decision was made to open an emergency gate to allow the crowd in.

As more supporters entered already crowded areas behind the goal and the areas to the sides, those already there were pushed forward and crushed against the high, wire-topped safety fences. The crush continued until a senior police officer ran onto the pitch to stop the game, and the rescue operation began.

*The public inquiry, inquest, criminal investigations and disciplinary action*

A public inquiry into the deaths by Lord Justice Taylor, which started in May 1989 and published an interim report in August 1989, criticised Sheffield Wednesday Football Club, their engineers and Sheffield City Council over safety issues, including poor signage and layout of the ground, but it said that the principle cause of the disaster was the failure of police control.    ➡

---

An investigation of possible criminal and police disciplinary offences was started after the interim report was published, but the Director of Public Prosecutions (DPP) concluded in August 1990 that there was insufficient evidence for a prosecution to be brought for any criminal offence.

In 1991, after a 90-day hearing, an inquest jury returned a verdict of accidental death and an attempt by families of the victims to have a judicial review of the inquest was rejected[1].

Disciplinary action against Chief Superintendent David Duckenfield the officer in charge of policing Hillsborough, and his deputy, Superintendent Bernard Murray, was abandoned as Duckenfield was too ill to undergo the disciplinary processes and he was allowed to retire, and the Police Complaints Authority (PCA) said it would be unjust to pursue a joint charge against Murray alone, in the absence of the more senior officer.

In April 1993, relatives of six of the victims were granted an application for a judicial review of the inquest verdicts, but the Divisional Court concluded that the Coroner's procedure and the jury verdict were correct.

A review of the evidence was carried out in 1997 after a television documentary claimed to have found new evidence, including pictures from a security camera which was thought not to be working, but a new public inquiry was ruled out by the then Home Secretary, Jack Straw.

*Failed manslaughter prosecutions*

In June 2000, both Duckenfield and Murray faced charges of manslaughter (and others) at Leeds Crown Court[3]. The case against them was brought as a private prosecution by The Hillsborough Family Support Group. Murray was found not guilty and the jury unable to agree a verdict for Duckenfield. The judge ruled that the case was over and there would be no retrial.

*Death of Harry Stanley*

In October 2005, the CPS announced that there was insufficient evidence to charge Chief Inspector Neil Sharman and Police Constable Kevin Fagan with any offence in relation to the fatal shooting of Harry Stanley in September 1999. Harry was shot dead in a London street by police who believed that he was armed with a gun. A member of the public had made a 999 call when they had seen him carrying a table leg wrapped in a bag. According to a report by the Independent Police Complaints Commission (IPCC), it bore a close resemblance to a sawn-off shotgun     ➡

The CPS had received a file on the case in 2000 and had concluded after reviewing the evidence that there was insufficient evidence to bring any criminal charges against the police officers involved. In March 2001, it considered the Stanley family's application for a judicial review of this decision in which they provided fresh evidence and confirmed it would review the case again, but again advised in December 2001 that there was insufficient evidence to bring any criminal charges against the police officers involved.

In October 2004 an inquest jury returned a verdict of unlawful killing, although this was later quashed. In line with the Attorney-General's guidelines into deaths in custody, the CPS again reviewed the case. As part of this review the reviewing lawyer requested the re-examination of some of the evidence and it was discovered that two bullet holes to the top left shoulder of the jacket that Mr Stanley was wearing when he was shot appeared to show that he may have been shot as he began to turn towards the officers, in contradiction to the statements provided by them. On this basis, the officers were arrested by Surrey Police on suspicion of murder, gross negligence manslaughter, perjury and conspiracy to pervert the course of justice, and misconduct in a public office.

In relation to gross negligence manslaughter, the CPS considered that it was arguable that the officers' haste and lack of planning led them to breach their duty of care to Mr Stanley and cause his death, but there was insufficient evidence to place before a jury to enable that jury to be sure the degree of negligence was gross. It said that gross negligence requires something beyond even serious mistakes and errors of judgement. (The CPS decided that there was insufficient evidence to prosecute anyone involved).

*Death of PC Sidhu[2]*

In April 2003, Metropolitan Police Commissioner Sir John Stevens and Lord Condon, who had retired in January 2000 appeared in the Old Bailey, following the death of PC Kulwant Sidhu and injuries to PC Mark Berwich. The two police officers had fallen through roofs while chasing suspects. They were charged with four offences under HSWA 1974, to which they both pleaded not guilty.

Parliament decided in 1997 that the chief officer of police should be named as the employer for the purposes of any prosecution under health and safety law.

The prosecution in the case said that there was no proper system in place regarding police officers going up on roofs and the court heard that there had been 69 cases of Metropolitan police officers falling from heights between June and November 2000. ➡

The jury in the case was unable to decide whether or not the Commissioners of the Metropolitan Police failed to ensure their officers' health and safety by establishing the right working practices and proper training in relation to the risk of serious injury when they went onto roofs in the course of their duties. The HSE said that it brought the prosecution because it 'found evidence to suggest that there were persistent failures by the Metropolitan Police to protect their officers while carrying out their duties' but it decided against seeking a retrial, saying it would not be in the public interest.

*Deaths of William Kadama and Gameli Akuklu*[3]

In July 2007, the Office of the Commissioner of Police for the Metropolis was fined £75,000 plus £50,000 prosecution costs and the London Borough of Barnet was fined £16,500 plus £10,000 costs for breaches of health and safety law following the deaths of two boys, 15-year-old William Kadama and 14-year-old Gameli Akuklu, who drowned in the swimming pool at the Metropolitan Police Training College, Hendon, North London in July 2002. A similar charge against the Metropolitan Police Authority (MPA) was not pursued – the HSE said that it is an administrative body, which oversees the provision of policing in London, but did not have day-to-day control of the running of the pool.

The boys were participating in a summer play scheme that involved a swimming activity at the Police College. The HSE said that its investigation into their deaths uncovered serious deficiencies in the operation of the swimming pool by the Metropolitan Police Service, and poor control of the summer play scheme by the London Borough of Barnet.

Following the prosecution, the HSE advised organisers of youth activities and swimming pool operators to review their procedures to ensure safety of participants at swimming events during the forthcoming school holidays.

Ron Wright, HSE principal inspector, said:

'Pool operators need to make sure that there are enough lifeguards for the size of the pool and the activities taking place. Play scheme organisers need to establish the swimming ability of the children involved and the suitability of the activity and pool.'

Comprehensive HSE guidance on managing health and safety in swimming pools to assist pool operators and pool hirers to put in place appropriate safety precautions is available from HSE Books: *Managing health and safety in swimming pools* (HSG179).    ➡

*Death of Jean Charles de Menenez[4]*

Following an investigation by the Independent Police Complaints Commission (IPCC) into the circumstances surrounding the death of Mr Jean Charles de Menezes, the CPS decided to prosecute the Office of Commissioner of Police for an offence under ss 3 and 33 of HSWA 1974. The unarmed Brazilian man was shot dead by police on 22 July 2005 after being mistaken for a suicide bomber in the wake of the 7 July 2005 bombings and the later failed bombing attempts two weeks later.

In this case, the HSE was not involved in the investigation into the death. Instead, the decision to prosecute for alleged health and safety offences was reached by the CPS.

The offences considered by the CPS included murder, manslaughter, forgery, and breaches of health and safety legislation, but it said that there was insufficient evidence to provide a realistic prospect of conviction against any individual police officer.

The CPS explained that the two officers who fired the fatal shots did so because they thought that Mr de Menezes had been identified as a suicide bomber and that if they did not shoot him, he would blow up the train, killing many people.

In a press release explaining the charging decision with regard to the fatal shooting, Stephen O'Doherty, senior lawyer from the CPS Special Crime Division set out that:

'In order to prosecute those officers, we would have to prove, beyond reasonable doubt, that they did not honestly and genuinely hold those beliefs. In fact, the evidence supports their claim that they genuinely believed that Mr de Menezes was a suicide bomber and therefore, as we cannot disprove that claim, we cannot prosecute them for murder or any other related offence. While a number of individuals had made errors in planning and communication, and the cumulative result was the tragic death of Mr de Menezes, no individual had been culpable to the degree necessary for a criminal offence.'

But he went on to say that the operational errors indicated that there had been a breach of the duties owed to non-employees under HSWA 1974, by the Office of Commissioner of Police and a prosecution under that Act was therefore authorised, although he made clear that this was not a prosecution of Sir Ian Blair in his personal capacity, but of the Office of Commissioner, as the deemed employer of the Metropolitan Police officers involved in the death of Mr de Menezes.

¹   Taylor, Peter: The Hillsborough Stadium Disaster 15 April 1989 interim report London, HMSO, August 1989 (The final report was published in January 1990: Taylor, Peter. The Hillsborough Stadium Disaster 15 April 1989 Final Report, London, HMSO, January 1990).
²   See HSE Press Release 27 June 2003.
³   See HSE Press Release 13 July 2007.
⁴   See Crown Prosecution Service Press Release 17 July 2007. As was widely reported, at the beginning of November 2007, the Metropolitan Police was found guilty of endangering the public and fined £175,000 with £385,000 costs.

## Deaths in Custody

**14.18**    The issue of deaths in custody proved to be the most controversial aspect of CMCHA 2007. The prison population is now at a record level. In October 2007, it reached 81,333 prisoners, and overcrowding has been blamed for an increase in prison deaths. Figures produced for the first time in September 2007 by the Forum for Preventing Deaths in Custody showed that there were nearly 600 deaths in custody in the year 2006–07, with 351 of these deaths among detained mental patients. Although 279 of these were from natural causes, 41 were the result of apparent suicides, and in prisons, 71 of the 162 deaths were self-inflicted or for reasons other than natural causes.

After a considerable battle between the government and the House of Lords, the offence will apply where an organisation owed a duty of care, under the law of negligence, to the person who died, reflecting the common law offence of gross negligence manslaughter.

### What CMCHA 2007 says

**14.19**    A relevant duty of care arises where the organisation is responsible for the safety of person in custody or detention (CMCHA 2007 s 2(1), (2)). Various forms of custody and detention are covered, including prisons, the custody area of courts and police stations, immigration detention facilities, prison escort arrangements, secure accommodation for children and young people; and detention under mental health legislation.

There is also provision for the categories of people to whom a duty of care is owed because they are in custody or detention to be extended by the Secretary of State. However, extension of the offence to deaths in custody will not come into effect on the 6 April 2008, but within three to five years after this time.

### The View of Civil Liberties and Human Rights Groups

**14.20**    In May 2007, Inquest, along with other human rights groups Liberty, Justice and the Prison Reform Trust produced a briefing as the Corporate Manslaughter and Corporate Homicide Bill was being debated: *Corporate Manslaughter and Corporate Homicide Bill Briefing for House of Commons consideration of Lords amendments Deaths in* *custody* which outlined that all four organisations 'strongly support the Bill which we consider to provide a long-overdue opportunity for Parliament to fill a significant gap in the criminal law'.

The briefing set out the problems with the law as it stood:

'Between 1995–2005 INQUEST's casework and monitoring service has highlighted over 2000 deaths in police and prison custody. Many of these deaths have raised issues of negligence, systemic failures to care for the vulnerable, institutional violence, racism, inhumane treatment and abuse of human rights.

'Despite a pattern of cases where inquest juries have found overwhelming evidence of unlawful and excessive use of force or gross neglect, no police or prison officer has been held responsible, either at an individual level or at a senior management level, for institutional and systemic failures to improve training and other policies. This is even the case when inquests return 'unlawful killing verdicts'.

'Since 1990, 10 'unlawful killing' verdicts have been returned by inquest juries but none of them has led to a successful prosecution. While inquests can provide a verdict and the coroner can suggest remedial measures under rule 43 of the Coroners Rules 1984, these recommendations have no binding force.

'The Government also points to public inquiries as an alternative route of accountability – but it refused to hold public inquiries into the deaths of both Zahid Mubarek and Joseph Scholes. In both cases, [Cf *R (oao Amin) v Secretary of State for the Home Department*[1]; *R (Scholes) v Secretary of State for the Home Department*[2]], the Government fought the families' attempts to have a public inquiry held in the civil courts.

'Without a legal victory by the family, the Zahid Mubarek Inquiry would not have been held. Without a similar verdict in the ongoing *Scholes* case, it is very unlikely that a public inquiry will be held. An inquiry – for which a family have had to fight – held years after a death, is in any event not sufficient in itself to provide an effective deterrent against gross negligence causing deaths in custody.'

It went on to say:

'We believe that in an appropriate and severe case a corporate manslaughter prosecution could be the only appropriate way of holding organisations to account and providing justice to bereaved families.'

Commenting on the passing of CMCHA 2007, including deaths in custody, Inquest said:

'The Act is also a victory for deaths in custody campaigners. After extensive lobbying by INQUEST, working with Peers and a coalition of penal reform and human rights NGOs, the remit of the Act has been extended to cover prison and police cell deaths. The government resisted this extension heavily but was defeated by the House of Lords on five occasions and eventually forced to concede. The Act gives a three-year delay period for the law covering deaths in custody to come into force. INQUEST will be monitoring the provisions being put in place to deal with the legislation.'

Zahid Mubarek was murdered by a racist inmate he was forced to share a cell with at Feltham Young Offenders Institution in 2000. The report of the Public Inquiry into the events that lead to his death is available at www.report.zahidmubarekinquiry.org.uk.

Joseph Scholes hanged himself in hanged himself in Stoke Heath Young Offenders Institution in 2002, nine days into a two-year sentence for street robbery.

Inquest described him as a very deeply disturbed young boy, and called for a Public Inquiry into his death. Deborah Coles, Co-Director of the organisation, commented on the case saying:

'We know from INQUEST's casework that child deaths are too often linked to failings in the community, the inappropriate use of penal custody for vulnerable children, inadequate treatment whilst in custody whereby the institutions are unable to care for the vulnerabilities of those that they detain. Child deaths in custody raise thematic issues that need to be addressed in a joined up manner through a properly resourced inquiry so that appropriate recommendations are made to ensure that lessons are learned and safeguards put in place to protect the lives of children in the future. The public interest case for a judicial inquiry remains urgent and pressing.'

Inquest's website is at www.inquest.org.uk.

1    [2003] UKHL 51, [2003] 4 All ER 1264, [2004] 1 AC 653, [2003] 3 WLR 1169.
2    [2006] EWCA Civ 1343, [2006] All ER (D) 188 (Oct).

# Appendix

## Corporate Manslaughter and Corporate Homicide Act 2007

*Corporate manslaughter and corporate homicide*

**1   The offence**

(1)   An organisation to which this section applies is guilty of an offence if the way in which its activities are managed or organised—

    (a)   causes a person's death, and

    (b)   amounts to a gross breach of a relevant duty of care owed by the organisation to the deceased.

(2)   The organisations to which this section applies are—

    (a)   a corporation;

    (b)   a department or other body listed in Schedule 1;

    (c)   a police force;

    (d)   a partnership, or a trade union or employers' association, that is an employer.

(3)   An organisation is guilty of an offence under this section only if the way in which its activities are managed or organised by its senior management is a substantial element in the breach referred to in subsection (1).

(4)   For the purposes of this Act—

    (a)   "relevant duty of care" has the meaning given by section 2, read with sections 3 to 7;

    (b)   a breach of a duty of care by an organisation is a "gross" breach if the conduct alleged to amount to a breach of that duty falls far below what can reasonably be expected of the organisation in the circumstances;

    (c)   "senior management", in relation to an organisation, means the persons who play significant roles in—

        (i)   the making of decisions about how the whole or a substantial part of its activities are to be managed or organised, or

        (ii)   the actual managing or organising of the whole or a substantial part of those activities.

(5)   The offence under this section is called—

  (a)   corporate manslaughter, in so far as it is an offence under the law of England and Wales or Northern Ireland;

  (b)   corporate homicide, in so far as it is an offence under the law of Scotland.

(6)   An organisation that is guilty of corporate manslaughter or corporate homicide is liable on conviction on indictment to a fine.

(7)   The offence of corporate homicide is indictable only in the High Court of Justiciary.

*Relevant duty of care*

**2    Meaning of "relevant duty of care"**

(1)   A "relevant duty of care", in relation to an organisation, means any of the following duties owed by it under the law of negligence—

  (a)   a duty owed to its employees or to other persons working for the organisation or performing services for it;

  (b)   a duty owed as occupier of premises;

  (c)   a duty owed in connection with—

    (i)   the supply by the organisation of goods or services (whether for consideration or not),

    (ii)   the carrying on by the organisation of any construction or maintenance operations,

    (iii)   the carrying on by the organisation of any other activity on a commercial basis, or

    (iv)   the use or keeping by the organisation of any plant, vehicle or other thing;

  (d)   a duty owed to a person who, by reason of being a person within subsection (2), is someone for whose safety the organisation is responsible.

(2)   A person is within this subsection if—

  (a)   he is detained at a custodial institution or in a custody area at a court or police station;

  (b)   he is detained at a removal centre or short-term holding facility;

  (c)   he is being transported in a vehicle, or being held in any premises, in pursuance of prison escort arrangements or immigration escort arrangements;

  (d)   he is living in secure accommodation in which he has been placed;

(e)   he is a detained patient.

(3)   Subsection (1) is subject to sections 3 to 7.

(4)   A reference in subsection (1) to a duty owed under the law of negligence includes a reference to a duty that would be owed under the law of negligence but for any statutory provision under which liability is imposed in place of liability under that law.

(5)   For the purposes of this Act, whether a particular organisation owes a duty of care to a particular individual is a question of law.

The judge must make any findings of fact necessary to decide that question.

(6)   For the purposes of this Act there is to be disregarded—

   (a)   any rule of the common law that has the effect of preventing a duty of care from being owed by one person to another by reason of the fact that they are jointly engaged in unlawful conduct;

   (b)   any such rule that has the effect of preventing a duty of care from being owed to a person by reason of his acceptance of a risk of harm.

(7)   In this section—

"construction or maintenance operations" means operations of any of the following descriptions—

   (a)   construction, installation, alteration, extension, improvement, repair, maintenance, decoration, cleaning, demolition or dismantling of—

      (i)   any building or structure,

      (ii)   anything else that forms, or is to form, part of the land, or

      (iii)   any plant, vehicle or other thing;

   (b)   operations that form an integral part of, or are preparatory to, or are for rendering complete, any operations within paragraph (a);

"custodial institution" means a prison, a young offender institution, a secure training centre, a young offenders institution, a young offenders centre, a juvenile justice centre or a remand centre;

"detained patient" means—

   (a)   a person who is detained in any premises under—

      (i)   Part 2 or 3 of the Mental Health Act 1983 (c 20) ("the 1983 Act"), or

      (ii)   Part 2 or 3 of the Mental Health (Northern Ireland) Order 1986 (SI 1986/595 (NI 4)) ("the 1986 Order");

   (b)   a person who (otherwise than by reason of being detained as mentioned in paragraph (a)) is deemed to be in legal custody by—

      (i)   section 137 of the 1983 Act,

      (ii)   Article 131 of the 1986 Order, or

      (iii)   article 11 of the Mental Health (Care and Treatment) (Scotland) Act 2003 (Consequential Provisions) Order 2005 (SI 2005/2078);

   (c)   a person who is detained in any premises, or is otherwise in custody, under the Mental Health (Care and Treatment) (Scotland) Act 2003 (asp 13) or Part 6 of the Criminal Procedure (Scotland) Act 1995 (c 46) or who is detained in a hospital under section 200 of that Act of 1995;

"immigration escort arrangements" means arrangements made under section 156 of the Immigration and Asylum Act 1999 (c 33);

"the law of negligence" includes—

   (a)   in relation to England and Wales, the Occupiers' Liability Act 1957 (c 31), the Defective Premises Act 1972 (c 35) and the Occupiers' Liability Act 1984 (c 3);

   (b)   in relation to Scotland, the Occupiers' Liability (Scotland) Act 1960 (c 30);

   (c)   in relation to Northern Ireland, the Occupiers' Liability Act (Northern Ireland) 1957 (c 25), the Defective Premises (Northern Ireland) Order 1975 (SI 1975/1039 (NI 9)), the Occupiers' Liability (Northern Ireland) Order 1987 (SI 1987/1280 (NI 15)) and the Defective Premises (Landlord's Liability) Act (Northern Ireland) 2001 (c 10);

"prison escort arrangements" means arrangements made under section 80 of the Criminal Justice Act 1991 (c 53) or under section 102 or 118 of the Criminal Justice and Public Order Act 1994 (c 33);

"removal centre" and "short-term holding facility" have the meaning given by section 147 of the Immigration and Asylum Act 1999;

"secure accommodation" means accommodation, not consisting of or forming part of a custodial institution, provided for the purpose of restricting the liberty of persons under the age of 18.

**3    Public policy decisions, exclusively public functions and statutory inspections**

(1)    Any duty of care owed by a public authority in respect of a decision as to matters of public policy (including in particular the allocation of public resources or the weighing of competing public interests) is not a "relevant duty of care".

(2)    Any duty of care owed in respect of things done in the exercise of an exclusively public function is not a "relevant duty of care" unless it falls within section 2(1)(a), (b) or (d).

(3)    Any duty of care owed by a public authority in respect of inspections carried out in the exercise of a statutory function is not a "relevant duty of care" unless it falls within section 2(1)(a) or (b).

(4)    In this section—

"exclusively public function" means a function that falls within the prerogative of the Crown or is, by its nature, exercisable only with authority conferred—

(a)    by the exercise of that prerogative, or

(b)    by or under a statutory provision;

"statutory function" means a function conferred by or under a statutory provision.

**4    Military activities**

(1)    Any duty of care owed by the Ministry of Defence in respect of—

(a)    operations within subsection (2),

(b)    activities carried on in preparation for, or directly in support of, such operations, or

(c)    training of a hazardous nature, or training carried out in a hazardous way, which it is considered needs to be carried out, or carried out in that way, in order to improve or maintain the effectiveness of the armed forces with respect to such operations,

is not a "relevant duty of care".

(2)    The operations within this subsection are operations, including peacekeeping operations and operations for dealing with terrorism, civil unrest or serious public disorder, in the course of which members of the armed forces come under attack or face the threat of attack or violent resistance.

(3)    Any duty of care owed by the Ministry of Defence in respect of activities carried on by members of the special forces is not a "relevant duty of care".

(4)    In this section "the special forces" means those units of the armed forces the maintenance of whose capabilities is the responsibility of the Director of Special Forces or which are for the time being subject to the operational command of that Director.

## 5    Policing and law enforcement

(1)    Any duty of care owed by a public authority in respect of—

    (a)    operations within subsection (2),

    (b)    activities carried on in preparation for, or directly in support of, such operations, or

    (c)    training of a hazardous nature, or training carried out in a hazardous way, which it is considered needs to be carried out, or carried out in that way, in order to improve or maintain the effectiveness of officers or employees of the public authority with respect to such operations,

is not a "relevant duty of care".

(2)    Operations are within this subsection if—

    (a)    they are operations for dealing with terrorism, civil unrest or serious disorder,

    (b)    they involve the carrying on of policing or law-enforcement activities, and

    (c)    officers or employees of the public authority in question come under attack, or face the threat of attack or violent resistance, in the course of the operations.

(3)    Any duty of care owed by a public authority in respect of other policing or law-enforcement activities is not a "relevant duty of care" unless it falls within section 2(1)(a), (b) or (d).

(4)    In this section "policing or law-enforcement activities" includes—

    (a)    activities carried on in the exercise of functions that are—

        (i)    functions of police forces, or

        (ii)    functions of the same or a similar nature exercisable by public authorities other than police forces;

    (b)    activities carried on in the exercise of functions of constables employed by a public authority;

    (c)    activities carried on in the exercise of functions exercisable under Chapter 4 of Part 2 of the Serious Organised Crime and Police Act 2005 (c 15) (protection of witnesses and other persons);

    (d)    activities carried on to enforce any provision contained in or made under the Immigration Acts.

## 6 Emergencies

(1) Any duty of care owed by an organisation within subsection (2) in respect of the way in which it responds to emergency circumstances is not a "relevant duty of care" unless it falls within section 2(1)(a) or (b).

(2) The organisations within this subsection are—

(a) a fire and rescue authority in England and Wales;

(b) a fire and rescue authority or joint fire and rescue board in Scotland;

(c) the Northern Ireland Fire and Rescue Service Board;

(d) any other organisation providing a service of responding to emergency circumstances either—

(i) in pursuance of arrangements made with an organisation within paragraph (a), (b) or (c), or

(ii) (if not in pursuance of such arrangements) otherwise than on a commercial basis;

(e) a relevant NHS body;

(f) an organisation providing ambulance services in pursuance of arrangements—

(i) made by, or at the request of, a relevant NHS body, or

(ii) made with the Secretary of State or with the Welsh Ministers;

(g) an organisation providing services for the transport of organs, blood, equipment or personnel in pursuance of arrangements of the kind mentioned in paragraph (f);

(h) an organisation providing a rescue service;

(i) the armed forces.

(3) For the purposes of subsection (1), the way in which an organisation responds to emergency circumstances does not include the way in which—

(a) medical treatment is carried out, or

(b) decisions within subsection (4) are made.

(4) The decisions within this subsection are decisions as to the carrying out of medical treatment, other than decisions as to the order in which persons are to be given such treatment.

(5) Any duty of care owed in respect of the carrying out, or attempted carrying out, of a rescue operation at sea in emergency circumstances is not a "relevant duty of care" unless it falls within section 2(1)(a) or (b).

(6)   Any duty of care owed in respect of action taken—

(a)   in order to comply with a direction under Schedule 3A to the Merchant Shipping Act 1995 (c 21) (safety directions), or

(b)   by virtue of paragraph 4 of that Schedule (action in lieu of direction),

is not a "relevant duty of care" unless it falls within section 2(1)(a) or (b).

(7)   In this section—

"emergency circumstances" means circumstances that are present or imminent and—

(a)   are causing, or are likely to cause, serious harm or a worsening of such harm, or

(b)   are likely to cause the death of a person;

"medical treatment" includes any treatment or procedure of a medical or similar nature;

"relevant NHS body" means—

(a)   a Strategic Health Authority, Primary Care Trust, NHS trust, Special Health Authority or NHS foundation trust in England;

(b)   a Local Health Board, NHS trust or Special Health Authority in Wales;

(c)   a Health Board or Special Health Board in Scotland, or the Common Services Agency for the Scottish Health Service;

(d)   a Health and Social Services trust or Health and Social Services Board in Northern Ireland;

"serious harm" means—

(a)   serious injury to or the serious illness (including mental illness) of a person;

(b)   serious harm to the environment (including the life and health of plants and animals);

(c)   serious harm to any building or other property.

(8)   A reference in this section to emergency circumstances includes a reference to circumstances that are believed to be emergency circumstances.

**7   Child-protection and probation functions**

(1)   A duty of care to which this section applies is not a "relevant duty of care" unless it falls within section 2(1)(a), (b) or (d).

(2) This section applies to any duty of care that a local authority or other public authority owes in respect of the exercise by it of functions conferred by or under—

    (a) Parts 4 and 5 of the Children Act 1989 (c 41),

    (b) Part 2 of the Children (Scotland) Act 1995 (c 36), or

    (c) Parts 5 and 6 of the Children (Northern Ireland) Order 1995 (SI 1995/755 (NI 2)).

(3) This section also applies to any duty of care that a local probation board or other public authority owes in respect of the exercise by it of functions conferred by or under—

    (a) Chapter 1 of Part 1 of the Criminal Justice and Court Services Act 2000 (c 43),

    (b) section 27 of the Social Work (Scotland) Act 1968 (c 49), or

    (c) Article 4 of the Probation Board (Northern Ireland) Order 1982 (SI 1982/713 (NI 10)).

*Gross breach*

**8     Factors for jury**

(1) This section applies where—

    (a) it is established that an organisation owed a relevant duty of care to a person, and

    (b) it falls to the jury to decide whether there was a gross breach of that duty.

(2) The jury must consider whether the evidence shows that the organisation failed to comply with any health and safety legislation that relates to the alleged breach, and if so—

    (a) how serious that failure was;

    (b) how much of a risk of death it posed.

(3) The jury may also—

    (a) consider the extent to which the evidence shows that there were attitudes, policies, systems or accepted practices within the organisation that were likely to have encouraged any such failure as is mentioned in subsection (2), or to have produced tolerance of it;

    (b) have regard to any health and safety guidance that relates to the alleged breach.

(4) This section does not prevent the jury from having regard to any other matters they consider relevant.

(5) In this section "health and safety guidance" means any code, guidance, manual or similar publication that is concerned with

health and safety matters and is made or issued (under a statutory provision or otherwise) by an authority responsible for the enforcement of any health and safety legislation.

*Remedial orders and publicity orders*

**9    Power to order breach etc to be remedied**

(1)    A court before which an organisation is convicted of corporate manslaughter or corporate homicide may make an order (a "remedial order") requiring the organisation to take specified steps to remedy—

(a)    the breach mentioned in section 1(1) ("the relevant breach");

(b)    any matter that appears to the court to have resulted from the relevant breach and to have been a cause of the death;

(c)    any deficiency, as regards health and safety matters, in the organisation's policies, systems or practices of which the relevant breach appears to the court to be an indication.

(2)    A remedial order may be made only on an application by the prosecution specifying the terms of the proposed order.

Any such order must be on such terms (whether those proposed or others) as the court considers appropriate having regard to any representations made, and any evidence adduced, in relation to that matter by the prosecution or on behalf of the organisation.

(3)    Before making an application for a remedial order the prosecution must consult such enforcement authority or authorities as it considers appropriate having regard to the nature of the relevant breach.

(4)    A remedial order—

(a)    must specify a period within which the steps referred to in subsection (1) are to be taken;

(b)    may require the organisation to supply to an enforcement authority consulted under subsection (3), within a specified period, evidence that those steps have been taken.

A period specified under this subsection may be extended or further extended by order of the court on an application made before the end of that period or extended period.

(5)    An organisation that fails to comply with a remedial order is guilty of an offence, and liable on conviction on indictment to a fine.

**10    Power to order conviction etc to be publicised**

(1)    A court before which an organisation is convicted of corporate manslaughter or corporate homicide may make an order (a "publicity order") requiring the organisation to publicise in a specified manner—

    (a)   the fact that it has been convicted of the offence;

    (b)   specified particulars of the offence;

    (c)   the amount of any fine imposed;

    (d)   the terms of any remedial order made.

(2)   In deciding on the terms of a publicity order that it is proposing to make, the court must—

    (a)   ascertain the views of such enforcement authority or authorities (if any) as it considers appropriate, and

    (b)   have regard to any representations made by the prosecution or on behalf of the organisation.

(3)   A publicity order—

    (a)   must specify a period within which the requirements referred to in subsection (1) are to be complied with;

    (b)   may require the organisation to supply to any enforcement authority whose views have been ascertained under subsection (2), within a specified period, evidence that those requirements have been complied with.

(4)   An organisation that fails to comply with a publicity order is guilty of an offence, and liable on conviction on indictment to a fine.

*Application to particular categories of organisation*

## 11   Application to Crown bodies

(1)   An organisation that is a servant or agent of the Crown is not immune from prosecution under this Act for that reason.

(2)   For the purposes of this Act—

    (a)   a department or other body listed in Schedule 1, or

    (b)   a corporation that is a servant or agent of the Crown,

is to be treated as owing whatever duties of care it would owe if it were a corporation that was not a servant or agent of the Crown.

(3)   For the purposes of section 2—

    (a)   a person who is—

        (i)   employed by or under the Crown for the purposes of a department or other body listed in Schedule 1, or

        (ii)   employed by a person whose staff constitute a body listed in that Schedule,

    is to be treated as employed by that department or body;

    (b)   any premises occupied for the purposes of—

        (i)   a department or other body listed in Schedule 1, or

(ii)   a person whose staff constitute a body listed in that Schedule,

are to be treated as occupied by that department or body.

(4)   For the purposes of sections 2 to 7 anything done purportedly by a department or other body listed in Schedule 1, although in law by the Crown or by the holder of a particular office, is to be treated as done by the department or other body itself.

(5)   Subsections (3)(a)(i), (3)(b)(i) and (4) apply in relation to a Northern Ireland department as they apply in relation to a department or other body listed in Schedule 1.

## 12    Application to armed forces

(1)   In this Act "the armed forces" means any of the naval, military or air forces of the Crown raised under the law of the United Kingdom.

(2)   For the purposes of section 2 a person who is a member of the armed forces is to be treated as employed by the Ministry of Defence.

(3)   A reference in this Act to members of the armed forces includes a reference to—

(a)   members of the reserve forces (within the meaning given by section 1(2) of the Reserve Forces Act 1996 (c 14)) when in service or undertaking training or duties;

(b)   persons serving on Her Majesty's vessels (within the meaning given by section 132(1) of the Naval Discipline Act 1957 (c 53)).

## 13    Application to police forces

(1)   In this Act "police force" means—

(a)   a police force within the meaning of—

(i)   the Police Act 1996 (c 16), or

(ii)   the Police (Scotland) Act 1967 (c 77);

(b)   the Police Service of Northern Ireland;

(c)   the Police Service of Northern Ireland Reserve;

(d)   the British Transport Police Force;

(e)   the Civil Nuclear Constabulary;

(f)   the Ministry of Defence Police.

(2)   For the purposes of this Act a police force is to be treated as owing whatever duties of care it would owe if it were a body corporate.

(3)   For the purposes of section 2—

(a)  a member of a police force is to be treated as employed by that force;

(b)  a special constable appointed for a police area in England and Wales is to be treated as employed by the police force maintained by the police authority for that area;

(c)  a special constable appointed for a police force mentioned in paragraph (d) or (f) of subsection (1) is to be treated as employed by that force;

(d)  a police cadet undergoing training with a view to becoming a member of a police force mentioned in paragraph (a) or (d) of subsection (1) is to be treated as employed by that force;

(e)  a police trainee appointed under section 39 of the Police (Northern Ireland) Act 2000 (c 32) or a police cadet appointed under section 42 of that Act is to be treated as employed by the Police Service of Northern Ireland;

(f)  a police reserve trainee appointed under section 40 of that Act is to be treated as employed by the Police Service of Northern Ireland Reserve;

(g)  a member of a police force seconded to the Serious Organised Crime Agency or the National Policing Improvement Agency to serve as a member of its staff is to be treated as employed by that Agency.

(4)  A reference in subsection (3) to a member of a police force is to be read, in the case of a force mentioned in paragraph (a)(ii) of subsection (1), as a reference to a constable of that force.

(5)  For the purposes of section 2 any premises occupied for the purposes of a police force are to be treated as occupied by that force.

(6)  For the purposes of sections 2 to 7 anything that would be regarded as done by a police force if the force were a body corporate is to be so regarded.

(7)  Where—

(a)  by virtue of subsection (3) a person is treated for the purposes of section 2 as employed by a police force, and

(b)  by virtue of any other statutory provision (whenever made) he is, or is treated as, employed by another organisation,

the person is to be treated for those purposes as employed by both the force and the other organisation.

**14   Application to partnerships**

(1)  For the purposes of this Act a partnership is to be treated as owing whatever duties of care it would owe if it were a body corporate.

(2)     Proceedings for an offence under this Act alleged to have been committed by a partnership are to be brought in the name of the partnership (and not in that of any of its members).

(3)     A fine imposed on a partnership on its conviction of an offence under this Act is to be paid out of the funds of the partnership.

(4)     This section does not apply to a partnership that is a legal person under the law by which it is governed.

*Miscellaneous*

**15    Procedure, evidence and sentencing**

(1)     Any statutory provision (whenever made) about criminal proceedings applies, subject to any prescribed adaptations or modifications, in relation to proceedings under this Act against—

(a)     a department or other body listed in Schedule 1,

(b)     a police force,

(c)     a partnership,

(d)     a trade union, or

(e)     an employers' association that is not a corporation,

as it applies in relation to proceedings against a corporation.

(2)     In this section—

"prescribed" means prescribed by an order made by the Secretary of State;

"provision about criminal proceedings" includes—

(a)     provision about procedure in or in connection with criminal proceedings;

(b)     provision about evidence in such proceedings;

(c)     provision about sentencing, or otherwise dealing with, persons convicted of offences;

"statutory" means contained in, or in an instrument made under, any Act or any Northern Ireland legislation.

(3)     A reference in this section to proceedings is to proceedings in England and Wales or Northern Ireland.

(4)     An order under this section is subject to negative resolution procedure.

**16    Transfer of functions**

(1)     This section applies where—

(a) a person's death has occurred, or is alleged to have occurred, in connection with the carrying out of functions by a relevant public organisation, and

(b) subsequently there is a transfer of those functions, with the result that they are still carried out but no longer by that organisation.

(2) In this section "relevant public organisation" means—

(a) a department or other body listed in Schedule 1;

(b) a corporation that is a servant or agent of the Crown;

(c) a police force.

(3) Any proceedings instituted against a relevant public organisation after the transfer for an offence under this Act in respect of the person's death are to be instituted against—

(a) the relevant public organisation, if any, by which the functions mentioned in subsection (1) are currently carried out;

(b) if no such organisation currently carries out the functions, the relevant public organisation by which the functions were last carried out.

This is subject to subsection (4).

(4) If an order made by the Secretary of State so provides in relation to a particular transfer of functions, the proceedings referred to in subsection (3) may be instituted, or (if they have already been instituted) may be continued, against—

(a) the organisation mentioned in subsection (1), or

(b) such relevant public organisation (other than the one mentioned in subsection (1) or the one mentioned in subsection (3)(a) or (b)) as may be specified in the order.

(5) If the transfer occurs while proceedings for an offence under this Act in respect of the person's death are in progress against a relevant public organisation, the proceedings are to be continued against—

(a) the relevant public organisation, if any, by which the functions mentioned in subsection (1) are carried out as a result of the transfer;

(b) if as a result of the transfer no such organisation carries out the functions, the same organisation as before.

This is subject to subsection (6).

(6) If an order made by the Secretary of State so provides in relation to a particular transfer of functions, the proceedings referred to in subsection (5) may be continued against—

(a) the organisation mentioned in subsection (1), or

(b)   such relevant public organisation (other than the one mentioned in subsection (1) or the one mentioned in subsection (5)(a) or (b)) as may be specified in the order.

(7)   An order under subsection (4) or (6) is subject to negative resolution procedure.

## 17    DPP's consent required for proceedings

Proceedings for an offence of corporate manslaughter—

(a)   may not be instituted in England and Wales without the consent of the Director of Public Prosecutions;

(b)   may not be instituted in Northern Ireland without the consent of the Director of Public Prosecutions for Northern Ireland.

## 18    No individual liability

(1)   An individual cannot be guilty of aiding, abetting, counselling or procuring the commission of an offence of corporate manslaughter.

(2)   An individual cannot be guilty of aiding, abetting, counselling or procuring, or being art and part in, the commission of an offence of corporate homicide.

## 19    Convictions under this Act and under health and safety legislation

(1)   Where in the same proceedings there is—

(a)   a charge of corporate manslaughter or corporate homicide arising out of a particular set of circumstances, and

(b)   a charge against the same defendant of a health and safety offence arising out of some or all of those circumstances,

the jury may, if the interests of justice so require, be invited to return a verdict on each charge.

(2)   An organisation that has been convicted of corporate manslaughter or corporate homicide arising out of a particular set of circumstances may, if the interests of justice so require, be charged with a health and safety offence arising out of some or all of those circumstances.

(3)   In this section "health and safety offence" means an offence under any health and safety legislation.

## 20    Abolition of liability of corporations for manslaughter at common law

The common law offence of manslaughter by gross negligence is abolished in its application to corporations, and in any application it has to other organisations to which section 1 applies.

*General and supplemental*

## 21 Power to extend section 1 to other organisations

(1) The Secretary of State may by order amend section 1 so as to extend the categories of organisation to which that section applies.

(2) An order under this section may make any amendment to this Act that is incidental or supplemental to, or consequential on, an amendment made by virtue of subsection (1).

(3) An order under this section is subject to affirmative resolution procedure.

## 22 Power to amend Schedule 1

(1) The Secretary of State may amend Schedule 1 by order.

(2) A statutory instrument containing an order under this section is subject to affirmative resolution procedure, unless the only amendments to Schedule 1 that it makes are amendments within subsection (3).

In that case the instrument is subject to negative resolution procedure.

(3) An amendment is within this subsection if—

   (a) it is consequential on a department or other body listed in Schedule 1 changing its name,

   (b) in the case of an amendment adding a department or other body to Schedule 1, it is consequential on the transfer to the department or other body of functions all of which were previously exercisable by one or more organisations to which section 1 applies, or

   (c) in the case of an amendment removing a department or other body from Schedule 1, it is consequential on—

   (i) the abolition of the department or other body, or

   (ii) the transfer of all the functions of the department or other body to one or more organisations to which section 1 applies.

## 23 Power to extend section 2(2)

(1) The Secretary of State may by order amend section 2(2) to make it include any category of person (not already included) who—

   (a) is required by virtue of a statutory provision to remain or reside on particular premises, or

   (b) is otherwise subject to a restriction of his liberty.

(2) An order under this section may make any amendment to this Act that is incidental or supplemental to, or consequential on, an amendment made by virtue of subsection (1).

(3)    An order under this section is subject to affirmative resolution procedure.

**24    Orders**

(1)    A power of the Secretary of State to make an order under this Act is exercisable by statutory instrument.

(2)    Where an order under this Act is subject to "negative resolution procedure" the statutory instrument containing the order is subject to annulment in pursuance of a resolution of either House of Parliament.

(3)    Where an order under this Act is subject to "affirmative resolution procedure" the order may not be made unless a draft has been laid before, and approved by a resolution of, each House of Parliament.

(4)    An order under this Act—

(a)    may make different provision for different purposes;

(b)    may make transitional or saving provision.

**25    Interpretation**

In this Act—

"armed forces" has the meaning given by section 12(1);

"corporation" does not include a corporation sole but includes any body corporate wherever incorporated;

"employee" means an individual who works under a contract of employment or apprenticeship (whether express or implied and, if express, whether oral or in writing), and related expressions are to be construed accordingly; see also sections 11(3)(a), 12(2) and 13(3) (which apply for the purposes of section 2);

"employers' association" has the meaning given by section 122 of the Trade Union and Labour Relations (Consolidation) Act 1992 (c 52) or Article 4 of the Industrial Relations (Northern Ireland) Order 1992 (SI 1992/807 (NI 5));

"enforcement authority" means an authority responsible for the enforcement of any health and safety legislation;

"health and safety legislation" means any statutory provision dealing with health and safety matters, including in particular provision contained in the Health and Safety at Work etc Act 1974 (c 37) or the Health and Safety at Work (Northern Ireland) Order 1978 (SI 1978/1039 (NI 9));

"member", in relation to the armed forces, is to be read in accordance with section 12(3);

"partnership" means—

(a)    a partnership within the Partnership Act 1890 (c 39), or

(b)    a limited partnership registered under the Limited Partnerships Act 1907 (c 24),

or a firm or entity of a similar character formed under the law of a country or territory outside the United Kingdom;

"police force" has the meaning given by section 13(1);

"premises" includes land, buildings and moveable structures;

"public authority" has the same meaning as in section 6 of the Human Rights Act 1998 (c 42) (disregarding subsections (3)(a) and (4) of that section);

"publicity order" means an order under section 10(1);

"remedial order" means an order under section 9(1);

"statutory provision", except in section 15, means provision contained in, or in an instrument made under, any Act, any Act of the Scottish Parliament or any Northern Ireland legislation;

"trade union" has the meaning given by section 1 of the Trade Union and Labour Relations (Consolidation) Act 1992 (c 52) or Article 3 of the Industrial Relations (Northern Ireland) Order 1992 (SI 1992/807 (NI 5)).

## 26    Minor and consequential amendments

Schedule 2 (minor and consequential amendments) has effect.

## 27    Commencement and savings

(1)    The preceding provisions of this Act come into force in accordance with provision made by order by the Secretary of State.

(2)    An order bringing into force paragraph (d) of section 2(1) is subject to affirmative resolution procedure.

(3)    Section 1 does not apply in relation to anything done or omitted before the commencement of that section.

(4)    Section 20 does not affect any liability, investigation, legal proceeding or penalty for or in respect of an offence committed wholly or partly before the commencement of that section.

(5)    For the purposes of subsection (4) an offence is committed wholly or partly before the commencement of section 20 if any of the conduct or events alleged to constitute the offence occurred before that commencement.

## 28    Extent and territorial application

(1)    Subject to subsection (2), this Act extends to England and Wales, Scotland and Northern Ireland.

(2)    An amendment made by this Act extends to the same part or parts of the United Kingdom as the provision to which it relates.

(3)    Section 1 applies if the harm resulting in death is sustained in the United Kingdom or—

(a)    within the seaward limits of the territorial sea adjacent to the United Kingdom;

(b)    on a ship registered under Part 2 of the Merchant Shipping Act 1995 (c 21);

(c)    on a British-controlled aircraft as defined in section 92 of the Civil Aviation Act 1982 (c 16);

(d)    on a British-controlled hovercraft within the meaning of that section as applied in relation to hovercraft by virtue of provision made under the Hovercraft Act 1968 (c 59);

(e)    in any place to which an Order in Council under section 10(1) of the Petroleum Act 1998 (c 17) applies (criminal jurisdiction in relation to offshore activities).

(4)    For the purposes of subsection (3)(b) to (d) harm sustained on a ship, aircraft or hovercraft includes harm sustained by a person who—

(a)    is then no longer on board the ship, aircraft or hovercraft in consequence of the wrecking of it or of some other mishap affecting it or occurring on it, and

(b)    sustains the harm in consequence of that event.

**29    Short title**

This Act may be cited as the Corporate Manslaughter and Corporate Homicide Act 2007.

SCHEDULE 1
LIST OF GOVERNMENT DEPARTMENTS ETC

Section 1

*Assets Recovery Agency*

Attorney General's Office
Cabinet Office
Central Office of Information
Crown Office and Procurator Fiscal Service
Crown Prosecution Service
Department for Communities and Local Government
Department for Constitutional Affairs (including the Scotland Office and the Wales Office)
Department for Culture, Media and Sport
Department for Education and Skills
Department for Environment, Food and Rural Affairs

*Assets Recovery Agency*

Department for International Development
Department for Transport
Department for Work and Pensions
Department of Health
Department of Trade and Industry
Export Credits Guarantee Department
Foreign and Commonwealth Office
Forestry Commission
General Register Office for Scotland
Government Actuary's Department
Her Majesty's Land Registry
Her Majesty's Revenue and Customs
Her Majesty's Treasury
Home Office
Ministry of Defence
National Archives
National Archives of Scotland
National Audit Office
National Savings and Investments
National School of Government
Northern Ireland Audit Office
Northern Ireland Court Service
Northern Ireland Office
Office for National Statistics
Office of the Deputy Prime Minister
Office of Her Majesty's Chief Inspector of Education and Training in Wales
Ordnance Survey
Privy Council Office
Public Prosecution Service for Northern Ireland
Registers of Scotland Executive Agency
Revenue and Customs Prosecutions Office
Royal Mint
Scottish Executive
Serious Fraud Office
Treasury Solicitor's Department
UK Trade and Investment
Welsh Assembly Government

**NOTE**—Entry "Assets Recovery Agency" prospectively repealed by the Serious Crime Act 2007, s 74(2)(g), Sch 8, Pt 7, para 178.

SCHEDULE 2
MINOR AND CONSEQUENTIAL AMENDMENTS
Section 26

*Coroners Act 1988 (c 13)*

**1**

(1)    The Coroners Act 1988 is amended as follows.

(2)    In the following provisions, after "manslaughter" there is inserted ", corporate manslaughter"—

    (a)    section 11(6) (no finding of guilt at coroner's inquest) (twice);

    (b)    subsection (1)(a)(i) of section 16 (adjournment of inquest in event of criminal proceedings);

    (c)    subsections (1)(a) and (2)(a) of section 17 (coroner to be informed of result of criminal proceedings).

(3)    In section 35(1) (interpretation), after the definition of "Greater London" there is inserted—

""person", in relation to an offence of corporate manslaughter, includes organisation;".

*Criminal Justice Act 2003 (c 44)*

**2**

In Schedule 4 to the Criminal Justice Act 2003 (qualifying offences for purposes of section 62), after paragraph 4 there is inserted—

*"Corporate manslaughter*

**4A**

An offence under section 1 of the Corporate Manslaughter and Corporate Homicide Act 2007.'

**3**

(1)    Schedule 5 to that Act (qualifying offences for purposes of Part 10) is amended as follows.

(2)    After paragraph 4 there is inserted—

*"Corporate manslaughter*

**4A**

An offence under section 1 of the Corporate Manslaughter and Corporate Homicide Act 2007.'

(3)    After paragraph 33 there is inserted—

*"Corporate manslaughter*

**33A**

An offence under section 1 of the Corporate Manslaughter and Corporate Homicide Act 2007.'

*Criminal Justice (Northern Ireland) Order 2004 (SI 2004/1500 (NI 9))*

**4**

In Schedule 2 to the Criminal Justice (Northern Ireland) Order 2004 (qualifying offences for purposes of Article 21), after paragraph 4 there is inserted—

*"Corporate manslaughter*

**4A**

An offence under section 1 of the Corporate Manslaughter and Corporate Homicide Act 2007.'

# Index